Presidential Travel

Presidential Travel

The Journey from George Washington to George W. Bush

RICHARD J. ELLIS

UNIVERSITY PRESS OF KANSAS

© 2008 by the University Press of Kansas

Published by the University Press of Kansas
(Lawrence, Kansas 66045), which was
organized by the Kansas Board of Regents
and is operated and funded by Emporia State
University, Fort Hays State University, Kansas
State University, Pittsburg State University,
the University of Kansas, and Wichita State
University

Library of Congress Cataloging-in-Publication Data

Ellis, Richard (Richard J.)
  Presidential travel : the journey from George
Washington to George W. Bush / Richard J. Ellis.
      p.   cm.
  Includes bibliographical references and index.
  ISBN 978-0-7006-1580-3 (cloth : alk. paper)
  1. Presidents—United States—History.
2. Presidents—Travel—History. 3. Presidents—
Protection—United States. 4. Visits of state. I. Title.
  E176.1.E47 2008
  973.09′9—dc22

                                                2007046313

British Library Cataloguing-in-Publication Data is
available.
Printed in the United States of America
10 9 8 7 6 5 4 3 2 1

The paper used in this publication is recycled and
contains 50 percent postconsumer waste. It is acid
free and meets the minimum requirements of the
American National Standard for Permanence of
Paper for Printed Library Materials
Z39.48-1992.

Contents

Acknowledgments

Back in September of 2003, Fred Woodward proposed that I write a volume on the presidency that "would show how the United States has evolved from republican simplicity to present-day celebrity," how the president as first citizen became the president as political star. I thought the idea intriguing, though I worried that it perhaps ran the risk of degenerating into a predictable lament about the degraded state of contemporary American politics. Lewis Gould, to whom Fred also shopped the project, suggested a way of giving life to the idea: "look at the presidency when it gets out among the people." Lew even offered a title: "Outside the Bubble: The Presidency among the People." He allowed that the research for such a book would be "daunting," and suggested that consequently the project would require a person blessed with "stamina and youth."

Although I clearly lacked at least one of the requisite qualifications, the idea of a book on the history of presidential travel nonetheless appealed to me. Presidential travel seemed an obvious but underutilized lens through which to examine the evolving relationship between the president and the public, a topic that has long engaged me. A rich scholarly literature exists on the development of presidential rhetoric, but presidential travel has typically received only passing attention. How, I wondered, would the narrative of presidential history look different if travel was placed at the center of the story rather than relegated to its fringes?

From the outset, I had no intention of writing a definitive, comprehensive history of presidential travel. A chronological study of all presidential travel from George Washington to George W. Bush, I feared, would result in a book that would be dreadfully long, unavoidably repetitive, and exhausting for both author and reader. I preferred instead a study of presidential travel organized conceptually around questions to which I did not know the answers. When, I wondered, did the American public begin to pick up the tab for presidential travel? And why did nineteenth-century presidents never leave the country? Why, moreover, were presidents in the nineteenth century left so unprotected when they ventured outside the White House? Beyond these specific questions I also hoped the history of presidential travel might shed light on a paradox: namely, that the contemporary presidency is at once a more democratic institution than it was in the early republic and yet in many respects it is a more regal one as well.

Fred Woodward and Lew Gould deserve the credit for planting the seed, but they should not be blamed for the form I have given this book. Indeed at several junctures they tried in vain to divert me from my misguided course. If the narrative is still bogged down with too much detail it is definitely not for want of trying on Fred's part. And the large chunks of the history of presidential travel that I have left out are not missing because Lew didn't point them out to me. The existence of chapters 2 and 3 owes a great deal to Lew's insistence that I not leave a black hole between Monroe's tours and those of the late nineteenth-century presidents.

I also wish to single out Bruce Miroff for my sincere thanks. His appreciative comments on an early draft of the first chapter, presented at the Western Political Science Association meeting in the spring of 2005, buoyed my flagging spirits. I also benefited from his sage comments on the final manuscript, which not only offered encouragement but saved me from some embarrassing errors and helped to strengthen the narrative in several places.

I have been greatly aided in carrying out the research for this book by a small battalion of talented Willamette University undergraduates, who helped to compensate for my lack of youth and stamina. Most important was Alexis Walker, who read more reels of microfilm than any human being should ever be asked to do. Little wonder she is now being fitted for glasses. Also indispensable was the assistance of Kate D'Ambrosio, who, together with Alexis, spent the long summer of 2004 reading through every travel-related story they could find in the *New York Times.* Joey Mello was a tremendous help in the summer of 2005 in locating congressional debates that came to form the basis of chapter 5. Others who provided valuable research assistance at various stages of the project were Jenelle Woodlief, Katie Johannsen, Sarah Chalmers, and Olivia Saccomanno. None of them, I suspect, will be eager see another reel of microfilm anytime soon. Erin Dougherty, a former Willamette student, also helped by carrying out research at the Gerald Ford Library, as did Doris Kinney, who expertly mined the archives at the FDR Library.

It is not possible to identify every librarian who helped me with some aspect of my research, but I would be remiss if I did not thank Willamette University librarian Rich Schmidt, who helped me to obtain countless documents and reels upon reels of microfilm. My job was also made easier by Ford Schmidt's work in securing digitized newspaper collections, specifically the *New York Times* and Readex's Early American Newspapers collection. Credit for the latter acquisition also goes to my history colleague Seth Cotlar.

A number of scholars helped me at various stages by answering queries, including Daniel Preston, whose invaluable documentary history of the tours of James Monroe was an early catalyst for this project; Brendan Doherty, who generously shared data he had collected on presidential travel; and Jeff Jenkins and Eric Schickler, who dug up data on compensation for congressional travel. Others who patiently answered pestering queries are Barbara Oberg, Ted Frantz, Dallett Hemphill, Robert Johnstone, Sandy Moats, and Bob Withers. Also thanks to Fred Greenstein, who took an early interest in the project, offering encouraging words and sage counsel, not all of which I followed. Terri Bimes also offered useful suggestions on the chapter on Monroe.

Also deserving of special recognition are my daughter, Eleanor Ellis, whose careful editing and critical eye helped to improve the writing in countless ways, and Martha Whitt, whose professional and vigilant copy editing mended many a mistake.

And, finally, as always, I owe a huge thanks to the entire sterling crew at the University Press of Kansas. My respect for the dedication and skill that they bring to their craft grows with each book that I publish with UPK. I feel fortunate to have had them as constant companions on my authorial journey.

Introduction

On the first Monday of May in 1833, Andrew Jackson set out by steamboat for Fredericksburg, Virginia. The newly reelected president had been invited to lay the cornerstone for a monument to Mary Ball Washington, mother of the nation's first president. Accompanying Jackson on the 50-mile journey down the Potomac River were his nephew and personal assistant, Major Andrew Donelson, as well as several cabinet members. The steamer made a brief stop at Alexandria; among those who came aboard there was Lieutenant Robert Beverly Randolph. Five years earlier Randolph had been the navy's acting purser on one of the nation's most famous warships, the USS *Constitution*, but Randolph was fired by Jackson after an audit found that money had gone missing. The disgraced Randolph insisted that he had been wrongly accused and that the financial irregularities were the fault of his deceased predecessor.[1]

Upon boarding the ship Randolph sought out the president, and found him relaxing in his cabin, perusing the newspaper and puffing on a pipe. No guard manned the door and none of the president's companions made any effort to prevent Randolph from entering the room or approaching the president. Uncertain about the president's identity, Randolph asked Jackson whether he was the president. Jackson allowed that he was and apologized for not standing on account of "a pain in [his] side." Thinking that the visitor was taking off his glove to shake hands with him, Jackson bent forward. Randolph, however, had removed his glove not to greet but to strike the president. "You have injured me," Randolph declared, before "dash[ing] his hand" into Jackson's face. Randolph was then quickly spirited off the boat by "some ruffian confederates," leaving a stunned president to nurse his wounds.[2]

The modern reader marvels that an individual could wander into the president's private cabin, walk directly up to the chief of state, calmly remove his glove, and hit the president square in the nose. Even more surprising still is that this individual, having smacked the president hard enough to draw blood, was able to leave the boat without being apprehended or arrested. But perhaps most telling is not the incident itself but its aftermath: Randolph got away scot-free. Federal authorities were powerless to prosecute the act and Virginia refused to do so. There was nothing that Jackson could do about the assault except privately vent his frustration at the "disgrace" that Virginia had brought upon itself and the country for failing to act against Randolph. To be sure, after Jackson left office there was a belated effort to bring Randolph to justice, but by that time—nearly five years after the attack—Jackson was no longer willing to press the case against his assailant.[3]

The Randolph incident offers a glimpse into the presidency that was but is no more. This book tells the tale of that transformation. In the early republic, Americans celebrated that their chief executive was not enveloped by an armed guard, court, or retinue. To be sure, there were early attempts to make the president appear more royal—by giving him a fancy title, for instance. However, most Americans pointed proudly to the lack of regal trappings surrounding the executive. The president, it was often said, was the "first citizen" of the republic. Today, the president strives mightily to appear as a man of the people, but he cannot escape the handlers and guardians who keep him a safe distance from the people. The president must be protected from the people he represents. We have difficulty imagining it any other way.

Yet we cannot quite bring ourselves to admit it either. We are not accustomed to thinking of past political institutions and practices as more open or more democratic than those of the present era. Our nation's history is typically told in terms of the forward march of democracy: slavery abolished, women given the right to vote, segregation outlawed, civil rights extended, the voting age decreased. Americans believe in progress. Democracy, we tell ourselves, is on the march, at home and abroad. But the history of the American presidency cannot easily be shoehorned into this progressive narrative.

Jackson's presidency figures prominently in the narrative of democratic progress, especially his inauguration ceremony in which unruly crowds of people from all walks of life pressed inside the White House to greet the president, drink his liquor, and eat his food. One senator described the event as a "regular Saturnalia. . . . The mob broke in, in thousands—Spirits black, yellow and grey, poured in in one uninterrupted stream of mud and filth." The sight of "a mob of boys, negroes, women, children, scrambling, fighting, [and] romping" in the presidential mansion appalled polite society. One Washington matron clucked that the president was "nearly pressed to death and almost suffocated and torn to pieces [by the crowd] in their eagerness to shake hands with Old Hickory." Elites watched helplessly as the "rabble" muddied the furniture and smashed the china.[4]

But if Jackson's inauguration is a measure of raw, untamed democracy then we've gone in the reverse direction ever since. The wild events of that day tell us less about the progressive democratization of the presidency than they do about the gulf that separates the Jacksonian era presidency from the carefully scripted presidency of today. President George W. Bush need never fear of being "nearly pressed to death" by his admirers—the Secret Service sees to that. No mob is permitted to occupy the White House, even for a day. Tourists are carefully guided through the White House, much as they might be guided through any royal palace in Britain. Today, the inauguration ceremony more closely resembles the choreographed coronation of a king than it does the "raving Democracy" that marked the celebration of Jackson's inauguration.[5]

In the early nineteenth century, presidents were routinely spotted walking or riding through the capital. Jackson's predecessor, John Quincy Adams, regularly took an early morning swim in the Potomac, in the buff, without any protective detail. Nobody mobbed the president but no one needed to protect him either—though on one occasion a female journalist reportedly held Adams's clothes hostage in order to obtain an interview. One did not have to be a member of Congress or fat cat contributor to see the president. At appointed times during the week, the White House was open to citizens who wished to see the president, shake his hand, exchange pleasantries, or press their case for a government job. There was no Secret Service or chief of staff and no surveillance cameras, checkpoints, or massive iron gates.

Although a president is more protected and less accessible today than he was two centuries ago, he is also, ironically, better known and more widely recognized. The first photograph of a president was not taken until the 1840s, and not until the end of the nineteenth century did newspapers begin to include photographic images. Many nineteenth-century Americans were, as a result, hard-pressed to recognize the president. Randolph felt he needed to ask Jackson his identity before assaulting him. James Monroe's 1817 tour included a stop at small inn in Altona, New York, and while the inn's owners instantly knew that the travelers "were people of great importance from the rich attire of the servants and the splendid coaches and horses," they did not recognize Monroe as the president of the United States. Only later in the evening, after sharing supper with his hosts, did "the President ma[k]e himself known" to his hosts. When James Polk visited New York City in 1847, to take another example, the president was reportedly "mistaken by many persons" for one of his traveling companions, Alabama Senator Dixon Hall Lewis. These people "went away declaiming" that President Polk—a relatively slender man of 5 feet 8 inches—was "the fattest man they ever did see."[6]

Even by the time of Woodrow Wilson's presidency it was apparently still possible for the president to go unrecognized by his fellow citizens. In the summer of his first year as president, Wilson cruised down the Potomac on the presidential yacht to the famous revolutionary battlefield site of Yorktown. He "talked freely with more than a score" of Yorktown residents without anyone "so much as suspect[ing] that he was the President." When he came ashore, some "negroes lounging around the wharf" hailed him as "uncle" but did not recognize him. Wilson walked into the village store to buy some postcards without a glimmer of recognition from the man who served him. Outside the store were another three or four men "propped back in chairs," and none of them had any inkling who their visitor was, despite exchanging pleasantries with Wilson about the stifling heat. A clerk at the county courthouse retrieved some documents that Wilson requested without suspecting that he was serving the president. Even the sheriff, with whom Wilson talked at the courthouse, did not recognize the president, even though a poster bearing "an excellent . . . lithograph likeness" of Wilson hung on a nearby wall. Only as the president was preparing to leave Yorktown was he at last recognized by a precocious "tiny Virginia girl," who proceeded to give the president a free tour of a historic house near the battlefield.[7]

Admittedly by Wilson's time, this sort of encounter struck many people as an oddity, a reflection less of the presidency than of the nation's benighted backwaters. That was clearly the spirit in which the *New York Times* covered the story, which it placed prominently in the upper left-hand corner of the front page. Newsreels—which were used for the first time in the 1912 campaign—and newspaper photographs spread the president's image across the country. And yet the Yorktown incident still suggests the gulf separating the presidency of the early twentieth century from the presidency of the early twenty-first century. It is virtually impossible to imagine President George W. Bush or President Bill Clinton traveling to any village in the nation without being instantly recognized. If their face didn't give them away, their protective entourage certainly would.

The paradox, then, is that the president today is more visible but less accessible, more recognizable but less reachable. Americans in the twenty-first century cannot help but see and hear their president. His image and his voice are everywhere, inescapable to all but the most determined recluse. The contemporary presidency, as Bruce Miroff has suggested, monopolizes the public space in a way that is fundamentally unlike the nineteenth-century presidency.[8]

This book is not a jeremiad, not a call to go back to a simpler or more innocent time. It describes a political world that we have left behind, for better and for worse. The past is not a model for the future, but recovering a forgotten past can reveal aspects of the present that are sometimes obscured or taken for granted. In these pages the reader will not find a cure for what ails the American presidency and polity, only the beginnings of a diagnosis.

BEYOND THE WHITE HOUSE

When we think of the presidency, we usually think first of the White House. For over 200 years, it has been the preeminent symbol of the American presidency. The covers of countless presidential textbooks are adorned with a representation of the White House, and an impressive photograph of the presidential abode graces the cover of the field's flagship journal, *Presidential Studies Quarterly*. Yet the president is not a prisoner of the White House. He spends many of his waking (and sleeping) hours outside its storied walls. In fact, modern presidents have typically spent between one-third and one-half of their time away from the White House.

To be sure, much of a president's time away from the White House is spent at isolated retreats. Camp David in Maryland's Catoctin Mountains has been a favorite presidential retreat since Franklin Roosevelt first used it during World War II. Ronald Reagan spent over 500 days at Camp David. George W. Bush's use of Camp David has only been slightly behind Reagan's record-setting pace; during his first five and a half years Bush visited over 100 times for a total of 331 days. During that same period Bush also visited his ranch in Crawford, Texas, 56 times for a total of 374 days. In other words, roughly 700 of Bush's first 2,000 days in office were spent at Camp David or at his ranch in Texas. Richard Nixon, who had two retreats in addition to Camp David—one in San Clemente, California, and the other in Fort Biscayne, Florida—spent over 40 percent of his presidential days at one of these three well-protected compounds.[9]

Presidents in the early republic, too, escaped the capital for significant segments of time, particularly during the summer months. John Adams and Thomas Jefferson, for instance, both spent about a quarter of their time in office outside of the nation's capital. Every summer Adams left for his home in Quincy, Massachusetts, and Jefferson departed for his beloved Monticello. Although the Civil War afforded few opportunities for the president to leave the capital, Lincoln still managed to spend a quarter of his presidency in residence at the Soldiers' Home, a "charming rural retreat" on the outskirts of the District.[10]

There is more to presidential travel, of course, than escaping summer heat or seeking a secluded spot. Presidents also travel to achieve political objectives. These include articulating administration policies, cultivating or dramatizing popular support, putting public pressure on other politicians, boosting the president's reelection chances, and bolstering the electoral prospects of other candidates in the president's party. In recent years at least, presidents have traveled a tremendous amount in pursuit of political objectives. Between 1981 and 1999, presidents made about sixty domestic trips annually, for an average of around eighty days of traveling each year. These figures, moreover, exclude presidential appearances within Maryland and Virginia, which account for a significant additional amount of presidential travel. During this same twenty-year period, presidents also averaged about twenty-two days of foreign travel a year. All told, presidents in the 1980s and 1990s spent well over one hundred days a year traveling the country or traversing the globe.[11]

Not surprisingly, presidents today travel much more than presidents of yesteryear. It took John Adams two weeks to travel the 300 miles that separated the capital of Philadelphia and his home in Quincy, while George W. Bush can travel over 600 miles an hour in Air Force One. Yet from the beginning, presidents have placed travel at the service of politics. President George Washington had been in office less than half a year when he undertook a monthlong tour of New England that took him through Connecticut, Massachusetts, New Hampshire, and Maine. The following year Washington journeyed to Rhode Island after that state finally ratified the Constitution, and the next year he embarked on a two-month tour of the South, during which he visited Maryland, Virginia, North Carolina, South Carolina, and Georgia. Each of these tours was designed to serve Washington's preeminent political objective: to consolidate national authority and to promote popular identification with the new nation and its new government.

Aided by the advent of the railroad, nineteenth-century presidents traveled all across the country, particularly following the Civil War. Andrew Johnson's notorious "swing around the circle" in 1866 took him to nine states, reaching as far west as St. Louis; by the end of his term he had visited fourteen states. Ulysses Grant was even more adventurous, visiting twenty two states and territories, and getting as far west as Salt Lake City. The only states outside of the South not to receive a visit from Grant were Minnesota, Wisconsin, Kansas, Oregon, California, and Nevada. Grant strategically steered clear of the old Confederacy, paying only the briefest of visits to northern Virginia. Grant was on the road—or, more precisely, the rails—so often that questions were raised in Washington about his "absenteeism." Rutherford Hayes, the first president to make it all the way to the Pacific Ocean, traveled so frequently that wags dubbed him "Rutherford the Rover." During his many trips, Hayes visited thirty states and six territories. The only nonsouthern state that he neglected to visit was Maine, the home state of James G. Blaine, Hayes's chief rival for the Republican nomination in 1876.[12]

Presidents continued to travel extensively in the last decades of the nineteenth century and the opening decades of the twentieth century. During his two terms, Theodore Roosevelt visited every state and territory in the union. Roosevelt's successor, William Howard Taft, traveled even more often, journeying an average of nearly 30,000 miles a year by train. Woodrow Wilson traveled less, but still covered an impressive 87,000 miles, and that doesn't count his two trips to Europe that kept him out of the country for more than six months. By twentieth-century standards, Warren Harding, Calvin Coolidge, and Herbert Hoover may have been relatively light travelers, but each of them still traveled over 32,000 miles by train. Franklin Roosevelt traversed 243,827 miles by rail during his nearly thirteen years in office, or roughly the distance between the earth and the moon. FDR also traveled another 100,000 miles by sea and air.[13]

Given the amount of time presidents spend traveling, it is striking that more attention has not been devoted to the subject. As political scientist Michael John Burton recently noted, there is a lamentable "dearth of scholarship on presidential travel." Political science, observes Burton, particularly "lacks an understanding of [presidential travel's] history and conduct." Perhaps this dearth owes something to the sense that the history of presidential travel is best left to coffee table books and railroad buffs. Whatever the reason, the deficiency is unfortunate because presidential travel provides an important window into the changing relationship between the president and the people. In writing a history of presidential travel I have sought to illuminate not only an aspect of the history of the American presidency but of American democracy as well.[14]

THE ARGUMENT

In a nation suspicious of executive power, it has long been important for presidents to mingle with the people. Traveling outside of the capital draws the president physically and symbolically closer to the people. But it has also been important for presidents to avoid the trappings of monarchy. Fancy carriages, impressive retinues, triumphal receptions, even popular adulation triggered deep-seated fears of monarchy, particularly because the carriages, retinues, and processions readily evoked in the Anglo-American imagination the specter of the "royal progress," in which the monarch traveled around the British countryside. Those fears were as important as rudimentary transportation technology in explaining why early presidents did not travel more.

Despite his immense personal popularity, President Jefferson never embarked on the sort of tour undertaken by Washington. In contrast to Washington, who visited each of the original thirteen colonies, Jefferson as president never visited any state apart from his native Virginia, which he traveled through every summer on his way home to Monticello. Throughout his presidency, Jefferson pointedly shunned the accouterments of monarchy that his supporters identified with the Federalists. At his first inaugural, he dramatized his "republican simplicity" by refusing the customary horse and carriage, instead walking to and from his inauguration. Whereas Washington typically traveled in an elegant coach with liveried attendants, Jefferson customarily rode a horse, accompanied by a single servant.[15]

Chapter 1 focuses on James Monroe's two ambitious tours: the first, a three-and-a-half-month tour of the North that took him to thirteen states plus the territory of Michigan; the second, a nearly four-and-a-half-month tour through eight southern states. Monroe's challenge was to devise a mode of presidential travel that would be seen as dignified but not monarchical. When Washington traveled he had been insulated from criticism by his immense personal prestige, but Monroe, though well respected, could not count on his revolutionary exploits to shield him from partisan sniping. Anxious to avoid any sinister echoes of the royal progress, Monroe announced his determination to travel as a "private citizen." Although he recognized that a president could not in fact travel as a private citizen, the pose was a shrewd way of assuaging republican fears of monarchy.[16]

Americans in the early republic did not want the president parading like a monarch, but nor did they want him campaigning like a mere politician. Stumping for the White House was deemed undignified. The office of the president "should neither be sought nor declined," as James Polk put it in accepting his party's nomination in 1844. On the one hand, then, Americans wanted reassurance that their president traveled as one of them, unburdened by monarchical pretensions. On the other hand, they wanted a president who would eschew ordinary political ambition and rise above partisan passions. Not a monarch yet not a party politician either. Nineteenth-century presidential travel required presidents to tack between the Scylla of monarchy and the Charybdis of electioneering.[17]

For Monroe and Washington, charges of monarchy were more to be feared than accusations of electioneering. Both men were elevated to the presidency without serious political opposition, and both toured the nation in order to unify it. Both aspired to be "a president above party," transcending society's divisions and erasing its political factions. The rise of organized, national political parties and competitive presidential elections in the late 1820s and the 1830s changed the political calculus of presidential travel. Although presidents still had to worry about being taken to task for regal preening, they now had to worry more about being censured for electioneering. Chapter 2 examines how two presidents in the Jacksonian era—Andrew Jackson and Martin Van Buren—navigated between the demands stemming from their role as party leader and the norms accompanying their position as head of the nation.

Every president between Jackson and James Buchanan toured the nation (except the unfortunate William Henry Harrison, who died before getting the chance), and none found it easy to be both head of the party and head of the nation. Each received partisan invitations to travel and was confronted with the unpleasant choice of disappointing fellow partisans or inviting the opposition charge that the president was degrading his office. In a highly competitive political environment, presidents were buffeted between the insistence that they avoid electioneering and the demand that they keep their eyes fixed on their party's fortunes in upcoming state and national elections. Partisan and electoral calculations were an important component of presidential travel during the Jacksonian era, but presidents who openly advertised their partisan objectives ran the risk of being tarred as unfit for the high office of the presidency, as Van Buren and later, more spectacularly, Andrew Johnson discovered.[18]

Only a few decades separate Monroe's tours from those of the Jacksonian-era presidents, yet a political and cultural chasm separates travel in the two eras. Although Monroe was widely praised for his "plain republican" manner, his receptions were generally characterized by a stiff formality. The dignified Monroe bowed to those who were introduced to him. The people drew near the president but rarely touched him or grasped him by the hand. During the Jacksonian period, many of the forms remained the same, particularly the town's welcoming address and the presidential response, but the space between president and people had been diminished and democratized. Bowing gave way to handshaking. Common people expected or at least hoped to touch the president, even if they had not been introduced. On tour, Monroe was invariably addressed formally, as Mr. Monroe, the President of the United States, the Chief Magistrate or, on occasion, His Excellency. In contrast, as we see in chapter 3, the crowds of people who swarmed to meet President Zachary Taylor greeted him as "Old Zack."[19]

During the Jacksonian era, the president was commonly hailed as "a man of the people" and heralded, by Democrats at least, as a direct representative of the people and executor of the popular will. The ideology of republicanism had been premised upon executive restraint, tethering the president through strict construction of the Constitution and deference to the people's elected representatives in Congress. Jacksonian ideology, in contrast, ushered in a populist vision that empowered the president to act in the name of the people. Whereas republicanism taught eternal vigilance against the encroachments of monarchy, the emergent democratic sensibility seemed to dissolve those fears of executive power in the solvent of democracy. How, after all, could a popularly elected president be confused with a king?

The rise of democracy provided a rationale not only for presidential power but for presidential travel as well. A man of the people, after all, should mingle with the people. And the people's agent should speak not only for the people but with the people. Democratic rhetoric, however, collided with older yet enduring conceptions of what was appropriate behavior for the individual occupying the nation's "highest office." Andrew Johnson's "swing around the circle," a focal point of chapter 3, highlights the pitfalls that awaited the president who failed to attend to the demands of presidential dignity and decorum. Aptly dubbed "the last Jacksonian" by historian Kenneth Stampp, Johnson tried to turn his tour into a rousing populist crusade against scheming politicians, but found himself roundly rebuked for descending into the "muddy gutters of political vituperation" and forgetting "the dignity of his station."[20]

Most presidents, however, will worry less about the fate of Andrew Johnson than the fate of a John Quincy Adams, Martin Van Buren, or George Herbert Walker Bush, all presidents who were seen as lacking a common touch. In a democratic age, the most damaging charge against a president is not that he has acted in a vulgar or undignified manner but that he is aloof or distant, out of touch with the people's interests and wants. The sharp reactions to Johnson's tour marked the behavioral boundaries beyond which a nineteenth-century president on tour could not go, but most Americans continued to insist that the president remain close to the people. On this point, republican and democratic sensibilities converged.

Nineteenth-century Americans were inordinately proud that their presidents did not need to be protected from the people. That presidents could travel without bodyguards was a mark of the superiority of a democratic republic. Monarchs, emperors, and despots understandably feared the people over whom they ruled and so needed armed protection when they traveled outside the palace. But freely elected presidents had no reason to fear the people and so did not require protection from them, or so Americans believed. Chapter 4 explores the persistence of this tenet of American political thought even in the face of the assassinations of Abraham Lincoln in 1865 and James Garfield in 1881. Only after the assassination of William McKinley in 1901, the third president killed in 36 years, did Americans finally reconsider and authorize permanent protection for the president.

In choosing to protect the president, Americans made a fateful decision that helped to set the nation on the path toward the regal presidency that nineteenth-century Americans had strenuously worked to avoid. There are few political leaders in the world today who travel with more elaborate protections or a larger entourage than the American president. Chapter 4 charts the growth of presidential protection and examines the ways in which protecting the president on his travels created a safe distance between the president and the people, a distance that in the nineteenth century would have been criticized as undemocratic and indeed monarchical.

To dispel fears of monarchy President Monroe had set out on his tour not only without ceremony or entourage but with the intention of paying for his own travel. Neither the Constitution nor Congress provided the president with a travel allowance or even a mode of transportation. Washington toured in his personal carriage, and Jefferson owned the horse that carried him around the capital and home to Monticello. The absence of a public subsidy for travel acted as a brake on early presidents' traveling ambitions.

The advent of the railroads not only revolutionized the speed of presidential travel but transformed its financing as well. Whereas Washington and Monroe largely paid their own travel expenses, presidents who traveled by rail benefited from the generosity of the railroads. During the latter half of the nineteenth century, presidents essentially traveled as guests of the railroads. Not until after the abolition of the "free pass" system in 1906 was presidential travel made a public responsibility. One hundred and seventeen years after Congress had voted itself a mileage allowance the president was at last given a travel allowance of his own.

Chapter 5 surveys the financing of presidential travel, from Monroe's time to our own, but its central focus is the debates in Congress between 1906 and 1910 about the propriety of taxpayers paying for presidential travel. Although these debates were laced with partisanship, they nonetheless raised fundamental questions about the relationship of the president to the people and the role of travel in facilitating that relationship. In defending taxpayer-financed presidential travel, proponents were compelled to articulate the democratic purposes of presidential travel in a more systematic way than had been done before. Their arguments prevailed, but not all of the opposition's criticisms were answered. In particular, proponents had no sound riposte to the concern that taxpayers would be subsidizing travel that was designed to advance partisan aims. Defenders of the plan could answer only that they were sure no president would behave in such an undignified way—but few if any believed that.

Having taxpayers pay for presidential travel is surely preferable—or at least more democratic—than relying on the personal wealth of presidents or powerful private interests to pay for a president's travel. But democracy also requires transparency and accountability. And there is typically little of either in the travel expenditures of modern presidents. The cost of modern presidential travel is enormous but largely hidden from public view, dispersed as it is across countless departments and agencies. Finding out who accompanied the president can be as difficult as uncovering the costs associated with a trip. In contrast, the travel expenses of members of Congress and their staffers are an open book to the public and the press. Ironically, then, having taxpayers pay for presidential travel has made the presidency more regal even as it also made it more democratic.

Among the conventions governing nineteenth-century political travel was a taboo against foreign travel. Domestic travel was regarded as a welcome opportunity for presidents to talk with the people who had elected them, but foreign travel was seen in an altogether different light. Nineteenth-century Americans did not want their president mingling with royalty, visiting great palaces, exchanging bows with kings and queens. Republicans feared the seductions of the court as well as the "entangling alliances" that Washington warned against in his Farewell Address. The president's republican simplicity could best be guarded by keeping him far away from the corrupting influence of the Old World.

Chapter 6 examines the erosion and breakdown of this taboo in the early twentieth century. The central focus is Woodrow Wilson's momentous, precedent-breaking trip to Europe in 1919 and the controversy it engendered. The debate unleashed by Wilson's travel, like the debate over the funding of presidential travel a decade earlier, reveals sharply contrasting visions of the president's place in the American political system. The norm that proscribed foreign presidential travel not only kept the president tethered to American shores but it presupposed and bolstered a restrained American role in the world. Supporters of the norm understood that global leadership, as Alexis de Tocqueville had predicted, would dramatically increase the power of the American executive. The president could not be the leader of the Free World without transforming the presidency's role in the political system. If the taboo against presidents traveling abroad was a means of avoiding the development of a regal presidency, the taboo's breakdown spelled the demise of the nineteenth-century vision of a restrained, republican presidency.[21]

Changing transportation technologies, of course, have played a pivotal role in the changing patterns of presidential travel in the twentieth century. When Wilson traveled to Europe aboard the *George Washington*, an ocean liner the length of two and a half football fields, the voyage took nine days. Four decades later, President Dwight Eisenhower made the same trip by jet in nine hours. Jet aircraft enabled presidents to travel the globe in ways that would have been impractical if not inconceivable before. That much is obvious. Less obvious, however, are the paradoxical effects airplanes had on domestic presidential travel.

Chapter 7 explores the paradox that plane travel enabled presidents to travel further and faster than ever before but at the same time helped to make the president more remote from many Americans. Trains were much slower than planes but took presidents through countless small towns and hamlets. In the late nineteenth and early twentieth centuries, crowds of people from the surrounding countryside would come to see the president pass through and to hear him speak. Presidents felt an obligation to stop and address the crowds or at least to acknowledge them. The airplane, in contrast, enabled presidents to bypass towns and villages that did not serve their political interests and instead to head straight for the large metropolises or the carefully selected photo-op. The rest of the nation could watch the president on television.

Train travel was as well suited to the republican presidency as Air Force One is to the regal presidency. Cross-country travel aboard a train typically entailed a punishing schedule of stops and speeches, handshakes and greetings. Barely an hour would go by before the president would appear before an audience, and in between appearances the president often met with welcoming committees composed of prominent local citizens. The train symbolized the president's accessibility to the people. In contrast, Air Force One projects the power and majesty of the presidency. The president literally soars above the people, he out of their sight and they out of his. The plane, as one former White House adviser puts it, is "a traveling court," and "it is all oriented toward making sure the president has what he needs." Rather than provide an escape from the insulated White House bubble, Air Force One recreates the bubble in the air.[22]

The concluding chapter reflects on the rise of the regal presidency and takes as its starting point the paradox that a nation born in a revolutionary struggle against monarchy has created a presidency with so many prominently regal features. The nineteenth-century presidency was constrained and shaped by republican fears of a regal presidency. Nineteenth-century Americans were constantly on their guard against presidents exercising monarchical prerogatives, corrupting and influencing the legislature, or adopting the trappings and entourage of a court. This was why nineteenth-century presidents were denied even a rudimentary staff and encouraged to defer to the will of the legislature. Jefferson broke with the precedent established by George Washington and delivered his annual messages in writing rather than as a speech because Republicans worried that the practice of having the executive appear before the legislature to deliver an address aped monarchical practices. Underlying Jefferson's decision was not fear of a rhetorical presidency but a regal one.[23]

Travel in the nineteenth century was, among other things, a way for presidents to forge and to dramatize their connection to the people. Mingling with their fellow citizens enabled presidents to demonstrate their republican credentials and to dispel fears of monarchy. To be sure, memories of the "royal progress" complicated matters. There was always a fine line to be walked between an enthusiastic reception and servile adulation, between republican dignity and monarchical pomp. There was always the danger too that critics would find the transportation luxurious or extravagant. But presidents deflected this criticism by traveling, as much as possible, in "republican simplicity," without a large sycophantic entourage or threatening military guard. Speaking with the people, shaking hands, patting heads, kissing babies—all were useful ways of showing how far the president was from a monarch.

Presidents today still shake hands and kiss babies and deliver speeches on their travels. They try to appear as men of the people, just as nineteenth-century presidents did. They attempt, too, to use travel to show that they are not prisoners of the White House. Presidents today, however, are caught in a Catch–22, for they cannot travel without dramatizing the regal character of the contemporary presidency. They cannot leave the Secret Service behind or travel without an entourage any more than they can ground Air Force One and book a ticket aboard United Airlines. Moving a president today is a hugely complex operation that makes Queen Elizabeth I's royal progresses look like a casual romp in the countryside. Some of the "sprawling, regimented travel establishment" is hidden from public view but enough is visible that presidents find it difficult to travel without underlining their special privileges and accenting the distance that separates them from the people. Instead of demonstrating the president's connection to the people, presidential travel ends up reinforcing the image of a regal presidency.[24]

The Origins of Presidential Travel: The Tours of George Washington and James Monroe

In early April 1817 the newly inaugurated president, James Monroe, penned a letter to his friend and former assistant Nicholas Biddle, informing him that he had decided to undertake a tour of the northern United States. Not since George Washington had a president embarked on a tour of the nation, and Biddle was enthusiastic about the new president's plans. In Biddle's view, "Ever since the time of Gen. Washington, the President has unfortunately appeared to the nation too much like the Chief Clerk of Congress, a cabinet man, stationary at his desk relying exclusively on Secretaries, & invisible except to those who seek him." Biddle believed that it would "be highly gratifying to the community to see the Chief Magistrate examining for himself, & taking care that the great operations confided to him are not marred by the negligence or infidelity of agents." For Biddle, Monroe's tour would make the presidency more visible and help to change the way the people viewed the office.[1]

Monroe's initial purpose in undertaking the tour, however, was not to make the president more visible but rather to inspect the nation's fortifications along the northeastern coast and the northern border with Canada. Foremost in Monroe's mind was the debacle of the War of 1812. As secretary of state (and, for a while, secretary of war as well), he had observed at close quarters the perils of an inadequate national defense. He had been among those who had fled the capital in August 1814 as the British army sailed up the Chesapeake Bay, marched into Washington, D.C., and torched the Capitol and White House. The war had tested republican doctrine and found it wanting. State militias, the country discovered, were inadequate for national defense. A stronger navy was needed, as were better coastal defenses and improved roads and canals for transporting troops and materials. Building on a national scale required the federal government to become more involved than Jeffersonian orthodoxy had hitherto allowed. Or so Monroe (and James Madison) believed were the war's lessons.

Following the end of the war, President Madison had pressed Congress to improve the nation's defenses, especially along the eastern seaboard. Congress approved funds "to establish a chain of fortifications, along the coast . . . and to establish Naval Depots and Dock-yards" at regular intervals. When Monroe assumed the presidency he immediately made the building of these fortifications a priority. His aim in taking the tour, as he explained to Congress at the end of his eight years in office, was to "be better enabled to judge of the Reports, which might be made, through the proper Departments, by the Engineers & Naval Commissioners, appointed to survey the Coast, respecting the Sites, & nature of those works." But Monroe's aim was not only to improve his ability to make sound decisions, it was also to shape public opinion. "By making this inspection in person," Monroe explained, "I might . . . draw the public attention more forcibly to the object." With the war over, the danger was that the American people would forget the lessons of the war and lapse back into old republican habits. The tour would help to focus the nation's attention on the federal government's responsibility to maintain a strong national defense.[2]

Today Monroe's tour is most commonly remembered—when it is remembered at all—as the "goodwill tour" that ushered in the so-called Era of Good Feelings.[3] And in fact the tour was quickly transformed into a celebration of the submerging of party differences. Federalists vied with Republicans to show their respect for the nation's first magistrate, a particularly important symbolic act in New England, where some Federalists had seriously entertained the possibility of secession in 1814. For New England Federalists this was a chance to affirm their commitment to the nation—"to work out the stain of the Hartford Convention," as one Federalist put it—while for Monroe it was an opportunity to reaffirm national unity in the wake of a divisive and often disastrous war.[4]

The great fanfare and elaborate ceremony with which Monroe was greeted across New England were not part of his original plan. Of course, he expected to be noticed; indeed, only by being in the public spotlight could he succeed in directing national attention toward the need for expanded fortifications. But Monroe strove to lower the trip's profile. He left his family in Virginia and did not ask any members of his administration to accompany him, apart from General Swift, head of the Army Corps of Engineers—the administrative unit responsible for the construction and maintenance of coastal fortifications. Leaving Washington, D.C., Monroe's only companions were a couple of servants and his nineteen-year-old personal secretary. Monroe was determined to travel "in the character of a private citizen," avoiding parades and public dinners, and even paying for the trip out of his own pocket.[5]

It did not take long for Monroe to realize that his hope of traveling the country as a private citizen was wildly unrealistic. Upon arriving in Baltimore, the first stop on his tour, he was greeted by "a vast cavalcade of citizens several miles from the town and escorted into the city." Crowds of people, like "an agitated sea," seemed to envelop the president wherever he went. The morning after the president's arrival, the *Baltimore Patriot* reported that the people of Baltimore did "not feel disposed to gratify" the president's well-advertised wish "to avoid all parade." The citizens of Baltimore were not alone. Fancy carriages, military escorts, triumphal arches, ringing bells, and booming cannons marked the president's arrival in towns all along the eastern seaboard. In Boston, an estimated forty thousand people "lined the streets and filled every window along the route" to watch the presidential procession snake its way toward the Boston Common, where "the official welcoming party" awaited.[6]

The press of people was constant. It seemed that everyone wished to pay tribute to the president. He was feted and toasted at countless public dinners, granted an honorary degree at Harvard College, and made a fellow of the Literary and Philosophical Society of New York. He was addressed by delegations from the Society of Associated Mechanics in New Hampshire, a group of clergymen in Maine, and the Society of the Cincinnati in Massachusetts, New York, and Pennsylvania. Virtually every village and town through which Monroe passed prepared a welcoming address, and the president was expected to respond to the address with a speech of his own. Monroe estimated that he had "been compelled to answer four or five addresses in a day, . . . not one of which I had seen, or heard, till read." The constant impromptu speech-making and negotiating of crowds of people meant the traveling was far more taxing than he had anticipated.[7]

In short, the president of the United States could not possibly travel the country as a private citizen. The president was a "distinguished character" to whom citizens wished to pay tribute. A visit from the president, moreover, was a novelty for most Americans; Washington was the only other president to tour the nation and that had been a quarter century earlier. A bemused John Adams reported that in Boston "there is no other theme of conversation at present," a sentiment echoed by Rufus King (Monroe's defeated opponent in the 1816 presidential election), who observed that in New York City "we have no other topic of Communication except that of the Pr[esident]'s tour." Everyone, agreed one of New York City's leading merchants, was "all in a flutter" at the president's arrival.[8]

Monroe was faced with the choice—as he later told Jefferson—of "either returning home, or complying with the opinion of the public." And that, of course, was no choice at all. To spurn the accolades and invitations would have meant giving "serious offense," both personal and political. Monroe submitted to the inevitable and used the parades and processions as a means to focus attention on the themes of national unity and strength that he had highlighted in his inaugural address. But if it was obvious from the outset that a president would not be able to travel as a private citizen, why then did Monroe initially believe that he could?[9]

The editor of Monroe's papers suggests that this was because the "experience of the preceding sixteen years had taught him that he could do so." Presidents Jefferson and Madison had regularly traveled between their Virginia homes and the capital without attracting great notice. And in the District of Columbia, observe the editors, "the president moved about the city as freely as any other resident." But surely there is more to it than that. For experience would also have taught Monroe that President Washington's tours—by far the closest parallel to what he was proposing to do—had been highly visible events, accompanied by elaborate pomp and ceremony. Monroe would also be keenly aware that members of his own party had been fiercely critical of the monarchical trappings of the Washington and Adams administrations. And nothing was more monarchical than "the royal progress"—the term used to describe the practice of monarchs touring the kingdom. Monroe's determination to travel as a private citizen was neither naivete nor a mistaken calculation. Rather it was a way of touring the nation while also assuaging republican fears of monarchy.[10]

THE ROYAL PROGRESS

The royal progress had been a central part of the British monarchy in the sixteenth century. Queen Elizabeth I went on "progresse" almost annually during her forty-four-year reign. Accompanied by an immense retinue of court officials, counselors, courtiers, clergymen, and countless servants, the queen would literally take the court to the country. "Up to six hundred strong, with heralds in the lead and lumbering baggage carts bringing up the rear, the court would set off over provincial roads to show Gloriana to her people." A typical progress began in the middle of summer and lasted about seven weeks, with overnight stops in about two dozen different locales, generally the homes of wealthy, well-connected lords and ladies. So common were these royal travels that many a great house was designed or redesigned so as to accommodate the monarch's needs.[11]

When the queen's progress took her through a town, she was generally met with an oration to which she would offer a few gracious words in response. Towns might also prepare triumphal arches for the queen to pass through, or offer a play for the queen's entertainment. When the queen and her retinue stayed at a country estate, the host was expected to offer the queen not only a generous gift but a ceremonial pageant in praise of her majesty. Historian Malcolm Smuts relates an incident from 1591 that illustrates how far the nobility would go to please their visiting queen. Hearing that her majesty

> was moving toward one of his small country residences . . . [the Earl of Hertford] hired 280 workmen to erect a small village to house the court and construct the setting for a pageant. They dug a pond in the shape of a crescent moon of Diana, goddess of chastity. In it stood an island fortress and a ship, to symbolize England and her navy, and a huge snail made of trimmed hedges, to represent the queen's enemies. When Elizabeth arrived, water deities came out of this enchanted pool to pay homage in song and verse to the mistress of the seas. Then the ship and fortress attacked the snail with blazing cannon, blowing it up in a profusion of fireworks.

The queen must have appreciated the earl's efforts as she stayed for three days.[12]

Despite the substantial expense attached to hosting the queen and her traveling party, members of the landed aristocracy were generally eager to have the queen stay with them, both because it enhanced their reputation in the local community and because they hoped it would prompt the queen to look more favorably upon them. A visit from the queen also provided the host with a degree of access to the monarch that was impossible in the more regulated environment of the court. The host had the chance both to curry royal favor and to request royal favors. Towns also welcomed a visit from the monarch for it gave local officials the opportunity to ask for her majesty's assistance "in strengthening the civic economy, especially the harbors, markets, and industries, as well as in adjudicating local disputes."[13]

For the queen, the progresses served myriad political purposes. Whether the host was a private individual or a group of town officials, the progress enabled Elizabeth to cultivate personal bonds between herself and influential local notables and families. The visits also allowed the queen to gather first-hand information, whether about the needs of a particular area of the country or the state of military defenses in port towns such as Southampton or Dover. The elaborate public ceremonies that attended her arrival in towns and villages effectively dramatized and projected her royal authority. By affording her subjects the opportunity to see her majesty in all of her royal splendor, Elizabeth forged a powerful public image of an accessible yet magnificent monarch.[14]

The royal progress gradually declined in size and importance over the course of the seventeenth and eighteenth centuries. In part this reflected a shift in the balance of power between the monarch and the landed aristocracy. As the power of the monarchy declined, the landed gentry were less willing to foot the bill for royal travel. In part, too, it reflected opposition from those within the royal household who resented both the expense and the disruption to court life that resulted from the monarch traveling. Always attuned to her popularity, Elizabeth believed the effort well worth the expense. But the Stuart monarchs of the seventeenth century put far less stock in cultivating public support and used the royal progress less frequently and less strategically than Elizabeth had. By the eighteenth century, the royal progress had fallen out of fashion. The first of the Hanoverian monarchs, George I, disliked England and spent as little time as possible there. George II, like his father, spoke German and counted few friends among the English landed nobility.[15]

Although by the eighteenth century the royal progress was no longer a central part of the display of monarchical power, it continued to resonate in the Anglo-American world. The term "progress" continued to carry the connotation of "a state journey made by a royal or noble personage," particularly a journey accompanied by pomp and ceremony. Although King George III was not known for his journeys across England, the progress remained linked in the Anglo-American mind to the regal display of power and magnificence. In the new United States, where republicans kept a vigilant watch for the sprouts of monarchy, traveling presidents had to be careful to avoid the appearance that they were trying to recreate the magnificent royal progress of the Tudors.[16]

George Washington was a national hero before ever setting foot in the presidential office. He was revered for his military leadership during the American Revolution and for the way he relinquished his powers when the war was over. The framers who created the presidency took it for granted that Washington would be the office's first occupant. Public support for the unanimously elected new president seemed boundless. The French chargé d'affaires told his government at the beginning of 1790 that "never has the citizen of a free country enjoyed among his compatriots a confidence as pure and as universal. In more than one hundred gazettes, often very licentious, published daily in the United States, his name has constantly been respected; in an assembly composed of so many heterogeneous individuals as is that of Congress, he has always been spoken of with veneration."[17]

On the morning of October 15, 1789, about two weeks after the adjournment of the first session of the first Congress, Washington left the nation's capital for a month's tour through the states of New England. Although universally admired, Washington was anxious to avoid the sort of fanfare that could make his trip resemble a royal progress. The aim of the tour, he explained, was merely "to acquire knowledge of the face of the Country . . . and the temper and disposition of the Inhabitants towards the new government." He also hoped the tour would make him "more accessible to numbers of well-informed persons, who might give him useful information and advice on political subjects." To this end, he kept his traveling party small: six servants and a couple of personal assistants. Informed by Massachusetts Governor John Hancock of the elaborate arrangements being made for the visit, Washington politely thanked the governor for "the honor intended" but said that he preferred his tour to be "without any parade, or extraordinary ceremony." The president also turned down Hancock's invitation to stay with him, explaining that "from a wish to avoid giving trouble to private families" he had decided to decline any invitations to stay at private residences, preferring instead to pay his own way at taverns and public houses.[18]

The governor reluctantly acceded to Washington's choice of lodgings, but would not budge on the parade and ceremony, which, he told Washington, were "tokens of respect" that "answer[ed] the expectations of my Constituents." Hancock's constituents were not disappointed at the grand spectacle that greeted the president's entrance into Boston; even Washington conceded that the reception was "in every degree flattering & honorable." He was met at Cambridge by the Massachusetts lieutenant governor, Samuel Adams, and the state's Executive Council, and escorted to Boston where he was introduced to the selectmen of the town. The presidential procession, Washington reported in his diary, passed through the Citizens classed in their different professions, and under their own banners, till we came to the State House; from which, across the Street, an Arch was thrown; in the front of which was this Inscription—"To the Man who unites all hearts" and on the other—"To Columbia's favourite Son.". . . . This arch was handsomely ornamented, and over the Center of it a Canopy was erected 20 feet high with the American Eagle perched on the top. After passing through the Arch, and entering the State House at the So. End & [as]cending to the upper floor & returning to a Balcony at the No. End—three cheers was given by a vast concourse of people who by this time had assembled at the Arch. Then followed an ode composed in honor of the President; and well sung by a band of select Singers—after this three Cheers—followed by the different Professions, and Mechanics in the order they were drawn up with their Colours through a lane of the People which had thronged abt. the Arch under which they passed. The Streets, the Doors, Windows & Tops of the Houses were crouded with well dressed Ladies and Gentlemen.

Washington found there was little he could do to prevent such demonstrations and so determined to enjoy what he must endure. Towns across New England welcomed their president with odes sung in his honor, the discharge of artillery, the parading of state militia, welcoming addresses by local officials, escorts in and out of town, elegant public dinners, and cheering crowds.[19]

Although Washington at times seemed uneasy with the ostentatious show of respect, his fellow citizens did not seem to share those concerns. But Washington—ever sensitive about appearances—was right to be apprehensive. For while the president's personal reputation shielded him from criticism, there were already murmurings of complaint about the "royalist trappings" of the administration. When the first Congress convened back in April 1789 they began by debating what to call the president. Vice President John Adams believed a "a royal or at least princely title" was necessary "to maintain the reputation, authority, and dignity of the President," and a majority of the Senate evidently agreed, proposing the president be referred to as "His Highness, the President of the United States of America, and Protector of the Rights of the Same." The House refused to go along, believing that such a title was inappropriate for an elected leader of a republic. William Maclay, a senator from western Pennsylvania who spearheaded the Senate opposition, saw in such efforts a determination on the part of some "to run into all the fooleries, fopperies, finches, and pomp of royal etiquette."[20]

Maclay and Adams also clashed in the opening days of Congress about how to refer to the president's inaugural address. On the Senate floor Adams referred to Washington's inaugural address as "his most gracious speech," an appellation customarily used to describe the British monarch's speech to Parliament. When the phrase turned up in the minutes, Maclay asked his colleagues to strike the words.

"The words prefixed to the President's speech," he explained, "are the same that are usually placed before the speech of his Britannic Majesty." The words, Maclay predicted, would "give offense," for "we have lately had a hard struggle for our liberty against kingly authority" and consequently "everything related to that species of government is odious" to the people. Despite the vice president's strenuous resistance to Maclay's proposal, the Senate agreed to drop the offending words.[21]

Maclay was also among those who expressed misgivings about the president's Tuesday afternoon levees at which select individuals were introduced to the president, and polite bows and pleasantries were exchanged. No chairs were placed in the room so that none might make the mistake of sitting in the president's presence. Washington's dress set the "high tone" of the event. He was outfitted "in black velvet ordered from Europe at $5 a yard, along with yellow gloves, silver knee buckles, and glistening dress sword in a white leather scabbard." In December 1790, Maclay wrote in his diary that "the practice [of the levee] . . . considered as a feature of royalty, is certainly antirepublican. This . . . escapes nobody. The royalists glory in it as a point gained. Republicans are borne down by fashion and a fear of being charged with a want of respect to General Washington." Maclay then allowed himself a forbidden thought. "Would to God this same General Washington were in heaven! We would not then have him brought forward as the constant cover to every unconstitutional and unrepublican act."[22]

In 1790, such subversive thoughts were best kept to oneself. But over the next few years the whispers and private thoughts of a few became more audible and widespread. In February 1793, just months after Washington's unanimous reelection, the radical editor Benjamin Franklin Bache informed his father that the president's levees were now "generally censured." A month earlier Bache's *General Advertiser* had published a satirical advertisement that sought a "poet laureate" for the administration. The successful candidate would have to be accomplished at writing about "Monarchical Prettiness," including "levees, drawing rooms, stately nods instead of shaking hands, titles of offices, seclusion from the people, &c., &c." Many who had previously joined in extravagant birthday celebrations for the president now swore off such celebrations, which they said smacked of monarchy. In the pages of the *General Advertiser*, "Mirabeau" identified ten features of the Washington administration that were ushering in monarchy and aristocracy. Chief among them were fancy titles, grand levees, celebrating the president's birthday, "establishing a ceremonial distance between the officers of the government and the people," and "parade of every kind in the officers of government, such as pompous carriages, splendid feasts, and tawdry gowns."[23]

At the time Washington embarked on his second tour in April 1791—this one a two-month journey through the southern states—concerns about the monarchical pretensions of the administration were still generally subdued. Opposition barbs were aimed at Vice President Adams's alleged penchant for fancy titles, but Washington was generally beyond public reproach. Still Washington's tour did attract some critical commentary that foreshadowed the more frontal attack on monarchical practices that would emerge in another eighteen months. Only ten days into the trip, Bache's *General Advertiser* expressed disapproval that "the President, on his journey, is still perfumed with the incense of addresses. However highly we may consider the character of the Chief Magistrate of the Union, yet we cannot but think the fashionable mode of expressing our attachment to the defender of the Liberty of his country savors too much of Monarchy to be used by Republicans, or to be received with pleasure by a President of a Commonwealth."[24]

Certainly a number of the addresses to "his Excellency"—as Washington was frequently called—were fit for a king. In Fredericksburg, Maryland, for instance, town officials told Washington: "We have the fullest confidence in divine Benevolence that the disposer of all good will be graciously pleased long to continue you in health and reward you both here and hereafter with blessings adequate to your Merit." The addresses to the president, moreover, were as carefully scripted and painfully formal as anything a monarch might receive. At each location Washington knew precisely what was going to be said. The welcoming address was submitted beforehand to the president's aide who then made a copy of the message and drafted a reply for the president to sign. When the president arrived in a town, invariably accompanied by an official escort that had met him at an agreed-upon location some distance from the city boundary, the town's representatives "would read aloud their original address and present it to the president with due ceremony, and then [Washington] would read his official reply and likewise deliver it to the officials."[25]

Washington's entourage was minuscule by the standards of British monarchs, but the style in which he traveled was impressive nonetheless. On his tour of the South he took only a personal secretary and four servants, but each of the servants— a "valet, two footmen and coachman"—was "attired in red and white livery." The "chariot" in which Washington traveled was even more impressive.

> Painted white, the coach had beautiful designs of the four seasons . . . painted on the doors and front and back. The Washington coat-of-arms, within ovals, was painted on the quarter panels. There were four Venetian blinds on the sides in the shape of quarter-ellipses, and four others—two each front and back— rectangular in shape. There were glass windows in the front of the coach. The whole framework and springs were gold plated, as were the door handles and the moldings around the roof. . . . The coach was pulled by four, matched white horses, their harnesses of red leather and gold.

At the time of his two tours Washington's magnificent coach and horses seemed to attract only favorable comment, but within eighteen months the coach and the horses had become an important symbol of the monarchical pretensions of the administration. In January 1793, for instance, the *General Advertiser* published a mocking commentary from a "Farmer" who had traveled to Philadelphia to get a glimpse of George III's son Prince Edward, who was said to be driving around the capital city in an elegant coach. "I met the coach," the correspondent reported, "and to my utter surprize and disappointment, who should it be but the President of the United States: Ah! Thought I to myself the times are changed, and have changed with them the plain and republican General Washington into a being which my neighbour . . . took to be a Prince."[26]

Charleston, the largest city on Washington's southern tour, entertained the president in a high style that would not have been completely out of place in the court of George III. In preparation for the president's weeklong visit, "every head and every hand" in the city was "anxiously occupied, each in their proper station, from the governor to the mechanic." Upon his arrival, the president was rowed across the harbor by twelve smartly dressed captains on a splendid barge outfitted for the occasion; painted on the boat's side were the words "Long live the president." Accompanying the president were some forty vessels packed with a "gay throng of richly dressed ladies and gentlemen," including two boats carrying a choir that welcomed Washington in song:

He comes! He comes! The hero comes.
Sound, sound your trumpets, beat your drums,
From port to port let cannons roar,
His welcome to our friendly shore.

On his second day in Charleston the president attended a large public banquet, where he was seated beneath "a beautiful triumphal arch, from which was suspended a wreath of laurel." The following evening, the president was treated to a magnificent ball, which featured, Washington noted in his diary, "256 elegantly dressed and handsome ladies." What Washington did not record, but others did, is that the ladies wore ribbons "with different inscriptions expressive of their esteem and respect for the president," including "Long live the president," "He lives, the guardian of his country's rights," "Virtue and valor united," "Rejoice, the hero's come," and "Shield, oh! shield him from all harm." Adding to the splendor of the evening was a "beautiful arch of lamps" that illuminated the entrance of the building, atop which were the words *Deliciis Patriae* [Beloved by the nation]. A company of fusiliers standing guard at the gates of the building added to the "splendid elegance" of the evening.[27]

The following evening's entertainment—a musical concert—was possibly grander still. Washington left no record of his impressions of the music, but he was undoubtedly dazzled by the female company. "There were at least 400 lad[ie]s," Washington marveled, "the Number & appearances of wch. exceeded any thing of the kind I had ever seen." The large hall was elaborately decorated; pillars "ingeniously entwined with laurel" and walls adorned with Latin mottos in praise of the president as well as one in English: "With grateful praises of the hero's fame / We'll teach our infants' tongues to lisp his name." "So much beauty and elegance," noted one observer, "were never before displayed in this country."[28]

The next day the president again attended a ball in the evening, this one at the governor's home where he mixed with what he described in his diary as a "select company of ladies." Washington did not mention that instead of the usual "elaborate floral headdresses and imposing feathers" the ladies "wore handsome fillets or bandeaux upon which was drawn or painted Washington's portrait, with the national colors entwined." Little wonder that some Americans were beginning to grouse about "the vileness of the adulation paid to Washington," and to fret that such hero worship was setting the nation on the well-worn path to monarchy and aristocracy.[29]

In sum, the pageantry of Washington's tours, though largely praised at the time, nonetheless contributed to growing unease about the monarchical and aristocratic pretensions of the Federalists. As the Republican opposition emerged as a potent political force in 1793, Federalist efforts to envelop the president in "royal pomp and circumstance" became a primary target in the Republican battle against "Monocrats," as Jefferson dubbed the Federalists. The potency of this critique may explain why neither Adams, Jefferson, nor Madison attempted to emulate Washington's tour. Traveling among the people on Washington's model still looked too much like a monarchical progress to be acceptable in a republican nation. The challenge for Monroe was to come up with a republican model of traveling among the people.[30]

MONROE'S FIRST TOUR

Monroe announced his intention to travel as a private citizen in an attempt to dispel the specter of monarchy that still haunted the republican imagination. The fifth president of the United States was popular, but he did not possess the commanding prestige that had shielded the nation's first president from criticism. As a politician with strong connections to the most doctrinaire wing of the Republican Party, Monroe was instinctively sensitive to the need to avoid behaviors that could be interpreted as incipient monarchy.

It helped that Monroe eschewed the elaborately decorated, privately owned carriage that had transported President Washington. Instead Monroe rode in public stagecoaches or on horseback. Although he might not be able to travel as a private citizen, many Americans found it reassuring that their president "appeared in the dress of a citizen." Over and over, observers commented approvingly on the "republican simplicity" and "plainness" of Monroe's dress and deportment. The editors of a Pennsylvania newspaper, for instance, accented his "extremely plain . . . dress and behaviour." They felt sure that "to a man of his appearance the fulsome addresses which have been presented to him & the parade that has been made to receive him . . . must be extremely irksome." The editors sympathized with the president, who "is conducted into town like a state prisoner, . . . compelled to wait for the performance of ceremonies which he dislikes." Monroe's plain republican appearance and his much-publicized desire to avoid processions and parades helped to inoculate him against charges of monarchical pretensions.[31]

The president's defenders were quick to underline that Monroe had explicitly requested that towns avoid public spectacles. Three weeks into the tour, for instance, the *National Intelligencer*, the administration's "semiofficial" newspaper, allowed that some of its readers might reasonably think that the president's excursion had been accompanied by "too much of the pomp of military and civil parade." The *Intelligencer* confessed it shared those concerns, but reminded its readers that "so far from courting such transitory honors, the President himself endeavored to avoid them; and that the offerings of respect, and ebullitions of joy on his arrival in Philadelphia and New York particularly, were the spontaneous evidences of the respect and attachment of a patriotic people." Monroe could not be faulted for having "secured . . . a strong hold in the affections of the American people."[32]

Monroe's supporters also emphasized how unlike the president's tour was from anything one might witness in Europe. The *American Telegraph* marveled at the contrast between Monroe's tour and the "situation of an European sovereign," who would be "guarded by thousands of his slaves" while living in constant "dread [of] the pistol and the poniard of the lurking assassin." How different the situation was for Monroe, who "unattended but by only a few of his particular friends and servants has made a journey of 2000 miles, not only with security, but without fear and molestation." The president's "only body guard" was "the love the people bear their government and its officers." To the editors of the *Telegraph*, this was the defining "difference between despotism and liberty—between a government founded for the benefit of the rulers and a government established for the good of the people." Monroe's tour induced similar reflections on the wonders of American democracy from the *Georgetown Messenger*: "We cannot contemplate this individual citizen, elevated by the suffrages of a free people to the chief executive office of the country, passing through the several states unprotected, save by the affection which surrounds him, and not make the comparison between his happiness and that of—for instance, the Prince Regent of England. Stones and bullets are the greetings received by the one tho' buttoned in a military coat, and mailed in arms; whilst spontaneous and grateful applause, sent forth by an enlightened and happy people, are bestowed on the other." Whereas in Europe the sovereign needed an armed entourage whenever he ventured beyond the palace gates, in the United States the president could travel "fearlessly and comparatively alone, through the whole extent of the Union."[33]

The receptions that greeted Monroe, the president's backers insisted, bore no relation to the slavish adulation bestowed upon European monarchs. As the *Baltimore Patriot* explained, "These effusions of respect and gratitude are unlike the adulation of fawning courtiers, and bear no resemblance to that adoration which ignorance and superstition proffer to the legitimate majesty of despots." In Europe the respect shown to the monarch was born either of "that cringing servility which proceeds from the fear of a crowned head" or "that idolatry and ignorance which would extol to the heavens the infamy of titled greatness." But in the United States the displays of respect were "the unbought expressions of regard, emanating from the bosoms of a free people." The *National Intelligencer* emphasized the same point, noting that "the public respect, which now surrounds [President Monroe] is not . . . the heartless sycophancy of courtiers, the babyish worship of titles, or the superstitious adulation which is paid by ignorance to prescription." Instead it was "the homage of republican people to the government of their choice." Celebrations in Monroe's honor represented not an unrepublican fawning over the executive but a celebration of democracy. "It was in fact," the lawyer Edward Bangs wrote to Nathaniel Howe, "bending the knee, not to a man, but to the Majesty of the People concentered in him."[34]

On this interpretation, far from representing a vestige of monarchy, Monroe's tour heralded the emergence of democracy. In a monarchy the people were kept at a safe distance from the monarch, but in a republic touring the nation brought the president and people closer together. As the *New Hampshire Gazette* observed, "our citizens, in republican simplicity, meet and converse with their President, face to face, hand in hand. No royal diadems, no court sycophants, no military guards, as in nearly all other countries, keep the people at a useless, gazing, distance." When the American Society for the Encouragement of American Manufacturers favored the president with an address, the group emphasized that the president's tour signaled "a new era in the history of society." In times past and in other parts of the globe, "the influence of the Magistrate is felt, only from the operation of his laws, or through the instrumentality of his subordinate agents; while on the other hand, he derives his information through intermediate channels, but our happy Constitution places the people and their officers in such relations to each other, that they may have a mutual and direct intercourse—and we now behold the first Magistrate of a great Nation, seeking at its source, the information, which will enable him to know the wants and wishes of the country." By touring the nation, the president forged direct bonds between himself and his fellow citizens in a manner befitting a democracy.[35]

Not everyone, however, was sure that the tour was promoting republicanism, whatever Monroe's intentions. Skeptics warned that an "excess of ceremony" was "incompatible with the simplicity of republican manners and independence of republican principles." The New York *Columbian* was one of many newspapers to warn against welcoming celebrations that "ape monarchy, with all of its parade." Judging by newspaper accounts, the *Columbian*'s editors groused, "you would suppose that the tour of a republican chief magistrate through these states was the procession of the 'autocrat of all the Russias,' through his empire." In a similar vein, Henry Meigs wrote to his father condemning "this ridiculous aping of Rotten Monarchy." "So much parade as is threatened," Meigs complained, "savors but little of Republican plainness.... Those who offer the adulation are belittled by it and ... belittle the object of their adulation."[36]

Probably the most influential critic of Monroe's tour was Thomas Ritchie, editor of the *Richmond Enquirer*. Ritchie's anxieties about the tour became particularly pronounced as Monroe made his way through the Federalist stronghold of New England. On July 17, as New England feted the president, Ritchie's *Enquirer* expressed "disgust" at the accounts of the president's tour that filled the eastern papers: "So much parade—such bombastic accounts of who [the president] breakfasted or dined with; his cortege, and coteries, and collations, and balls; mixed up with such ridiculous and parasitical accounts of 'Mrs. Harrison Gray Otis's mansion,' 'The splendid mansion of Mr. Speaker Bigelow,' &c. &c." Ritchie could hardly believe this was America. "Are these the manners of republican citizens? Is this the description of the trip of an American officer in the discharge of his Executive duties? Or are we in England, where 'the great man' scarcely moves without a herald at his heels?" Ritchie largely absolved Monroe of blame. The president, he allowed, was "an honest man—of a warm and generous heart—and if we do not most grossly mistake him, one of the plainest men that ever sat in the chair of any state." But whatever Monroe's intentions, such events "suit not him, nor the office which he fills, nor the people, whose agent he is."[37]

Ritchie's chastising did not escape Monroe's attention. On August 5, the president wrote to his son-in-law and political confidant, George Hay, expressing apprehension that his receptions in upstate New York would "give much offense to Mr. Ritchie, & bring on me something more than an implied attack from that quarter." Monroe described being "met at each village en masse" by the entire population of the surrounding area, passing under "19 triumphal arches" that had been erected over a bridge. The entire town was illuminated, though he knew nothing of it until the morning, "having gone to bed early in consequence of much fatigue." The president insisted that he had been as powerless to control his reception in these villages as he had been in the earlier segments of his tour. "The military," he assured Hay, "had nothing to do in this business. It was exclusively the act of the citizens."[38]

Monroe's fears were justified. On the same day that Monroe penned his letter, Ritchie blasted "all the idle pageantry, [and] all the ridiculous and noxious pomp" that accompanied the president's tour. Ritchie did credit Monroe's tour with having contributed to the "political calm" that had settled over the country, but he also believed that hopes of an enduring era of good feelings were a chimera. Party spirit, he warned, "never can perfectly die." There would always be a division between those men "fond of distinction, of titles, of privilege, unwilling to associate with their fellow-citizens, thinking themselves better than the mass of the people, leaning toward an aristocracy in government." And with such men, Ritchie cautioned, "it is impossible for the friends of equal rights to hold communion. They must declare war against them." Monroe's policy of reaching out to the Federalists, although valuable for calming party spirit, was dangerous to the republic in so far as it tried to conciliate those who were irreconcilably opposed to republican government.[39]

Ritchie's admonitions were calculated to warn Monroe against drawing too close to New England's Federalists. Suspicions of the Federalists' intentions in welcoming Monroe (as well as of Monroe's intentions in traveling to New England) were particularly strong in the West, nowhere more so than in Henry Clay's Kentucky. Clay himself ridiculed the homage paid to Monroe: "The people of those parts through which the President passed, rise en masse, as the audience at the Theatre Francais or Covent Garden, upon the entrance of the Sovereign, to greet, to honor, and to salute him." The "pomp and ostentatious parade" obscured the Federalists' partisan aims and betrayed their monarchical leanings. The *Kentucky Gazette* minced no words about the motives behind "this pompous parade of Federal regard for our republican president." It was "a stratagem, an artifice, a shallow plot to gain the good will of the chief magistrate, to persuade him that they, who never hitherto ceased to persecute him, are his best friends, and mean to support his administration; thereby hoping to obtain a share of executive appointments, and ultimately, if possible, to displace the republican party from the national councils." The *Gazette* expressed confidence that Monroe "will guard against their deceitful acts," but the message was a pointed reminder to Monroe to remember his true friends and not to have his head turned by Federalist adulation.[40]

Monroe's tour was unnerving not only to fervent Republican partisans. Even more measured and less fiercely partisan voices, such as the *Niles Weekly Register*, were uneasy about much of the tour's pomp and ceremony. The paper's editor, Hezekiah Niles, did not find fault with Monroe, for he "travels as privately as he can, except he were to pass on incognito." The president's "dress and manners have more the appearance of those supposed to belong to a plain and substantial, but well informed farmer, than such as, from our perverted notions, are attached by many to a personage so distinguished." Nor could he blame the people for "desiring to see and pay respects to their chief magistrate." And yet Niles's unease was palpable. Three weeks into the tour, the editor explained that the *Weekly Register* did not intend to "follow the president step by step, and retail all the chit-chat stuff that appears in the papers about him," for such reports were "as irksome to the republican mind and manners of Mr. Monroe as to the people at large." Niles reiterated that there was nothing wrong with the people paying their "marks of respect . . . to the chief magistrate on a tour of duty," but admitted that "there is more of pomp and parade given to it by the people than the fitness of things requires." However, Niles considered his paper "a sort of journal of official proceedings," and so felt compelled to cover the president's tour. The president's traveling was news.[41]

Several months into the tour, the *Weekly Register* felt compelled again to explain its coverage of the tour and to distance itself from the tour's unrepublican aspects.

"Several of our friends," Niles wrote, "have good humoredly queried, whether the plain republican character of the *Weekly Register* was not rather compromitted [*sic*] by the space allowed in its pages to accounts of the forms and ceremonies attending 'the President's tour.'" Niles's verdict was that the paper had not compromised its principles. The paper merely recorded things that "belong to the history of the manners and feelings of the times." But Niles also made it clear that his own views were "entirely repugnant to the pompous proceedings of his eastern brethren." Such adulation and gawking were not only unrepublican but prevented the president from carrying out his "tour of business." "Encompassed with a crowd—at every hour intruded upon, and beset at every turn and corner by an idly gazing multitude," the president could neither perform his public duties nor even have "a moment at his own disposal." As a record of official proceedings the *Weekly Register* would continue to cover the president's tour, but Niles cautioned darkly that "there is danger in pomp and parade."[42]

In New York, the *National Advocate*, which began by defending the "suitable demonstrations of respect" that were being planned for the president's visit to New York, adopted a more cautionary note as the president's tour stretched on. After two weeks of the tour, the *Advocate* reported approvingly that Monroe "has been received, not with the pageantry of a monarch, claiming, by hereditary right, the homage of his subjects, but with the spontaneous friendship and sincere affection of his fellow-citizens, who, in paying that respect due to their chief magistrate, substantially honored the officer of their own creation." The paper applauded, too, "the simple and unaffected manners of the President" and marveled at a nation in which the chief magistrate could leave "the seat of government on public business, without guards, retinue, or even suite, but merely attended by a secretary and a few friends, accommodating himself with the usual conveniences for travellers." But a month later, with the president now in the heart of New England, the paper's celebratory tone shifted. The editors now distanced themselves from "the tea parties, coteries, processions, and all that assemblage of anti-republican ceremonies, so uncongenial with the character and disposition of the people of this country." They claimed to have anticipated that once the president left New York and crossed "the line into the eastern states, the President would fall in with people of a different character—with men 'who were the last to fight,' during our late war, and at present the 'first to fawn.'"

> We knew the attachment of the good people in that quarter to every thing
> partaking of the principles of the good old English monarchy, and expected
> to see every thing carried on in a truly royal style, short of ribbons, stars
> and garters—and, with the last exception, the arrangements on the occasion
> equaled any ceremonies prepared for the sovereigns of Europe which we
> either saw or read of. . . . The more we deliberate on the style of the addresses

presented to him, the more we witness the unmeaning pomp and extravagance of the people, the stronger and more insurmountable is our disgust. To see the president handsomely and respectfully received would have afforded real pleasures to his real friends; for they know his merits—but to see him addressed as a monarch, creates pain and indignation. Who is to blame? The president? Not so! We have read every reply of his which we deemed genuine; he never ceases to speak of our republican institutions and form of government; he never ceases to recommend a devotion to the Union, the constitution and the laws—there is nothing about him but what is purely republican. It is the people of those states who are thus setting a dangerous example to the rising generation; who are tainting the young mind with displays of pomp and majesty, and which impairs the vital principles of freedom of whom we have so much cause to complain.[43]

If some Republicans began by defending the president's tour only to become increasingly nervous at the sight of the president cozying up to the Federalist establishment, many Federalists began by disparaging the president's tour but ended by defending it in the face of Republican criticisms. The Baltimore *Federal Republican*, for instance, initially greeted the announcement of Monroe's tour by grousing that it was "a very expensive mode of ascertaining how little the good people of the U. States care about him." But faced with Republican criticism of the president's reception in New England, the paper reversed direction, vigorously defending the "attentions that have been shewn to the President." Had New England allowed the president "to pass their dwellings like a man who had run away from his creditors," the newspaper complained, the Federalists would have been charged by their opponents with having treated the president with "personal incivility and disrespect." The president, the *Federal Republican* insisted, had been rightly received "with cordiality and kindly greetings" that were appropriate for the man who had been "elevated . . . to the highest office in the gift of the nation."[44]

Theodore Dwight's *New York Daily Advertiser* exercised a similar about-face. Although never as hostile to the idea of the tour as the *Federal Republican*, the *Daily Advertiser* did express disapproval early on that "officious people have taken such unwearied pains to make . . . [the president's] private journey . . . a matter of great notoriety." But as the criticisms of the tour's "pomp and parade" intensified in the South and West, Dwight shifted to defending the president's tour and mocking its critics. Perhaps, Dwight sarcastically suggested, a constitutional amendment was needed to protect the president from being "contaminated" by monarchical easterners. The amendment would state the president "shall not be at liberty to travel through the eastern and northern States for business or pleasure, for and during the term he may be in office, [and shall] . . . be obliged to live like the 'King Bee' in the center of his constituents, and be wound up in the mazes of public affairs." The president, Dwight intimated, needed to travel among all the people if he was to be the people's president. Otherwise he would become a prisoner of the Washington establishment or a tool of his party's most fevered partisans.[45]

Partisanship colored and complicated all aspects of the president's tour. But beneath the partisan jockeying and maneuvering was genuine uncertainty about the proper way to receive a president, and how the president, consistent with republican simplicity, should travel among the people. Indeed serious questions were raised about whether the president of the United States even needed to venture out beyond Washington, D.C. Was he vainly seeking "to be puffed, and flattered" or, worse, cynically seeking popularity in a bid to get reelected?[46] Or was it, as one of the president's defenders maintained, essential for the president, who "presides at the head of our government," to gain "an acquaintance with the state of society . . . so that his administration may be strictly impartial and beneficial to us all"?[47]

Monroe's tour of New England did not settle these questions but his "plain republican" appearance certainly helped to shield him from the criticisms that his trip invited. By venturing into the heart of Federalist New England with a message of national conciliation, Monroe could not avoid stirring Republican anxieties about a dilution of party principles. Republicans, moreover, had spent decades honing their critique of the monarchical and aristocratic pretensions of the Federalist Party, and a presidential tour of New England that featured "salutes, the ringing of bells, the triumphal arches, the scattering of flowers, and the elegant displays of the drawing room, and the tea-party" was bound to provoke a critical Republican response. The president's well-advertised pledge to travel as a private citizen enabled Republicans to absolve their president of blame and instead hold the Federalists accountable for the tour's monarchical pomp.[48]

MONROE'S SECOND TOUR

In 1819, when Monroe embarked on his second great tour, this time through the southern states, the politics of the tour were markedly different. Because Monroe's destination was the reliably Republican states of the South and West, there was far less anxiety among Republicans that the pomp and parade would induce the president to abandon his friends or water down his political principles. Thomas Ritchie's *Richmond Enquirer*, for instance, uttered not a single critical word during the tour, even when the president was in cities such as Charleston and Savannah, where the celebrations greeting the president were every bit as ostentatious as they had been in New England. Northern newspapers occasionally tweaked the South and West for emulating what they had previously condemned, but their criticism was aimed not at the style of the president's tour but at the hypocrisy of their opponents.[49]

However, the propriety of the president's tour did become an object of contention in a few places, particularly in Kentucky where the leading newspapers of Lexington engaged in a war of words. The president's tour was barely a week old when the

Kentucky Gazette—a newspaper allied with Speaker of the House Henry Clay, who generally opposed the Monroe administration for reasons personal and political—chided the citizens of Savannah for making "plans of pomp and parade." The president, the *Gazette* allowed, "should be respectfully received" but "sycophantic adulation, such as was displayed eastwardly in his last tour, ought to be sickening to the heart of a republican." The *Gazette* predicted that when the president arrived in Kentucky, he would receive "a plain and welcome reception" but "no civic wreaths will be presented—no triumphal arches will be erected—no flowers strewed in his walk."[50]

The *Western Monitor* strongly rebuked the *Gazette*. It was only natural, the *Monitor* countered, "for the citizens of a free republic" to feel gratified at having "an opportunity of personal intercourse with their illustrious chief magistrate." It was proper, too, "to exhibit to the distinguished visitor—without servility or adulation indeed, but with hospitality and respectful politeness—every possible mark of attention, calculated to render his journey agreeable, and to evince the esteem and affection of his fellow citizens." The *Monitor* reminded readers of "all the whining and grumbling of certain pseudo-republicans" during Monroe's first tour. These critics had maintained that such a tour was "not only unnecessary, but absolutely improper, as his presence was said to be constantly required at the seat of government." The *Monitor* insisted, on the contrary, that the tours performed a valuable function for American democracy. Not only was there a benefit to having the president personally survey the nation's defenses—a point the *Gazette* seemed willing to concede—but there was also

> much good to be anticipated from the mere circumstance of association and intercourse between the President and his fellow citizens. A familiar intercourse with every individual, in so short a time is indeed impracticable, but almost every man—at least in the considerable towns through which the President passes—may, either directly or indirectly, associate with him. If he cannot converse with him himself, in order to form an idea of his character, he can obtain at least through the medium of some of his friends, who have enjoyed such an opportunity, a tolerably accurate acquaintance with him.

There was, in short, nothing unrepublican about making a fuss of a president; in fact by tightening the bond between people and president the tour was an essential component of democracy.[51]

Lexington's *Kentucky Reporter* sided with the *Gazette*. Having received reports of the president's splendid reception in Charleston, South Carolina, the *Reporter* regretted that "the Southern people have disgraced themselves as much as the people of the East, by the disgusting aristocratic pomp with which they . . . received" the president. In the *Reporter*'s judgment, the president should never have left the capital since "the duties of his office require him to be [there] at all times." The *Reporter* urged the citizens of the West to resist the poor example set by their fellow citizens in the eastern and southern states. Treat the president with "respect and politeness," the newspaper pleaded, but there should "no pomp—no parade and adulation," nothing that departed "from the simplicity and integrity of republican manners and principles."[52]

The *Monitor* allowed that it had no interest in "unmeaning pomp," "mere ostentation" or "fawning . . . adulation," but warned against the opposite danger of failing to show the proper respect and hospitality due to the president. There was a "danger of our being too scrupulous—of our being [so] afraid of being thought servile, as to be wanting in politeness, and thus affording still further ground for the erroneous impression, that we are generally opposed to the administration of Mr. Monroe." Alarm about unrepublican pomp and parade, the *Monitor* suggested, was really a cover for a partisan agenda that aimed to embarrass the president. Not to show the president the civility and respect he had been offered elsewhere in the nation would be to mark the people of the town as "nothing better than boors and clowns."[53]

Although the debate about the president's tour was sharper in Lexington than in the rest of the country, the behavior of the citizens of Lexington was little different than the behavior of citizens elsewhere in the nation. Lexington did what virtually every town had done upon receiving word that the president would be passing through—its citizenry formed a committee of arrangements "to make preparation for [a] proper reception," which included providing a military escort into town, lodgings and entertainment, a public address welcoming Monroe, and a public dinner in the president's honor. The *Gazette* objected strenuously to the committee's plan "to make a military parade . . . and march out to escort [the president] to [his] lodgings," reminding the town's citizens that "Lexington was not silent on the subject of pomp displayed, when Mr. Monroe made his eastern tour." If Lexington followed through on the reception planned by the committee of arrangements, "our citizens will hereafter be compelled to seal their lips, with regard to shew and ostentation." Otherwise, Lexington would seem hypocritical in the eyes of the nation, condoning in themselves what they had condemned in others.[54]

On July 2, the president arrived in Lexington, and a scene that had been repeated countless times before was reenacted. As President Monroe (accompanied by General Andrew Jackson) drew within about 4 miles of Lexington he was met, at a prearranged spot, by the committee of arrangements and a troop of cavalry. When the party got closer to the town, it was joined by light infantry, a rifle corps, and selected citizens. The all-male procession then approached the town in a carefully arranged order: first, the military escort, followed by the president (on horseback) and his aides and servants, and then Jackson and his suite. Behind them was the committee of arrangements, and finally, bringing up the rear, a "cavalcade of citizens." At the outskirts of the town, "the procession was saluted by a discharge of cannon" from an artillery company, followed immediately by a ringing of the bells of the courthouse and various churches. An artillery company joined the procession as it made its way through the city's main streets, which were "thronged with orderly and gratified spectators." The windows, too, we are told, "were crowded with smiling faces," and "female taste and beauty were on every side displayed." By the time the procession reached the president's lodgings it numbered over a thousand people. Never before, boasted the *Monitor*, "has so large and respectable a procession been witnessed in this town."[55]

During Monroe's four days in Lexington, two substantial addresses were delivered to the president, both of which he answered at some length. The first of these occurred when Monroe and his entourage visited the fledgling Transylvania University, where they were greeted by an address from the school's president. The second welcoming address was delivered by the chair of the committee of arrangements on behalf of the citizens of Lexington. The president's replies to both addresses indicate that he was sensitively attuned to the controversy that had been stirred up by his tours. That controversy spurred the president to use his speeches to articulate, more clearly and more publicly than he had before, why he saw the tours as important to his presidency and to the nation.

Although the Constitution did not command the president to travel beyond the capital, he considered it his duty "to become acquainted with the wants and interests of every section of the Union." However, the tour was about more than just information gathering. It provided an opportunity for a "great and unusual intercourse with my fellow-citizens." Traveling allowed the president and citizens not just to see each other but to become "personally acquainted." And this "free intercourse between the Chief Magistrate of this Union and his fellow-citizens," Monroe explained, "is not only in strict accord with the principles of the Constitution, but it is a duty enjoined on him by these principles." He admitted that when he first set out on tour he neither sought nor anticipated these personal interactions, but now believed that even if he had the power or "right to repress them"—which he did not think he did—that he would not "promote the interest of my country by exercising it." To those who worried about his traveling, he reminded them that "In honoring their Chief Magistrate, a free people honor themselves, since he holds his trust from them, and performs its duties for their advantage." The tour was democracy in action: "it is peculiarly consistent with the principles of our government that the chief magistrate should be known as intimately as possible by the mass of the people: to other governments it belongs for rulers to keep themselves aloof and distinct from those, whose interest they are bound to promote."[56]

Monroe's Lexington addresses are of interest not only for their principled defense of the democratic nature of presidential travel, but also for their forthright articulation of the link between his tour and his administration's policy objectives. Monroe stressed that the recently concluded war had taught us that "numerous fortifications" were necessary to protect "the peace of our interior, and of the inland frontier, against savage warfare." In addition, the federal government had an obligation to preserve and civilize the Indian nations, as well as to secure public lands—"a fund of vast resource to the nation"—from "intrusion." His tour was undertaken to better realize these policy objectives, both by gauging for himself the conditions and sentiments in the interior and by helping to "draw the attention of my fellow citizens to these great objects."[57]

Prompted by the address delivered on behalf of the citizens of Lexington, Monroe also articulated his position on federally sponsored internal improvements. The speech by the chair of the committee of arrangements expressed the town's hope that the president's travel through the interior will have "increased & firmly established, by your daily observation, [your conviction] in favor of the great national importance of internal improvements and domestic manufactures, and their intimate connexion with the harmony, strength, and prosperity of our federal system." The question of the proper federal role in funding internal improvements (roads and canals, for instance) was among the most contentious issues within the Republican Party, dividing the nation along regional and ideological lines. In the western interior, where roads were poor, the people generally favored federal financing of internal improvements, while in eastern states, where roads were better, there was less support. Those who were strict constructionists believed the Constitution did not authorize the federal government to subsidize the building of roads or canals within a state's boundaries, while others who took a more expansive reading of the Constitution argued that such activities were well within the scope of the federal government's power. Monroe had political reasons to be cautious, but he did not reject or even sidestep the invitation to talk about his administration's policy with respect to internal improvements.

Monroe allowed that his journey through the western interior had brought many issues to his attention, chief among those "relating to manufactures and internal improvement." Monroe professed himself to be "decidedly friendly" to both, "believing . . . that success in each . . . will . . . promote the national welfare." With regards to internal improvements, the president informed the citizens of Lexington that "after a deliberate and full investigation of the powers of the general government" he had determined that Congress did not, under the federal Constitution, possess the power to adopt an extensive system of federally funded internal improvements. However, the president put himself on record as earnestly desiring a constitutional amendment that would "obtain an enlargement of the powers of Congress, so as to give full effect to such a system." The president promised the citizens of Lexington that his "best efforts will not be wanting" to achieve this end.[58]

The president's speech, as well as the speech delivered to the president on behalf of the citizens of Lexington, contradicts political scientist Jeffrey Tulis's claim that "policy-oriented" presidential rhetoric was proscribed by nineteenth-century norms. Neither the citizens of Lexington nor the president showed any reluctance to talk about public policy. Nor was the Lexington speech unique. At many stops along his tour of the South and West Monroe spoke about policy, as did the citizens who addressed him.[59]

In Frankfort, Kentucky, for instance, the speech delivered to Monroe on behalf of the citizenry did not shy away from policy. The citizens of Frankfort pointedly drew attention to the region's economic hardships: "the miserable and almost ruined state of our western manufactures, which now oppresses the interior." They reminded the president that Kentucky's "distance from markets renders the enhanced value given to our products by manufactures (now lost in favor of foreigners) an object of profound concern." And so the town appealed to the president, "as one of the guardians of the public weal," to give "this great and vital interest of the west the attention which we sorely feel it to require." Monroe did not hesitate to join the conversation. He allowed that "our manufactures have received a check, which is very sensibly felt in this quarter of our union." The entire nation, he continued, had an interest in encouraging domestic manufactures, since an economic slowdown in one region or sector of the economy would reverberate throughout the nation. Finally, he reminded the citizens of Frankfort that Congress was giving this issue its "unremitted attention" and he pledged to do all he could "to cooperate in any measures" that would be likely to alleviate the problem.[60]

Often, as in Frankfort, the president took his cue from the welcoming address. On at least three occasions in South Carolina—in Georgetown, Charleston, and Beaufort—the welcoming address praised the recently signed treaty with Spain that would cede Florida to the United States. In turn, the president affirmed the importance of acquiring Florida in making the United States more secure and prosperous. In Augusta, Georgia, the welcoming committee approvingly noted Monroe's attention to strengthening the nation's military defenses in the wake of the deficiencies highlighted during the War of 1812. This prompt brought a hearty concurrence from Monroe, who affirmed "the necessity of being better prepared" for war and reiterated how his personal inspection of military defenses across the nation would advance this policy.[61]

To be sure, Monroe's speeches are a far cry from the speeches presidents routinely make today. Monroe largely portrayed his tour as helping him to implement and administer policies that had been laid down by Congress. Unlike a modern president, he was not "going public" in order to put pressure on Congress to act. However, there is no evidence from Monroe's tour that people expected the president to avoid policy-oriented speech; indeed they invited such speech and received it. Nowhere in the press reactions to the president's tour is there any hint of disapproval about the president speaking about public policy. A few disagreed with the positions he articulated—the *Kentucky Gazette*, for instance, differed with Monroe about his "constitutional scruples" on federally funded internal improvements—and many praised the positions he took, but no newspaper took the position that it was inappropriate for the president to speak publicly about public policy.[62]

The debate triggered by Monroe's two great tours was generally not about whether and how the president should speak to the people; it was not, in other words, about the rhetorical presidency. Rather the debate was about whether and how the president should travel amongst and interact with the people. It was, in short, a debate about the proper relationship between the president and the people, about the place of the presidency in a democratic republic. Monroe's tour provoked important reflections about the place of the presidency in the political system, reflections focused not on the propriety of presidents speaking but the propriety of presidents traveling.

Among the most interesting of these reflections came from the editors of Charleston's *Southern Patriot*. The paper's editors allowed that the sight of a president engaging "in a tour of observation" that was "connect[ed] with the objects of his administration" was "a novel and interesting spectacle." They allowed that some had "distinctly hinted at the impropriety" of such a tour. They conceded, too, that "some of the external show and parade" might appear to bear some resemblance to "the aspect of monarchy, in some of its outward splendours." But the appearance was misleading, for the tour no less than the public demonstrations of respect were, in their "real spirit and objects," hallmarks of a democratic republic, not a monarchy.[63]

The "arbitrary monarch" has little incentive to travel among the people because he rules by fiat and "executes through his ministers." In a "popular government," however, it was proper that knowledge of "public interest and opinion" should be acquired by "personal examination and comparison" on the part of the president. In a democracy the president's responsibility for policies is "direct," and so "his lights must be ample." In "a government of force" the ruler "may receive the particulars of his empire, by which he regulates his policy, from scanty to corrupt sources, and through imperfect channels," but the president "must, if he would preserve his reputation, draw on a richer fund of knowledge, or gather the materials of his administration from sources more exact and comprehensive." The monarch did not need to get it right to survive, but a president, who bears direct responsibility for the laws he proposes, needs reliable information about the effects laws are having and the conditions of the country. In order to protect what political scientist Richard E. Neustadt famously called the president's "power stakes," the president could not rely on the reports of underlings but must see for himself the people and land he has been charged with governing.[64]

Moreover, in a republic of diverse interests it was essential that a president acquire a deep sympathy and appreciation for the different mores and interests that prevailed in different sections of the country. Traveling in the "different parts of our widely extended Republic" was a way for the president to "correct the influence of local attachments" and rise above "sectional resentments." Representatives sent by localities to the national legislature are invariably "impressed with the importance of the particular interest which they imagine they appear there to represent, strong in their mutual jealousies, ardent in their local attachments, obstinate and uncompromising in their opinions." Their judgment clouded by particular "passions and prejudices," representatives were "incapable of large and liberal views of public policy." Adopting an "enlarged view" of the public good was "part of the function and duty of the Chief Magistrate." For in the American political system, only the president was in a position to "survey the whole field of politics with an exact, and comprehensive eye" and "to weigh and compare the diversities of opinion, of interests, of wishes, or pursuits; to propose, in short, in the spirit of an enlarged wisdom and enlightened sense of the public advantage, those measures of legislation for the good of the whole, that tend to bind the whole in the strong ligaments of interest and patriotism." The president could not serve this function if he remained trapped behind his desk in Washington, D.C. "Personal observation and comparison" were "indispensible."[65]

Monroe would have been more cautious than the *Southern Patriot*—certainly he would have avoided describing the president as a "fountain of light" or "the source and centre of intelligence in our federal system." But the arguments Monroe advanced on behalf of his tour were fundamentally the same. To be president of all the people he needed to know all regions of the country, not just his native Virginia. As he explained to the citizens of Nashville, Tennessee: "Every part of our Union . . . has an equal claim to the attention of the Chief Magistrate." The knowledge he gained "of the national resources" and "the acquaintance . . . he form[ed] with his fellow-citizens in every quarter" of the nation were "not only in strict accord with the principles of our constitution, . . . but [would] have a very salutary influence, in guiding the measures of his administration." Presidential traveling was not an idle luxury or a vain conceit but was essential to governance in a democracy.[66]

CHAPTER TWO

The Life of the Party: The Tours of Andrew Jackson and Martin Van Buren

Partisans of Andrew Jackson gathered in Hartford, Connecticut, on January 8, 1833, to celebrate the defeat of Henry Clay in the recently concluded presidential election. The day's festivities began on a sober and serious note, with an afternoon lecture at the Universalist church by William M. Holland, a professor at Washington College (now Trinity College) who would later pen a campaign biography for Martin Van Buren. After the oration, some three hundred Jackson enthusiasts formed a procession and made their way to a gaily decorated hall where dinner and music awaited. After dinner the toasts began. First they drank to the "glorious eighth" of January, when Jackson had led the Americans, "untaught and inexperienced in war," to victory over the "veteran legions" of Britain in the fabled Battle of New Orleans. Next they drank to the 1832 election: "the triumph of truth and principles over coalitions, factions, bargains, fraud, falshood [sic], and corruption." They drank, too, to popular sovereignty, the federal union, Jackson, Vice President Van Buren, freedom of speech, and the elective franchise. In all, fourteen "regular toasts" were announced and then drunk, each accompanied by "the discharge of Cannon and music from the Band." Then began the "volunteer toasts," a continuous course of toasts in praise of Democratic principles and politicians, each of which was greeted with drained glasses and boisterous cheers. The *Hartford Times* recorded seventy such toasts, but confessed that despite its best efforts it had not been able to record them all.[1]

Among those called upon to offer a toast that evening was Andrew Judson, a prominent Democratic lawyer and politician from Windham County. Instead of a toast, Judson presented a resolution. He proposed that the assembled appoint a committee "whose duty it shall be, to signify to Andrew Jackson, President of the United States, our veneration of his character—our approbation of his administration, and invite him, at such time as shall suit his convenience, to visit New England." The gathering roared its approval and agreed on the names of six stalwart Connecticut Democrats—including Judson—to tender the invitation. Among the others named to the committee was arguably the state's most influential Democrat, John M. Niles, who was both the founding editor of the *Hartford Times*, the town's only significant pro-Jackson newspaper, and the town's postmaster general, a position to which

Niles had been appointed by Jackson in 1829. After the invitation and committee had been agreed upon, the increasingly raucous toasting and drinking resumed.[2]

These were exciting times for Connecticut's Democrats. Eight years earlier the state had been virtually a one-party state and popular participation was anemic. Only 15 percent of Connecticut's eligible voters (a category that excluded those who were not taxpayers) bothered to vote in the 1824 presidential election, and support for Jackson was nonexistent. In 1828, Jackson finished fifty percentage points behind John Quincy Adams in a contest in which only about one-quarter of Connecticut's eligible voters cast ballots. By 1832, however, Jackson had sliced the margin of defeat in Connecticut to twenty points, and voter turnout approached 50 percent. Jackson showed similar gains throughout New England. In Vermont, for instance, Jackson lost by only ten points; four years earlier he had lost by five times that amount. Jackson actually carried New Hampshire and, more surprisingly, Maine, a state he had lost by twenty points in 1828.[3]

Jackson's reelection and his creditable showing in New England energized Connecticut's Democrats. The night before the "great Jackson festival" on the eighth of January, Democrats at localities across the state had convened to select delegates to attend a district convention, which in turn selected delegates to attend the state convention to be held in Hartford on the last day of January. The fledgling Democratic Party had used the convention system for several years to nominate candidates, but never before had there been such optimism in the party's ranks. The delegates who gathered in Hartford resolved that the "present times and circumstances" were "peculiarly auspicious for the reestablishment of the Democratic party in this state." For the first time, Democrats nominated a candidate for governor. The convention also offered up six candidates for Congress, including three of the individuals who had been charged with tendering Jackson an invitation to visit Connecticut. One of those three was Andrew Judson, whose idea the invitation had originally been.[4]

The bustle and excitement of the district and state conventions perhaps explain why Judson and his fellow committee members did not get around to writing the invitation to Jackson until February 5. As instructed, the committee extended their fellow citizens' invitation and conveyed their strong approval of the president's "leading measures." The president's "triumphant" reelection, the committee wrote, was an endorsement of the president's policies and an opportunity for "extending those measures to their beneficial results." The committee pointed with special pride to Jackson's vote total in Connecticut, which was nearly triple what it had been in 1828.[5]

The letter and the invitation placed Jackson in uncharted territory. Was it proper for the president to accept a partisan invitation from a partisan body? Was it acceptable for the president of the United States to travel as the head of a party? Washington, who was twice elevated to the presidency by a unanimous vote, never had to confront these questions on his tours. Partisanship did color reactions to Monroe's tours—particularly from Republicans who feared that by courting New England Federalists Monroe might sacrifice or dilute the party's core principles—but, like Washington, Monroe traveled as a president above party. Monroe had faced only token opposition in the election of 1816, and in 1820 he ran completely unopposed. If Washington's tours took place before the first party system—pitting Jeffersonian Republicans against Federalists—had formed, Monroe's tours were conducted when the first party system lay in ruins. Both Washington and Monroe could travel as presidents above party because they journeyed through a nation that was effectively a one-party system.

Whereas Monroe toured the nation in hopes of extinguishing the embers of party feeling, Jackson was invited to travel by buoyant partisans eager to promote their party's fortunes. Jackson's victories in 1828 and 1832 had been decisive but both elections were fiercely contested, particularly in battleground states such as New York, New Jersey, and Ohio, where the average margin of victory was under 3 percent. These close elections had helped to bring the parties to life, just as the lopsided contests in the first two decades of the nineteenth century had undermined the abortive first party system.[6]

Partisan attachments, to be sure, had yet to harden. Jackson encountered parties that were less well organized than they would be just a decade later, and partisan loyalties that were less deep-seated and intransigent. A national politics structured around partisanship was emerging but had not yet reached its maturity. In 1832, many states were still far from competitive—Jackson won 100 percent of the votes in Georgia and Alabama and virtually the same in Tennessee—whereas by the end of the decade, vibrant two-party competition characterized the politics of virtually every state. Still the political system of 1832 was clearly not the system envisioned by the founding fathers.

Of course, the framers of the Constitution were not naive. They expected that society would be riven by rival factions, interests, and regions. That was part of the rationale for checks and balances and separation of powers. But neither were the framers clairvoyant. They did not anticipate the emergence of an organized two-party system capable of mobilizing masses of people and structuring their voting choices. The framers imagined the president as a man above party, a leader who would rise above the competing factions and rival groups in society to represent the enduring interests of the nation. The emergence of organized political parties did not spell the demise of the framers' vision; indeed by making the president the head of state the framers ensured that the ideal of a president above parties would persist. But the emergence of a competitive party system gave the president a role the framers had not foreseen: head of a political party. The collision between the president's new role as party leader and the older norm that a president should be above parties created a dilemma for the traveling president and for the communities receiving him.

Something else had changed since the days of Monroe and Washington. When Monroe was elected in 1816 about half the states still allowed the state legislature rather than the people to choose presidential electors. By contrast, when Andrew Jackson was reelected in 1832 every state but South Carolina chose its presidential electors by a vote of the people. Property and taxpayer restrictions on voting by white males, which were customary in Monroe's time, were becoming increasingly uncommon. And the competition for the presidency was bringing voters to the polls in much larger numbers. In 1832, 55 percent of eligible voters turned out to decide the contest between Jackson and Henry Clay; in contrast, when Monroe was reelected in 1820 it is estimated that less than 1 percent of white males voted. A little over one hundred thousand votes were cast when Monroe won reelection, whereas over one million two hundred thousand votes were cast when Jackson was reelected. Jackson, in short, inhabited a political universe that was both more democratic and more partisan than anything Monroe had experienced. And this new political universe posed new challenges for traveling presidents.[7]

JACKSON'S 1833 TOUR

The invitation to Jackson from Connecticut's Democrats in 1833 was a sign of this new political universe. Jackson was being invited to tour New England, just as Monroe and Washington had. But unlike Washington and Monroe, Jackson was being invited by a partisan group. The president-above-party model of the late eighteenth and early nineteenth century would have suggested that Jackson decline such an avowedly partisan invitation. Yet after conferring with advisers, Jackson accepted.[8]

On March 15 the administration's mouthpiece, the *Washington Globe*, published the committee's invitation and Jackson's response. Jackson thanked the committee for its "flattering letter" and for their approbation of "my character and the course of my administration." Although Jackson was unable to say definitively when he would be able to take up the invitation, he indicated that he hoped to do so this year or the next. The *Globe* was more specific, however, suggesting that the president would likely "comply with the wishes of his New-England friends during the approaching season of comparative leisure"—that is, when Congress adjourned for the summer. A visit from the president, the *Globe* predicted, would quickly dispel those "violent prejudices against him" that had been fostered by the opposition and would show the people of New England "how much they have been deceived."[9]

Word that Jackson might be traveling north spread quickly. Democratic committees across the northeast drafted similar invitations.[10] Even before the *Globe* had published the correspondence between Jackson and the committee of Connecticut Democrats, a committee of Boston Democrats had sent Jackson a letter inviting him to visit their city to celebrate the Fourth of July. A few weeks later the Massachusetts state legislature, which was dominated by Jackson's political opponents, authorized the appointment of a joint legislative committee that would "make all suitable arrangements in the name and behalf of the State, for the proper reception of the President of the United States." At stake in these dueling invitations was whether the president was to be received as the leader of a party or the president of all the people.[11]

The action of the Massachusetts legislature precipitated a bitter fight within the Democratic Party over whether the president should allow himself to be received by a legislative body dominated by the opposition. The legislature's invitation was immediately condemned by the *Hartford Times*, which warned that Jackson's "friends [will not] wish to see him surrounded by his opponents, clothed with official authority from federal legislatures." Instead the president would want to have direct "intercourse with the people, and to take by the hand the independent freemen who ... have proved themselves ... devoted to republican principles." The views expressed in the *Hartford Times* were subsequently "copied into nearly all the republican papers in New England, as containing the sentiments of the republican party." So widely were they disseminated that many did not know where the views had originated. Some mistakenly attributed the remarks to the *Globe*, forcing the administration's organ to disavow the sentiments and to insist that the president would travel as the president of all the people and would welcome courtesies from both political friends and enemies.[12]

The *Globe's* disavowal induced a sharp rebuke from some Democratic editors. The *New Hampshire Patriot*, New Hampshire's leading Democratic paper, interpreted the *Globe's* comments that "the President should know no parties among us" as evidence that its editor "knows little of the state of parties ... in New England." If, upon arriving in Boston, the president "is to throw himself into the hands of a committee appointed by the Massachusetts legislature," the *Patriot* asked, "what chance will his friends stand of seeing him?" The *Patriot* insisted that "the men who bore [Jackson's] name to the ballot boxes, would rather forego the pleasure of seeing him at all than be indebted [for an introduction] to the courtesy of men, whose curses and revilings of the President are not yet cold." Moreover, the *Patriot* worried about the parallel between Jackson's tour and the tour of New England that Monroe had undertaken two decades earlier. The *Patriot* had no interest in burying partisan differences or ushering in an "era of good feelings": "If the President's visit is to produce such a state of things as did the visit of Mr. Monroe—if it is to result in conciliating his opponents and discarding his old friends, [then] much as we desire to see him, we had rather he would not come at all." The *Patriot* praised the *Hartford Times* for having expressed sentiments that "every democratic editor in New England" would proudly defend.[13]

The *Globe* tried to reassure nervous Democrats that it had no desire to see the president's visit result in "conciliating his opponents and discarding his old friends." The *Globe* meant only that the president "would not decline the civilities of those who were disposed to consider political differences as no bar to the performance of the courtesies which belong to social relations." The *Patriot*, however, was in no mood to be conciliated. The *Globe* was "at liberty to prize the lip-service of the hypocritical revilers of the President, as pure and unalloyed patriotism," but the *Patriot* was not so easily taken in by the opposition's self-serving, disingenuous antics.

> That sort of courtesy, or if you please, politeness, which makes men canting hypocrites . . . we heartily despise. If the thousand and one calumnies which they have uttered against this man of the people, be true, they never ought to take him cordially by the hand. . . . If, on the contrary, they are false, the authors ought not to presume to look him in the face; while those who have been deceived, should first acknowledge their error, and publish their recantation. We are unwilling to see men degrade themselves by acting the part they do not feel. . . . [F]or high-minded men, who claim the reputation of sincerity, uprightness, and singleness of heart, to hail with cordiality a man whom they, without recantation, have branded as a traitor . . . is among the most contemptible of all abominations.

The *Patriot* again recalled the specter of Monroe's tour, in which the president's "old democratic friends were unceremoniously thrust aside" while the "first to welcome him" were those for whom "the worst word in their vocabulary had been once too good for him."[14]

Things got particularly nasty in Portsmouth, New Hampshire, where the parties sparred over the proper way to receive the president. On May 14, the city's main Democratic paper, the *New Hampshire Gazette*, announced a meeting of the "Democratic Republicans of Portsmouth," for the purpose of selecting "a Committee of Arrangements from among the political friends of the President of the United States." The ten-person committee was to meet Jackson "at Newburyport, Boston, or elsewhere, and present him with the cordial salutations of the Democratic party," and then accompany him to Portsmouth where the committee would "introduce him to the municipal authorities of the town." The committee was also tasked with determining whether Portsmouth's Democrats, "as a party," should make "any other definite provision for the reception and accommodation of the President." The gathering of Portsmouth's Democrats also passed a resolution naming five Democrats to serve with the town's five selectmen as "a committee for the purpose of making suitable preparations, at the expense of the town, for the reception and accommodation of the President." Among the five Democrats named was Abner Greenleaf, editor of the *Gazette*, postmaster of the town, and a close ally of Levi Woodbury, Jackson's secretary of the navy.[15]

The resolution immediately attracted strong criticism. At a town meeting the following evening, the resolution was enacted only after the five Democratic names were dropped, thereby leaving the arrangements in the hands of the town's elected representatives. The opposition assailed the Democrats' efforts to "take the business out of the proper persons' hands,—and make it an exclusive party affair." Particularly galling was that the Democrats had tried to make the reception "at the 'expense of the Town,'—thus making the Town pay the fiddler, while only the Party should dance." The main opposition organ, the *Portsmouth Journal*, resorted to an imaginary dialogue between a "Union Man" and an "Exclusive" man to ridicule the Democratic position.

> Union Man: Do you think the Old General means to come this way?
> Exclusive: Certainly he will.
> U: Well, we shall all be glad to see him.
> E: What do you mean by *all*?
> U: The Citizens generally. All wish to show him proper respect.
> E: That will never do. The party sent for him, and he is coming to see the Party. If we let all the people come into the show in common, we shall only be like so many peas in a peck. The President won't see that we differ any at all from the multitude. Nay, there may be some danger, that when he comes to appoint any new officers from this place, he may remember some man here, who has been voted out of The Party, while he forgets the whole of us. . . . I voted for him, and huzzaed for him, and supported him through thick and thin. . . .
> U: I voted for him too. But I voted for him as President of the United States and not as the President of any Party. Men, who voted against him when he was a Candidate, may surely be allowed to show him civility, now he is President.
> E: If he was to make no distinctions between his supporters and opponents, I had rather he would never come at all. . . . I hope he will turn off to Concord, unless *we* can do the whole business *ourselves*.[16]

The public backlash placed Portsmouth's Democrats on the defensive and they scrambled to explain their actions. They had no intention of monopolizing the president during his stay in Portsmouth. Instead, the *Gazette* explained, Democrats "simply ask the pleasure, as his old friends and supporters . . . to meet and accompany him to Portsmouth and introduce him" to the appropriate civic authorities. The president's invitation to visit the northern states had, after all, come from "his political friends at Hartford" and so "it was highly proper, that he should be noticed by his political friends, as such, in the various places he should visit." Certainly there was "no impropriety in their sending such a delegation to meet him." Moreover, the partisan committee was not asking for the town to pay its expenses; the cost would instead be covered by the president's "political friends." The town's citizens were only being asked to pay the cost of the civic reception.[17]

However, the *Gazette* had more difficulty defending the resolution to add five

Democrats to the town committee. Yet defend it they did. First they argued that the Democratic Party was not "fairly represented in the municipal authorities of the town." Nobody on the Portsmouth Board of Selectmen could be counted among the party faithful. As a result, Democrats had "reason to suspect an intention to shut out the early friends of the President from any participation in the reception." They wished to avoid a repeat of Monroe's visit two decades earlier when Federalists in control of the town council managed to take the business of greeting the president "out of democratic hands" and select a prominent Federalist, Jeremiah Mason, to deliver the welcoming address. The Democratic aim, in short, was the modest one of having "some representation in the reception of the President." Otherwise Democrats would be compelled to "pay their part" while the opposition "carr[ied] down the dance."[18]

The town's selectmen tried to defuse the standoff by naming a host of Democrats to the official committee of arrangements, including five of the ten who had been selected by the Democratic nominating committee to escort Jackson from Boston to Portsmouth. Moreover, instead of having Mayor Ichabod Goodwin, a strong Jackson critic, deliver the welcoming address, the selectmen chose William Claggett, who had supported Jackson in the recent election. However, the town authorities' conciliatory steps did not succeed in appeasing the Democrats.[19]

The five Democrats were only willing to serve on the town's committee of arrangements if the selectmen would give their blessing to the party committee traveling to Boston and allow it to introduce the president to the town authorities. When the selectmen refused, the five Democrats declined to serve. Several other Democrats also resigned from the town's committee of arrangements in protest or, perhaps, for fear that they would be read out of the Portsmouth Democratic Party for cooperating with the town authorities. The *Gazette* now railed not only against the hypocrisy of "federalists" but also the infidelity of a "twaddling clan" of "nominal" Democrats, political "mongrels" utterly lacking in political principles. Having begun as a war of words between Jackson's supporters and his opponents, the battle mutated into a bitter contest among Jackson's supporters.[20]

On June 22, less than a week before Jackson was expected to arrive in Portsmouth, the *Portsmouth Journal* published a letter signed "Jacksonites" that condemned the "few ultra exclusive and ultra Simon-Pure Democrats" who were sabotaging the president's visit. The letter writer, a member of the town's committee of arrangements, assured the public that the "utmost harmony prevails in the Committee . . . , a majority of whom are Jacksonians." Moreover, "the political opponents of the President on the Committee have been disposed to yield every thing to the wishes of the Presidents's political friends." True, some Jacksonians had left the committee because the selectmen "refused to agree to their peremptory demand to go out and make a party address to the President, and receive him as a party man." But they had been replaced by "other Jacksonites entertaining more liberal and correct National views" of the relationship between the president and the people. "The great body of the Jackson Republicans of Portsmouth," the letter writer predicted, "will unite with cordiality and harmony, under the municipal authorities in giving our patriotic and illustrious President a hearty welcome. . . . Should a very few wander out of town to address the President as mere partizans, [Jackson] will no doubt treat them civilly, as his manners are affable and polite, though he may regret their futile attempt to mar the general joy which his visit inspires."[21]

Far from spreading joy, the letter fueled the intraparty squabble. The *Gazette* had "no difficulty" identifying the author of the letter as William Claggett, who had been selected to deliver the official welcoming address. Claggett's claim that the Democratic committee had desired to have the town pay for a partisan greeting was, the *Gazette* fumed, "as false, as he is false to his late political friends." Claggett, the *Gazette* reminded readers, had initially "hung upon J. Q. Adams' skirts," only letting go after "all hopes of being appointed to office under a federal administration was lost." His support of the tariff and the Bank, the *Gazette* noted, was an indication of just how out of step he was with the principles of the president and the party.[22]

Jackson's "true" friends would not allow themselves to be deterred from their plan of meeting and being introduced to the president "as political friends." A subcommittee of their own committee of arrangements—led by Abner Greenleaf— journeyed to Boston to meet Jackson and extend their invitation to the president. The opposition press reported that the committee received a cold shoulder from the president; that in fact a "gentlemen of the President's suite, high in office, told the committee it would not do, for them to be introduced as a party committee." The *Gazette* emphatically denied the rumor, insisting that the president had graciously received the partisan delegation and communicated, through his private secretary Andrew Donelson, that he would be "happy of an introduction to them" when he reached Portsmouth. The truth probably lay somewhere in between. Although Jackson was happy to meet his political allies, he could not have been eager to land in the middle of an internecine party feud.[23]

The town could not prevent the Democratic committee from meeting the president or from inviting the president to Portsmouth. However, they could prevent the committee from using a public building. The Democratic committee of arrangements wanted to use Jefferson Hall for Jackson's visit but the civic authorities refused permission, arguing that the space was needed by the military companies that would be in town for the president's visit. It appeared the real reason was that the town's committee of arrangements did not want anything to compete with the civic reception it planned to hold in Franklin Hall. Under intense pressure, however, the town authorities relented and allowed the Democrats to use Jefferson Hall. Having secured the hall, the Democratic committee immediately wrote to Jackson, who was then in Concord, inviting him "to meet his political friends for the purpose of an introduction, at Jefferson Hall, at such time after his arrival as may best suit his convenience."[24]

Jackson's reply surprised everybody. On account of his poor health, he would not be able to continue his tour and was instead compelled to return immediately to the capital. There is no question that the tour had taken its toll on Jackson's health. When Jackson arrived back in Washington, D.C., on July 4, his aide Major William B. Lewis confessed that "he was seriously alarmed at [the president's] feeble and emaciated appearance." But many wondered whether the suddenness of Jackson's decision also owed something to his desire to avoid the intraparty spat in Portsmouth. The *Portsmouth Journal* allowed that the president's health may have been "a sufficient reason for terminating his tour," but wondered that even if Jackson had been in good health "would he have consented to visit a place where his reception would have produced a scene of disorder and confusion?" The actions of a "small division of the Jackson party," insisted the *Journal*, were "not only indecorous and unbecoming, but must have been viewed with disgust" by Jackson, who "came as the President of the whole people, and not to gain party proselytes."[25]

Although the *Journal* is likely correct that Jackson was displeased if not actually disgusted with Democratic squabbling in Portsmouth, the president's tour was far from the nonpolitical or nonpartisan event that the *Journal* suggested. From the outset the *Journal* had posed the choice as whether the president should "appear like a President of the Nation" or as "a narrow partizan." But in fact the president traveled as *both* party chief and chief executive. Not only did Jackson receive and accept invitations from partisan groups in cities across the northeast, but he traveled in the company of other Democrats. In both respects, Jackson's tour was unlike the self-consciously nonpartisan tour undertaken by Monroe.[26]

Throughout his New England tour, Jackson was flanked by other members of the administration, each of whom was a loyal Democrat. Among those who accompanied Jackson on all or part of the journey were Vice President Van Buren, Secretary of State Louis McLane, Secretary of War Lewis Cass, and Secretary of the Navy Levi Woodbury. Very often the state and local politicians who accompanied Jackson were Democrats as well. When Jackson entered Hartford, Connecticut, for instance, the presidential procession was a veritable who's who of prominent Democrats, including not only Van Buren, Cass, and Woodbury, but also the newly elected Democratic governor of New York, William Marcy, and the newly elected Democratic governor of Connecticut, Henry Edwards. In addition, Jackson was shadowed by two of Hartford's prominent Democrats, John Niles and Gideon Welles, who had been deputized by the town's committee of arrangements to meet Jackson in New York City and escort him to Hartford.[27]

Jackson's willingness to accept invitations from openly partisan groups raised Democratic hopes that "unlike Mr. Monroe, Gen. Jackson will give the *preference* to his friends." In contrast to Monroe, who had been "so closely guarded ... by the gentlemen federalists 'in gloves and ruffled shirts,'" Jackson, predicted the *New Hampshire Patriot*, "will not shrink from the grasp of the hard hands which bore his name to the ballot boxes, nor spurn the warm hearts of our hardy yeomanry, who have stood by him through two campaigns." The difference, for the *Patriot*, was not just between Jackson's readiness to privilege his political friends and Monroe's desire to bury partisanship but also between the stiff formality and elitism of Monroe's tour and Jackson's willingness to accept the warm embrace of the people.[28]

In fact, a marked contrast between Monroe's visit and Jackson's was on display from the outset. In Philadelphia, the second stop on Jackson's tour, the arrangements were directed almost entirely by the president's political friends. When Jackson disembarked from the steamboat that had carried him from Baltimore, he was immediately ushered into an open carriage where he was seated next to Henry Horn, a Jackson loyalist who orchestrated much of the president's visit. A year earlier, Horn, then a member of Congress, had been "called to the Chair" of a meeting of Philadelphia Democrats in support of Jackson's veto of the national bank. The president's veto had placed Horn in a particularly difficult spot since Horn had—along with almost the entire Pennsylvania delegation—supported the bill to recharter the bank, which was headquartered in Philadelphia. At the public meeting Horn declared his unequivocal support for Jackson's veto; his vote in favor of the bank, he said, had been motivated solely by his desire to reflect the views of his Philadelphia constituents. Jackson's veto and Horn's loyalty to the president probably cost him his seat; in the 1832 election the first-term congressman lost to the pro-bank and anti-Jackson candidate, James Harper.[29]

When the citizens of Philadelphia gathered on May 18, 1833, to make "the necessary arrangements for the patriotic reception" of Jackson, Horn was again "called to the Chair." Although this mass meeting was not designated as a party meeting, it was attended exclusively by those who supported Jackson. The resolutions adopted at the meeting empowered Horn to select a sixty-person committee of arrangements.[30] The delegation from the committee of sixty that traveled to Baltimore to meet Jackson and accompany him to Philadelphia was composed entirely of Jackson supporters. Upon arriving in Philadelphia, the president placed himself "in [the] charge" of Horn and the committee of arrangements. It was not until two days after his arrival that Jackson was formally introduced to the elected city authorities, most of whom, including the mayor, were anti-Jackson.[31]

The committee of arrangements wanted the citizens of Philadelphia to have an opportunity not only to see Jackson but to greet him, so they announced that after Jackson had been introduced to the civic authorities in Independence Hall the people would be given the chance to meet him. A huge crowd turned out, "waiting anxiously for an opportunity to shake hands with the Chief Magistrate." The area surrounding the hall, according to the *American Sentinel*, was "filled, for nearly three hours, with a mass, crowded together almost to suffocation." When the official introductions within the hall were over, the doors were flung open and a desperate scramble of "pushing and jamming" ensued as citizens pressed for "a chance of a shake" of the president's hand. The scene, according to one account,

> bordered on the ludicrous. . . . The crowd made a rush to the hall, which nothing short of bayonets would have resisted. Shaking hands soon became out of the question, and at last a nod to each was beyond endurance. The President sank on a sofa, and the crowd still increasing, each one was as anxious to make his escape as to enter. The only resort was the back windows, from which issued *pelle-melle* a motley group of soldiers, sailors, and citizens, in every variety of dress, and by a leap of about four feet, joined the crowd without, to relate their perils and escape.[32]

To some of Jackson's critics, the reception in Philadelphia was evidence of the "degeneracy of the age in taste, feelings, and principles." Many in the opposition complained particularly about the "rude party exclusiveness" that marked the president's visit in Philadelphia and elsewhere. The president, the *Niles Weekly Register* lamented, was "hemmed round about by exclusive partizans" who "forbid . . . the approach of some of the most virtuous or venerable persons in the United States" and "cast . . . him into scenes of senseless noise and unreflecting obtrusion." Democratic partisans were accused of holding the president "like a prisoner in bonds" or, worse, parading him "as if he were a wild beast to be exhibited gratis." Either way, it was demeaning to the presidency.[33]

Partisan sour grapes? Most certainly. Yet Jackson's reception in Philadelphia undoubtedly did look markedly different from that which Monroe had received in the same city sixteen years earlier. Then there had been no mass meeting to decide upon a committee of arrangements; instead there was a meeting of the "civil officers of the general and state governments." The committee charged with welcoming Monroe to Philadelphia was made up entirely of state and federal office-holders. Although Monroe was cheered by "a great concourse of citizens" upon his arrival in Philadelphia, there was nothing like the boisterous crowds and frenzied scramble that occurred at Independence Hall upon Jackson's visit. Some private citizens paid their respects to Monroe personally, but they generally did so at Monroe's hotel lodgings and in strict observance of early nineteenth-century decorum—including bowing rather than shaking hands. The citizens who had the opportunity to greet Jackson in Independence Hall were those who pushed and shoved the hardest, whereas those who approached Monroe in his hotel had been the city's most distinguished and respected gentlemen. Deference definitely wasn't what it used to be.[34]

Conservatives sensed the change. Philip Hone, once the mayor of New York City, marveled at the throng of New Yorkers who turned out to welcome the president. Jackson, the elitist Hone confessed in his diary, was "certainly the most popular man we have ever known." George Washington had been revered as the "Father of His Country," but the people kept a respectful distance. He was "too dignified, too grave for their liking, and men could not approach him with familiarity." Jackson, in contrast, was "The Man of the People." "Here is a man," Hone observed, "who suits [the people] exactly. He has a kind expression for each—the same to all, no doubt, but each thinks it intended for himself." Jackson was, in short, a democratic politician.[35]

Both the president's allies and adversaries understood that Jackson's popularity was a potent partisan weapon. Hence the National Republicans' generally unenthusiastic response to the prospect of Jackson's tour and the Democrats' welcome embrace of it. The *Georgetown Gazette* was hardly alone among Democratic newspapers in predicting that Jackson would "convert many by his travels." At a minimum, Democrats believed, the Old Hero would sway the undecided. Jackson's visit, noted the *Boston Statesman*, afforded citizens the opportunity "of seeing [Jackson] as he is, without the intervention of any false and dangerous medium to pervert the vision or bewilder the audience." Particularly in New England, the *Statesman* explained, the "enemies of Democracy" used their superior wealth and control of newspapers to distort the public mind. Traveling enabled Jackson to forge a direct, unmediated relationship with the American citizenry, and thereby "dissipate that cloud of prejudice" and rally people to the Democratic cause.[36]

Although partisan calculations and ambitions permeated the president's tour, Jackson remained highly conscious of the need to avoid turning the tour into an openly partisan mission. Unlike Monroe, who spoke frequently, and often at length, about public policy, Jackson kept his public remarks to a bare minimum. So brief and inconsequential were Jackson's remarks that newspapers rarely bothered to record what the president said. Typically, a reader of the newspapers learned only that Jackson made "a short, but appropriate and feeling reply." Even in Concord, New Hampshire, speaking to a legislature dominated by Democrats and flanked by the state's two most prominent Democrats—Levi Woodbury and Isaac Hill—Jackson said little, and what little he did say avoided any hint of partisanship. His hosts, too, tended to avoid open declarations of partisanship in Jackson's presence. Aboard the steamboat to Philadelphia, Jackson sat down to a "very splendid dinner" with a host of prominent Philadelphia Democrats, yet only a single, innocuous toast was drunk. George Mifflin Dallas, a prominent Jacksonian who had been the mayor of Philadelphia as well as a U.S. senator, offered: "Unvarying health—unfading glory to the welcome guest of Pennsylvania." It was the sort of toast that had often been offered to President Washington.[37]

Mifflin's toast was a tribute to the continuing hold of the president-above-party ideal. The avoidance of open partisanship also reflected the conventions of the presidential tour. Although the committees escorting and welcoming Jackson were sometimes predominantly or even exclusively of the president's party, the committees typically claimed—Portsmouth excepted—to represent the citizenry of the town and not just the citizens of one party. Even when delivered by a fellow Democrat, the welcoming speech extended to the president almost always avoided the divisive or controversial questions of the day. Much about Jackson's tour was familiar from the tours of Monroe and Washington: the elaborate processions and parades, the welcoming committees, the thunderous cannons. The *National Intelligencer's* caustic verdict was not altogether unwarranted: "it is all one dull, unvarying sameness of military parades through the streets, white handkerchiefs at the windows, graceful bowing in return, very natural weariness on the part of the President closing each day's ceremonies, and then *de capo*."[38]

But all the ritualistic pomp and ceremonial parades should not obscure the strategic objectives and political dimensions of Jackson's tour. One issue loomed particularly large: nullification. On November 24, 1832, South Carolina had declared the tariffs of 1832 and 1828 to be "null [and] void" in the state of South Carolina. In response, on December 10, 1832, Jackson issued the Nullification Proclamation, an uncompromising refutation of South Carolina's assertion of authority. No state, Jackson insisted, could nullify federal laws or secede from the Union. "To say that any State may at pleasure secede from the Union," Jackson declared, "is to say that the United States are not a nation." The president's nationalistic message was received particularly warmly in New England, a region that had rarely been enamored of states' rights.[39]

Everywhere the president traveled in New England, particularly in Massachusetts and Connecticut, he encountered the words of his famous toast at a Jefferson Day dinner in 1830: "The Union. It must be preserved." Towns erected arches emblazoned with the president's rebuke to the nullification doctrines championed by his then–vice president John Calhoun. In Norwich, Connecticut, the civic procession welcoming Jackson included several hundred women, "each of whom bore a banner inscribed with the words of the memorable toast." The triumphal arches and even the women adorned with inscribed ribbons and banners were familiar from the tours of Washington and Monroe; the novelty was that the arches and banners greeting Jackson affirmed the president's words and endorsed his policy.[40]

From the outset, Jackson saw the tour as a way to underline the themes of national unity and federal supremacy that he had laid down in the Nullification Proclamation. That was why he had asked South Carolina Democrat Joel Poinsett to join him on his journey through New England. Poinsett, who would be appointed secretary of war in the Van Buren administration, had played a vital role in mobilizing Unionist forces in South Carolina and providing Jackson with intelligence about political developments in the Palmetto State. Traveling with one of the most prominent public faces of South Carolina Unionism by his side, Jackson broadcast his position on nullification to an appreciative New England audience.

In cities and towns across New England, the speeches welcoming Jackson high-

President's Visit.

The President will be met at the Bridge by the Committee of Arrangements, preceded by the Chairman, when the latter will greet the President in the name and in behalf of the citizens of the town. He will then take a seat in the President's Barouche, when the Procession will immediately be formed in the following order:

Order of Procession.

Military Escort.

Aid. | Chief Marshal. | Aid.

Committee of Arrangements.
MARSHALS.

President of the United States,
Accompanied by the

Vice-President, and the Chairman of Com. of Arrangements.

Mr. Woodbury, { Secretary of the Navy

Mr. Cass, { Secretary of War.

Maj. Donaldson, { President's Private Secretary.

Col. Earle, { Of the U. S. Army.

MARSHALS.

Members of Congress.

Delegates and Gentlemen attending the President.
MARSHALS.

Clergymen.

Revolutionary Officers & Soldiers.
MARSHALS.

Citizens generally.
MARSHALS.

☞The Procession will move down Water street to Green street—up Green, to Summer street—through Summer street, across Main, to Winter street—thence to Pecker street, through said street, to Capt. Caldwell's dwellinghouse—thence across to How street, down to Water street—thence to Main street, to the Hotel, where the President will be addressed in behalf of the town by I. R. HOWE, Esq.

☞Those citizens who wish to unite in forming a procession on the above occasion are requested to assemble for that purpose on the Green, in front of the First Parish Meetinghouse, *at five o'clock,* on Tuesday afternoon.

JACOB HOW, *Chief Marshal.*

Haverhill, Monday Evening, June 24, 1833.

☞No Carriages of any description will be permitted to stand in any of the streets in which the procession is to move, during its progress.

SELECTMEN'S NOTICE.

The Selectmen hereby give notice that measures have been taken to prosecute all persons who shall violate the Law relative to the SELLING and FIRING of Squibs, Crackers, &c. next Tuesday afternoon and evening.

Parents, Masters, and Guardians are therefore particularly requested to give their attention to this subject, and prevent the Boys under their charge from any infraction of said Law. A due regard to the comfort of the illustrious Guests, the character of the town, and respect for the majesty of the laws require that this enactment be rigidly enforced on the present occasion.

By order of the Selectmen,

JOHN HUSE, *Chairman.*

CAVALCADE.

Those Citizens who may be disposed to join in a Cavalcade or Citizens' Escort in honor of the President, are requested to assemble on horseback at or near the Store of Amos Parker, Esq. in Bradford, *precisely at five o'clock,* on Tuesday afternoon.

A broadside announces the order of procession for President Andrew Jackson's visit to Haverhill, Massachusetts. Due to illness, Jackson made a late change to his route that required bypassing Haverhill. (Archive of Americana collection, published by Readex, a division of NewsBank, in cooperation with the American Antiquarian Society) lighted his stance on nullification. None more directly than the Newport, Rhode Island, committee that praised Jackson for having "outreasoned, repudiated, and repelled, the heresies of nullification and secession." And none more grandiloquently than the famous orator Edward Everett, who welcomed Jackson on Bunker Hill by noting his fellow citizens' "unanimous approbation of the [president's] firm, resolute, and patriotic stand . . . in the late alarming crisis of affairs, in order to preserve that happy union under one constitutional head." In Roxbury, Massachusetts, the brief welcome closed in rhyme: "And may his powerful long arm remain nerved. Who said—The UNION—it *must* be preserved." To which Jackson responded: "It shall be preserved, Sir, as long as there is a *nerve* in this *arm.*"[41]

The timing of Jackson's tour was masterful. Even without the Nullification Proclamation, Jackson would have been enthusiastically received in cities like Philadelphia, New York, and Concord. But especially in Massachusetts, where antiadministration sentiment ran strong, Jackson's repudiation of nullification helped to elevate his reception well above the merely polite or coldly civil. Some among the president's opponents even appeared to hold out hope that the trip "could make [Jackson] a yankee," especially now that he had "come over to the creed of our Webster." Seeing the region's thriving manufactures and prosperous towns might soften the president's opposition to protective tariffs, while traveling on the area's well-maintained roads might lead the president to rethink his position on federally sponsored internal improvements.[42]

The president's tour hoisted Jackson's opponents onto the horns of a dilemma. On the one hand, they did not wish to show disrespect toward the nation's popular chief executive and open themselves up to the charge that they were mean-spirited partisans. On the other hand, if they cooperated in the celebration of the president, they risked bolstering Jackson's popularity. And a popular president, they understood, was a more formidable opponent. They knew that Democrats would be quick to interpret enthusiastic cheering for Jackson as an endorsement of the president's and the party's policies. Indeed that is exactly what had happened on the president's first stop, in Baltimore. The "immense crowd," crowed the *Baltimore Republican*, showed not only the people's regard for the man but their "approbation . . . of his measures." Because the president was not above party but was instead the party's head, strengthening the president meant fortifying his party as well.[43]

Jackson, too, confronted a delicate situation. One the one hand, his fellow Democrats looked to him to energize the partisan base and win over the undecided. Jackson, moreover, shared this partisan agenda. He was committed, as he told Van Buren shortly after his reelection, to "strengthen[ing] the democratic party." In addition, the president was about to unleash the second front in the bank war by ordering the removal of deposits from the national bank and distributing those monies to "pet banks" across the country. Jackson anticipated massive resistance to this daring initiative, and the tour provided an opportunity for him to impress his opponents—

and his wavering allies—with his popularity, even in the opposition's northeastern strongholds.

On the other hand, explicit partisan appeals or speech making would have been incongruous with the conventions of the presidential tour. The president was the guest of the town, not of a party. By appearing as a narrow partisan, Jackson would have risked forfeiting the prestige and influence that stemmed from his role as the nation's symbolic head and the representative of all the people. Jackson was a force to be reckoned with in part because he spoke in the name of "the people," not just those people who had voted for him. Open partisanship, paradoxically, could undercut the popularity Jackson needed to achieve his partisan agenda.[44]

In a 1963 study of Jackson's tour, historian Fletcher Green concluded that "the formal, nationalistic presidential tours of Washington and Monroe had been transformed by Jackson into a highly partisan, political campaign." However, Green's judgment that Jackson's tour was "distinctly political and partisan rather than formal, official, and nationalistic in nature" is misleading. For Jackson's tour was, in some respects, as formal and nationalistic as Monroe's. What made Jackson's tour distinctive was that it combined the political and the official, the partisan and the nationalistic. Jackson, in sum, traveled as both party head and chief of state.[45]

TRAVELS TO THE HERMITAGE

Jackson's presidential travels were not limited to his 1833 tour of New England. Four times as president, Jackson made the long journey back to his home in Tennessee: in 1830, 1832, 1834, and 1836. Every president since Washington had returned home during the summer months, but Jackson was the first who hailed from outside of Virginia or Massachusetts. He was also the first to encounter massive crowds en route, and the first to use the journey for political purposes. Jackson's travels to the Hermitage truly did, at times, resemble a "highly partisan, political campaign."

Jackson's first trip back to the Hermitage came close on the heels of his veto of the Maysville Road bill, an action that he was warned would lose him political support in the West where federal funding for internal improvements was popular. Yet as Jackson made his way into the interior he encountered enthusiastic crowds and warm welcomes. In Cincinnati—just 50 miles west of Maysville, Kentucky—six thousand people jammed along the shores of the Ohio River to welcome the president. To Jackson, such receptions were evidence, as he wrote to an adviser in Washington, that "the veto is working well, widely different to what our enemies anticipated."[46]

The evening before Jackson was scheduled to arrive in Cincinnati, he was met by a Democratic welcoming committee, which had been "appointed at a public meeting of the friends of the present administration ... [from] the city of Cincinnati and county of Hamilton, Ohio." The seventeen-person committee, accompanied by a musical band, had hired an elegant steamboat in order to greet the president en route and escort him more than 100 miles down the Ohio River to Cincinnati. The chairman of the committee was General William Lytle, an old friend of Jackson's whom the president had appointed Surveyor General of the Public Lands in the states of Ohio, Indiana, and Michigan. After the president's vessel and the committee's boat had been "lashed together," Lytle delivered a brief address in praise of the president's veto. "The measures of your administration generally," Lytle proclaimed, "are cordially approved, and especially your reasons for disapproving of the bill appropriating the public funds of the nation for constructing local roads." He assured Jackson that "although a few may have made your veto on the Maysville . . . bill a pretense for leaving our ranks, we are convinced that our real strength has been increased rather diminished by that document."[47]

Jackson replied with a speech recapping the basic argument of his veto message. He regretted that he had been compelled to issue a veto, but he could not allow "the adoption of a policy calculated to extend the action of the General Government to the local concerns of the States, and to confound all distinction between the powers of Congress and those reserved to the people." The Maysville Road had been "purely of a local nature" and so it was inappropriate for the federal government, which had been "formed for general purposes," to bestow money upon this project. Jackson showed no reluctance to speak in defense of his administration's policy, but even before this partisan audience he was careful to cast himself in the role of unifier rather than partisan divider. His actions were necessary because he was "acting for the whole, and not [for] a part of our Union."[48]

Although Jackson hesitated to don the hat of party chief, he made no effort to distance himself from the partisan welcoming committee. The committee enveloped Jackson throughout his time in Cincinnati. The president even stayed overnight at the committee chairman's "noble mansion." Had Jackson wished to shake loose his Democratic entourage he would have had difficulty doing so, for the committee's officeholders and office-seekers were determined to cling closely to the coattails of the party's popular standard bearer. Only when the president reached Louisville did the committee finally part from the president, leaving him to make the remainder of his trip by horse and carriage.[49]

Partisan passions were running particularly high when Jackson returned to the Hermitage in the summer of 1832. He left the capital on July 22, a week after Congress had failed to override his veto of the national bank. The impending election was on everybody's mind, and Jackson's political friends in places such as Nashville, Tennessee, and Lexington, Kentucky, pressed him to attend partisan dinners in his honor. Conscious of the taboo against electioneering, Jackson declined these invitations and avoided making any speeches. Presidential partisanship stopped at the campaign's edge.[50]

But the norm against campaigning for the presidency did not stop Jackson from greeting his political friends and mixing with large crowds of well-wishers. Although refusing to attend a public dinner in Nashville, he did consent to come to town to "meet [those who had invited him] and shake my old neighbors and friends by the hand." Similarly, while turning down the offer to attend a partisan barbecue in Lexington, he nonetheless consented to stop there for two nights in order to meet his fellow citizens. Upon his approach to Lexington, Jackson was met by an enthusiastic crowd of some five thousand people. As the president made his way into town, reported one observer, "it was almost impossible to keep back the crowd who pressed up to the carriage window to take him by the hand." And while Jackson did not deliver any campaign speeches, he apparently did give away "all the locks [of hair] he could spare" to female admirers.[51]

On the return leg, which commenced on September 18, Jackson visited many more towns, particularly in Kentucky, the home state of Jackson's opponent Henry Clay. Jackson had carried Kentucky by only a single percentage point in 1828, and with Clay at the top of the ticket the task of holding the state had become much more difficult. The close partisan contest in Kentucky had been underscored in the recently concluded August election in which turnout reached nearly 75 percent and the Democrats carried the governorship by the slenderest of margins. Historian Robert Remini perhaps exaggerates in claiming that the president "was literally escorted by mobs on his entire journey through Kentucky," but it is true that Jackson was greeted at county lines across the state and escorted by citizens on horseback for much of his journey through Kentucky. As Jackson approached a town, the escort would typically increase in size and the speed of the travel would slow as Jackson stopped to greet citizens. One individual who joined in escorting Jackson to Mount Sterling—a town about 30 miles east of Lexington—estimated Jackson's escort had grown to three hundred men on horseback by the time they reached Mount Sterling and reported that "we had frequently to stop, in order that ladies and the old men on the road might be presented to the President." Jackson seemed in no hurry to get back to Washington, D.C. Whereas the trip to the Hermitage in July had taken him only about two and a half weeks, the return trip lasted over a month. Not until October 19, just a few weeks before election day, did Jackson finally arrive at the capital. As Remini wryly concludes, "For a man who was not supposed to do any campaigning, Jackson saw an awful lot of people on his trip back to Washington."[52]

In 1834, with his reelection now behind him, Jackson felt less constrained by the need to avoid explicitly partisan meetings. Almost as soon as he arrived at the Hermitage, a delegation of Nashville Democrats invited him to attend a public dinner. In 1832 he had declined an invitation from the same group, but this time he accepted. The dinner was attended by fifteen hundred people, each "well dressed and truly Republican." A toast to the president's health was all the excuse Jackson needed to offer a prepared toast of his own: "The true Constitutional currency, gold and silver coin. It can cover and protect the labor of our country without the aid of a National Bank, an institution which can never be otherwise than hostile to the liberties of the people, because its tendency is to associate wealth with an undue power over the public interests." The toast was a clear and succinct statement of Jackson's economic policy.[53]

Jackson's last trip home as president, in the summer of 1836, saw him assume the mantle of party head in a more open way than ever before. If in 1832 Jackson had been careful to avoid the appearance of electioneering, he now campaigned openly to help his vice president, Martin Van Buren, particularly in Tennessee where Van Buren faced an uphill battle to carry the president's home state. The newly formed Whig Party was running Tennessee native son (and former Democrat) Hugh White as one of its three presidential candidates (Daniel Webster and William Henry Harrison were the other two), and Jackson desperately wanted to avoid Tennessee—a state he had carried three times—slipping into the opposition column. On August 20, Jackson attended a "great dinner and barbecue" in Nashville, where he shook hands with and greeted upwards of four thousand Tennesseans. At the dinner he offered a stirring partisan toast to "Republican Tennessee:— Her motto, 'principles not men'—She will never abandon her good old Jeffersonian Democratic Republican principles, which she has so long maintained and practiced, to throw herself (on any occasion) into the embraces of the Federalists, the Nullifiers, or the new born Whigs." Jackson's toast, which was a direct attack on White, "the new born Whig," was greeted with "deafening thunders of applause" from the partisan audience.[54]

At the urging of Speaker of the House of Representatives James Polk, Jackson also traveled to Columbia, Tennessee, to attend a partisan meeting of some five thousand Democrats. Here Jackson offered more than a succinct toast in praise of the Democratic nominee and the party's principles. After listening to "a lengthy and flattering address" from a leading Columbia Democrat, Jackson "stepped to the speaker's rostrum" to address the party faithful: "You have said that my election was depicted to the country as a worse calamity than war, pestilence, or famine. The feelings which employed such language were not prompted merely by a wish to injure me. They had a higher ambition to gratify. They aimed at the prostration of the principles which the country had decided should be brought into operation." They had aimed their barbs at Jackson, in other words, not simply out of personal malice but because he was the head of a political party. The barbs directed at Jackson, however, were nothing compared with those directed at his successor.[55]

VAN BUREN TOURS NEW YORK

From the outset of his political career, Martin Van Buren had worked to create a strong Democratic Party. Unlike many of his contemporaries, Van Buren believed that party competition was vital to the health of a democratic political system. Writing to James Madison in 1822, President Monroe had castigated parties as the "curse of the country" and was proud that party divisions had "cooled down or rather disappeared" during his administration. In his 1825 inaugural address, President John Quincy Adams celebrated the eradication of the "baneful weed of party strife" and called for his fellow citizens to discard "every remnant of rancor against each other" and to make "talent and virtue alone" the sole criteria for public advancement. For both Monroe and Adams, the president's role was to rise above parties and—as Adams explained shortly before taking office—"to bring the whole people together in sentiment as much as possible." Van Buren, however, rejected the premise that lay beneath such thinking. For Van Buren the choice was not between partisan conflict and national harmony. Instead the choice was between political conflict grounded in personalities and factionalism, on the one hand, and a politics structured as a democratic contest between rival principles and public policies, on the other hand. In Van Buren's view, parties made politics more accountable and helped to knit together a nation that might otherwise fracture along regional lines. An important part of the president's role therefore was to lead his party.[56]

But even Van Buren, who believed parties were a positive good, did not believe that the president could or should behave as a mere partisan. When he traveled north in the summer of 1839, he tried, as Jackson had in 1833, to balance the roles of party leader and head of state. But for the Little Magician the task was more difficult than it had been for the Old Hero. Jackson was a popular war hero, whereas Van Buren was a professional politician who had been the leader of New York's Democratic Party since the early 1820s. Making Van Buren more vulnerable still was an economic downturn that had divided Democrats, emboldened the opposition, and damaged Van Buren's public standing. But the most important difference was that Jackson had toured New England the year following his reelection, whereas Van Buren embarked upon his tour of New York the year before he planned to run for reelection. As a result, Van Buren's 1839 tour invited charges of partisan electioneering that Jackson had largely been able to avoid in 1833.

At the outset of the tour, Van Buren seemed set to tear a page from Monroe's playbook by traveling virtually as a private citizen, "discarding every thing like form and parade" and avoiding partisanship. Unlike Jackson, whose 1833 tour was anticipated and advertised for several months beforehand, Van Buren set out on his trip with relatively little advance warning. In Baltimore he alighted from the train and stepped into his waiting carriage "without the good people of the city being aware of his presence." When he arrived in York, Pennsylvania, the following day, the town had not yet had time to prepare a formal welcome. The town's "Democratic citizens" invited Van Buren "to partake of a public dinner," but he declined their offer, opting instead to stay in his lodgings where "citizens without distinction of party, called upon him *en masse*, to pay their respects." The president's arrival the next day in the Pennsylvania state capital of Harrisburg was also "rather unexpected," according to the *Harrisburg State Capitol Gazette*. Democratic state legislators, who learned of

Van Buren's plan to pass through the state capital only after the president had left Washington, D.C., hurriedly convened to tender Van Buren an invitation to dine with them. Van Buren again declined, preferring instead to receive informal visits from "as many of the *people* as he could conveniently shake hands with."[57]

There was little in Van Buren's first week on the road to suggest that the nation had changed all that much from the days of Monroe. The intention to travel in "the simplicity of a private citizen" was the same, as was the language in which Van Buren was praised. The Democratic press lauded his "republican simplicity," his "unostentatious manner," and the way in which he "meets his fellow-citizens as one of them." And, as with Monroe's tour, as word spread of the tour it became more difficult to avoid formal ceremonies and processions. Committees insisted on the honor of escorting the president along his route. At the village of Womelsdorf, for instance, Van Buren was greeted by a committee of citizens from Reading who had been appointed to escort the president the remaining 10 miles into town. As the president drew near Reading, his escort was joined by civic authorities and "a large number of citizens in vehicles, on horseback, and on foot." Van Buren was given "a beautiful cream colored horse" on which he could traverse the last few miles into town, and his entrance was hailed "by the ringing of all the bells in the town." Local newspapers of both parties swelled with pride at the magnificent scene. The *Berks and Schuylkill Journal*—a "decided whig paper"—gushed over the president's "graceful horsemanship" and the "dignity of his deportment." Van Buren, the *Journal* boasted, was "received, not as the successful candidate of party—but as the President of the United States, the Chief Magistrate of a great nation, chosen by the voice of a Free People." The *Reading Democratic Press* agreed that "on this occasion all party wrath and bitterness were deposed, and with smiling faces and warm hearts, ALL men joined in doing honor to the Chief Magistrate of the nation."[58]

But 1839 was not 1817. Unlike Monroe, Van Buren received a stream of explicitly partisan requests and invitations. Upon arriving in Easton, Pennsylvania, Van Buren was handed a letter from a committee that, "on behalf of the people of Northampton county," welcomed the president to a community that "for nearly half a century has stood forth firm and fearless in her undeviating support of democratic men and democratic measures." As was the case in York and Harrisburg, Van Buren was invited to attend a partisan dinner, an invitation that he again declined. In a letter, Van Buren explained that his refusal was motivated both by "considerations affecting my official position" as well as a "long cherished preference for a less ceremonious interchange of salutations with my political friends." Van Buren would be happy to meet his political friends but not as part of a separate or formal party event. Yet even while Van Buren was careful not to appear in a purely partisan capacity, he used the letter to make a barely veiled campaign appeal for the German vote, emphasizing the "great advantages" the nation was receiving "from the great number of

German emigrants who are daily making this the land of their adoption" and stressing "the high opinion" he had "long entertained of the German character, the hospitality, industry, and courtesy."[59]

The pressure to travel as the head of party came not only from the president's political friends but also from the political opposition. In New York especially, many Whigs were loathe to join in welcoming a Democratic president, particularly one who had been the architect of the rise of the state's Democratic Party. And particularly not the year before a presidential election. In the state capital of Albany, Democrats' effort "to get up [a] no party reception" for the president met with withering scorn from Thurlow Weed's *Albany Evening Journal.* "The Whigs of Albany," the *Journal* insisted, "are not disposed to make a tail for Mr. Van Buren's kite." For years, Van Buren and the Democrats had abused the Whigs, stigmatizing them "as 'Bank Whigs,' 'Biddle Whigs,' 'Federalists,' [and] 'Abolitionists.'" Now, incredibly, Whigs were being asked "to unite with them in magnifying Van Buren!" Only "curs kiss the rod with which their masters scourge them." A party president, argued the *Evening Journal,* deserved only a partisan welcome.[60]

Almost from the moment it was learned that Van Buren would travel to New York, Whigs suspected a "political campaign" was in the cards. Democrats, they felt certain, would use the president's trip for "calling out and displaying" the Democratic Party. Although Van Buren repeatedly turned down Democratic offers to attend public dinners, his written replies to these invitations sometimes veered onto partisan ground. For instance, when York's Democrats extended their invitation to Van Buren "as a mark of personal respect, and also of the approbation of his course as President of the U. States, especially in relation to the custody of the public money," Van Buren felt obliged to respond. Disagreements about the administration's banking policies were to be expected, Van Buren noted, but he was confident that "these differences are . . . yielding to a more correct understanding of the subject, . . . and the time is not . . . very distant when [his policies] will receive the cordial assent of all disinterested persons." Van Buren's "electioneering letter" was immediately jumped on by opponents as further evidence that the president is "traveling upon an election tour" and that "the Sub-Treasury is his electioneering hobby."[61]

Nor were the president's critics wrong. Van Buren's decision to return to New York for the first time since his election in 1836 was steeped in political and electoral calculations. The Empire State was indispensable to Van Buren's reelection, but it could no longer be counted on to vote Democratic. The Panic of 1837 and the ensuing economic downturn had produced "stunning gains" for the Whig Party. Van Buren blamed bankers and speculators for the nation's economic ills and championed the "separation of bank and state" as the cure. Many of New York's Democrats, including Governor William Marcy and *Albany Argus* editor Edwin Crosswell, were wary of Van Buren's plan to deposit public monies in an "Independent Treasury." Conservative Democrats, led by Senator Nathaniel Tallmadge, were openly hostile.

Divisions in the party led to Marcy's defeat in 1838 and the election of William Henry Seward, the state's first Whig governor. By the early summer of 1839, however, the economic picture had brightened and most Democrats—including Marcy and Crosswell—were lining up in support of Van Buren's Independent Treasury plan. Van Buren hoped that by traveling to New York he could help to pull together the party he had led for so long, and secure the support of the state without which he could not hope to be reelected.[62]

The partisan dimensions of the tour were evident from the moment Van Buren touched shore in New York City, where he was greeted by Tammany leader John W. Edmonds, who welcomed the president on behalf of "your Democratic Fellow Citizens." Speaking "in the name of those who are . . . the supporters of your principles and your policy," Edmonds offered a sustained defense of the administration's policies. Opposition to Van Buren's Independent Treasury was to be expected since every "great reform" encounters resistance from "the attachment of private interests." "All who thrive by a system, however evil" and "all who attain power by legislation, however unjust . . . unite against the reformer." Having denigrated opposition to the centerpiece of the administration's domestic policy as little more than the self-serving resistance of the powerful, Edmonds then lauded the skill with which Van Buren had handled the state's border conflicts with Canada. In conclusion, Edmonds looked forward to "the period when the measures of your administration shall receive the . . . unbiased and united approbation" they deserved. That is, to the day when Whigs finally admit that they had been in error.[63]

Edmonds's welcome came as no surprise to Van Buren. The Tammany chief had written to Van Buren several times in late June to notify him of the arrangements that were being made. Indeed it was Edmonds who advised Van Buren that he should arrange to arrive on July 2. Moreover, Edmonds had sent Van Buren a copy of his address so that the president would have time to compose a response. The speech Van Buren delivered in answer to Edmonds's welcome was not extemporaneous. He had written it out beforehand, and he chose his words carefully. The president began by gratefully acknowledging the "cordial reception on the part of my democratic fellow-citizens" of New York, and thanked them for their "approbation" of his "official conduct" as president. He was particularly gratified by Edmonds's praise for the Independent Treasury, which showed "a very mature and just consideration of the subject." For Van Buren, the question was ultimately whether government was to work "for the safety of the many or the aggrandizement of the few." The opposition wanted the public's money to be controlled by "private corporations, irresponsible to the people," whereas the administration wanted it to be in the hands of the people and their elected representatives. Van Buren promised to adhere to the Democratic principle of "the greatest good to the greatest number." Following the script provided by Edmonds's speech, Van Buren closed by defending the administration's course in negotiating territorial disputes along the Canadian border.[64]

For New York's Whigs, the speech confirmed what they had long suspected and many had been saying for weeks: Van Buren "comes among us a politician and not as President of the United States." Those who had urged their fellow Whigs not to participate in the president's reception felt vindicated, while those who had encouraged Whig participation felt betrayed that the president had chosen to appear as "the mere head of a paltry party." Van Buren's speech emboldened several Whig-controlled town councils to refuse the president an official civic welcome. Among these was the council of Hudson, the town in which Van Buren had begun his political career nearly thirty years earlier. The Hudson council explained that they could not appropriate public monies "for the glorification of party men, or the furtherance of party measures." Nor could they "lend the influence of [their] official stations" for partisan purposes. Instead they drew up a resolution declaring it "plain ... that Mr. Van Buren's tour is one of a political and partizan character" and that therefore "the Mayor and Common Council of the city ... do not feel bound by any consideration of justice, prudence, or hospitality, to expend the people's money ... for the purpose of aiding political partizans in their endeavors to carry out their favorite schemes."[65]

For Democrats, however, the breach of decorum was on the Whig side. The "gross illiberality and discourtesy" of the Whig council in Hudson was evidence of the "unabashed malevolence" that Whig politicians had long shown toward Van Buren. In New York City, too, Whigs had betrayed a narrow partisanship. Democrats pointed out that the newly elected Whig governor had rudely declined to join in welcoming Van Buren to New York City. Moreover, most of the city's "Whig press had for weeks labored earnestly to prevent their side from joining in, [insisting that] if the President came at all ... he should be received by his political friends." It was rank hypocrisy, then, for Whigs to criticize the president's political friends for extending Van Buren a partisan welcome. Moreover, the Whigs were forgetting the careful "dividing line" that had been erected "between the different proceedings of the day."

> At Castle Garden, he was received by his political friends, and by them alone. He was welcomed by them there, and then their work was done. After the ceremonies at the Garden, the reception was by the military and the people, without distinction of party; so was the procession through the streets, and so too were the proceedings at the City Hall, where he was received by the Mayor and Common Council, and thenceforth he became their guests. His reception at the Garden, by his friends, was avowedly such; but after that, every proceeding was without distinction of party.

Van Buren traveled as both head of the party and the head of state, and so long as the line separating the two roles remained distinct there was no breach of custom or decorum. It would be bad form to deliver a partisan speech to an official audience, the Democrats seemed to concede, but there was nothing wrong with the president tailoring a partisan message to an audience of political friends.[66]

During the week that Van Buren stayed in New York City, he saw a great deal of his political friends and allies. Much of his time, as historian Donald Cole points out, was "spent . . . in the company of radical Democrats," who were among the most enthusiastic backers of the president's Independent Treasury plan. One evening, the president even accompanied a prominent radical to the Bowery Theater, the centerpiece of the city's "lower-class world of rough amusement." Well-heeled Whigs like Philip Hone were appalled that the president of the United States consented to fraternize with the "Loco-foco rabble," but Van Buren was less interested in what moneyed Whigs were thinking than in securing the political support of the city's workingmen.[67]

Over the next several months Van Buren would travel as far north as Plattsburgh and as far west as Buffalo. At countless stops along the way, Van Buren was greeted with a welcoming address to which he dutifully offered a reply. Some of the welcoming addresses were strongly partisan in tone, particularly where the audience was made up largely of fellow Democrats. Others avoided current politics and focused instead on Van Buren's prepresidential career, typically singling out for praise the role that Van Buren had played in liberalizing the state's suffrage requirements. Van Buren's replies varied widely, depending on the welcoming address, the audience, and local politics. His speeches were at times partisan and at other times conciliatory, sometimes merely a gracious thank you, sometimes a vigorous defense of administration policy. Throughout the tour Van Buren tried to act presidential without abandoning his party or his policies.[68]

One of Van Buren's most notable speeches came in Schenectady, another town in which the Whig common council had resolved not to receive the president. The welcoming address, delivered by a respected local judge, began by acknowledging the partisan divide, welcoming Van Buren "notwithstanding the diversity of sentiment that prevails between members of the two great parties . . . as to some of the measures of your administration." Even those who differed with the president, the judge continued, owed Van Buren respect as "the representative of the majority of the People of the United States." Taking his cue from the magnanimous welcome, Van Buren offered a defense of principled partisanship and a warning against allowing honest differences of opinion to degenerate into "personal hatred, or to infringe upon the courtesies of civilized life." All sides, Van Buren allowed, desire to promote "the public good." But unanimity could not be "reasonably expected" with "respect to the principles and measures" that individuals and parties pursue in their attempt to realize the public good.

The constitution of man, and the nature of public questions, on the contrary, render a diversity of views in regard to [principles and measures] almost a matter of moral necessity; and the conflict which such a division of sentiment invites, when it is divested of personal malignity, is by no means a public evil. The discussions and investigations it calls out are eminently useful to the cause of truth, and every public man is more or less benefitted, in the discharge of his official duties, by the close supervision to which it subjects him. No administration deserves to stand, which is not content to have all its measures subjected to the severest ordeal of free and manly public criticism.

Parties were inevitable, and the president was therefore necessarily a party head. Suppressing partisan conflict was not only bound to fail, it was positively harmful. Democratic accountability required parties and presidents to lay out their principles.[69]

At times, Van Buren did lay out his Democratic principles. In Troy—a third town in which a Whig-dominated council had refused to sanction Van Buren's welcome—the president was welcomed by a Democrat and former congressman, Job Pierson, who praised the president's Independent Treasury for seeking "to place the guardianship of the revenues of the Union in the hands of those who owe their elevation to the people themselves, and are directly responsible to them." In pursuing this and other measures, even in the face of intense opposition, Van Buren had shown his steadfast commitment to "those political principles maintained and avowed by Jefferson and Madison, and revived and restored by your immediate predecessor in office." In his reply, Van Buren did not feel it necessary to defend his policies, which he had "often explained" and his friends had "nobly defended." But nor did he try to change the subject. Prior to his election, Van Buren had placed before the country "an exhibition of the principles upon which, if elected, it was his intention to administer the government." And once in office he had "endeavored to carry [these principles] into practical operation." The people had delivered the president a mandate to pursue his policies.[70]

Perhaps Van Buren's most partisan speech came in Onondaga County, where he again took his cue from the welcoming address. Before a heavily partisan crowd, Major Burnet contrasted the "courtesy and tolerance" Van Buren showed "towards his political opponents" with the "the bitterness of party asperity and malignity" evinced by the other side, which had consistently "misinterpreted and misrepresented" the president's action. The "envy and hatred" that had been directed against Van Buren was, in a sense, a badge of honor, for the same feelings of jealousy and hate had been "directed against [his] illustrious predecessors, devoted to the same political faith and pursuing the same policy." Burnet was confident that the people, "the final arbiters of public men and measures," would vindicate Van Buren's course just as they had vindicated Jackson's.[71]

In his reply, Van Buren acknowledged that the "inveterate malignity with which [he had] been pursued by his political opponents ... at every step" of his political career was a matter that had been frequently brought to his attention in the course of his tour. He had no objection to partisan attacks so long as they were motivated by a sincere "regard to the real good of the country." Indeed if partisan contests could be raised "to the standard of reason and justice . . . our political discussions would . . . become a blessing to the country."

> But when it is quite manifest that those by whom the conduct of a public officer is arraigned are resolved to condemn his acts in any event; when they only desire to know which side of a public question he espouses in order to take their own position against him; when all considerations of comity and right are merged in an absorbing desire to expel him from office and when nothing so much mortifies and enrages them as that he should decide or adopt measures that redound to the good of the country; in all such cases it appears to me an act of inexcusable weakness on the part of the public functionary to suffer what such opponents may say or think of him to give him a moment's care or unease.

There was no point in paying attention to what his "enemies" said since their intention was not "to get at the truth and to approve what is really right" but simply to attack whatever the administration proposed.[72]

Van Buren took solace in Burnet's observation that the misinformation spread by Whig newspapers showed that he had not given up the people's cause. "These continual attacks . . . from the same quarter," Van Buren told the approving crowd, "are like beacons" of light, which allow even those living "in the remotest corner of the land" to see his fidelity to the democratic faith. So long as the people "continue to hear the hootings of the common enemy, they know that their confidence is well placed. It is only when those attacks cease," Van Buren continued, "that their suspicions are aroused, and seldom, indeed, without ground." In other words, the "unceasing assaults" upon the president were a sign that he was doing the people's work and not giving in to the powerful interests.[73]

At other points on the tour, Van Buren was careful to avoid partisanship, even when the welcoming address seemed to invite an avowal of partisan principles. In the president's hometown of Kinderhook, for instance, Major Mordecai Myers endorsed the course Van Buren's administration had taken on a host of contentious matters, from "Indian affairs, to the abolition question, . . . to the management of our foreign affairs, . . . and to the important question of an Independent Treasury." Mordecai acknowledged that "it is not to be expected that . . . all should think alike on matters of great national concern; nor is it desirable that we should." Moreover, he allowed that the minority could play an important part in checking "hasty and improvident legislation." But the opposition of the Whig Party was founded on "no settled principles" apart from a knee-jerk opposition to "the recommendation of the executive and the will of the majority." This type of opposition only "clogs the wheels of government, retards the progress of public business, [and] involves the country in useless expense." Mordecai assured Van Buren that so long as the "polar star" of his administration was the principle that "the greatest good should be done to the greatest possible number" he would retain the public's confidence. In his reply, Van Buren thanked the major but refused to be drawn into politics, preferring instead to reminisce about his early days in Kinderhook.[74]

Where the welcoming committee and address avoided partisanship, so too did Van Buren. In the village of Cherry Valley, for instance, the committee charged with inviting and receiving Van Buren was composed of eight Democrats and eight Whigs, and the welcoming address, delivered by Levi Beardsley—a conservative Democrat with strong misgivings about the Independent Treasury—scrupulously avoided the divisive issues of the day. Although "differing in opinion as to men and measures," Beardsley intoned, the town's citizens "cheerfully unite as freemen in tendering their welcome to the Chief Magistrate of this Republic." Beardsley stressed that it was "one of the excellencies of our republican institutions, that party conflicts, though often embittered, do not necessarily convert the contending parties into enemies, or preclude their uniting in testimonials of respect to those whom a majority of the people (the only legitimate source of power) 'delight to honor.'" Van Buren took his cue from Beardsley, praising the "obvious sincerity" with which the citizens of Cherry Valley had "foregone their political differences" in welcoming him. In front of a crowd made up of citizens of both parties, Van Buren played the Chief Magistrate rather than the head of party.[75]

But there was no avoiding that Van Buren was also the head of a party, and that as such he was a divisive figure. Some towns, such as Cherry Valley, put aside their political differences for the day of welcome, but more often party divisions were on public display. In Poughkeepsie, for instance, the Whigs "stood aloof from" the proceedings, leaving the welcome in "the hands of [the president's] political friends." In the small village of Keeseville, the president's visit occasioned great excitement but it was only "the dwellings and shops *belonging to the republicans* [that] were illuminated with great taste and splendor." Democrats were clearly much happier to see the president than were Whigs.[76]

Many of the forms surrounding presidential travel, such as the illuminated buildings, were unchanged from the days of Washington and Monroe, but they had been refashioned to suit a more partisan era. Triumphal arches, for instance, punctuated Van Buren's tour, just as they had Washington's and Monroe's. However, unlike the celebratory platitudes that adorned the arches under which Monroe and Washington passed (recall Boston's paean in 1789 to "To the Man who unites all hearts"), the messages on the arches that had been prepared for Van Buren were often explicitly political and partisan. Arriving in Greenbush, for instance, Van Buren was met with an arch across the street, "resting upon hickory trees for columns, upon which was inscribed the . . . motto: 'The People's Money, where the People can control it.'"

On the reverse side of the arch were the words: 'The greatest good of the greatest number.'" Even carriages in the civic procession sometimes carried a partisan message, as in Onondaga, where a carriage "displayed . . . a volunteer flag, bearing the . . . words 'An Independent Treasury.'"[77] In contrast, then, to the tours of Washington and Monroe, which had chiefly celebrated loyalty to the nation and promoted national unity, Van Buren's tour provided an occasion for Democrats across New York to parade their political persuasion.

PRESIDENT OF ALL THE PEOPLE

The divergent reactions to Van Buren's tour reveal how much the emergence of organized political parties had complicated presidential travel. Monroe's preeminent challenge while on tour had been to reassure his fellow citizens that he was not aping monarchical practices. Van Buren, too, had to fend off charges that he was "play[ing] the Monarch," but his main difficulty was navigating the conflict between his partisan supporters, who urged him to raise high the party banner, and his political opponents, who insisted he should appear as "president of all the people." Van Buren and his supporters hoped to use the president's trip to energize and organize his political base. His opponents hoped either to tether him to a nonpolitical conception of his role that would restrict his political maneuvering or, alternatively, to use the nonpolitical norm as a stick with which to beat him for violating accepted canons of presidential behavior.[78]

In the early republic, the vision of a president above party rested on widespread distrust of what George Washington, in his Farewell Address, called "the baneful effects of the Spirit of Party." The presidency was seen as a place for men of high character whose disinterested judgment would not be distorted by parties. Although the framers of the Constitution rejected monarchy, their vision of a virtuous president standing above party bore an unmistakable resemblance to an idealized conception of monarchy. The acceptance of political parties as legitimate instruments of democratic governance paved the way for a more democratic understanding of the presidency, one that envisioned the president as a partisan politician rather than a regal head of state. Just as Monroe's commitment to republican simplicity helped to move the presidency away from a monarchical model, so Van Buren's willingness to embrace the role of party leader promised to remake the presidency in a less regal image.[79]

But a funny thing happened on the way to the modern presidency. The monarchical side of the presidency proved remarkably resilient. Just as pomp and ceremony did not in fact give way to republican simplicity, so the ideal of a president above party survived even after the nation accepted that parties and partisanship were necessary to democracy. Indeed the nonpartisan ideal prospered. Partisan squabbles only seemed to feed the public's hankering for a president who would rise above the party contest. And presidents found they often benefited enormously from downplaying partisan appearances. After all, the argument that people must rise above party or that the nation cannot afford party differences—for instance, that "politics stops at the water's edge"—usually translated as: Congress should stop bickering and instead follow the president's lead. What chief executive would settle for the job of party head when he could don the regal robes of head of state?

Admittedly, most Americans view the president through the lens of a political party. Adherents of the president's party are invariably more approving of his performance than are adherents of the opposing party. Sometimes, these differences are immense; other times they are more muted. George W. Bush's approval rating among Republicans, for instance, has never dropped below 70 percent, whereas his approval among Democrats has frequently wallowed in single digits. In contrast, Gerald Ford, who inspired neither the same adulation among his Republican base nor the same hatred among his Democratic opponents, experienced closer to a 30-point gap between evaluations rendered by the two side's partisans. The absence of public opinion polls in the nineteenth century prevents us from specifying precisely the partisan basis of nineteenth-century Americans' evaluations of presidential performance. However, given the central role that parties played in organizing political life and disseminating political information in the nineteenth century, it seems safe to assume that partisan lenses colored public judgments of the presidents in ways that were at least as significant as they are today.

Intense partisanship, however, coexisted with the public expectation or hope that the president should be something more than a mere partisan. The president was the acknowledged head of his party, yet he was also expected to be "the president of all the people." The tension between these roles was never so exquisitely felt as when a president was on the road, traveling among and speaking to the people, his supporters as well as his opponents. When the Whig Zachary Taylor embarked on a tour during his first year in office, he vowed that he "would endeavor to conform to the views and carry out the wishes of the party that elected him." Democratic editors immediately pounced on the statement, expressing shock that any president "could descend so far as to proclaim himself degraded from the Presidency of the United States." Feeling the sting of such criticism, Taylor tried to clarify his views the following day: "I conceive that I am the President of the United States, and not of a particular party. I consider the majority of the people the sovereigns of this great Republic, and I will carry out their wishes, be them Democratic or be them Whig."[80]

Taylor's statement clarified little, but it does provide a caution against assuming that the responsibilities of party leadership were simply laid atop an older, more elitist ideal of nonpartisanship. Rather, the framers' nonpartisan ideal was itself reshaped by democratic politics. After Jackson, presidents increasingly couched their claims to be above party in populist language. Empowered by elections, presidents claimed to speak for "the people." The president, as Woodrow Wilson expressed it in

1908, "is the only national voice in affairs. . . . He is the representative of no constituency, but of the whole people. When he speaks in his true character, he speaks for no special interest." Or, as political scientist Clinton Rossiter expressed the point a half-century later: "The President is the American people's one authentic trumpet." The language is populist, but the vision is regal: the president stands above special interests and discordant factions, and sounds the true and enduring sentiments of the people. Just as a king was supposed to do.[81]

Democratic Manners and Presidential Dignity: The Tours of Zachary Taylor and Andrew Johnson

"Old Zack! How are you old feller?" was the indecorous shout from the first man in Lancaster, Pennsylvania, to grasp Zachary Taylor's hand through the open railcar window. "I'm well, and how are you?" was the beaming president's quick response. One cringes to imagine the contemptuous stare that such ill-mannered familiarity would have received from the first president of the United States. And James Monroe, for all of his "plain republican" habits, would have found such behavior baffling. Citizens did not greet Washington or Monroe by their first name, let alone a nickname. And neither Washington nor Monroe typically shook hands with their fellow citizens, and certainly not in the streets. Instead they generally bowed politely to those citizens fortunate enough to be introduced to them.[1]

Unimaginable in the time of Washington, this kind of familiar exchange between president and citizen was celebrated in the Jacksonian era as a measure of the president's democratic sympathies and close connection with the people. Andrew Jackson, who was widely known as Old Hickory or, alternatively, the Old Hero, was the first president to be called by a nickname. Zachary Taylor went by Old Rough and Ready as well as Old Zack; James Polk was called Young Hickory; William Henry Harrison was famously Tippecanoe or just Old Tip. To friends, Martin Van Buren was the Little Magician, though his enemies preferred the Sly Fox or Little Van. And, of course, throughout the North, Abraham Lincoln was Old Abe or, alternatively, Honest Abe. The nicknames—apart from Van Buren's—symbolically shrunk the distance between leader and followers, making the leader appear to be one of the people.[2]

Shaking hands with the citizenry fulfilled much the same function. Handshaking between gentlemen was not uncommon in the eighteenth century, but only social equals shook hands in polite society. In the latter part of the eighteenth century, however, handshaking crept into the political arena as a way for the gentry to appeal for the votes of their social inferiors. A 1771 pamphlet warned voters against the "forced smiles, hearty shakes by the hand, and deceitful . . . enquiries after your wife and family" that self-interested politicians used to gain election. Handshaking between candidate and voter became more common in politics but not necessarily accepted by all. In the fall of 1816, for instance, a Federalist newspaper in Massachusetts complained of the "handshaking–whiskey treating–electioneering gentry of all parties."[3] Like many of their social class, Washington and Monroe associated handshaking with a distasteful electioneering that had no place in the presidency.

The norm against electioneering for the presidency would prove to be amazingly resilient, lasting, in an admittedly weakened form, into the early twentieth century. Nineteenth-century presidential candidates were generally expected to stand for election, not run for it. In contrast, the stigma against presidential handshaking disappeared quickly, an early casualty of what historian Sean Wilentz describes as "the democratic ferment of the 1820s." When Monroe's successor, John Quincy Adams, traveled to Baltimore in 1827, for instance, he received about two thousand visitors during the course of one evening. "They came in a continual, unceasing stream," Adams wrote in his diary. "I shook hands with them all, and among them all there were not twenty whom I had seen before." "Many," Adams added, "told me they hoped I should be re-elected." Adams clearly regarded it as somewhat strange and more than a little distasteful that a man in his position was called upon to shake the hands of so many people he did not know, including some who were "very much in liquor." After a life of exchanging dignified bows with foreign dignitaries, shaking hands with his fellow citizens was a ritual that the Harvard-educated Adams "got through awkwardly" at best.[4]

Although the same age as Adams, Jackson had none of his predecessor's awkwardness with the emergent democratic political culture. Jackson was widely seen as "a man of the people," a term that nobody ever used to describe Adams. In 1840, the Whig Party turned the tables on the Democrats, casting Van Buren as the effete aristocrat and Old Tip as the man of the people. To be successful, presidents needed to show they had democratic manners, that they were at home among the people. And there were few better ways of demonstrating that popular touch than a presidential tour.

However, drawing too close to the people had its dangers as well. Although citizens wanted their president to be comfortable shaking hands, exchanging small-talk, and mingling freely in their midst, they also wanted him to be something more than a mere politician, a huckster, a stump speaker. Presidents were expected to be dignified. Even toward the end of the nineteenth century, it was not uncommon for a president to be addressed as "his Excellency." Presidents faced a dilemma: draw too close to the people and face charges of behaving with an undignified vulgarity, coarseness, or even demagoguery; swerve too far from the demos and set off shouts of royalty and monarchism.[5]

This chapter examines two presidential tours from the mid-nineteenth century: Zachary Taylor's little-known trip through Pennsylvania and New York in 1849 and Andrew Johnson's infamous "swing around the circle" in 1866. Both tours were designed to demonstrate the president's connection to the people and to bolster the president's political agenda. Although Taylor's tour was cut short by illness, it nonetheless illustrates the democratization of manners that had reshaped the relationship between president and people in the first half of the nineteenth century. Johnson's tour, in contrast, dramatizes the salience of presidential dignity. The heavy price that Johnson paid for breaching the bounds of appropriate decorum was a lesson not lost on his successors in the latter part of the nineteenth century.

Zachary Taylor departed from Washington, D.C., on August 9, 1849. Affixed to the rear of the waiting train was "a large, new and elegant car" that had been provided by the Baltimore and Ohio Railroad company "for the exclusive use" of the president. Taylor, however, "respectfully declined" to use the special car, preferring instead, the *Baltimore Sun* reported, to take "his seat in common with other passengers." Like Monroe, Taylor let it be known that he did not want to be met with elaborate public receptions or parades. He was, he said, "going to visit the sovereigns, and wished to do it in a very quiet way." Also like Monroe, Taylor professed a desire to avoid an entourage, having resolved "to go among the people, as one of the people, free and untrammeled." The president did not wish, explained a supportive newspaper editor, to be "restrained from a free communication with [the people] by any of the customary forms." The words were not dissimilar to those Monroe might have chosen, but Taylor interacted with his fellow citizens in a way that Monroe would likely have regarded as unbecoming the president of the United States.[6]

Taylor reached his first scheduled stop, the city of Baltimore, at a little past seven in the evening. As he stepped onto the railway platform, his appearance was greeted by "an earthquake of cheers and shouts," especially, we are told, "from the numerous body of mechanics who had assembled from the various workshops." The president immediately found himself enveloped in a dense crowd of admirers, each one of whom was intent on shaking his hand. Although not a career politician, Taylor knew what to do. He "returned their warm grasp" and, according to the *New York Herald*'s correspondent, "seemed particularly happy in seizing the hands of the roughest among them, telling them that he had left Washington . . . to see the sovereigns, and . . . he was determined to feel them also."[7]

Three decades earlier, when Monroe arrived in Baltimore at the outset of his northeastern tour, there was also plenty of popular enthusiasm and excitement. But there was no shaking of hands, nor was there good-natured banter between the chief executive and the crowd that had gathered to glimpse the nation's fifth president. Monroe's welcome was stiffer, more scripted. The president was escorted into town by cavalry from the First Baltimore Hussars as well as by a "large concourse of citizens on horseback." Upon his arrival, reported the *Baltimore Patriot*, "several of the aged and most respectable citizens attended the president, and welcomed his appearance in Baltimore." People cheered Monroe enthusiastically and watched the many military regiments that had been called out to parade for review, but the president and the people generally remained a dignified distance from each other.[8]

The gulf in manners between the tours of Monroe and Taylor is even more evident in Taylor's reception the following evening in Lancaster, Pennsylvania. In some ways, the scene was a familiar one. Hours before Taylor's arrival, the streets of Lancaster "were thronged with thousands, the buildings gayly decorated with flags, the ladies standing all ready at the windows with their white handkerchiefs, the cannon all loaded and pointed, the cavalcade dancing to martial music." But as soon as the president's train arrived the scene was quite unlike anything Monroe had faced. "In an instant," reported the *Philadelphia News*, "the car containing the President was literally surrounded with human beings, both inside and outside, each trying at one and the same time the capacity of his lungs and the utmost extension of his arms and fingers." It was only "with much difficulty" that Taylor was finally pried loose from the grip of the immense crowd, estimated at around eight thousand people, and bundled into the carriage that took him to his downtown hotel.[9]

Early the next morning Taylor renewed his acquaintance with the people of Lancaster and the "yeomen and mechanics" who had "poured in" from the surrounding areas, "all impelled by the common desire to see and feel Old Zack." When Monroe toured the northeast he had visited mostly fortifications, but Taylor headed immediately for Lancaster's main market, where he "mix[ed] familiarly with the country people." However, "the throng about him" became "so great [that] he was soon obliged to beat a hasty retreat." By eight in the morning Taylor was back at his hotel where he received the ladies of Lancaster, and then at nine "the doors were thrown open" to the men, "who rushed in without order, and pressed upon each other, to the great danger of life and limb." Taylor tried at first to shake hands with each person, but "the tide flowed upon him so turbulently," reported that the *Philadelphia Public Ledger*, "that it was impossible for him to grasp the hands of those who presented themselves," and so they had to "be content with a smile and a nod." According to the *Lancaster Examiner and Herald*, Taylor had been obliged to stop shaking hands because "the hearty grasp of his visitors would have squeezed his hand to a jelly." But even after "Old Zack" had given up on shaking hands, noted the *Philadelphia News*, he still "had a ready reply" for the "rough and quaint salutations" of each person who greeted him.[10]

The arduous work of shaking hands was often noted by observers of the tour, particularly after Taylor was taken ill at Harrisburg on August 12. One Harrisburg correspondent wrote that "the exercise of shaking hands with fifteen or twenty thousand a day . . . is exceedingly fatiguing." The president's right hand, the correspondent observed, "is already becoming lame, so that he is obliged to put a part of the labor upon the left." Although clearly weakened by diarrhea and fatigue, the president was determined to continue the ordeal of seeing and feeling the people.

At Shippensburg, Pennsylvania's governor, William Johnston—who accompanied Taylor throughout the president's two-week tour of the Keystone State—told an exuberant crowd of thousands that he had warned the president that "if he attempted to shake hands with all, he would not have a hand nor an arm left on his body." The president's reply, reported Johnston, was "that so long as he had a hand or an arm left, he should give it to the people who had reposed confidence in him." The crowd erupted in cheers of approval at this testimonial to Taylor's democratic manners.[11]

At times, Taylor's health prevented him from mixing with the people in the manner he had hoped. When the train stopped at Mechanicsburg on August 13, for instance, Taylor was "too feeble to go among the crowd," as he had planned, but instead "could only hold familiar conversations with them from his seat." The president "apologized for being unable to see them more intimately and to descend among the crowd," but he compensated by "allow[ing] them to seize him by the hands, the arms and the shoulders." Later that same day, after a bout of vomiting, the president was weaker still and was compelled in Newville to delegate the "duty of shaking hands" to the governor, though reportedly there was "a most determined stampede" among some of the "ladies and young girls" who "commenced kissing the 'dear old man' . . . within an inch of his life." Even less restraint was shown by the huge crowd that awaited his arrival in Chambersburg, the last stop on that grueling day. Even before the president's car had come to a halt, it was "literally swarming with old men and young." Those who reached " 'Old Zack', as they affectionately called him, came near tearing him completely asunder" as they pressed to shake his hand or "catch him by the arms and shoulders and hug him." So eager were the people to see and feel Old Zack that they ignored "the earnest remonstrance" of Governor Johnston and the "pale and haggard appearance of the president." It appeared to one concerned correspondent that "the crowd would have succeeded in carrying [Taylor] off in their arms, but for timely interference."[12]

Accounts of Taylor's tour, at least in the Whig Party press, repeatedly highlighted not only the physical contact between the president and the people but also the easy familiarity with which they addressed each other. At one "small settlement," for instance, Taylor is reported to have stopped at a tavern where the "rough but honest men, in their short sleeves and aprons, . . . assured by the open countenance of the General, . . . gathered round him, and talked with freedom and familiarity." The president is repeatedly described as "mingling" freely with crowds of people. The *Greensburg Intelligencer*, for example, praised Taylor for the way in which "he mingles with, and converses freely with all, [making] everyone feel perfectly at home in his company." Admirers in Pittsburgh noted that even after crowds had begun to disperse, Taylor "was still quietly walking from group to group, chatting familiarly with all he met." The president, observed the *Lawrence Journal*, "was as familiar with the people as any farmer in Lawrence county could be to his neighbor."

And the people reciprocated, addressing the president, noted a correspondent for the *New York Tribune,* just as "they would have done a long-lost brother, husband, or son."[13]

The civic ceremonies invariably addressed the president by the formal title of "Mr. President," but the crowd's exuberant shout was generally "Hurrah for Old Zack." According to a correspondent who followed Taylor through western Pennsylvania, the president did "not appear to have any other name" than Old Zack. The Whig press told of countless incidents like the one at Harrisburg where a "rough looking man, with a straw hat, stepped up to the side of the cars, and patting the President on the shoulder said 'Old Zack, if you do as well at Washington as you did at Buena Vista, we shall be satisfied.'" Or the greeting at Mechanicsburg, where the president was hailed by the crowd with "cries of 'Come out Old Zack, and let us see you.'" It is as difficult to imagine President Washington or President Monroe being hailed in such familiar terms as it is President Clinton or President Bush.[14]

Many of these stories were undoubtedly embellished by a Whig press determined to portray Taylor in a positive light. Not surprisingly, Democratic newspapers offered a starkly different narrative of the president's tour. Taylor's reception in Baltimore, for instance, was reported to be "cold" and the crowd "meagre." His appearance on the hotel portico was said to have produced "a few sickly cheers akin to the chirpings of a brood of chickens with the pip." Even where the crowds were undeniably large, the people were rendered in the Democratic press as passive bystanders in a gaudy political spectacle. In Harrisburg, for instance, we are told that the president was "put in an open barouche and escorted through the most fashionable and stylish part of the town for about an hour, with an evergreen crown on his head and a hoop, trimmed with dahlias, round his shoulders, in imitation of the victors in the Olympic games." Afterwards he "retired to the Whig head-quarters . . . to dine." In Bedford Springs, the *Democratic Union* insisted, "the gentry . . . took charge of [the president], and gave him a grand ball, but the hard-handed forge and furnace men of Bedford county never saw him." Paraded by his partisan handlers before "gaping crowd[s]," the president was prevented from touching or talking with the ordinary people of the state.[15]

If Whigs and Democrats could not agree on the character of Taylor's tour, they did agree on what a presidential tour should look like. The Whigs praised Taylor for his intimate, physical contact with the people, symbolized most emphatically by the handshake: the "cordial grasp of the toil-hardened laborer" or the "warm grasp of the yeomen of our Commonwealth." The Democrats, in contrast, faulted Taylor for allowing a genteel distance to separate president and people. The criticisms of Taylor no less than the praise pointed to a relationship between president and people that was supposed to be unmediated and familiar. The rhetoric of both parties was premised on the belief the president's political strength was rooted in the strength of his connection with the people.[16]

Many Whigs were confident that Taylor's tour had bolstered the president's political standing. The *Pittsburgh Gazette*, for instance, reported that "by mixing with his fellow citizens" the president had "greatly increased his personal popularity" and made himself "at this moment, invincible in Pennsylvania." The same optimistic note was sounded by the *New York Herald*, which observed that Taylor's "benevolent, plain manner makes [him] friends at once," even among "the strongest democrats." As an example the *Herald* quoted a "hardy looking 'son of the soil'" who, after meeting the president, declared "I've seen Old Zack, and I'll be d—d if ever I vote for any one else. He took right hold of my hand and said God bless you, and he can't be a bad man if he said that."[17]

Some Democrats were concerned that Taylor might indeed be winning converts with his folksy manner. A Whig paper gleefully reported the prediction offered by a Democrat who, after watching the president's enthusiastic reception in Harrisburg, suggested that if Taylor continued "through Pennsylvania [then] no other man could carry the state while he was living." Democratic newspapers, however, scoffed at such judgments as barely disguised Whig propaganda. They predicted instead that although Taylor's "electioneering errand" had been "arranged altogether for political effect . . . by the whig plotters," it would end up hurting the president and his party more than it helped. Democrats mocked Taylor's public speaking. Many of the president's speeches, they suggested, could barely be heard by any but those on the speakers' platform. And when the former general could be heard, reported the *Pittsburgh Daily Post*, he spoke "so bunglingly" that all people "not over filled with Whig enthusiasm, blushed for the honor of the Republic." At Lancaster, snickered the *Post*, the people witnessed the "humbling spectacle" of "the President of our great nation . . . unable to address the people," opting instead to allow Governor Johnston to act as "the mouth-piece of his Excellency."[18]

Democrats were right that Taylor, a career military officer, was no orator. Before assuming the presidency, Taylor had never delivered a political speech or even voted. Nor did he have a natural aptitude for public speaking that might compensate for his lack of practice. Although not a compelling orator, Taylor nonetheless spoke frequently, answering welcoming addresses much as Monroe and Van Buren had. Prior to the complete breakdown of his health just outside Erie on August 24, Taylor delivered over two dozen speeches to Pennsylvania audiences. Sometimes these speeches were only bland acknowledgments of thanks, but often they communicated his position on important issues facing the state and the nation. Taylor also had a number of formal and informal issue-oriented conversations with groups of citizens.[19]

By far the most important issue in Pennsylvania was tariffs. The state's coal and iron industries were mired in depression, and economic discontent ran strong. Anxiously eyeing the upcoming fall elections, Pennsylvania's Whigs were making support for higher tariffs the centerpiece of their fall campaign. The tariff, as one prominent Pennsylvania Whig noted, "is the one question upon which the Whigs have always carried Pennsylvania, and it is the only one upon which it can be carried." The president, however, had yet to commit himself to a rate hike. The state's party leaders begged Taylor to use the tour to signal his endorsement of an increase in tariffs; otherwise, they warned, Whig candidates would face a "catastrophe" in the October elections.[20]

Taylor insisted that the tour was entirely nonpolitical. The "sole purpose" of the trip, he informed the welcoming committee that greeted him at the Pennsylvania state line, was "obtaining a more intimate knowledge of the various sections of our Union, of their various pursuits and interests." Yet the path that Taylor had charted through Pennsylvania as well as New York belied the administration's claim that the "journey was not for political purposes." Ten of the fourteen counties on the Pennsylvania itinerary had voted for the president in 1848; this in a state in which two-thirds of the counties had voted Democratic. Moreover, both Pennsylvania and New York were critical to Taylor's reelection plans. Had either state gone Democratic in 1848, as they narrowly had in 1844, Lewis Cass would have been the nation's twelfth president. Taylor had won Pennsylvania, which generally leaned Democratic, with only a hair over 50 percent of the vote, and he carried New York despite garnering less than 48 percent of the popular vote, thanks largely to the presence of third-party candidate Martin Van Buren, who split the Empire State's Democratic vote.[21]

The political dimensions of the tour were clear from the moment Taylor reached the Pennsylvania state line, where the welcoming address was delivered by the state's first-ever Whig governor, William F. Johnston. A former Democrat who had recently left the party over tariffs, Johnston urged Taylor to pay close attention to the "means calculated to encourage" Pennsylvania's industries, a thinly veiled plea for higher tariffs. At the end of the day, Taylor heard the same message in more explicit terms from Thaddeus Stevens, who had been selected by the residents of Lancaster to deliver their town's welcoming address. Stevens would later become one of the most powerful Republicans in the House of Representatives—a thorn in Lincoln's side and the bane of Andrew Johnson—but in the summer of 1849 he was still a newly elected and relatively unheralded Whig congressman. Although firmly antislavery, Stevens did not talk to Taylor about that. Instead he talked economic policy. Stevens applauded Taylor for touring the state and directed the president's attention to the state's economic needs: "May you traverse every portion of Pennsylvania—learn its capabilities—see its prosperity and its sufferings [and] observe how large a portion of its untold treasures are yet buried in the bosom of the earth." Stevens pressed Taylor to embrace the Whig program. Pennsylvania, he said, "hopes that after full examination you will come to the conclusion that the labor of the people is entitled to the *protection of the nation*," and that the state's "great interests are worthy of *the fostering care of government*." The language and the policy prescriptions were unmistakably Whiggish. Recognizing that he risked crossing the line between bipartisan welcome and partisan plug, Stevens excused himself on the grounds that Pennsylvanians were agreed on the tariff. "I would not touch debatable ground," he explained, but "in this hope I believe every Pennsylvanian agrees."[22]

In his reply to Stevens, Taylor reaffirmed his desire to "witness in person [the state's] agricultural, manufacturing, and mining operations." He expressed, too, his gratification that "the People have welcomed me, without distinction of party" and reminded the citizens of Lancaster that he traveled among them "in a plain and unostentatious manner." But Taylor did not rest on republican ceremony; instead he took up Stevens's invitation to talk about economic policy, assuring his audience that "no one takes a deeper interest in . . . the great industrial interests of Pennsylvania— her agriculture and manufactures, her iron and coal" than he did. He vowed that as president he would "heartily cooperate with the National Legislature in recommending or carrying out such measures" as would promote those interests.[23]

Secretary of State John Clayton praised the president's remarks, which he anticipated would "produce a great effect in Pennsylvania," but Taylor's comments were still too equivocal for many anxious Pennsylvania Whigs, who pressed the president for more explicit assurances of his support for higher tariffs. Taylor complied in Pittsburgh, where he met with "a number of the Iron Masters" before taking a tour of more than a dozen of the city's factories and mills. The deputation of industrialists conveyed to the president the "ruinous" harm that the Democrats' tariff reductions had visited on the region's coal and iron industries, to which Taylor responded that he was "decidedly in favor of a permanent protective tariff, founded on specific duties, and discriminating in favor of American Labor." Moreover, he indicated that the Walker Tariff of 1846 "had been unfortunate for the country, and while he was not in favor of prohibitory duties, he desired to see such a modification of our revenue laws as would afford a reasonable and fair protection to all the manufactures, and industrial interests of the country." After Pittsburgh, nobody was left wondering about the president's position on tariffs.[24]

Taylor left Pittsburgh by carriage the following morning, arriving in the town of Beaver at the end of another arduous day of traveling. Located along the Ohio River near the western border of Pennsylvania, Beaver was closer to Ohio than to Pittsburgh, and as in many western towns the issue of transportation—what was known in the language of the day as "internal improvements"—loomed large. Whereas welcoming addresses in industrial towns like Lancaster and Pittsburgh had highlighted the tariff, the Beaver welcoming address accented internal improvements: "Our system of internal improvements connecting with the Atlantic—with the great northern Lakes, and by the Ohio with the great valley of the Mississippi, requires but a comparatively small outlay on the part of the general government, in a judicious improvement of our rivers and harbors to complete it and make it perfect." Taylor seized on the invitation to declare his support for federally funded internal improvements. "So far as internal improvements are concerned," he told the citizens of Beaver, "I am strongly in favor of a system by which we shall have good harbors and navigable rivers; and will do everything proper to produce a result so desirable."[25]

Tariffs and internal improvements were not the only important policy questions that Taylor broached while on tour. After leaving Beaver the president headed north for Mercer, where he met with a delegation of citizens from Warren, Ohio. Settled largely by New Englanders, Warren was traditionally a Whig stronghold, but fears about the expansion of slavery had pushed many of the area's citizens into the arms of the Free Soil Party in 1848. The strength of the Free Soil Party throughout northeastern Ohio (known as the Western Reserve) had crippled the Whig Party and tipped the state to Cass in 1848, and the meeting with the Warren delegation provided the president a useful venue in which to reassure northern Whigs who were nervous about his position on slavery. During a "free and general conversation" with the delegation—which included the editor of the *Trumbull County Whig*—Taylor declared "that the people of the North need have no apprehension of the further extension of Slavery." He also assured them that "the necessity of a third party organization on this score would soon be obviated."[26]

Whigs pointed to the president's willingness to speak plainly with the people about important issues as further evidence of his democratic manners. The *Beaver Argus*, for instance, praised Taylor for not attempting "to conceal his opinions in his intercourse with the People." The *Argus*'s editor was equally impressed by the president's willingness to listen to people talk about public policy. Taylor had come, "as [he] should come, in a plain republican manner, to mingle freely amongst the people [and] to hear their view of public policy." A similar theme was sounded by the *New York Herald*, which lauded Taylor's willingness to go "to the people for their advice" rather than simply listen to what his cabinet tells him. In Pittsburgh, noted the *Philadelphia News* approvingly, the president "took all by the hand, and conversed freely with all, . . . and in all his conversations on public affairs, . . . which engrossed a large share of his time . . . , he evinced a knowledge, and expressed his views with a precision and plainness." A democratic leader traveled not only to see and to feel the people, but to converse with them, to talk to them and to listen to them.[27]

What Whigs saw as democracy in action, Democrats portrayed as an undignified "bid for votes." From the moment the president crossed into Pennsylvania, complained the Harrisburg *Democratic Union*, "the Whigs took sole charge of [Taylor] in all his movements and acts [and] told him what to say at each particular point." The Democratic Party flung at Taylor the same electioneering charge that Whigs had hurled at Van Buren a decade earlier, except that the transgressions of the war hero Taylor were largely attributed to the machinations of his political handlers whereas Van Buren, widely regarded as a wily politician, was held personally responsible for his political maneuvering.[28]

It is tempting to see this rhetoric as little more than rank hypocrisy and partisan gamesmanship. Eager to constrain or discredit Taylor, Democrats invoked the same conceptions of presidential dignity that the Whigs had pedaled when the Democrats controlled the White House. Meanwhile, Whigs, who while in the opposition had kept a vigilant watch against all violations of an austere standard of presidential propriety, now urged their president to mingle freely with the people and to communicate openly with them about public policy. Whether a speech was deemed undignified electioneering or a laudable, democratic communion between president and people depended less on principle than on partisan interests.

The sharply divergent partisan reactions to Taylor's tour suggest that there was no one, universally accepted norm that dictated political behavior when a president traveled. However, these contradictory responses do not mean that ideas were merely a cover for raw political interests. Instead, the language with which presidents were praised and condemned reveals the power that two contradictory ideas exerted on the nineteenth-century political imagination. On the one hand, people expected their president to be "a man of the people." He was to be the people's direct representative, their "servant," selected to "ascertain their wishes [and] to execute them." To see what the people see, and feel what the people feel, the president needed to move "amongst them like one of [them]." The populist vision of the presidential tour coexisted, however, with an alternative, older understanding of the presidency, one that preferred the president to keep a dignified distance from the passions that roiled a vibrant democratic community. While the president had to avoid the trappings of monarchy, he also needed to avoid descending to partisan stump-speaking. Unlike a mere politician, the president was not to chase after votes.[29]

Veer too far in one direction or the other, and a president immediately invited criticism from partisan opponents. Too much distance and a president attracted accusations that he harbored monarchical pretensions or was out of touch with the people; solicit the people too assiduously and charges of electioneering or demagoguery were immediately hurled at the president. No nineteenth-century president who toured the nation found this an easy gauntlet to run, but no president failed it as spectacularly as Andrew Johnson. If Taylor's tour showed how much Americans valued democratic manners, Johnson's showed just how much presidential dignity still mattered.

ANDREW JOHNSON'S "SWING AROUND THE CIRCLE"

Johnson's so-called "swing around the circle" is the most famous—or infamous—presidential tour of the nineteenth century. Even those who know little else about nineteenth-century presidential travel have likely heard of Johnson's disastrous excursion. When the House of Representatives drew up articles of impeachment against Johnson, the tenth article condemned the president's speech-making on tour for having "brought the high office of the President of the United States into contempt, ridicule and disgrace." Even if the president's "intemperate, inflammatory, and scandalous harangues" did not rise to the level of an impeachable offense, many agreed with Congress that the president's behavior showed a reckless disregard for "the dignity and propriety" of his high office.[30]

According to political scientist Jeffrey Tulis, Johnson was "the great exception." His popular rhetoric, writes Tulis, "violated virtually all of the nineteenth-century norms" regarding presidential speech-making. Tulis is undeniably correct that Johnson's tour transgressed accepted norms about presidential behavior, but there was also much that was conventional about his tour. Before we proceed to examine the unusual and occasionally bizarre features of Johnson's tour, it will be useful to delineate some of its more ordinary aspects.[31]

Johnson's tour began, as did much nineteenth-century travel, with an invitation. This one came from Chicago, an entreaty to participate in the dedication of a monument to Stephen Douglas. As soon as it was announced that the president would travel to Chicago, other cities extended invitations of their own and formed committees to arrange for a reception of the president "in fitting accordance with the respect due the Chief Magistrate of the Union." Towns placed on the presidential itinerary prepared a formal welcoming address, delivered usually either by the mayor or a distinguished citizen. At stops along the way, Johnson's train was boarded by delegations charged with escorting the president to their city or town. At Rochester, New York, for instance, a three-man committee from Cleveland clambered aboard the presidential train and accompanied Johnson the remaining 250 miles to Cleveland, and in Erie, Pennsylvania, Cleveland's mayor, city council, and a large committee of citizens joined the traveling party in order to escort Johnson the final 60 miles. The president's train, groused the *New York Tribune*, was so "constantly filled with committees [that] there was hardly standing room to be found in the cars."[32]

Johnson's tour, which began on August 28, 1866, created the same sense of high excitement and eager anticipation as previous presidential tours. Even in the largest cities, a presidential visit was a special occasion. On the eve of Johnson's tour, the *New York Tribune* observed that "the visit of a live President to this metropolitan city is an event of such rare occurrence as to be worthy of very extended and general celebration." The *Boston Daily Advertiser* agreed that "great and noisy crowds" were to be expected since "a real, live president is not to be seen out of Washington every day."[33]

In New York City, on the tour's second day, citizens turned out "en masse" to see Johnson, just as they had when Van Buren and Jackson visited the city. "With the arrival of the President," recorded the *New York Times*, "the huzzaing people flooded street and footpath, and occupied every foot of ground within seeing or hearing distance of the hotel. Railings were seized upon as pet places, and stoops, which [had been] sacred stepping places for aristocratic owners only, were swarmed upon by the plebian multitude." Even the anti-Johnson *New York Tribune* could not deny that the crowds were "loud and vociferous," the sidewalks "impassable," and the windows and doors "thronged" with women waving handkerchiefs and men waving hats. So dense was the mass of humanity and "so violently" did it "press . . . upon" the president's carriage that the procession had difficulty getting started. "Men rushed up and caught [the president] by the hand," the *Tribune* reported, "while cheer after cheer arose from the surrounding crowd."[34]

Later in the tour, even as criticism of his speeches mounted, Johnson continued to be received by enthusiastic crowds in many cities and small towns. In St. Louis, a city that had never before seen "a real, live president," the reception was almost rapturous. Arriving by steamboat—aboard the *Andy Johnson*—the president was, according to the *Natchez Daily Courier*, met by "one mass of admiring, enthusiastic, living beings."

> The president landed amidst swarms of people. Batteries of regular artillery fired salutes of honor; and at the head of a procession of military and civilians, two miles in length, the President and cortege moved through the principal streets of the city. . . . Every square by which it passed was crowded with people, and the houses, as well as the public buildings, were handsomely decorated. Triumphal arches were erected over the roads. . . . [I]n short, the enthusiasm was unrestrained and irrepressible almost beyond description.

According to the *New York Times*, the reception in St. Louis was "the most brilliant ovation ever tendered an American citizen by American people, and . . . the most magnificent spectacle ever witnessed in the West." Even discounting for the hyperbole of the pro-Johnson papers, it is clear that Johnson received a warm and sometimes rapturous welcome at many stops along his tour.[35]

In the tour's opening days, crowds seemed as eager to see and touch Andy Johnson as they had been Old Zack. At Baltimore, "every foot of standing room in the depot was crowded, and until the starting of the train there was a tremendous scramble among the people to get a shake of the hand from the President." When the president's train stopped briefly at Havre de Grace in Maryland, people again "hastened forward to shake hands" with the president. At the next stop in Wilmington, the president appeared on the rear platform of the train, where he at first bowed "to the enthusiastic thousands." But "the surging multitude" were not content to have their cheers exchanged with bows. The crowd pressed insistently forward toward the president's car, and many succeeded in "struggling through the dense mass to shake hands with the President."[36]

At stops all along the president's route was evidenced what the *New York Times* described as "the universal American tendency to shake the hand of the lion of the day." The constant handshaking got to be too much for two of Johnson's traveling companions, General Ulysses S. Grant and Admiral David Farragut. At Cayuga Lake they both asked "to be excused from shaking hands" on account of their hands being "badly swollen from the exercise of the previous day." The crowd, however, reported the *New York Tribune*, "would not be refused." The president, who bore the brunt of the handshaking ordeal, never complained about it, at least not publicly. Unlike generals and admirals, presidents could not be seen to shrink from the people's embrace.[37]

Johnson's supporters, like Taylor's, played up the value of having the president "mingle freely with the people." For the *New York Times*, the tour was an opportunity for the people to see Johnson as he really was rather than as he had been rendered in the opposition press. Since Johnson was "in all respects a man of the people," opined the *Times*, "he cannot but be glad of a temporary escape from the army of supplicants by whom the White House is besieged, and a chance of talking with the multitude who are not politicians, and have no especial liking for politicians' tricks." In traveling through the country, the *Times* continued, Johnson "will hear from merchants. . . . He will exchange ideas with honest, hard-handed industry, and will gather strength from the association with those who furnished fighting material" during the Civil War. By bringing the president "directly in contact with popular ideas and feelings," the tour would promote "free communication" between the president and the people.[38]

So enthusiastic was the *Times* about Johnson's tour that it urged him to undertake a second tour, this one through the South. Let the president "appear before the Southern people," "indulg[ing] in such intercourse with them as [he] had" with the people of the northern states. Such a visit, the *Times* predicted, would yield the most "beneficent and desirable" results. After the president received an invitation to extend his tour to New Orleans, the *Times* renewed its call for a southern tour. Traveling to New Orleans, the *Times* again insisted, would enable the president to "speak plainly to the people of the South," just as he had spoken plainly with the people of the North. For the *Times*, as for other pro-Johnson organs, the president's willingness to talk "familiarly with the people" about "national affairs" was a sign of his credentials as a democratic leader.[39]

"THE DIGNITY OF HIS STATION"

While the *Times* portrayed Johnson's tour as evidence of his close connection with the American people, the opposition predictably attacked the tour as thinly veiled electioneering. The public's contradictory expectations about appropriate presidential behavior made this much inevitable. The narrowest of lines separated a frank discussion of national affairs, which was to be applauded, from unseemly talk of politics, which was beneath the dignity of a president.[40]

No president on tour could realistically expect to please both his opponents and his supporters. Republicans who disliked the president's Reconstruction policies— called Radical Republicans, an unfortunate label that has stuck to this day—were bound to pounce on anything that smacked of politics. Had Johnson said nothing he would still have received a cold shoulder from many in the opposition. Before the president had even begun his tour, in fact, Republican-controlled city councils in Wilmington and Philadelphia had decided not to tender the president an official welcome. The receptions in these cities were organized instead by the president's supporters, largely Democrats.[41]

But if partisan maneuvering and charges of electioneering were familiar enough, much that transpired on Johnson's tour was far from typical. By this time Americans were, as the *National Intelligencer* put it, "accustomed to turn out to see and hear their Chief Magistrate," but they were not accustomed to watching or hearing their president behave the way Johnson did. Even many of his erstwhile supporters were dismayed to find Johnson acting in a manner that they deemed beneath "the dignity of his station."[42]

The problem was not that Johnson spoke about public policy. As we have already seen, presidents since Monroe had done so without being pilloried let alone impeached. Many of Johnson's supporters were in fact eager to use the tour as an opportunity to affirm the president's policies, specifically his commitment to bring the southern states back into the Union with all possible speed. In New York City, where the Democratic Party was strong, the Board of Aldermen not only voted to extend Johnson the hospitality of the city but endorsed the president's policies as "eminently wise, national and conciliatory." When the board's resolution was taken up in the Common Council, a Republican member proposed to amend it by removing the policy endorsement from the presidential welcome, but the council, by a two-to-one margin, rejected the amendment so that its members too could use Johnson's visit as an occasion to express their support for the president's Reconstruction plans.[43]

A common way of understanding Johnson's tour is that "in the beginning all went well," and only when the president reached Cleveland on the evening of September 3 did things turn sour. Certainly many of Johnson's supporters initially perceived the tour to be a great success. William B. Phillips, an editorial writer for the *New York Herald*, wrote to the president on the 3rd: "We are all rejoicing at the extraordinary good effect of your journey to Chicago." Publicly the *Herald* expressed the same optimism. The president, noted the *Herald* approvingly, possesses "a magnetic manner over the people" and "the extraordinary power of touching the popular heart of every class." Through his tour the president had awakened the people to the dangers that the Radical Republicans posed to the nation. The popular acclaim that Johnson received "everywhere on this journey," predicted the *Herald*, meant that the people would "give the victory to the administration . . . in the coming fall election."[44]

It is true that the crowds that heard Johnson speak during the first week generally greeted his words enthusiastically. At Philadelphia, when he spoke from the balcony of the Continental Hotel, "the termination of almost every sentence" was "roundly applauded." Resounding cheers met his declaration that the people would "at the

President Andrew Johnson arrives at Philadelphia's Continental Hotel, where he spent the first night of his tour, August 28, 1866. (New York Public Library)

proper time and at the ballot box restore the country" so that "it will stand again redeemed and regenerated." Cheers, too, met Johnson's insistence that the people, in whose hands the government rested, could readily "bring the class of men who call themselves politicians" to account for their actions. Although Johnson did not name names, his rhetorical questions invited the crowd to do so. "Who is it in power holding the tyrant's rod over you?" thundered the president. A voice from the crowd shouted back obligingly: "Thaddeus Stevens." When Johnson told the crowd he had not intended to say as much as he did, the crowd encouraged him to "Go on, go on" and "Say more." On this occasion, at least, Johnson did not heed the crowd and kept the speech relatively brief, at least when judged by the loquacious standard of his subsequent speeches.[45]

The praise Johnson received from supportive newspapers and the applause he received from sympathetic crowds suggest that Johnson's "swing around the circle" did not immediately shock the sensibilities of all northern people. Many northerners, particularly Democrats, bitterly resented congressional Republicans for continuing to exclude the southern states from representation in the national legislature. These people were more than happy to have the president assail Congress and to hear him make the case for a speedy reintegration of the South. But that the president's words

President Johnson speaks from the rear of the train in his "Swing around the Circle." (Prints and Photographs Division, Library of Congress)

were cheered by many northern Democrats and some conservative Republicans does not mean that "all went well" during the tour's opening week. Such a judgment ignores the sharp criticisms of the tour well before Johnson spoke in Cleveland.

Typical was an editorial comment in the *Milwaukee Daily Sentinel*, published September 1, two days before the president's arrival in Cleveland. The *Sentinel* did not deny that the president could "properly and consistently with the dignity of his station traverse the country and receive ovations and banquets." But Johnson, complained the *Sentinel*, had "laid aside the character and dignity of President and assumed the character of partisan and stump orator," and so he was "entitled to no more respect than any other stump orator of equal merit." Although the president might have "a legal right to go about trying to influence elections," it violated "the proprieties of his station" for the president to "leave his magisterial mantle at home and make an electioneering tour through the country." The *Sentinel* was particularly upset at the president's "shamefully abusive language." Speaking from a New York Hotel balcony at nearly midnight, for instance, Johnson had told a crowd that he would defend the Union and the Constitution against "the traitors in the North" with the same vigor that he had fought "the rebels of the South." Although the sympathetic audience that listened to the speech gave the president "long and continued applause," the *Sentinel* believed the speech showed Johnson to be a "scheming demagogue" who was "dishonoring the office of President."[46]

The president's speech in Albany, on August 30, was also strongly condemned by the Republican press. As in Philadelphia and New York City, it was not what Johnson said in answer to the formal welcome that attracted criticism. Johnson generally kept his replies to official welcoming addresses short and dignified. What attracted Republican criticism in the tour's opening week were generally the speeches the president delivered from hotel balconies, often late in the evening and in response to serenades from Johnson supporters. At Albany, he appeared on the hotel balcony at about eleven o'clock at night, prompted by a serenade organized by a "Johnson Club." Before a large and sympathetic crowd, Johnson delivered one of his trademark speeches, sharply attacking Congress and continually inviting audience response and affirmation.

He began, as he did in so many of his speeches, by insisting that he had no intention of making a speech and that he appeared before them "not . . . in an official character" but merely as a "fellow-citizen." He portrayed himself, as he had in New York City, as the innocent victim of a campaign of "slander and calumny" begun by "a mercenary and subsidized Press" that had "attempted to poison the public mind." He repeated his insistence that he would fight the nation's enemies, whether they were from the North or the South. If those in the South had tried to subvert the Union by tearing it in two, those in the North were trying to destroy the nation by consolidating all power in the hands of the national legislature. Radical Republicans accused him of being a traitor, but he was willing to put his case to the American people. He had always been willing to let the people be his judge and jury. He had no political ambitions but was striving only to do his duty and to promote the reconciliation of the states. What, he asked the crowd, stood in the way? What remained to be done? "Hang Thad Stevens" came back the answer, to great laughter. What remained to be done, Johnson pressed on, was for the people "to do their duty at the ballot-box."[47]

Republicans were hardly surprised that Johnson had chosen to use his trip to Chicago "to open a political campaign." It was something to be "regretted"—as an August 30 New York Tribune editorial expressed it—but it was not unexpected. But after the president's speeches at Philadelphia, New York City, and Albany, the tenor and tone of the Republican criticism shifted markedly. "Many persons," reported the Auburn Advertiser, "felt embarrassed by the partisan character of the harangues uttered" and by the fact that the president of the United States was "making [an] exhibition . . . of himself." On September 1, Horace Greeley's Tribune complained that the president's speeches were an offense against "propriety and decency." The problem was less the electioneering than the intemperate language. Johnson, the Tribune grumbled, "made harangue after harangue charging the great body of those who elected him with being 'opposed to a restoration of the Union;' and saying of them, 'I intend to fight out the battle with Northern traitors.'" It was improper for the president, the "guest of the people," to use "this sort of language."[48]

But it was not only Johnson's partisan opponents who were becoming uncomfortable with his rhetoric. The New York Evening Post, a moderate Republican paper that had been generally supportive of Johnson's policies, also signaled its unhappiness with the president's "indecorous language and injudicious conduct." Although the *Post* "strongly sympathize[d]" with Johnson's goal of quickly admitting "loyal representatives of the Southern States . . . to their seats in Congress," it insisted that the president could only achieve that result through "reasoning" and "persuasion." The loyal citizens of the North, warned the *Post*, were "disgusted to hear him . . . denouncing Congress . . . as traitors, rebels, usurpers." By arousing "such a storm of indignation through the country," the *Post* worried, the president was undermining the very cause he was seeking to advance.[49]

The "storm of indignation," in short, struck well before Johnson reached Cleveland. However, that brewing storm gathered gale force winds when Johnson arrived in Cleveland, a strongly antislavery city and a political stronghold of the Radical Republicans. The crowds that heard Johnson speak in New York had generally greeted the president warmly, applauding politely when not cheering enthusiastically. But as soon as Johnson crossed the Ohio border, the tenor of the reception changed. In Ashtabula, the president's first stop in the Buckeye State, the president was prevented from speaking by the crowd's "laughing and cheering." Johnson arrived in Cleveland at about nine o'clock in the evening and was taken directly to his hotel. Around ten o'clock he appeared on the balcony to address the large crowd that had gathered outside the hotel.[50]

"I CARE NOT FOR DIGNITY"

The speech began much like all the others, with Johnson again declaiming any desire to give a speech and insisting that he appeared before them "as an American citizen simply, and not as the Chief Magistrate clothed in the insignia and paraphernalia of state." Mentions of Grant and Douglas brought cheers from the crowd. Johnson then linked himself to Lincoln, that "distinguished fellow-citizen who is now no more." A sarcastic voice from the crowd cried out "unfortunately." In New York the crowd's assent and approval had been the lifeblood of Johnson's rhetoric. Now, for virtually the first time, the voices from the crowd were skeptical, even heckling ones. Rather than sidestep the comment or soften his rhetoric, Johnson immediately shot back: "Yes, unfortunate for some that God rules on high and deals in right." Press reports indicate that the line brought cheers from the crowd, but the suggestion that both John Wilkes Booth and Johnson were God's chosen instruments was hardly likely to play well with any northern audience, let alone in an antislavery bastion like Cleveland. Johnson compounded his problems by trotting out his familiar attack on the Republican press, that "subsidized gang of hirelings and traducers." If Lincoln were still president, Johnson insisted, the partisan press would have "poured out" their "vials of wrath" on him just as they were now doing to Johnson. Johnson's claims brought angry shouts of denial from the crowd. "Never," shouted some. "Three cheers for the Congress of the United States," bellowed another. Johnson waded deeper into the fight. Forgetting his earlier claim that he had not come to deliver a speech, he now claimed that his "object in appearing before" them was to engage in an exchange of views and of "ascertaining, if we could, who was wrong."[51]

He challenged the crowd, as he had done many times before, to name one pledge that he had ever violated, one place where he had ever departed from the platform upon which Lincoln and he were elected. Previous crowds had roared their approval, but offered the chance to name Johnson's transgressions Cleveland's citizens were only too ready to oblige: "How about New Orleans?" shouted one, a reference to the bloody events of the past summer in which thirty-four blacks and three whites were killed by former Confederates who were trying to prevent the Radical Republicans from convening a constitutional convention that had as its aim the enfranchisement of blacks. That was followed immediately by other voices: "Hang Jeff. Davis" and then a shout of "Hang Thad. Stevens and Wendell Phillips." "Why not hang Thad. Stevens and Wendell Phillips," agreed Johnson.[52]

The situation was deteriorating rapidly, and the exchanges became angrier. "I called," Johnson bellowed, "upon your Congress that is trying to break up the Government." Not *the* Congress, but *your* Congress. Johnson's aggressively adversarial posturing induced near mayhem: "You be d—d," shouted one. "Cheers mingled with hisses," and "great confusion" ensued. "Don't get mad, Andy," came a cautionary shout from the crowd. But Johnson had lost his way. "I will tell you who is mad," yelled back the president. "Whom the gods wish to destroy, they first make mad." The performance was enough to make even his friends wonder whether he was indeed mad, or perhaps drunk.[53]

After briefly collecting himself, promising to "permit reason to resume her empire," Johnson descended again into the gutter of personal vituperation. Those in the crowd who were responsible for the "discordant notes," he charged, were just as much traitors as Jefferson Davis, Wendell Phillips, and Thaddeus Stevens. And cowards, too. For while brave Americans fought and died for their county, these "cowardly" hecklers remained safely at home, paying others to fight in their stead so they could spend the war "speculating and committing frauds on the Government." They only "pretend," Johnson sneered, to show respect for the loyal soldiers who spilled blood and lost limbs on the battlefield. Johnson's tirade brought outraged cries of "Is this dignified?" The president was undeterred: "You may talk about the dignity of the president," he responded. "I care not for dignity."[54]

This was too much even for the president's strongest supporters, even for those who loathed Thaddeus Stevens and the Radical Republican agenda. In a September 7 editorial entitled "The President's Mistake," the *New York Times*, one of the president's most steadfast backers, disavowed the president's remarks. Johnson's comment that he "did not care about his dignity," opined the *Times*, was "greatly to be regretted." For "the American people care very much about it and can never see it

A drawing published in Harper's Weekly on October 27, 1866, depicts President Johnson's September 3 speech in Cleveland. Behind Johnson is the shadowy presence of the long-faced secretary of state, William Henry Seward. (Provided courtesy HarpWeek, LLC)

Johnson's lack of respect for the dignity of his office is wickedly satirized by Thomas Nast. On the right of the picture, Seward holds Johnson's coat as Johnson prepares to brawl with the crowd. (Provided courtesy HarpWeek, LLC)

forgotten without profound sorrow and solicitude." The president's behavior had "startled and bewildered" even the "thousands and tens of thousands" who shared the president's political objectives. The *Times* rejected the fiction that the president was "speaking or traveling as a simple citizen." Johnson was the president of the United States, whether he was in Cleveland or Washington, D.C. Therefore he must "be just as considerate, just as calm and just as dispassionate in the one as in the other." Granted, the president had encountered "a good many men of rude manners and a very low conception of the proprieties of such occasions" and "he has been subjected . . . to taunts and reproaches more or less disrespectful and insulting." But it was a "great mistake" for the president to respond or even take notice of these individuals. "The President of the United States," the *Times* counseled, "cannot enter upon an exchange of epithets with the brawling of a mob, without seriously compromising his official character and hazarding interests too momentous to be thus lightly imperiled." It was also a grave mistake, the *Times* warned, for the president to suggest that "the great body of the people in the North who dissent from his views are enemies of the Union or are seeking consciously to destroy it." The president should quit calling his opponents traitors and start to "allay their unjust apprehensions, calm their aroused resentments and moderate the passions" that were coursing through the body politic. Johnson should act more like a president and less like a politician from "a Border State during a heated political contest."[55]

Johnson, however, never reacted well to criticism. The public rebuke in the *Times* had no more effect than the words of caution he received in private from trusted advisers. His friends and his enemies, he believed, underestimated his oratorical powers. Moreover, in Johnson's view, only a coward backed down from a fight. As he told the crowd in Cleveland, "when attacked my plan is to defend myself." And defend himself he did, often belligerently. The day after the Cleveland speech, the president's train stopped in Elyria, Ohio, where Johnson delivered "one of his usual speeches" before a crowd of several thousand that "listened respectfully to all that was said." When Johnson's barbed attack on Congress drew a groan from somebody in the crowd, the president immediately shot back: "you will groan worse than that before you get through. The *damned* always groans." Later that same day, at Norwalk, Johnson's call for healing the nation's wounds was met with a hectoring reminder of the shameful events in New Orleans. Angrily, Johnson demanded "to see that man's face" and then, when the crowd obligingly drew back, he denounced the man as "a craven, mean looking fellow." Johnson had done precisely the same thing toward the end of his Cleveland speech, when he had demanded that one of his hecklers "come out here where I can see you," taunting the man that he was the type of coward who would shoot a man "in the dark . . . when no one is by to see."[56]

Prior to Cleveland, partisan criticism of the president's "low electioneering" had generally not affected the willingness of crowds to let Johnson speak. After Cleveland, however, Johnson often had great difficulty getting people to listen respectfully. In Battle Creek, Michigan, the president found it difficult to be heard above the "hoots" from the crowd. In Bloomington, Illinois, his speech was repeatedly disrupted by insistent cheers for General Grant. In Madison, Indiana, he was again prevented from speaking by the crowd. At Pittsburgh, where Johnson spent the night of September 13, his attempt to speak from the hotel balcony was thwarted by the crowd's "unearthly yells and groans, mingled with cries of 'Grant, Grant,' 'Farragut, Farragut,' 'shut up,' 'go on,' 'go to hell,' 'dry up,' 'put him out,' 'New Orleans,' and so on." Unable to quiet the crowd, Johnson was "ultimately compelled to retire" without delivering his speech. Earlier that day the president received an equally rude reception from a crowd in Steubenville, Ohio, where the "hootings and groans and huzzas" of the crowds also made it impossible for Johnson to speak.[57]

Disgrace turned to tragedy in Indianapolis. The president was introduced from the hotel balcony to "a few groans, hurrahs for Johnson, cries for Gen. Grant, and some rude remarks." As Johnson began to speak he was pelted with cries of "Stop" and "Go on," chants of "Grant, Grant," and hostile shouts of "We want nothing to do with traitors." Johnson tried to quiet them, promising to keep his remarks short, but to no avail. "Shut up! We don't want to hear from you, Johnson," cried out one, and again the crowd began to chant Grant's name, while the president's supporters called out for Johnson. Realizing that he would be unable to address the crowd, Johnson gave up, and returned inside the hotel. The president's retreat did not quiet or disperse the largely Republican crowd, which "amused" itself by continuing to call for Grant and Farragut and groan for Johnson. Furious Democrats—who had organized the mile-long procession from the train station to the hotel—began calling Republicans and blacks by "all kinds of filthy and abusive names," and the Republicans retaliated by "by calling Democrats traitors, Rebels, &c." Pushing and shoving ensued, someone fired a shot, and then there were more shots, leaving one man dead and several others injured, including a reporter for an Indianapolis newspaper.[58]

These scenes of mob violence elicited sympathy for Johnson in some quarters. In Newark, Ohio, the president was greeted by a supportive crowd and a sign that read "We Stand by Andrew Johnson—No Indianapolis here." The Cleveland city council entertained a resolution apologizing for the crowd's disruptive behavior, though the Republican-dominated council defeated the measure. The *National Intelligencer* attributed the "mob violence" that the president encountered in Cleveland and Indianapolis to the "fierce intolerance" of the Western Reserve and the "desperate party spirit" of Indiana's capital. The real problem, the president's defenders insisted, was not the president's words but the provocateurs that had been set among the crowd to cause havoc.[59]

Republicans countered that the president had only himself to blame. The "disgraceful" scenes that had occurred throughout the tour, noted the *Auburn Advertiser,* were a direct result of the president's "ribald, false and slanderous speeches." The president "wallows in the political gutters," and "it is only tit for tat, for any bully and blacguard [sic] in a crowd, to splash back with the same sort of filth he splashes upon the Congress." If no president had ever been received in such a rude manner, agreed the *Albany Evening Journal,* it was because "none had descended to the low and pitiful standard" that Johnson had adopted. In practicing "the base arts of a demagogue; the disgusting swagger of a backwoods rough; the coarse and vituperative slang of the most vulgar," Johnson had "degrade[d] his office in the sight of the world."[60]

Condemnation of Johnson was not limited to the Radical Republican press. Perhaps the most damaging and conspicuous defection was James Gordon Bennett's *New York Herald.* An early cheerleader for Johnson and his tour, the *Herald* became increasingly critical of Johnson as the tour progressed. By the end of the tour, Johnson had lost Bennett's support. On September 23, a week after the president had returned to Washington, the editor explained his change of heart. "It is mortifying to see a man occupying the lofty position of President of the United States descend from that position and join issue with those who are draggling their garments in the muddy gutters of political vituperation."[61]

A few diehard Johnson supporters tried to spin the president's behavior as evidence of his "fearlessness," but in the North at least the great majority seemed to agree with the *North American and U.S. Gazette* that Johnson had "committed a grave offense against official dignity." The spectacle of the president of the United States "bandying epithets with men in the crowd," opined the *New York Independent,* was "mortifying," even "humiliating." A president could be celebrated as a man of the people, but he could not forget that he was not merely one of the people. As the nation's chief magistrate he was expected to carry himself with a dignity befitting that high station. Forfeiting "the insignia and paraphernalia of state" was not just an error of manners but a strategic mistake. For the president's powers of persuasion derived not only from his connection to the people but also from the respect and authority that inhered in his role as the head of state.[62]

In the early stages of the tour, the Republican press often expressed the view that, notwithstanding the president's inappropriate "partisan harangues," the people owed the nation's chief executive a dignified reception. That had "been the custom," noted the *Albany Evening Journal*, "from the earliest days of the Republic, and it is too good a custom ever to be ignored."[63] Although Johnson was snubbed early on by Republican officials in Wilmington and Philadelphia, each of the many towns on the New York itinerary extended the president an official welcome and a respectful hearing. However, the events of the tour's second week—especially Johnson's Cleveland speech, the riot in Indianapolis, as well as a presidential diatribe in St. Louis—prompted many civic authorities to refuse to sanction a formal welcome for the president. The Cincinnati city council voted, by an 18 to 6 margin, to refuse Johnson "the hospitalities of the city." The same verdict was rendered by city councils in Chicago, Columbus, Indianapolis, Pittsburgh, and Springfield. Most tellingly of all, Baltimore's city council, which had graciously welcomed Johnson on the tour's opening day, refused to participate in Johnson's reception on the return leg on the grounds that he had "laid aside the dignity of the Presidential office."[64]

The snubs only sharpened Johnson's sense of grievance and righteousness and accentuated his reliance on populist rhetoric. In Pittsburgh, for instance, the president trumpeted the authorities' refusal to welcome him, showing off the slight as a badge of pride. "I feel honored," Johnson began, "in receiving this welcome, more especially as it emanates from the people—the people on whom I have always relied, who have tendered it to me . . . in defiance of those who here hold power and authority." The people were "the masters" of those officials who had "refused welcome to a fellow citizen and to the Chief Magistrate," and "a welcome from their masters," Johnson reiterated, was "peculiarly gratifying." A greeting that sprang spontaneously from the hearts of the people meant far more than one that had been orchestrated by scheming politicians "clothed with a little brief authority."[65]

Johnson's willingness to attack elected representatives in the name of the people betrayed his Jacksonian roots. Johnson understood the president to be the people's "tribune and champion," which is precisely how the Harrisburg welcoming committee hailed him. Rather than run from the label of demagogue, Johnson embraced it. If believing that "the great mass of the people . . . will do right" was a demagogical idea then he would gladly call himself a demagogue. If declaring "the great truth" that "the voice of the people is the voice of God" was demagogical then he was indeed a demagogue. If only, he thundered to great applause, there "were more demagogues in our land."[66]

The American people had never seen anything quite like this from a president on tour. A president denouncing political opponents as traitors. A president inciting crowds to hang a member of Congress. A president reveling in verbal fisticuffs. A president "who stooped to bandy words with the crowd." A president insisting he cared nothing for dignity. And now a president embracing the appellation of demagogue. If this was the face of democracy, then maybe the American presidency needed a little less democracy and a little more dignity. That at least was the sentiment of one of Johnson's traveling companions, the next president of the United States, Ulysses S. Grant.[67]

THE SEARCH FOR DIGNITY

Grant had dutifully agreed to accompany President Johnson on the pilgrimage to Chicago, the general's loyalty to his commander in chief outweighing his dislike of pageantry and speech-making. Having already alienated most congressional Republicans, Johnson desperately needed Grant's support and he worked assiduously to cultivate it. The president made Grant the nation's first four-star "General of the Army," and appointed Grant's father as a federal postmaster and Grant's eldest son to the military academy. Johnson wanted the popular war hero by his side during the tour, hoping that Grant's presence would be seen as an implicit public endorsement of his policies. The president's advisers, particularly Secretary of State William Henry Seward, also calculated that "in these reckless and violent times" the presence of Grant, as well as Admiral Farragut, would help to protect the traveling party from acts of sabotage or disruption.[68]

Grant's chief-of-staff, General John A. Rawlins, an Illinois native who had been a Douglas elector in 1860, was enthusiastic about a trip to pay homage to the Little Giant. But Rawlins, always attentive to his boss's political image, also saw it as an opportunity for Grant to boost his own political prospects. On the third day of the tour, Rawlins wrote to his wife in glowing terms about the party's reception.

> The ovations to the President have been very fine. . . . The one in New York [City] perhaps has never been excelled in this country. General Grant and Admiral Farragut came in for a large share of the cheering, I assure you. And I am now more than ever glad that the General concluded to accompany the President, for it will do Grant good, whatever may be his aspirations in the future, and fix him in the confidence of Mr. Johnson, enabling him to fix up the army as it should be, and exert such influence as will be of benefit to the country.[69]

Grant may have initially shared his aide's hopes, but he quickly came to regret his decision to accompany the president. In Auburn, on the tour's fourth day, Grant wrote to his wife that he was "getting very tired of this expedition and of hearing political speaches [sic]." Although he remained publicly mum, inwardly Grant fumed at Johnson's antics. From St. Louis, on September 9, Grant again wrote to his wife, explaining that he had "never . . . been so tired of anything before as [he had] been with the political stump speeches of Mr. Johnson." They are, he concluded, "a National disgrace." He urged his wife, however, not to show the letter to anyone as it was important for "the country's interest" that he retain the president's confidence.[70]

Although Grant was anxious to avoid publicly criticizing his commander in chief, he was not always the model of discretion. On September 7, the *New York Herald* published a report indicating that Grant had told others privately that he was "disgusted with this trip" and "at hearing a man make speeches on the way to his own funeral." Another journalist, this one with the *New York Tribune*, later reported that "soon after" leaving Buffalo on September 3 Grant confided to a friend that "the President has no business to be talking in this way" and that he would not have agreed to accompany the president if he "had expected any thing of the kind."[71]

Secretary of the Navy Gideon Welles, who was among the traveling party, attributed Grant's souring on Johnson to "the seductive appeals of the Radical conspirators" that the general encountered en route, in places like Detroit, Chicago, St. Louis, and Cincinnati. Welles also suspected that Grant was influenced by the antislavery views of his father, whom Grant visited in Ohio. The president had his own explanation for Grant's change of heart. Writing to a former aide in the final year of his presidency, Johnson explained that "Grant saw the Radical handwriting on the wall, and heeded it." The election results in Maine, which gave the Republicans a large increase in their majorities, were widely seen as a vindication of the Radical position and a repudiation of the president's policies. The general, in this view, deserted Johnson to save his own political neck.[72]

Although not without merit, these explanations ignore the pivotal role that Johnson's behavior played in alienating Grant. The election in Maine, after all, did not occur until Monday, September 10, by which time Johnson had already delivered his disastrous speeches at Cleveland (on September 3) and St. Louis (on September 8). The general's private communications show that virtually from the outset of the tour he was deeply disturbed by Johnson's rhetoric, which he regarded as beneath the dignity of the presidency. Election losses and the president's tumbling popularity certainly made it more advantageous for Grant to distance himself from Johnson, but their estrangement owed more to the fact that Grant had lost respect for a president who persisted in behaving in ways that Grant regarded as both self-defeating and improper.

That Grant's behavior was principled rather that opportunistic is evident from the manner in which he behaved once he was ensconced as president. Grant certainly traveled plenty. Indeed so much that the time he spent away from the capital became a minor political tempest. However, he spoke only when he could not avoid it and almost invariably kept his comments terse and noncontroversial. Grant understood that by refusing to be drawn into a speech he would disappoint many people. Listening to the cries of an eager crowd in Cincinnati, President Grant remarked to the mayor, who was preparing to introduce him: "There it is; you never can get half a dozen American citizens together without their wanting a speech." Sometimes he would deflect the crowd with a joke, as in Omaha, Nebraska, where having been introduced by the mayor as "the friend of free men, free speech, and free press, and last, but not least, . . . of free schools," Grant quipped that since "I am in favor of free speech, . . . therefore I want other people to do the talking." Other times, he used self-deprecation: "If I could speak as eloquently as my friend Judge McCalmont," Grant told a crowd in Franklin, Pennsylvania, "I should have pleasure in talking to you at greater length. As it is, I must content myself with again thanking you."[73]

Grant had a reason for his reticence, however, that went beyond his own inadequacies as a public speaker. The bitter animosities unleashed by the Civil War made it imperative that the president act as a dignified, unifying figure who stayed above the passions of politics. After thanking the citizens of Pittsburgh for their bipartisan welcome in October 1871, Grant revealed his hope that "the day is not far distant when our citizens will look up to the Executive as the President of the whole country, and not as the representative of any party or section." The president was a model, someone to whom the American people should "look up to." Johnson's transgression was that he had stepped off of the presidential pedestal and descended to the level of the crowd, recklessly stoking the people's passions and dividing the nation.[74]

Presidential dignity, Grant believed, required a degree of reticence and reserve. It did not mean, however, that presidents should avoid crowds altogether; indeed Grant seemed to enjoy being the center of attention. Nor did Grant attempt to revive a monarchical model in which citizens only gazed upon the nation's leader. In a democracy that would never do. Although he was a military man who had never held an elective office prior to assuming the presidency, Grant knew how to work a crowd. In the summer of the first year of his presidency, for instance, Grant took "a pleasure trip" on the Erie Railroad that brought him through Binghamton, New York, where the train stopped for five minutes to take on wood and water. Grant, according to a press account,

> stepped quickly out upon the hind platform of the train and commenced a lively hand-shaking with a promiscuous crowd, who were dashing against the train like a torrent from some precipice. The General made his hands play about after the manner of a tenor Swiss bell-ringer, shaking with both hands at the same time, crossing his arms and dodging about in all directions, to take every hand that was stretched out to him.

Wherever Grant went, he was met with crowds of curious people eager to shake the famous general's hand. Sometimes there were only a hundred or so hands to shake but occasionally the number climbed as high as five thousand.[75]

In the years after the Civil War, such indiscriminate handshaking was frequently bemoaned as undignified. An etiquette manual published in 1870, for instance, deplored the practice as an example of "democratic intrusiveness." When Grant visited Maine in 1871, the *New York Times* objected that the president had to submit "to the hand-shaking torture which the American people think it necessary to inflict on those whom they would honor." Two decades later, during the administration of Grover Cleveland, the *Brooklyn Standard-Union* condemned what it called the "Handshaking Evil." "What reason or common sense is there," the *Standard-Union* asked, "in compelling the president of the United States to submit . . . to have his right arm shaken until it aches?"[76]

Grant, too, had his doubts about handshaking, but he had the good sense to wait until after he left office to express them. In the summer of 1877, while traveling through the British Isles, the former president confessed to an interviewer that he thought handshaking was a "great nuisance and should be abolished." It was not so much undignified as grueling. "It not only makes the right arm sore," Grant explained, "but it shocks the whole system and unfits a man for writing or attention to other duties. It demoralizes the entire nervous and muscular system." However "laborious and injurious" the handshaking, presidents could not avoid the democratic ordeal without courting a reputation as distant or elitist, as President Benjamin Harrison discovered.[77]

Harrison believed that handshaking was both undignified and unhealthy; indeed he suspected that handshaking had played a part in the death of his grandfather, President William Henry Harrison. When the newly inaugurated Harrison (the grandson) received crowds with "his right hand pushed inside his Chicago Prince Albert coat, [and] his left hand behind him," the opposition seized upon it as evidence that he treated the people "in a very chilly manner" and that he was "cold and proud." Harrison's reluctance to mingle and shake hands with his fellow citizens helped to earn him derisive monikers such as the "human iceberg" and the "refrigerator." Presidential dignity was an asset, but not if it came at the cost of an apparent disdain for the American people.[78]

What sort of barriers should there be between the president and the people? Build the barriers too high and the president became vulnerable to charges that he was out of touch with the people or harbored monarchical pretensions; tear them down and the president appeared to be just another politician or, worse, a demagogue. Presidents were caught in a web of contradictory expectations and deep-seated cultural ambivalence. Harrison's reserve transgressed norms regarding democratic manners no less than Johnson's behavior transgressed norms governing presidential dignity and decorum. Johnson's tour helped to swing the pendulum of opinion, for a time, in the direction of dignified reserve, but a far more enduring change in the relationship between the president and the people was driven by a desire to protect the president from physical harm. Here there would be no pendulum, only a steady, incremental, irreversible move toward the construction of ever more imposing barriers separating the president from the people. Three presidential assassinations in thirty-five years—each of them coming when the president left the safety of the White House—would all but extinguish the nineteenth-century expectation that the president should mingle freely with the people.

CHAPTER FOUR

Protecting the President

"James Monroe—Our distinguished guest and estimable fellow-citizen. The Chief Magistrate and unbiased choice of a free people. Guarded by their love, he needs no other protection." With that toast the leading citizens of Frankfort, Kentucky, drank to their president. The small capital town of Frankfort was a long way—not only geographically but economically, politically, and culturally—from Boston, Massachusetts, but the citizens of Boston cast their greeting to Monroe in strikingly similar terms. They were, they told Monroe, "happy in the reflection that the personal safety of the Chief Magistrate of a Republican Government requires no other protection than what arises from the affections of his fellow citizens."[1]

The absence of bodyguards or protective entourage drew considerable comment during Monroe's tours, particularly when the president traveled through the northeast, where Federalist opposition and bitterness ran strong. Americans delighted in drawing an invidious contrast with the monarchical nations of Europe where the traveling sovereign "is closely locked in his coach [and] guarded on all sides with armed troops." A resident of Pennsylvania who was visiting Boston during Monroe's tour of that city marveled at "the sublime spectacle" of the leader of a nation traveling "through an immense country, with no guard but the love and respect of his fellow citizens, with no armour but that of the law, . . . and carrying no arms but those of the Constitution." How unlike the old world, where

> we behold the King of France guarded by five thousand Swiss, who are daily skirmishing with the French people; the Prince Regent of England assaulted and shot at by a mob on the short way from his palace to the Parliament House; the King of Spain surrounded by an army of Inquisitors and Monks, not daring to put his foot beyond the walls of his residence; the King of Sardinia trembling at the sight of a freemason, and planting through his dominions the rack and wheel to awe his subjects into submission; the King of Naples under the protection of twenty five thousand foreigners, who like the Janissaries of Constantinople keep him under their unbridled sway; the throne of Sweden invested by conspirators, who will not allow their Prince to enjoy a single night's rest; the King of Prussia denouncing as treason the Association of the Patriots, by whose exertions he was unable to regain his dominions; all the other European sovereigns relying for their security only on their standing armies, without whom they would lose the crown in less than a day.

Only in America did the chief executive need no protection from the people. Selected freely by and from the people, the president of the United States had no call for the military protection that European monarchs required.[2]

Throughout the nineteenth century Americans gave voice to this same conceit. When Jackson toured New England in 1833, the *New-London Gazette and General Advertiser* noted with pride that "he travels unarmed and unattended, but by his household, by day or night, through a land where every house he sees is his home, and every man he meets is already enrolled in his life guard." A decade later, when President John Tyler visited New York City, he brandished the absence of a protective detail as a sign of his republican credentials. After a warm welcome from the city's mayor, who noted approvingly that "no mercenary soldier protects [the president's] person, no hired voices cheer his presence," Tyler responded: "You have said truly that I have no hired vassals. God forbid that I ever should! My body-guard I desire to be the people, and none but the people. That is the body-guard that a plain, republican President of the United States can alone desire to have." More than three decades later, when Rutherford Hayes became the first president to visit California, readers of the *San Jose Times* opened the paper on the morning of September 15, 1880, to find an editorial puffed with pride that the president traveled without a military guard:

> Nothing so strongly illustrates the true freedom and happy security in
> this land of liberty . . . than the comparison naturally suggested by the
> untrammeled movements of our worthy President on his present long journey,
> when compared with the nervous precautions necessitated in monarchical
> countries, when the crowned head passes through its districts. In Russia . . . the
> Emperor is guarded at every point. When lately on a railroad journey, 40,000
> troops and 10,000 peasants lined the road. Fears for his safety are but too well
> grounded, as the frequent exploding of the unexpected mine but too grimly
> testifies . . . , so it is needful to have armed guards and lynx-eyed detectives
> wherever he goes. Happily, America has no such terrors for the head of her
> government. He journeys free from all dread of injury or even insult, through
> every part of our vast territory.

The ability of the president to tour the country without any protection was evidence that the president was a man of the people and that the United States was a just and free society, the likes of which the world had never seen before.[3]

If the lack of protection for a president was a point of pride for Americans, the converse was also true. Protecting the president could not be done without relinquishing a cherished part of the story Americans liked to tell each other about the exceptional nature of their republican experiment. To accept protection would be to acknowledge that the American presidency was not so different from the British monarchy. That was why when a Charleston artillery battalion offered "to mount guard" for President George Washington during his stay in Charleston in 1791, Washington "politely declined . . . saying that he considered himself perfectly safe in the affection and amicable attachment of the people." And that was how Lieutenant Randolph could waltz into President Andrew Jackson's cabin aboard the *Cygnet* in 1833 and bloody the president's nose.[4]

Jackson had been deeply concerned about the consequences of Randolph's assault, particularly since Virginia showed little willingness to prosecute. The attack, he feared, will "compel us . . . to go armed, for our personal defence." It could "lead to, what I would sincerely regret, & which never shall happen whilst I am in office, a military guard around the President." Although Randolph was never punished— there was no federal law against attacking a president, and the federal government could not compel the state to prosecute Randolph—the attack generated little serious effort either to change the law or to improve presidential protection. The assault was seen as an oddity, rather than an invitation to rethink the relationship between the president and the people.[5]

Even more remarkable, an attempt on President Jackson's life two years later also brought no change in presidential protection. Jackson had been on his way out of a funeral service in the House of Representatives when a young man by the name of Richard Lawrence walked directly up to the president, drew a pistol from his coat, aimed it at the president's chest, and pulled the trigger. A loud bang was heard as the percussion cap exploded, but the gunpowder failed to ignite. The assailant had time to dig out a second pistol and fire again from close range, but again the gun misfired. A jury needed only ten minutes to find Lawrence, who believed that Jackson had prevented him from becoming the King of England, not guilty by reason of insanity. The unfortunate man was committed to an asylum.[6]

Many observers were inclined to see the hand of Providence in Jackson's miraculous escape, but no one seemed to think that the first assassination attempt on a U.S. president required altering the manner in which presidents moved about in public. Until the coming of the Civil War, presidential protection remained as lax and haphazard as it had always been.[7]

THE ASSASSINATION OF ABRAHAM LINCOLN

Almost from the moment Abraham Lincoln was elected president, the prospect of assassination hung over him. His election in 1860 immediately triggered a move toward secession across the Deep South. Six states—Alabama, Florida, Georgia, Louisiana, Mississippi, and South Carolina—seceded from the Union even before he had left Springfield, Illinois. Threats and whispered conspiracies surrounded the president-elect as he departed for the nation's capital on February 11, 1861. At countless stops along the nearly 2,000-mile journey, Lincoln appeared at the rear of the train with the aim, he told cheering crowds, "of seeing you and being seen by you."

The people implored Lincoln to speak, and he usually obliged. As David Donald observes, "the demands were so numerous that he became hoarse, and at times he lost his voice." In larger towns and cities, Lincoln descended from the train to deliver more formal addresses. In Columbus, Ohio, for instance, Lincoln addressed the state legislature before speaking to the citizenry from the capitol steps. The crowds that came to see the president were often immense. In Columbus, an estimated sixty thousand people "joined in the celebration." In Buffalo, the press of the crowd around the president was so intense that one of the president's traveling companions, Major David Hunter, dislocated his shoulder "in his efforts to protect the President-elect from his overenthusiastic observers."[8]

Protecting Lincoln from throngs of well-wishers was one thing, but protecting him from those who wished him harm was quite another. The Buchanan administration had not provided Lincoln with military protection; but several army officers, including Major Hunter, volunteered to accompany the president. In addition, Lincoln's longtime associate, Ward Hill Lamon, stuck close to the president-elect and served as his unofficial bodyguard. Over the final several hundred miles of the journey, flagmen were posted at road crossings and at half-mile intervals along the track to protect against sabotage.[9]

Upon arriving in Philadelphia on February 21, Lincoln was informed by detective Allan Pinkerton of an assassination plot against him. According to Pinkerton, the assassination attempt would take place in Baltimore, a hotbed of secessionist sympathizers. Rumors of secessionist plots to kill the president had been swirling around for months, but Pinkerton produced specific names as well as a time and a place. The president refused to alter his next day's schedule, but neither could he put the threat out of his mind. Speaking at Philadelphia's Independence Hall the next morning (and four days after Jefferson Davis's inaugural address in Montgomery, Alabama), Lincoln affirmed that the nation must be "saved" upon the principle of the Declaration of Independence, the principle "that in due time the weights should be lifted from the shoulders of all men, and that *all* should have an equal chance." "If it can't be saved upon that principle," Lincoln said, "it will be truly awful. I was about to say I would rather be assassinated on this spot than to surrender it."[10]

After traveling to Harrisburg, where he delivered an afternoon address to the Pennsylvania state legislature, Lincoln met again with his advisers to decide on the best course of action. Should the president carry on with his journey as planned or should he take evasive actions to foil the conspirators' plans? Pinkerton wanted the president to travel incognito, taking a special train back to Philadelphia, and then boarding another train that would take him through Baltimore in the middle of the night, so that he would arrive unannounced in Washington, D.C., in the early morning hours. Lincoln recognized that sneaking into the nation's capital could appear cowardly and thus undercut the image of resolve that he was looking to project. But in the end Lincoln reluctantly went along with Pinkerton's plan. Accompanied only by Lamon and Pinkerton, the president, absent his signature stovepipe hat, was shepherded secretly and undetected into Washington, D.C. As Lincoln had worried, the episode became the butt of scathing ridicule. Cartoons showed a ridiculous looking Lincoln disguised in a Scotch kilt and plaid cap. A protective military entourage might be monarchical, but sneaking away was worse. Both betrayed an unrepublican fear of the people.[11]

Lincoln learned his lesson from the episode. In the future he often failed to heed the advice of those who wished to protect him. He instructed his assistants to disregard letters that made threats against his life. He possessed, Noah Brooks observed, "an almost morbid dislike for an escort, or guide, and daily exposed himself to the deadly aim of an assassin." Most nights Lincoln wandered, often alone, over to the War Department to hear the day's latest military developments. Nights and early mornings he could be spotted walking around Washington, sometimes unaccompanied, sometimes with a single companion. Lincoln's family spent a great deal of time at a cottage called the Soldiers' Home on the outskirts of the capital, and the president sometimes made the 3-mile commute without an armed guard or even an escort. Lincoln also frequented the theater, again often without taking any protective measures. Lincoln's cavalier attitude toward his safety frustrated and even angered his friends, particularly Lamon. Upon discovering that the president had visited the theater accompanied only by the Massachusetts senator Charles Sumner, who had been famously caned to within an inch of his life on the Senate floor a few years earlier, and Baron Gerolt, an aged Prussian minister, an annoyed Lamon threatened to resign his post as marshal of the District of Columbia. Neither Sumner nor Gerolt, Lamon complained, "could defend himself against an assault from any able-bodied woman in this city."[12]

Some have seen in Lincoln's behavior a kind of death wish. Certainly he accepted that if someone wanted to kill him there was nothing he could do to prevent it. But there was more to this stoical attitude than a death wish or even resigned fatalism. For Lincoln also believed that such protection was inconsistent with a republican presidency. "It would never do," he explained, "for a President to have guards with drawn sabres at his door, as if he fancied he were, or were trying to be . . . an emperor." Armed guards and protective details were the stuff of emperors and monarchs, not democratic leaders. A large protective entourage, moreover, would be a sign of weakness, Lincoln argued, and would invite the very attacks it was meant to forestall. The president's source of strength was public support, and to ask for or even accept protection was to admit that a president could not trust the people. That was not a message that Lincoln wanted to convey, particularly at this time of national crisis.[13]

Not that Lincoln went without protection. In fact, compared to previous presidents he had far more armed guards and escorts, particularly during the latter half of the war. Concerns about the president's security led to unprecedented military protection at Lincoln's first inaugural. The carriage that conveyed Lincoln and James Buchanan up Pennsylvania Avenue was surrounded on all sides by a massive guard of soldiers. Sharpshooters were posted on rooftops, cavalry blocked off streets, and two artillery batteries were stationed next to the Capitol. The procession, David Donald writes, was "more like a military operation than a political parade." Indeed so dense was "the military enclosure" surrounding Lincoln that he was at times almost "completely hidden from the view of the crowds."[14]

In 1862, much to Lincoln's chagrin, the military commander of the District of Columbia detailed a "small detachment of cavalry" to accompany Lincoln on his travels to and from the Soldiers' Home. Walt Whitman observed Lincoln regularly on his commute from the Soldiers' Home into work at the White House and reported in August 1863 that Lincoln was invariably guarded by "a company of twenty-five or thirty cavalry, with sabres drawn and held upright over their shoulders." When the governor of Ohio visited Washington, D.C., he was so dismayed at the lack of military protection that he raised a select one-hundred-man company (one from each county in Ohio) called the Union Light Guard, which he then dispatched to the capital to guard the White House, War Office, Treasury Department, and other federal buildings. Another company raised in Pennsylvania stood guard on the south side of the White House. Soldiers were also detailed to guard the Soldiers' Home. The Washington metropolitan police force—prompted by Lamon—assigned four armed plainclothes officers, working in shifts, to provide the president with around-the-clock protection. They were to accompany the president whenever he left the White House and to be stationed outside Lincoln's upstairs private rooms at night.[15]

Although by war's end the White House was a much more secure place than it had been at the war's outset, Lincoln continued to be a difficult person to protect when he left the relative safety of the White House. On the afternoon of the fateful Friday night at Ford's Theatre, Lincoln took a lengthy ride through Washington in an open carriage, accompanied only by his wife. But spontaneous, unannounced excursions like this one were far less dangerous than routine or well-publicized trips. And Lincoln's plan to attend the evening performance of "Our American Cousin" was widely advertised ahead of time. Lamon had gone to Richmond, but before leaving he asked the president to "promise . . . you will not go out at night while I am gone, particularly to the theater." Lincoln was accustomed to Lamon's clucking over his safety and would only promise "to do the best I can." Secretary of War Edwin Stanton warned Lincoln not to go to the theater that evening because "it was too great an exposure." As usual, Lincoln ignored the cautions and warnings. He went to the theater, accompanied only by his wife; a young woman by the name of Clare Harris; her fiancé, Major Henry Rathbone; and the president's personal valet. The police officer who had been assigned to protect Lincoln met the presidential party at the theater and escorted the president and his companions up to the presidential box. Unfortunately, for reasons that remain unclear, the officer was not on guard when John Wilkes Booth approached the presidential box. The president's valet stood outside the door to the box, but he was neither armed nor trained to protect the president. Booth simply handed him his calling card, and the valet politely opened the door.[16]

Lincoln's murder shocked the nation, but the mystery is that he had not been killed earlier. Would-be assassins had thousands of opportunities to kill the president had they wished to do so. The assassination instantly transformed Lincoln into a martyred hero, but it did surprisingly little to change the way the nation protected the president. Lincoln's violent death was attributed to the unnatural passions unleashed by the Civil War. With secession defeated and the war now over, the nation could return to normalcy. Future presidents need not fear the fate that had befallen Lincoln. Or at least so people thought until 1881.[17]

THE ASSASSINATION OF JAMES GARFIELD

Few today remember James Garfield, but his murder in the summer of 1881 delivered a staggering blow to the nation. Lincoln's death had been understandable in terms of the unprecedented violence and suffering produced by the Civil War, but Garfield's death was much more difficult to comprehend. Its causes seemed mundane: office-seeking and partisan jockeying for advantage. Hardly the sorts of things for which people usually killed. Moreover, when Lincoln was assassinated it was plausible to see it as a freak occurrence. After all, no president before Lincoln had been gunned down. However, now in the space of sixteen years two American presidents had been shot and killed.

To see how little had changed since Lincoln's time, it is helpful to recall how easy it was for Charles Guiteau to kill President Garfield. Guiteau did have to rule out the White House. Not only was it crowded with people, but he had been barred from the building after visiting virtually every day during the spring to relentlessly press his claim for a government job. Outside the White House, however, Garfield was an easy target, since he had no bodyguard and frequently walked alone. Guiteau watched the president's comings and goings from a bench in Lafayette Park, from which he had an excellent view of the White House's front and side entrances. On the evening of Friday, July 1, Guiteau saw the president, completely alone, stroll out of the White House. Guiteau jumped up from his bench and followed, his newly acquired ivory-handled pistol pressed tightly in his hand. "I was several yards behind him," Guiteau later testified; it was a "splendid chance" to kill the president. But for some reason this troubled man passed up the chance, just as he had passed up a number of other, equally good opportunities to shoot the president at close range.[18]

The following morning, on July 2, Garfield was to depart on a lengthy tour that would take him through New York and New England. At about nine o'clock, Secretary of State James G. Blaine drove the president to the nearby train station in a

An artist's rendering of Garfield's assassination at the Baltimore and Potomac Railway Depot in Washington, D.C. (Prints and Photographs Division, Library of Congress)

two-seater carriage. The two most important men in the federal government then walked, side by side, from the carriage into the station, without any police protection, bodyguards, or even armed companions.[19]

Exactly two weeks earlier, Guiteau had waited at the same train station, following closely behind the president and his wife as they moved from their carriage to the train that was to take them to the New Jersey seashore. He had planned to shoot the president that day, but "the presence of Mrs. Garfield," he explained later, "deterred me from firing on him. She looked so thin and she clung so tenderly to the President's arm that I did not have the heart to fire upon him." If Mrs. Garfield had evoked sentimental feelings of sympathy in the disturbed mind of Guiteau, the sight of Blaine—whom Guiteau loathed—in intimate conversation with the president would have only stoked Guiteau's rage and righteousness. This time Guiteau had no last-minute feelings of mercy or hesitation. He walked up behind Garfield and shot him twice. It took Garfield an excruciating three months to die, but by September Guiteau had succeeded in his crazed plan to make Chester Arthur president.[20]

The assassination of Garfield challenged the way Americans thought about their country and political institutions. Assassination, Americans had hitherto believed, was something that afflicted the authoritarian nations of Europe and South America. It was a pathology born of corrupt aristocracies, decadent monarchies, military strongmen, anarchists, and revolutionaries. And indeed assassination attempts had become commonplace in other parts of the globe. Over the previous decade, the world had witnessed the assassination of the presidents of Peru, Ecuador, and Paraguay as well as the sultan of Ottoman Turkey and the czar of Russia. Since the American Civil War there had been failed attempts to assassinate emperors and monarchs in almost every European nation, including France, Spain, Germany, and Italy. Lincoln's murder could be explained away as an aberration, a product of the political divisions brought on by the Civil War. But the killing of Garfield was different. Guiteau was neither an anarchist nor a revolutionary. Born in Illinois, he was as much a product of American party politics as the president he shot.[21]

Garfield's attitude toward assassination had been much like Lincoln's. It "can no more be guarded against," Garfield told a friend, "than death by lightning; and it is not best to worry about either." After Garfield's murder, lightning strikes no longer seemed a satisfactory analogy. Two presidents killed in sixteen years was something the nation needed to worry about. But what should the country do about it? Some wanted to lynch Guiteau; most were content to see him hang. But the nation's anger and outrage were directed not only at Guiteau but at the political system. The culprit, many Americans decided, was the spoils system. Guiteau had been a "disappointed officeseeker," and Garfield's death was a grotesque and tragic result of the unseemly scramble for government offices. Reformers used Garfield's assassination to press for a change they had long sought: civil service reform. In January 1883, six months after Guiteau's execution, Congress passed the Pendleton Act. Although an important first step in achieving meaningful civil service reform, the act did nothing to address the fundamental cause of Garfield's assassination, which was not the spoils system but ease of access to the president. That would become clear twenty years later when a third American president was gunned down by a man armed only with a pistol.[22]

THE ASSASSINATION OF WILLIAM MCKINLEY

William McKinley's assassination in 1901 highlighted the continuing vulnerability of American presidents. To be sure, McKinley had not been unprotected in the way that Garfield had. Three Secret Service agents flanked the president as he shook hands with a huge line of visitors at the Pan American Exposition in Buffalo, New York. But none of the three federal agents, nor for that matter the "goodly number" of local detectives and police on guard nearby, spotted the danger posed by a man of modest height and unexceptional appearance. Leon Czolgosz waited his turn in line, raised his hand to the president, and shot him twice, in the stomach and chest, before two of the agents and some bystanders knocked the assailant to the ground.[23]

The Secret Service agents guarding McKinley had no statutory authority to protect the president. As a federal agency, the Secret Service dates from the Civil War when it was charged with protecting the nation's currency, particularly through ferreting out counterfeiting schemes. Although the Secret Service was drawn into counterespionage work, no Secret Service agent was employed to protect the president until 1894 when the newly appointed head of the agency, William Hazen, detailed two agents to protect President Grover Cleveland. Hazen's decision to deploy two service agents to the White House—a decision taken without consulting

Congress—was a response to information the agency had gathered about threats to Cleveland's life from some "suspicion persons who might be Western gamblers, Anarchists, or cranks." Information shortly thereafter about a possible plan to kidnap the president's family from their summer house in Buzzard's Bay, Massachusetts, led Cleveland's wife to ask Hazen to post several Secret Service agents at the residence. Hazen complied, apparently without asking the president, but when Cleveland arrived in Buzzard's Bay to find three agents guarding the house he made no objection. The following summer the same arrangement was made, again without consulting Congress and without any statutory authority for the detailing of federal guards.[24]

When McKinley took office, Hazen continued the small protective details he had initiated during the Cleveland presidency. Several agents were assigned to accompany the new president in public. A public uproar resulted, however, when an audit exposed the practice of using federal agents to guard the president's private home. Hazen was promptly reprimanded and demoted. Following on the heels of Hazen's demotion was the outbreak of the Spanish-American War, which prompted Congress for the first time, albeit on an emergency basis only, to authorize Secret Service protection for the president. America's defeat of Spain ended the emergency authorization, but the new Secret Service director, John Wilkie—a close friend of McKinley's—was unwilling to leave the president unprotected. Under Wilkie's direction the Secret Service had become the administration's "primary intelligence-gathering network" (the FBI was still almost a decade away from its creation), and Wilkie's agents were reporting that the president's life was in danger. And so it was that when McKinley appeared at the Pan American Exposition in September 1901 he was accompanied by three Secret Service agents as well as about one hundred security officers.[25]

McKinley's assassination sparked demands that Congress make permanent provision for presidential protection. Only three years earlier the head of the Secret Service had lost his job for trying to protect the president; now the pressure was on Congress to mandate that someone in the government be responsible for protecting the president. Seventeen bills relating to presidential protection were introduced in Congress after McKinley's assassination—seventeen more than had been introduced after the assassinations of Garfield and Lincoln.[26]

One such bill directed the secretary of war "to select and detail from the Regular Army a sufficient number of officers and men to guard and protect the person of the President of the United States." The bill's chief proponent was the powerful Republican chair of the Senate Judiciary Committee, George Hoar. The 76-year-old Hoar had been in the U.S. Senate for a quarter century and had spent nearly a decade in the House before that. McKinley was the third Republican president to be shot and killed in Hoar's adult life. Hoar believed that the army could provide a more effective protective force than a shadowy agency within the Treasury Department. As one senator who spoke in favor of the bill explained, the president "ought to be guarded by those whom we trust to do the fighting for the nation—by the cultivated officers, whose reputation is dearer than life and who would exercise eternal vigilance without any pause at any moment." Those whose "vocation is watching and fighting" were best equipped to protect the president from assassination.[27]

Others, however, objected to the idea of the president being guarded by the army. Using the army as a presidential guard, they claimed, was unrepublican. Florida Democrat Stephen Mallory, who had fought in the Confederate Army, insisted that it was "antagonistic to our traditions, to our habits of thought, and to our customs that the President should surround himself with a body of Janizarries or a sort of Praetorian guard, and never go anywhere unless he is accompanied by men in uniform and men with sabers as is done by the monarchs of the continent of Europe or as the King of Great Britain does with his household cavalry around him." Mallory contended that it was "not in keeping with our system and with the ideas which prevail among the people of this country that the Chief Magistrate, who is a civil official, should be surrounded with all the pomp and ceremony of an autocrat." Indeed it was not consistent with the president's own expectations. No president, Mallory maintained, would "care to have himself surrounded by such a bodyguard." For when the president travels he expects "to meet the people of the country whom he represents." The president, Mallory reiterated, would not allow himself to be "shut off from contact" with the American people by "a guard of soldiers."[28]

Edmund Pettus, an Alabama Democrat who had also served in the Confederate Army, countered that the bill did not require the "pomp of a bodyguard." Instead it empowered the secretary of war "to dress this guard of soldiers as he deems best." The military guard could thus be dressed in civilian clothes and remain relatively inconspicuous. The idea, Pettus explained, was to create "an efficient guard" comprised of a few well-trained men who could protect the president from an assassin. Had such a military guard been protecting President McKinley or President Garfield, Pettus felt sure that both would have escaped the assassin's bullet.[29]

Mallory remained skeptical. The Russian emperor was "surrounded all the time, not merely by a bodyguard, but by thousands of guards," yet that did not prevent the emperor from being assassinated. If an assassin has "made up his mind to achieve his objective at any cost," including the sacrifice of his own life, then it was difficult to protect even the most insulated and isolated of rulers. But the president could not be shielded from the people in the way an emperor or monarch could. "If a President goes among the people and allows crowds to approach in close proximity of his person he can not be protected at all times, at every instant of the ceremony that may be going on." Mallory reminded the Senate that McKinley had been flanked by armed personnel, but that did not stop a crazed and determined man from shooting him. Merely surrounding the nation's chief executive with "a bodyguard to keep the people from getting within speaking distance" of him would not solve the problem. Instead protection of the president needed to include "preventative" measures, by which Mallory meant chiefly surveillance of anarchists and of those suspected of being anarchists. And since the military was explicitly forbidden from investigating civilians, Mallory argued that protection of the president was best left to the Treasury Department, specifically the Secret Service, which could both provide discreet armed protection for the president and investigate threats against the president's life.[30]

Mallory's skepticism was echoed by Porter McCumber, a freshman Republican from North Dakota. McCumber agreed that no republican president "would go up the street under any circumstances with a bodyguard surrounding him." For McCumber, it was plain that "the only safeguard to the President of the United States is the love and affection of the people of the United States." Surrounding the president with a military guard or even an entire regiment would not only be ineffectual but counterproductive, for it would serve to alienate the president from the people's affections. By surrounding the president with guards and bayonets, emulating Old World practices, the law would create the sort of "prejudice against the governing power" that reigned in Europe. Moreover, it would contribute to the growth of anarchistic principles. The "fungus" of anarchy, McCumber reminded the Senate, "grew in the very shadow of the bayonets of the Old World and the walls and fortresses which guarded there." What was needed, McCumber stressed, was not an armed guard for the president but rather an orchestrated, aggressive government campaign to root out anarchy—a campaign "potent enough to absolutely destroy any attempt to propagate [anarchistic] theories of destruction against the Government of the United States." An anarchist killed McKinley, and so protecting the president required stamping out anarchists.[31]

Tennessee Democrat Edward Carmack charged that the bill would be "a dead letter" since no president would tolerate the sort of armed guard prescribed in the legislation. Certainly the current incumbent, Theodore Roosevelt, would not stand for such a guard. "If this were made obligatory upon him," Carmack argued, the president

> would climb out of one of the back windows of the White House and slip out of the back gate and dodge through an alley . . . in order to get away from his escort. He would not consent that every time he took a stroll, every time he took a horseback ride, every time he went to the theater, there should be a lot of military guards surrounding him; that when he is sitting in the box of the theater some man must stand there with a bayonet to keep anybody with evil intent from coming near his sacred person.

Such protection would be more than just personally "irksome"; it would prevent the president from carrying out his duties. What president would wish to travel the country "like the Czar of Russia or the Sultan of Turkey," prevented from interacting directly with the people he represents?[32]

Authorizing a military guard to protect the president was not the only part of Hoar's bill that drew sharp criticism. Objections were also raised against a provision that would have made killing the president a federal crime punishable by death. Nobody objected to the government killing a presidential assassin (the assassins of Garfield and McKinley had both been executed and John Wilkes Booth was killed by federal troops in a shootout), but many, particularly on the Democratic side, objected to making presidential assassination a federal crime. Opposition to this provision was based on two central points: first, that it violated states' rights, and second, that it violated equality before the law. That Democrats would worry about federal encroachment on states' rights is not surprising. More surprising was the objection that by legislating special punishment for those who killed or attempted to kill a president, the law violated equality before the law because it elevated the president above his fellow citizens.

In the view of the bill's critics, the president was not a "sacred person" nor was he the "sovereign of the country," and the law should therefore treat him the same as it treated every other citizen. To single out the president for special protection under the law, warned Mississippi Democrat Hernando Money, was to violate "the very foundation stone" of the American republic and to tread instead down the perilous path "toward imperial government." Democrat Anselm McLaurin, also from Mississippi, argued that when a president traveled to a state, "he goes there as a citizen, and is under the protection of the laws of [that state], just like any citizen in [that state] is under the protection of [its] laws." If the president should be assassinated while traveling, the assassin should "suffer the same penalty that would be inflicted upon him if he were to murder the humblest citizen." For the law to protect the president more than it did the humblest citizen was undemocratic.[33]

Republican supporters of the bill countered that the president was different. Killing a president was not like killing a regular citizen. It was "a crime against the United States Government," explained the Wisconsin Republican John Coit Spooner, and therefore it was "for Congress to prescribe the penalty." The punishment meted out to a presidential assassin or assailant, Spooner maintained, should not depend on the state in which the president happened to find himself at the time. To those who suggested that the president should be protected only when he was performing official duties, Spooner countered that the president was always on duty:

> I have not known any waking hour when it could be fairly said of the President that he was not in the discharge of executive duty. . . . I have never known any President to be on a purely pleasure trip. I have never known a President to be on any trip where he did not carry the burden of the Executive duty, and where he was not liable to be called upon and was not in fact called upon at almost any hour to discharge, by telegraph or otherwise, important Executive duties.

When a Democratic senator observed that he had known presidents to go "for a week duck hunting . . . away from all communication with the capital, away from the telegraph and from mail," Spooner was ready with a caustic reply, suggesting that perhaps the bill should be amended to read: "A bill to protect the President of the United States, except while he is duck hunting, or riding a horse, or sitting at a state dinner, or riding on the cars, or living in the Adirondacks, or seeking a little necessary recreation, and that you can shoot him at these or at any other times."[34]

The Republican majority succeeded in getting the presidential protection bill through the Senate on a nearly party line vote—only eight Democrats supported the bill, and just two Republicans opposed it. But in the House of Representatives the bill ran into an immovable wall of opposition. The House Judiciary Committee objected strongly to the provision lodging the protective function with the War Department. The secretary of war, the House committee feared, "may detail every man and officer in the Regular Army, under the pretense of protecting the President, dress them to suit his fancy, and send them abroad among the people to act under secret orders." Endowing the head of the War Department with this discretionary power posed a serious threat to "the liberties of the people." The House version of the bill did not call for any protective agency, but the House Judiciary Committee made clear that if a bill was to have such a provision it would be better to bolster the current Secret Service—under the control of the Treasury Department—than to have the duty of presidential protection fall to the army. In the end, the House and Senate failed to reach an agreement on the bill, and no change was made to the law. Not until 1906, well into Theodore Roosevelt's second term, did Congress finally pass a law that authorized the appropriation of funds "for the protection of the person of the President of the United States."[35]

However, Roosevelt did not go unprotected for the first six years of his presidency. Although Congress could not decide on who should protect the president, those in government did not doubt that the president needed some form of government protection. For the first time the secretary of the treasury directed the head of the Secret Service to protect the president. Wilkie was happy to comply, though in the absence of congressional authorization he was compelled to divert resources that had been designated for other parts of the Secret Service mission. Executive officers were forced to act on their own authority because Congress seemed unwilling to take the psychological plunge of acknowledging that a republic no less than a monarchy needed a guard to protect its chief executive.[36]

PROTECTING THEODORE ROOSEVELT

Although Congress was unable to agree on how to guard the president, McKinley's assassination had changed the discourse surrounding presidential protection. In the nineteenth century, protecting the president was something to be apologized for or hushed up. After McKinley's death, however, voices were increasingly raised in defense of protecting the president from the people.

Among the most respected of those voices was that of LeBaron Bradford Colt, the presiding judge on the First Circuit Court of Appeals. As the Senate prepared to debate Hoar's presidential protection bill in March 1902, Judge Colt delivered an address on "The Protection of the President" to the New Hampshire Bar Association. Colt indicted the nation's "appalling" record of presidential protection. By any comparative or historical standard, three presidents killed in thirty-seven years was a disaster. "The history of Europe for one thousand years," Colt intoned, "furnishes no parallel." No king of England had been assassinated in over four hundred years, and Colt counted only one French monarch assassinated in the previous three centuries. This was not because assassins hadn't tried to kill the rulers of Europe but because they had generally been thwarted. According to Colt, since the establishment of the U.S. government in 1789, there had been at least seventeen assassination attempts aimed at the ruler in France and another ten in England. The United States, in contrast, had witnessed only four such attempts. In comparison to Europe, then, the United States had witnessed far fewer assassination attempts but more assassinations.[37]

Colt disagreed with those who believed that the problem could be solved by keeping anarchists out of the country. Only McKinley's assailant had been an anarchist, and even in the case of McKinley's assassin the real cause, Colt argued, was not so much anarchism as it was an "unbalanced mind." Tighter immigration restrictions, which were being pressed aggressively in Congress, would not make the president safer. After all, each of the men who had killed or tried to kill the American president had been born in the United States. Instead, Colt emphasized, there needed to be a change in the way the president was guarded.[38]

The chief obstacle to making the president safer, in Colt's view, was the "sentimental notion that, because we are a democracy and the people have been accustomed, freely and on all occasions, to meet their Chief Magistrate, . . . to impair this time-honored custom would be unrepublican and savor of royalty." But the experience of the past four decades had shown that this was a dangerously misguided notion. In "the early days of the Republic" it was perhaps "reasonably safe for the President to mingle openly with the people," but conditions had changed and the nation needed to adapt to these changed conditions. The United States needed to emulate European nations, which had been far more successful in protecting their rulers. Colt was quick to add that it was not necessary for the president to "travel from place to place with the military pomp of some European rulers or with the gorgeous pageantry of Queen Elizabeth," but he insisted it was necessary to secure "reasonable safeguards appropriate to the simplicity and dignity of republican institutions." These safeguards included keeping "suspicious persons at a safe distance from the President." It was no coincidence, Colt pointed out, that "no assault has ever been attempted upon the President in the White House," where "reasonable precautions" had been taken to ensure the president's safety. Surely, Colt concluded, republicanism was not inconsistent with a presidential guard, or else "our boasted liberty [would] become the liberty of assassination."[39]

From the moment Roosevelt assumed the presidency in 1901, his protective detail attracted press attention. Although McKinley generally had Secret Service protection when he traveled, the press rarely mentioned it. In sharp contrast, newspaper stories of Roosevelt's travels and his summer stays at Oyster Bay frequently highlighted his Secret Service protection, with nary a suggestion of wrongdoing. Although Congress did not officially authorize Secret Service protection for the president until 1906, after McKinley's assassination such protection was taken as a given, even though it was still technically illegal.[40]

The increased visibility of the Secret Service was evident in a 1905 *New York Times* feature story on "The Men Who Guard the President." The profile began with an observation by an unidentified foreigner who had watched as President Roosevelt was driven into town from his Sagamore Hill home. "No outriders to clear the way— no military to impress the people," the foreign visitor marveled. "He seems not even to have protection." The foreigner gave voice to an American conceit dating back to the founding, but instead of seizing on this observation to celebrate the American political system, the *Times* story opined:

> Herein the foreign observer was mistaken. He did not notice several keen-looking men in the little group about the church door when the President entered, but he would have noticed them if there had been the slightest peculiar move toward the Chief Executive. They would have made their presence and their functions known by extremely rapid action. . . . They watch all trains that arrive at Oyster Bay. The stranger that comes to town is under their espionage, quite unknown to himself, until they are certain of his business and status. . . . The Secret Service men take no chances.

The *Times* interviewed several Secret Service agents stationed at Sagamore Hill, sympathetically relating the agents' efforts to protect the president and his family.[41]

Press accounts of Roosevelt's travels were liberally sprinkled with reports of the measures taken to protect the president. For instance, when Roosevelt came to Pittsburgh in 1902 to help the city celebrate the Fourth of July, the security arrangements were a front page story in the *New York Times*, under the headline "To Protect the President." Local officials, reported the *Times*, were "taking no chances on harm being done to President Roosevelt." To begin with, "a list of local Anarchists [was] furnished all police officers, [and] suspects . . . ordered to leave the city." Those suspects who "show[ed] themselves on the streets" were to be arrested. In addition, "detectives from all the leading cities [were] engaged to 'spot' visiting Anarchists," who were "to be locked up on sight until the President leaves the city." From the train

Two Secret Service men detailed to protect President Theodore Roosevelt at Oyster Bay. (Prints and Photographs Division, Library of Congress)

station to the park where the president was to speak, the parade route was roped off. Anyone crossing over the ropes during the parade, the police announced, would be arrested, as would anyone setting off fireworks "during the parade or within 300 yards of the President." Moreover, the president would not be allowed to shake hands with anyone in the crowd "even if he should request it."[42]

Security was tight too when Roosevelt visited Baltimore in June 1903 to attend a "grand concert" featuring six thousand singers. From the moment he alighted from the train he was cloaked in security. The president's carriage was surrounded by "a cordon of mounted policemen. . . . Ten of the officers rode close to the curbs of the streets en route, while a solid phalanx preceded the carriage and a squad followed. Along the route 400 picked men in uniform and plain clothes lined the curbs, so as to prevent any one approaching too near the Chief Executive's carriage." The same protective detail accompanied the president back to the train station after the concert. The city's police marshal explained that such preventative measures were necessary because "there are thousands of persons in the city, and it was thought possible that some anarchistic or utter crank might be among them." The police had no special information leading them to believe that anyone might attack the president, but they "deemed it wise to take every precaution."[43]

Even more elaborate precautions were taken on September 6, 1903, two years to the day that McKinley was shot, when Roosevelt left his summer residence at Oyster Bay to give an address at the opening of the state fair in Syracuse. A train carried Roosevelt and four Secret Service agents to a ferry, where they were joined by another twelve Secret Service agents. According to the *Times*, "no one was allowed near the [ferry], except members of the party" and no one was allowed in the ferry house until the boat had left. When the ferry landed in Manhattan a dozen detectives and another half dozen mounted police officers joined the president's party to escort the president across Manhattan Island to another ferry waiting to take the president across the North River to Hoboken where a special train awaited. The protective "cavalcade"—consisting of six carriages—drove the president rapidly across Manhattan to the ferry house where "again the most rigid rules prevailed," none being allowed in the ferry house until the ferry had departed. All of this was given front page coverage in the *New York Times*, under the headline "President Crosses City under Guard."[44]

The press account of Roosevelt's journey across New York City brought scathing letters from several readers. One writer, signing himself "Candor," thought it was "terribly humiliating" to read of the president "scurrying through the metropolis surrounded by a cavalcade of armed troopers." The president should instead have traveled through the city "without a single guard accompanying him . . . and all the people given a chance to see him pass through." Candor demanded to know whether we are "nearing the condition of a monarchy, where its crowned head is held in hate by its subjects." Roosevelt's armed guard was a disturbing sign of national decline. For surely the heroes of the Civil War—Grant, Sherman, Sheridan, and Lee—would never "have tolerated such an absurd display. . . . They were men without fear, and believed in the good-will of the people, and needed no breast plate to protect them from their friends." In accepting such protection, Roosevelt, "a man supposed to be devoid of fear," showed himself to be both a coward and undemocratic.[45]

Another letter to the editor lampooned Roosevelt for "rushing across the Manhattan Island in the evening surrounded by Secret Service men, and preceded and followed by a troop of clattering guards." Such behavior made the letter writer wonder whether "the hero of San Juan is afraid of his own people." Moreover, guarding the president in this ostentatious fashion smacked too much of "royalty to be appreciated by true Americans." The writer, who signed himself "American Citizen," contrasted Roosevelt's behavior with that of President Cleveland, who "permitted no clattering outriders, and if ever guarded by Secret Service men, secrecy was too well observed to have their presence turned into an advertisement."[46]

Other letter writers jumped to Roosevelt's defense. One pointed to "the fate of three Presidents in less than forty years" as a "sufficient answer to such diatribes." Another agreed that it was "a shame that such precaution is necessary," but recent history had shown that no "right-thinking person" could deny its necessity. The sad fact was that there were "crazy fanatics" in the United States, and so long as there were it would be necessary to protect the president. Imagine the "storm of indignation and protest" that would have erupted across the country if adequate pre-cautions had not been taken and the president had been assassinated as a result. To these observers, those who criticized presidential protection were naive at best, maliciously partisan at worst.[47]

Some, however, remained unpersuaded. To one letter writer it appeared that the lesson to be learned from Lincoln, Garfield, and McKinley was that an armed guard is not an effective protection. Instead, repeating a central tenet of republican thought dating back to the early republic, the writer maintained that the only "true and effective guard is that of freemen at every hand." The president should trust in the people to protect him rather than a " 'clattering guard' that excites the unbalanced mind to a fool's murderous 'dare.' " A military guard taught the chief magistrate to treat the people as suspects and potential murderers. In turn, the people learned to keep their distance. As evidence the writer quoted a longtime resident of Oyster Bay, who lamented: "We have known President Roosevelt's people, and were always openly welcome at the house. . . . Now, however, we are subjected to suspicion of an armed sentry. We are not murderers in heart or purpose, and resent the foul espionage of these paid policemen who are not our people, willing in every way to protect the president." The people protect their president out of love; the guards only because (and so long as) they are paid to do so.[48]

Such voices, however, were now in the minority and increasingly irrelevant. More common was the alarm produced by any apparent breach of security. A couple of months after Roosevelt's dash across Manhattan Island, his attendance at an uncle's funeral in New York City made page two of the *New York Times* beneath the headline, "Old Man Gets Past President's Guard." The guard, which included the president's usual Secret Service protection as well as five hundred city policemen, was unable to prevent an elderly man, at the close of the funeral service, from getting "near enough to the President to hand him a paper." The paper slipped to the president touted "the medical value of charcoal," which, the man promised, would "absorb all impurities in the blood, tumors, and cancers." The man was promptly arrested and found to be carrying three small cans of charcoal, which "had it been explosive material," opined the *Times*, could "have blown up the church and surrounding property." Although the man was harmless, the message conveyed by the story was that you can't be too careful.[49]

Protection was needed not only to guard the president against cranks and radicals but also against carelessness. The previous fall, when Roosevelt was touring New England, his carriage was struck by a trolley car. The accident had thrown the president from the carriage, and while he escaped with only some minor cuts and bruises, his bodyguard, Secret Service Agent William Craig, was killed instantly. Craig was the first Secret Service agent to die while protecting the president, and the tragedy brought national comment. How was it, people wanted to know, that more care was not taken to ensure the safety of the nation's president? The *Times* noted that we make a boast of the simple and democratic way in which the head of the Nation makes his journeys about the country. We smile at the precautions of armed escorts, pilot engines, and traffic suspension taken by foreign Governments to protect the person of the sovereign against accident and assault, and we stupidly congratulate ourselves that in this free Nation the President is everywhere safe among the People. But with no worse motive than that which may proceed from his ill-manners the motorman of the trolley car may be as dangerous as a dozen Anarchists and his onset as fatal as the explosion of a dynamite bomb. It is senseless and shocking that the person of the President should be exposed in this way.... There are reasons of the utmost gravity why the person of the Chief Magistrate must be shielded against all avoidable risks.

Roosevelt himself did not escape a chiding. The president, continued the *Times*, "has not the right to be guided by personal indifference to danger or to go about with no other or greater precautions than those which he has customarily observed, or rather disregarded in his journeyings as a private individual." The country, the *Times* concluded, "will look for an immediate taking to heart of the lesson of yesterday's accident and escape."[50]

In fact Roosevelt appreciated the role the Secret Service played, though less in protecting his life than in keeping unwanted individuals away from him. Writing to Henry Cabot Lodge in 1906, Roosevelt described his Secret Service detail as "a very small but very necessary thorn in the flesh." He admitted that "they would not be the least use preventing any assault upon my life," but thought it was "only the Secret Service men who render life endurable, as you would realize if you saw the procession of carriages that pass through [Oyster Bay], the procession of people on foot who try to get into the place, not to speak of the multitude of cranks and others who are stopped in the village." Roosevelt was right that the Secret Service played a crucial role in protecting the president's time during the months he spent at Oyster Bay. The newspapers were full of colorful stories of various oddballs trying to see the president only to be rebuffed by the agents stationed around Sagamore Hill. There was the "dangerous lunatic" who, armed with a loaded revolver, demanded to see the president about an engagement with the president's daughter. And there was the less threatening but more persistent "lady in blue" who was repeatedly frustrated by the Secret Service in her efforts to get to the president's home. When asked why she wanted to see the president, the diamond-clad woman would put "her finger mysteriously on her lips" and turn away. And, too, there was the elderly man who arrived in town and announced, "I am the devil and am going to see President Roosevelt." Needless to say, the Secret Service turned him away as well.[51]

The barrier that the Secret Service threw up around the president was justified on the grounds of presidential safety but, as Roosevelt acknowledged, its primary function, at least at Oyster Hill, was not to protect the president's life but rather to protect the president's time, not only from the distractions of harmless cranks and curious visitors but also from the attentions of office-seekers and even the press. Only those visitors who had received clearance from Roosevelt's secretary—first George Cortelyou and, by 1903, William Loeb—were allowed past "the guardians of the President." Although some townspeople complained about the sometimes heavy-handed ring of protection around the president, most seemed resigned to the fact that it was necessary to cordon off the president from the people, even his longtime neighbors. The president may have been a man of the people, but by the twentieth century there were clear limits to the extent to which he could safely mix with them.[52]

PROTECTING THE MODERN PRESIDENT

Modern Secret Service protection of presidents and would-be presidents did not emerge full-blown from the Roosevelt years. Many of the elaborate security arrangements that Americans associate with the contemporary presidency developed gradually, generally in response to assassinations and assassination attempts as well as to wartime threats.

In 1911 President William Howard Taft and his wife could slip out of the White House undetected in a "driving rain" on Christmas Eve and roam the capital streets unaccompanied, "dropping in at the homes of friends to wish them the compliments of the season." When the president's absence was at last noticed by the president's secretary, the Secret Service had no way of locating the missing president and first lady. Several hours later, relieved agents spied the president and his wife "trudging up the walk, dripping with rain but apparently delighted with their afternoon's escapade." Tellingly, the story was released to the press, perhaps because it showed the president's high spirits. Nobody seemed concerned that the episode might be seen as evidence of the incompetence of the Secret Service or the recklessness of the president.[53]

President Calvin Coolidge was less mischievous, but during the 1920s he often walked the streets of Washington, D.C., with only a single Secret Service guard for protection. Indeed his guard was evidently inconspicuous enough that "often [the president's] identity was never suspected" by those who passed him on the streets. "One story had it that on an icy Winter's day pedestrians on a downtown street noticed a thin man without an overcoat, gazing intently into a restaurant window where a girl was busily turning griddle cakes. As one passerby was pitying him for his apparent cold and hunger, the man turned and walked rapidly away, followed by another man in a greatcoat. The thinly clad one was the President." The thickly clad man was the Secret Service agent. Neither was recognized.[54]

Prior to World War I, a person could send the president threatening letters without fear of breaking a federal law. Secret Service protection of the president's family also began during World War I. Before the United States became a combatant in

World War II, anyone could wander freely through the White House grounds during the day. Not until 1951, after two Puerto Rican nationalists tried to kill Harry Truman, was the Secret Service given permanent authorization, and not until 1965, in the wake of the Kennedy assassination, did killing the president become a federal crime. Only after the assassination of Robert Kennedy in 1968 did Congress authorize Secret Service protection for presidential candidates.[55]

The size of the Secret Service today is unrecognizable from its spare beginnings. At the close of Theodore Roosevelt's eventful presidency, the agency's budget totaled a little over one hundred thousand dollars and most of that was spent on combating counterfeiting and forgery. As late as 1951 the Secret Service budget was still a relatively paltry three million dollars. But a quarter century later, in 1976, its budget had climbed to over one hundred million dollars. And by 2002 the Secret Service budget exceeded one billion dollars.[56]

The assassination of President Kennedy was a pivotal moment in the expansion of the Secret Service. The year before Kennedy's assassination the Secret Service budget stood at a little under five million dollars. Approximately 40 of the agency's 350 agents (the FBI, by way of contrast, had 6,000 agents at the time) were assigned to the White House protective detail. The remainder of the more than 300 Secret Service agents were scattered across sixty or so regional offices. Only when the president traveled would agents at a particular regional office become involved in protecting the president; the rest of the time their energies were devoted to the agency's century-old mission of fighting "the war against counterfeiting and against the theft and forgery of Government checks and bonds." Peacetime requests to beef up presidential security often met with a skeptical response. In 1962, for instance, the Secret Service sought funding for 58 additional agents, and the Republican National Committee immediately ridiculed the agency's request. Why should the public pay for Kennedy's "penchant for commuting from Hyannis Port, Palm Beach, Newport, and Middleburg" or for the First Lady's "safari into India"? Congressional Republicans echoed the same theme. Was the money required, Republicans inquired sarcastically, to guard the president's "ancestral estates" or perhaps to protect the much-photographed pony of the president's daughter, Caroline? In the end a skeptical Congress—controlled by Democrats—gave the administration only half of the additional agents it had requested.[57]

Kennedy's assassination transformed the political landscape. Requests that had seemed laughable now became unassailable. After Dallas, the nation's attention turned to understanding how the tragedy had happened and how it could have been prevented. Nearly everyone agreed that individual mistakes had been made, but a consensus also emerged that there were systemic problems that could be traced in part to a lack of resources. The agency needed more money for better training of agents, improved advance work, and more careful vetting of potential threats to the president. When, in 1964, the Secret Service submitted a $12.6 million budget request, including the addition of over 200 new agents (a 50 percent increase in the number of agents), no one objected, and the increase sailed through Congress. By 1973 the Secret Service had more than 1,200 agents, more than a threefold increase over the number at the time of the Kennedy assassination.[58]

The Warren Commission, which was charged with investigating the Kennedy assassination, had been strongly critical of the Secret Service's failure to take adequate preventative measures when the president traveled. The commission was disturbed that assassin Lee Harvey Oswald had not appeared on the service's list of names of people who were considered a potential threat to the president. The Secret Service responded to this criticism by greatly expanding the criteria it used in compiling its "trip file"—the list of individuals considered potential threats to the president. The result was a huge jump in the number of individuals that Secret Service agents needed to investigate and keep tabs on when the president traveled. Prior to Kennedy's assassination, there were typically only about one hundred names in the agency's trip file. By 1967 the file was reported to contain close to two thousand names, and by the mid-1970s estimates put the number of names on the list at around forty thousand. In 1962 the Secret Service received about one hundred "items of information" each month relating to presidential security. By 1967 it received more like seven thousand items a month, and by 1975 the agency received about two hundred thousand "pieces of information" every year from the FBI and local police authorities regarding people who were considered potentially dangerous to the president.[59]

Another area singled out for criticism was the agency's advance work. Nobody in the Secret Service had surveyed the buildings that flanked the presidential route or checked those who worked in the buildings. One such building was the seven-story Texas School Book Depository, from which Oswald shot President Kennedy. Why, the commission wanted to know, did the Secret Service not check out a prominent building directly in front of a spot on the route where the presidential motorcade would have to slow down to negotiate a turn? The failure to inspect the building, the commission learned, was not an oversight but rather part of the agency's standard operating procedure when the president traveled. "With the number of men available to the Secret Service and the time available," the agency's director explained in a confidential report written shortly after the assassination, "surveys of hundreds of buildings and thousands of windows is not practical. . . . Nor is it practical to prevent people from entering such buildings, or to limit access in every building to those employed or having business there." Only with "vastly larger forces of security officers," the agency insisted, could the Secret Service be expected to accomplish this level of advance work, and even then it might come at the cost of undermining the "purpose of the motorcade [which is] to let the people see their President and to welcome him to their city." Six months later, however, when the agency director James Rowley was asked whether there had been "a change in this regard in the procedures of the Secret Service," Rowley reassured the commission that there had been, though for security reasons he refused to elaborate, at least on the record. The Secret Service continues to refuse to disclose details relating to the logistics of advance work, but it is clear that the resources devoted to advance work today are many times greater than in Kennedy's time.[60]

The rapid growth in the cost and size of the Secret Service during the 1960s and 1970s was also fueled by the lengthening list of people the agency was required to protect. In 1962 the vice president and Speaker of the House were added to the list of those to be automatically provided Secret Service protection; in 1965 Congress authorized the Secret Service to provide lifetime protection of former presidents and their spouses; and in 1968 presidential candidates and presidential and vice-presidential nominees were given Secret Service protection. In 1971 the scope of Secret Service protection was expanded further to include visiting heads of state and foreign dignitaries, and in 1975 securing foreign diplomatic missions in the United States became a Secret Service responsibility.[61]

Although the past century has seen dramatic changes in the sophistication, scope, and size of the Secret Service, a basic tension has continued to characterize the relationship between the president, his protectors, and the public. Specifically, protection of the president is buffeted by two conflicting pressures: the desire to keep the president safe and the desire to make the president accessible. Presidential safety is obviously the paramount concern of the Secret Service; presidential accessibility brings no benefit to the agency, only costs, risks, and dangers. The president's safety matters also, of course, to the president and his family as well as to his supporters and the general public. But the president and the public also have an interest in the president being accessible, or at least being perceived as accessible. Throughout the twentieth century, presidents worried that the Secret Service's protective cocoon would make them appear to be out of touch with the people and thereby damage their chances of reelection or undermine their political clout. Citizens, too, have often expressed concerns that a tightly protected president more closely resembles a monarch than an elected leader.

Demands for increased presidential safety have been loudest and most insistent in the aftermath of assassinations and assassination attempts. In early 1965, for instance, members of Congress pressed Treasury Secretary Douglas Dillon about ways that Congress could mandate the president take certain precautions while traveling. Oklahoma Democrat Tom Steed, chair of the Appropriations subcommittee, broached the question of whether we were nearing the point "where we can put a limit on the number of places he will be allowed to visit in a given day." Given the dangers the president faced and the difficulties and expense of protecting him, it seemed to Steed that it was now necessary to talk about "a reasonable restriction" on the president's movement. Steed believed that the president should not be the one to decide what precautions he would take; instead "this ought to be something set for him." Dillon was sympathetic to the congressman's concern for the president's safety but although he thought it was "perfectly all right" [sic] for Congress to communicate its views to the president and to the nation, he insisted that Congress did not possess the legal authority to "say that the President cannot do this, that, or the other thing."[62]

Anxiety about President Lyndon Johnson's proclivity for plunging into crowds came to a head with the release of the Warren Commission's report a little over a month before the November 1964 election. Taking his cue from the report, Senate Majority Leader Mike Mansfield urged the presidential and vice-presidential nominees from both parties to avoid "exposing themselves unnecessarily . . . even if at times it means leaving a few hands unshaken or some autograph books unsigned." Press accounts reported disapprovingly that on his recent campaign stop in New England, "Johnson shook so many hands that he ended the long day with his own hand scratched and bruised." Typical of the press's scolding of Johnson was a column by columnist James Reston, who chided Johnson for his "rash and careless" behavior in his tour of New England. "He was not merely in touch with the crowd in Providence, Hartford, Burlington, and elsewhere," wrote Reston; "he was in the middle of it." How can the Secret Service protect the president, Reston asked, when Johnson insists on "scrimmaging with every crowd and shaking every outstretched hand?" Nobody was asking the president to remain "remote from the people in a bullet-proof cage" but, Reston argued, the president could "remain in touch with the people" without plunging into the midst of crowds. The president owed it to the presidency to show more good sense and greater caution.[63]

Johnson, however, was unmoved. Secretary Dillon, who had been appointed by Johnson to chair a four-person committee to study the Warren Commission's legislative recommendations, emerged from a 45-minute meeting with the president and was immediately asked by the press whether the question of "mixing with crowds" had come up. Dillon affirmed that the issue had been raised, but noted that the president "thinks he has a perfect right to meet the people, and he intends to go on doing so." The issue came up again at a presidential press conference a few days later. "In the light of the Warren Commission's report," the reporter began, would the president refrain from going "into the thick of the crowd" or at least avoid "undue exposure"? Johnson vigorously denied that the commission had recommended any such thing. The president quoted from the report at length, albeit selectively, to demonstrate his point.

> From George Washington to John F. Kennedy, such journeys have been a
> normal part of the President's activities. . . . In all of these roles, the President
> must go to the people. Exposure of the President to public view through travel
> among the people of this country is a great and historic tradition of American
> life. Desired by both the President and the public, it is an indispensable means

of communication between the two. . . . [H]is very position as representative of the people prevents him from effectively shielding himself from the people. He cannot and will not take the precautions of a dictator or a sovereign.

To bolster his case Johnson produced a letter from the director of the Secret Service, James Rowley, and eagerly read it to the press.

There has been much said concerning the dangerous risk involved when the President personally appears in and mingles with the crowds. The Secret Service is quite accustomed to working in crowds, and this responsibility does not make them nervous or jittery or worried. . . . The element of surprise which is gained during the impromptu appearances of the President, for example when he stops his car during a motorcade without notice, is often the most important deterrent to risk. . . . The crowd itself also offers some protection by covering the President. It also prevents a potential assassin from performing an act unnoticed and prevents the escape of the individual.

Rowley's letter, Johnson assured the press corps, represented "the feeling of all the people" who protect the president. It was classic Johnson overkill. Not content to affirm the importance of a democratically elected president traveling among and meeting with the people, he cajoled the Secret Service into affirming that the agency actually preferred the president diving into crowds.[64]

Johnson conveniently neglected to mention a memo that FBI director J. Edgar Hoover had prepared for him only ten days after the assassination. The memorandum emphasized the limits on presidential security but it also offered practical suggestions aimed at improving presidential security. The memo began by noting that presidential security was largely dependent on the president, specifically "the degree of contact with the general public desired by the President." Hoover operated from the premise that "absolute security is neither practical nor possible." To achieve "complete security would require the President to operate in a sort of vacuum, isolated from the general public and behind impregnable barriers. His travel would be in secret; his public appearances would be behind bulletproof glass." Clearly this would be unacceptable to any president. Although the president could not and should not be barred from the people, Hoover suggested that there were steps the president could take to minimize the threat of assassination. For instance, "the President's movements within crowds" could be kept "to a minimum." The president could "remain on the rostrum after public addresses, rather than mingling with the audience," and he could "avoid walking in public except when absolutely necessary." In addition, the president could use television in order to "limit public appearances . . . whenever possible."[65]

Johnson showed little interest in following or publicizing Hoover's recommendations. Despite the president's protestations to the contrary, his proclivity for wading into crowds in order "to press the flesh" continued to be a source of tension with the Secret Service. One agent speculated that the problem stemmed in part from "Johnson's he-man image of himself," which led him to resent "having agents around him all the time." Johnson, the agent explained, "didn't like the idea of needing 'protection' from anyone." Although Johnson's antics made him difficult to protect at times, Secret Service protection did in fact become much tighter after Kennedy's death.[66]

When President Johnson visited the World's Fair, for instance, in the spring of 1964, he was accompanied by "the heaviest security ever assigned to guard a President in peacetime." The day before the president arrived in New York, Secret Service and FBI agents as well as New York City police officers and the fair's private security agents "combed virtually every square yard of the 646-acre exposition grounds, studied every vantage point an assassin might use and searched through buildings to make sure no source of danger went undetected." The president arrived via helicopter and then drove the remaining two hundred yards to the speaker's platform in a closed limousine, through a cordon of hundreds of police officers, private security agents, and Secret Service agents who "stood almost shoulder-to-shoulder along the route." The three thousand spectators who gathered along the route watched behind barriers that kept them thirty feet away from the president's vehicle and the other twenty cars in the presidential motorcade. The relatively small number of onlookers may have owed something to the bad weather but was also due to the fact that the route the limousine traversed had not been divulged to the press or to the public beforehand.[67]

The heightened emphasis on security was evident for all to see at the inauguration of President Richard Nixon in 1969. Twentieth-century inaugurals, to be sure, had always been tightly guarded affairs. In the eyes of the Secret Service, the widely publicized and predictable nature of the inaugural route made the event particularly dangerous. Well before Kennedy's assassination the Secret Service was in the habit of closely checking buildings along the route of the inauguration parade. But Nixon's first inaugural, which took place less than a year after the assassinations of Robert Kennedy and Martin Luther King, Jr., saw presidential security reach unprecedented levels. Manholes were locked, roofs cleared, windows closed, confetti and streamers banned, and no one was allowed to enter a building along the route without special identification papers. So tight was the security that one observer was heard to grumble that Nixon "might as well have ridden by in a tank." Above the president hovered two helicopters jammed with Secret Service agents, ahead of him was a "flying wedge" of thirty policemen on motorcycles, and to the sides and rear were carloads of Secret Service agents. Agents also walked or jogged alongside the presidential limousine, and the streets were lined with thousands of police and military personnel. Scores of snipers, moreover, occupied strategic locations along the route. All told, the "protective force" was estimated to be around fifteen thousand people.[68]

Whereas the John F. Kennedy assassination—as well as the assassinations of Robert Kennedy and Martin Luther King, Jr.—bolstered support for enhanced presidential security, the Nixon administration fanned fears that the Secret Service was becoming a "palace guard." The concern was less that the Secret Service was helping to isolate a reclusive president than that the agency was being wielded as a political weapon against those the president did not trust or who he feared would embarrass him. In September 1973, for instance, the *Washington Post* reported that the Secret Service had been ordered by the president to wire-tap the phone of the president's brother even though the brother posed no threat to the president's life. Instead the president feared that his brother's financial dealings might embarrass him, as they had in the 1960 presidential campaign. The Secret Service also came under heavy criticism for confiscating anti-Nixon signs wielded by protesters or removing protesters, even when neither the protesters nor their signs posed a physical danger to the president. In addition, at the request of Nixon's aides and personal friends, the Secret Service authorized a host of improvements to Nixon's personal homes in San Clemente and Key Biscayne that seemed to bear more relationship to the president's comfort than his security. It was hard to see how a new swimming pool cleaning machine or an ice-making machine made the president safer.[69]

Nixon's use and abuse of the Secret Service altered, albeit briefly, the public discussion about presidential security. Between 1963 and 1972, the public conversation largely followed the tracks laid down in the Warren report: how to augment presidential security without "even the suggestion of a garrison state." Disclosures of Nixon's political and personal uses of the Secret Service briefly deflected the attention of the media and political elites toward combating the abuses of imperial presidency. However, two dramatic attempts on the life of President Gerald Ford in September 1975 quickly transformed the public discourse once again. Worries about a "palace guard" were replaced by renewed concerns about inadequate security.[70]

Both assassination attempts occurred during visits to California. The first happened in Sacramento as Ford navigated the roughly 150 yards from his hotel to the state capitol where he was to deliver a speech. A relaxed Ford shook hands with people as he walked briskly through the park in front of the state capitol. As he slowed to shake more hands, a woman close enough to touch the president aimed a gun directly at him. Luckily, she failed to get a shot off before she was subdued by a Secret Service agent. Less than three weeks later, in San Francisco, the ordeal was repeated. Ford emerged from a hotel, greeted by a cheering crowd of several thousand people. As the smiling president stepped toward the waiting limousine, he reached to shake a few of the outstretched hands that were thrust toward him from behind the rope barriers. Almost immediately a shot rang out and a dazed president was shoved unceremoniously to the ground by Secret Service agents and then dragged into the waiting limousine, which immediately sped away. The first assailant, Lynette ("Squeaky") Fromme, had been unknown to the Secret Service prior to the assassination attempt, but Sara Jane Moore was very well known to the agency. In fact, the evening before she tried to kill the president the Secret Service had picked her up, confiscated her gun, and then released her. Although neither woman fit the Secret Service's profile of a dangerous assassin, either could easily have succeeded in killing the president. Fromme had been a mere two feet away from Ford, while Moore had an unobstructed view of the president's head and may have missed only because the calibration of the gun she had purchased that morning was marginally off.[71]

After the first assassination attempt, Ford received letters from people across the country expressing their concern for his safety and urging him to take more care when going out in public. One woman from Fort Collins, Colorado, advised Ford "*not* to mingle with the crowds anymore." That sentiment was echoed by a man from Fort Wayne, Indiana, who informed the president that his "personal appearances on television" were more valuable to citizens than "handshaking opportunities." Presidents, explained a Los Angeles man, were a natural "target for nuts" and so needed to "stay away from handshaking" and "think more of isolation between themselves and [the] public." A "concerned citizen" from Pennsylvania was bold enough to propose that "from this day forward, President Ford and *all* future Presidents" should avoid "going up to or into crowds to shake hands." Shaking hands, wrote another, was an "old-fashioned" political technique that the nation could no longer afford.[72]

The media joined in the chorus of concern. James Reston, who had chided Johnson for his reckless behavior a decade before, now found fault with Ford's proclivity for traveling across the country and mixing with crowds. Reston questioned whether "in this age of television, . . . these political handshaking strolls through uncontrollable crowds are not a little out of date and even a little phony." Waving at crowds and shaking hands were "an unnecessary diversion from his really serious Presidential responsibilities." Perhaps in "the old days," Reston continued, "there was a good argument . . . for Presidents to travel around this vast continental country just to remind the people that the President was a living and breathing human being." But that was no longer necessary. Television gave the president "instant contact with almost every homestead in every city and village in the land." In view of these technological changes, Reston argued that it was neither "good government [nor] good politics to spend so much time rushing around the country repeating old arguments and convincing the convinced at party rallies." Reston assured his readers that he was not asking the president "to fly around the county from one safe military base to another . . . or [to] speak always . . . from behind bullet-proof lecterns." But it seemed clear to Reston that there was no reason for a contemporary president "to stroll through parks and mobs" to show he was in touch with the people.[73]

Immediately after the first assassination attempt, Ford had insisted that it would not change the way he interacted with the American people. The day of Fromme's attack the president informed the press: "This incident, under no circumstances, will prevent me from contacting the American people as I travel from one state and community to another." The following week Ford felt compelled to respond to mounting public criticism of his heavy travel schedule and his penchant for mixing with crowds. In a prepared statement, Ford said he "must respectfully disagree" with those who suggested he should change his behavior. "The business of the Presidency is people," Ford insisted. The president could not "gain a sense of what is on people's minds by sitting in the safety of the Oval Office and looking at opinion polls. . . . Only by going around the country, . . . by meeting people face to face and listening to what they have to say can [the president] really learn how people feel and what they think." Ford stressed that he had "no intention of abdicating that responsibility" or "allowing the Government of the people to be held hostage at the point of a gun."[74]

On September 12 the president conducted an interview at a St. Louis television station, and the first two questions he received centered on his security. Ford was asked whether, "in the interest of national security, . . . [he] should modify [his] campaign style" and whether such campaigning was "a wise use of [his] time when there are so many problems" facing the nation. Traveling, Ford responded, was not a distraction from his presidential responsibilities. Rather travel enabled him to do his job better. "It's helpful," he explained, "to meet with the people, shake hands with them, get their questions." Moreover, it was also important for the people "to have an opportunity to see firsthand, close-up, their President." These direct connections were vital in restoring the people's trust in their leaders and their government. A president who sat "in seclusion in the Oval Office" would lose the trust of the people and lose touch with them as well. Traveling was not just about campaigning, then, but about governing and solving the nation's problems. There were risks to presidential travel, to be sure, but those risks, Ford emphasized, had to be balanced against the important purposes that travel served in the "political life" of the nation.[75]

The second assassination attempt initially seemed to make Ford even more publicly defiant. Within minutes of arriving back at the White House, the president met with reporters to announce that he would not "cower in the face of a limited number of people who want to take the law into their own hands." The American people were "good people," Ford said, and they deserved "a dialogue [with] their President." And that dialogue required "talking with one another, seeing one another, shaking hands with one another."[76]

Not everyone had such a charitable interpretation of why the president insisted on mixing with crowds and shaking hands. A Stanford University psychiatrist, David Hamburg, suggested that such handshaking served no purpose beyond addicting presidents to "a God-like sense . . . of adulation." Ron Nessen, the president's press secretary, was asked to comment on that assessment at a press briefing two days after the second assassination attempt. He dismissed the professor's assessment as naive. "I don't think [the professor] knows very much about the purposes of Presidential travel," commented Nessen. The president travels so that he can communicate his views "directly to people . . . in hopes [the people] will prod Congress into action" on important legislation. In addition, Nessen pointed out, the president considered it important to "hear what people have to say to him directly," as he did on his visit to Stanford, where he met with 25 law students who told the president what they "think he is doing wrong."[77]

Although the White House could easily sidestep a reductionist psychological explanation of the president's behavior, Ford could not so easily avoid the friends and advisers who urged him to take greater care. The president did not wish to appear afraid of the prospect of assassination, but neither did he wish to appear reckless. At the same press conference in which Nessen defended the president against Hamburg's psychological assessment, he also "broadly hinted" that Ford had "already begun to reduce his close contacts with large crowds." Ford continued to insist he would keep traveling, but he now promised to "keep my communications open . . . not in any foolhardy spirit, but by every prudent and practical means." At the same time, Ford requested that Congress appropriate thirteen million additional dollars to fund 150 new Secret Service agents in order to enhance presidential protection.[78]

The president's new tone brought approving noises from many in the nation's press. The editors of the *New York Times*, for instance, were clearly pleased that the president's "strong initial refusal" to change his ways had "apparently been tempered." The *Times* noted that not only had there been "sharply stepped up" security in Ford's recent trips to Illinois, West Virginia, and New Jersey, but that the president had conspicuously "declined to wade into crowds with his normal fervor." The editorial's headline, "A More Secure President," intimated both that the president would be safer by being more cautious around crowds, and that his decision to accept enhanced protection suggested a psychologically "more secure" leadership than the macho bravado that Ford displayed initially.[79]

It is not surprising that assassinations and assassination attempts prompt calls for enhanced presidential security and for greater caution on the part of the president. However, such reactions are far from automatic. After President Ronald Reagan was shot outside the Washington Hilton Hotel in March of 1981, there was a predictable flurry of congressional investigations and questions about how a crazy man like John Hinckley could have got within twenty feet of the president and fired six shots, hitting the president and three others in the president's party. How was it that Hinckley, who had been arrested in 1980 for possessing three handguns and fifty rounds of ammunition as he boarded a plane in Nashville, Tennessee (where President Carter was giving a speech at the time), had not been in the Secret Service files? Others wanted to know why the 3,500 AFL-CIO delegates to whom Reagan spoke had to pass through rigorous security checks before entering the hotel, but there was no similar security check for the crowd of several hundred who gathered outside the hotel. However, unlike after the two attempts on Ford's life, the attempted assassination of Reagan was not accompanied by calls in the media for the president to limit his public exposure. On the contrary, many in the media cautioned that the event should not be used to justify limiting the president's exposure.[80]

The *New York Times*, for instance, which had badgered President Ford about his casual mingling with crowds and his hectic travel schedule, took a different tack with Reagan. In an editorial published just two days after the assassination attempt, the *Times* cautioned against those who "are beginning to say America must do more to protect its President." This was an "understandable reaction," but the *Times* questioned whether it was wise, particularly since the balance between security and access is "already well tilted toward security." There is, the *Times* opined, a "price to be paid for encapsulating Presidents even more. It would mean a different kind of Presidency and, necessarily, a different kind of Presidential campaign—changes that would create their own dangers for Presidents and public." To those who thought that in an age of television there was no need to expose the president to the dangers inherent in public appearances, the *Times* warned that "if all that's on a camera is a packaged President inside his White House bubble, the public's eyes would soon become as glazed as the bubble" and the president would soon become out of touch "inside his magnificent, airless isolation booth." Presidents are politicians and what makes a good politician are the "invisible antennae" that are "sensitive to public vibrations." Presidents, the *Times* concluded, "learn from trying out ideas on real people. They learn from the spontaneous reactions of live audiences, not ones carefully picked for enthusiasm. Interacting with the public adds a whole dimension, however hard to measure, to a President's understanding. To think of cutting that off, even for benign reasons, is hasty. Though not as palpable, suffocation is no less a threat than the bullet."[81]

The media's reaction was also motivated by a fear that the administration would use the assassination attempt to limit journalists' access to the president. Hinckley after all had managed to get so close to the president only because he had slipped unnoticed into the press section. Moreover, at the moment of the shooting the president had been responding to a question from a reporter, not shaking hands with a crowd. The fears proved justified. After Reagan recovered and resumed traveling, the press found themselves kept at a safe distance from the president. Prior to the assassination attempt, when the president arrived or departed on an airplane, reporters were usually close enough to ask the president questions. After the assassination attempt, however, that was no longer possible because of the distance the reporters found themselves from the president. The White House justified the change as a security measure, but it also served the administration's political interest in limiting embarrassing questions and unscripted answers. When reporters tried shouting out questions from afar, it just made the press appear rude. The cameras only captured Reagan's genial smile and a cheery wave. Not for the first time, the demands of security dovetailed with the political interests and proclivities of the president.[82]

THE "REGAL TREATMENT"

In today's age of terrorism, one can hardly underestimate the dangers faced by a president. Although only one president has been assassinated since the Secret Service was given the duty of protecting the president, Ford's and Reagan's survival owed much to fortune (and advances in medicine, in Reagan's case). Equally lucky was President-elect Franklin Roosevelt, who was fired on five times at Bayfront Park in Miami without being hit; the mayor of Chicago, Anton Cermak, was not so fortunate—he was shot in the stomach while shaking FDR's hand, and died several weeks later. The Secret Service's record is far from flawless, and yet the agency has done a remarkable job keeping the president safe. Take away that protection and it is doubtful that any president today would survive long.

There is, of course, no danger of that. As the *Times* pointed out in 1981, the balance is "well tilted toward security." Presidents can, of course, still be shot and killed. And presidents can and do override security considerations in favor of political objectives. But presidents today are surrounded by more layers of protection than ever before in the nation's history. Gone is the time when presidents can drive down streets in open convertibles or take regular morning walks through the streets of the capital. Bullet-proof vests, bullet-proof glass, and swarms of muscular agents help protect the president from the people. The Secret Service still attempts to make protection as inconspicuous as possible in order to avoid the appearance of a "garrison state," but that is not easily done. There are not many inconspicuous ways of shutting down freeways—which is standard operating procedure to secure the safety of the presidential motorcade. Presidential security in the nineteenth century was sporadic and unsystematic; presidential protection today is pervasive and inescapable.

It would be misleading, however, to portray the president as a reluctant prisoner of the Secret Service. Of course, presidents and their families generally do not enjoy having their every step followed by guards. And presidents and their staffs have been known to chafe under the constraints the Secret Service imposes on public appearances. But the president and the Secret Service have a shared interest in creating a ceremonious distance between the chief executive and the public. In 1932, while Herbert Hoover was still president, a *New York Times* reporter shrewdly noted how the Secret Service had managed to make "happy use of a certain amount of fanfare in isolating and protecting" the president. This "limited regal treatment," as the *Times* termed it, has become much more pronounced over the subsequent 75 years. The imposing pomp and ceremony that envelops the contemporary presidency is well suited both to the Secret Service's need to secure the president's safety and to the president's desire to project an image of mastery and command. Both the image-makers and the security apparatus favor carefully scripted events over spontaneous, close encounters between the president and the people.[83]

From the vantage point of the twenty-first century, it is remarkable how doggedly nineteenth-century Americans adhered to a set of practices that left presidents dangerously unprotected. Their fears of monarchy appear exaggerated; their warnings against despotism almost histrionic; their vision of politics naive. Yet they were right on two counts. First, the president could not be protected from cranks and extremists without also making the president less accessible to ordinary people. Second, establishing a government agency whose mission it was to protect the president's life meant creating a formidable institution that had an overriding institutional incentive to constrict public access to the president. The rise of the regal presidency has many causes, but chief among them is that a regal president is easier to protect than a republican one.

CHAPTER FIVE

Paying for Presidential Travel

After President Monroe returned from his tour of the northern states in 1817, he was presented with a bill for his use of government mail coaches. The cost: one thousand nine hundred and twelve dollars. The president thought the charges excessive, and the postmaster general later confirmed that the charge for an "ordinary traveler" would not have exceeded five hundred dollars. Yet Monroe grudgingly paid the bill anyway, out of his own pocket.[1]

Having spent most of his life in public service, Monroe was not a wealthy man when he entered the presidency at the age of 58. Like many Virginia planters, he had large debts. What personal wealth he possessed was tied up in land, slaves, crops, and livestock. To raise the money he needed for his first presidential tour Monroe sold his furniture to the government—the furnishings of the President's House had been destroyed when the British torched the capital in 1814, and new furniture had yet to arrive from France. With the help of his $25,000 a year presidential salary, Monroe was able to buy back his furniture after the new furnishings were delivered.[2]

Monroe did not pay for his entire trip, though that had been his plan when he first declared his intention to tour the country as a private citizen. Local officials often insisted on paying for the president's lodgings. In New York City, for instance, Monroe asked to pay the bill for the "elegant apartments" that had been secured for him by the local committee of arrangements, but the city's representatives would not permit the president to pick up any part of the bill for its "spontaneous testimonial of respect to the first magistrate of our country." As Monroe later conceded, the cost of his tour "was much diminished by the hospitality and accommodation afforded me, throughout the Union, and especially in the principal Cities, where the expense was greatest." Such hospitality notwithstanding, Monroe expended all of the $6,000 he had drawn from his "furniture fund."[3]

The federal government in the early republic made no provision for financing presidential travel, even though the first Congress had provided legislators with a travel allowance to cover mileage to and from their district. Local governments helped to defray the costs of presidential visits, but these arrangements were ad hoc and often awkward for all parties concerned. Little wonder, then, that presidents in the early republic did not travel much. Indeed it is a wonder that they traveled at all. How did we get from a world in which it was unremarkable that a president would foot the bill for his travels to a world in which the idea is unimaginable? How and when did the nation come to believe that a president's travel should be paid for by the taxpayers of the United States?[4]

THE FREE PASS SYSTEM

The coming of the railroads revolutionized travel in the United States. Distances that had taken weeks by horse and carriage could be covered in days. Monroe never traveled more than 30 miles a day on his tours, whereas Rutherford Hayes could do 30 miles an hour by rail. Traveling great distances in the early republic was arduous and sometimes dangerous. On his southern tour, George Washington was transported across the Chesapeake Bay by a coach ferry, which ran aground twice in a storm. The president reported that he spent the night "in my greatcoat and boots in a berth not long enough for me by a head, and much cramped," before being rescued the next morning by a sailboat. His coachman nearly drowned trying to move the coach onto another boat. Rail travel had its own dangers but they did not begin to compare with the rigors of traveling by horse and carriage.[5]

Travel by rail had another advantage for presidents, one less often appreciated. Trains not only enabled presidents to travel great distances but to travel without paying. Railroads were heavily dependent on government largesse, and railway executives were therefore more than happy to transport public officials for free in hopes of getting favorable treatment from them. The so-called "free pass system" benefited all manner of public officials, but for the president it provided a useful way to meet the increasing public demand to see the chief magistrate without having to pay for it out of his own pocket.

Initially the railroads' practice of allowing public officials to ride free did not attract strong criticism. In the 1870s, however, railroads began to be seen as the central villain in the economic distress suffered by rural and small-town America. In 1887 Congress passed the Interstate Commerce Act, the first federal effort to regulate the railroads and the rates they charged. But the Interstate Commerce Commission (ICC) had minimal effect on the power of the railroads. To many it seemed that the ICC did the railroads' bidding. The ICC's failure to exercise meaningful regulatory review produced pressure on Congress to give the ICC real power, particularly the power to limit the rates charged by railroads. Reformers also wanted to end the stranglehold that they believed the railroads exercised in the halls of power. One key element of this influence, according to reformers, was "the free pass bribery system."[6]

In 1906, the federal government finally acted. At the urging of President Theodore Roosevelt, Congress passed the Hepburn Act, which gave the ICC the power to set the rates that railroads could charge. Among the act's other provisions was a section that forbid railroads from issuing free passes, except with specified exceptions. The indigent, disabled veterans, religious ministers, and physicians were among the exempted, but politicians and presidents were not. From that point forward, members of Congress, executive branch officials, and the president were to pay their own way when they traveled on the nation's rails.[7]

This new law posed an acute problem for the president. Presidents could not very well ride in a regular railcar. The lesson learned from the Lincoln, Garfield, and McKinley assassinations was that the president needed to be carefully protected. Having the president travel in the same car with other citizens would make the job of the Secret Service nearly impossible. The president also needed a quiet place to work while he traveled. An ordinary rail ticket could provide neither the safety nor the work environment to which the president had become accustomed. The free pass that presidents had received from the railroads was no ordinary rail ticket; instead it had typically entitled them to a special car or even an entire train.

By the late nineteenth century the accommodations provided to the president by the railroads had become almost lavish. In the spring of 1891, President Benjamin Harrison was transported free of charge on the Pennsylvania railroad in a train that was said to be unsurpassed "in beauty, convenience, [and] opportunities for luxurious ease." The "Presidential Special," which was to take the president on a nine-thousand-mile, five-week journey to the West Coast, consisted of five magnificent cars: the Aztlun, the Coronado, the New Zealand, the Ideal, and the Vacuna. The Aztlun included "furniture in olive plush, a library, a barber's shop, and a bathroom." The Coronado was the dining car, containing "tables of oak, curtains of green plush, seats of pearly grey velvet, [and] a silver service." The president's quarters were in the New Zealand, with blue plush upholstery and "a double drawing room set apart as a sleeping chamber" decorated in white and gold. The Ideal was graced with "six rooms, richly furnished, each room in wood different from that predominating in the other," and the Vacuna was an observation car in which the president could sit "in a sort of glass case" and view the countryside.[8]

Such "luxurious" travel arrangements attracted occasional criticism. The *New York Times*, which backed Grover Cleveland, reported on President Harrison's train under the front page headline, "Luxury for Mr. Harrison." Noting that the president would soon be traveling through Populist strongholds in the West and South, the *Times* speculated that "the distressed farmer," upon seeing "this glittering red, gold, and steel-blue parade," might well ask "who it is that is to pay for this royally handsome and comfortable train." As the president heads westward, the farmer will "behold [the president] in plate glass and velvet magnificence," knowing that it is the farmer, through higher railroad rates, "who will eventually pay all expenses of this trip."[9]

Such complaints, however, were generally dismissed as partisan carping. Most took it for granted that presidents needed or deserved these sorts of special arrangements. Presidents Cleveland, McKinley, and Roosevelt were all provided special cars and trains, courtesy of the railroad companies. These arrangements enabled the president to live and work on the train throughout the time he was away from Washington, D.C. He did not need to worry about where he was staying (or who was paying). There was no need for the awkward arrangements of the sort that Monroe had to negotiate. The president could make the occasional foray into town to give a speech or have a meal, but often he spoke from the rear of the train and ate and slept on the train as well.

In the spring of 1903, for instance, Roosevelt was furnished a special train by the Pennsylvania Railroad for a western tour that would take him 14,000 miles in about two months. The six-car train, "the Pacific Coast Special," was "specially decorated and equipped for the trip" and reputed to be one of "the finest ever run out of Washington." The president's private car, the Elysian, was "seventy feet of solid mahogany, velvet plush, and sinkingly deep furniture. It had two sleeping chambers with brass bedsteads, two tiled bathrooms, a private kitchen run by the Pennsylvania Railroad's star chef, a dining room, a stateroom with picture windows, and an airy rear platform for whistle-stop speeches." Among the other cars was the Atlantic, which boasted a barbershop, and the Gilsey, a dining car "stocked with champagne and cigars." Two other handsomely furnished cars were to accommodate the bevy of journalists, photographers, staff, and protective detail that accompanied the president, as well as prominent individuals who had been invited to join him along the way, including the presidents of Columbia University and the University of California and the poet and naturalist John Burroughs. All of the expenses for the two-month journey of the president and his guests were picked up by the railroads.[10]

The provision of the Hepburn Act abolishing the free pass system meant that the nation needed to devise a new way of funding presidential travel. No longer would presidents be able to rely on the largesse of the railroad companies. Who would pay for the cost of the special cars and trains that the president needed? Republicans in Congress quickly moved to remedy the situation by proposing that the president receive up to $25,000 a year to pay for his travel expenses as well as those of his "invited guests." House Democrats defeated the provision on a point of order, but Republicans returned a few days later with a revised proposal. The amended bill dropped the "invited guests" language but still gave the president up to $25,000 to cover his traveling expenses. The spending of the money was to be left to "the discretion of the President and accounted for on his certificate solely."[11]

THE HOUSE DEBATE

The revised proposal was introduced in the House on June 20, 1906 (ten days before the Hepburn Act was signed into law) and immediately encountered objections from Democrats. Ollie James, a young Kentucky Democrat, demanded to know what official duty, prescribed by the Constitution, required the president "to travel over the United States or leave the capital?" Shepherding the bill on the House floor was the veteran Minnesota Republican James Tawney, chairman of the House Appropriations Committee. Tawney conceded that the Constitution did not require the president to travel but noted that "the demands of the people may." The answer failed to satisfy James, prompting Tawney to suggest that the president might need to travel in his capacity as commander in chief. The Kentucky Democrat remained unpersuaded and asked Tawney to identify a single president who had left the capital "to command either the Army or the Navy."[12]

James pressed his advantage. He could see no need for a president to travel. The president's constitutional duty was "to communicate with both Houses of Congress suggesting needed legislation and not by stump speeches through the country." James was willing to concede the Republicans' point that Roosevelt had played an important role in mobilizing public support for the railroad rate bill but insisted that this influence was not because people heard the president speak but rather because they read his speeches. According to James, the president could have been just as effective in stirring public opinion had he communicated his messages to Congress, which was, he reiterated, "the constitutional manner of advising the House and Senate upon needed legislation." Thus even if public opinion leadership was an important presidential role, traveling and speaking were not necessary to carry out that role effectively.[13]

The Democratic assault upon the bill was joined by Alabama's Oscar Underwood, who argued that the bill was plainly unconstitutional. Article XI, section 6 of the Constitution explicitly stated that Congress could not increase or decrease a sitting president's salary nor could it grant him "any other emolument." Giving the president $25,000 to spend on travel, insisted Underwood, was "clearly" an emolument. Congress could authorize travel expenses for a future president but was prevented by the Constitution from granting the money to Roosevelt.[14]

The bill's floor leader was unmoved. He pointed out that Congress already provided the president with a carriage and horses for travel in the capital. What was the difference, Tawney asked, between appropriating money that enabled the president to visit Philadelphia and appropriating money to assist the president in getting around Washington, D.C.? The difference, Underwood responded, was that the Constitution did not prevent Congress from providing an emolument for a future president. Congress would be within its constitutional powers to provide the next president with a $25,000 travel budget; Congress was forbidden only to provide such a benefit to the incumbent president.[15]

But Underwood, like other Democrats, was interested in more than the narrow constitutional question of how to interpret Article XI, section 6. Underwood opposed appropriating travel money not only for Roosevelt but for any president. Like his colleague Ollie James, Underwood demanded to know why the president should be given free transportation when "his official duties do not require him to travel."[16]

Underwood's challenge brought New York Democrat William Bourke Cockran to his feet. Irish born and French educated, Cockran was a bit of a maverick, having bolted the Democratic Party in 1896 to campaign for McKinley. In 1900 he switched course and supported William Jennings Bryan. Cockran asked his fellow Democrat Underwood whether he thought that "when the President of the United States moves from one part of the country to another discussing public questions before his fellow-citizens, he is engaged in his own amusement or in the public service." Underwood quipped that it might be both, but Cockran would not let his colleague off the hook so easily. He pressed again: "Is it not a fact that Mr. Roosevelt's speeches within the last two or three years have been more fruitful in actual legislation, as in the railway rate bill, than any other single force that can be mentioned?" Underwood was reluctant to go that far, but under persistent questioning he conceded that Roosevelt deserved "a great deal of credit" and that "sometimes the President's trips about the United States were of advantage to the country." But Underwood added that not all of a president's trips had a public purpose. Sometimes, "the President takes a trip with his family to his summer home." And in any event, insisted Underwood, the public purpose could be served as well by the president giving a speech in the capital as in Chicago or San Francisco. For "the utterance of a President of the United States has a world's audience no matter where he makes it." Cockran reacted in disbelief. Surely the effectiveness of the president's speeches had been greatly aided by "his circulation among the people." Finding it difficult to dispute Cockran's point, Underwood retreated to safer ground: the bill, he reiterated, violated the constitutional prohibition of Article XI.[17]

Sensing that he had Underwood on the run, Cockran articulated more fully the political vision that animated the legislation. "In the operation of our constitutional system," Cockran intoned, "the President has become the chief leader of public thought and exponent of public opinion." The president of the United States had become an important source of ideas for new legislation and was no longer "a mere executive charged with enforcing the laws." Hence "the circulation of the President throughout the country aids practically and decisively in promoting salutary legislation by giving direction to public opinion." And so it followed that the expenses the president "incurred in rendering such important public service [should] be borne out of the public Treasury."[18]

Cockran's sweeping claims about the place of the presidency in the political system prompted a sharp rebuke from Underwood. Every public official, including members of Congress and the president's cabinet, Underwood argued, contributes to these "great discussions." Why should an exception be made for the president? Why should the president be given a special fund for traveling when others did not receive money for that purpose? Cockran was ready with the obvious retort: "Would the gentleman deny mileage to Members" of Congress. Members had to return home each year, Underwood retorted, whereas the president was expected to live in the White House. The president therefore did not have the same need for travel as members of Congress. Cockran enjoyed his next question: Where in the Constitution did the honorable senator from Alabama find the provision requiring the president to be "confined to any particular spot" in the United States? Underwood admitted there was no such provision, but observed that the "very fact that Congress has provided a home, furnished and maintained for the President at the capital of the United States, shows the law contemplates he shall reside here."[19]

Cockran tried to return the discussion to the pragmatic question at hand. If the railroads were to be forbidden from paying for a president's travel and if the government would not pick up the tab, then the president would no longer be able to travel "for the purpose of meeting the people and giving an account of his stewardship." The expenses of such travel "would be ruinous if paid out of his own pocket." Underwood denied this. The president after all had a handsome annual salary of $50,000, ten times the salary of a member of Congress. And all the president's living expenses, apart from his food and clothing, were paid for by the government. A president could easily afford to travel among the people, certainly more easily than other members of the government. Moreover, Underwood maintained, the president likely would not have to dip into his salary to cover the costs of traveling. For "where the President goes out to meet the people . . . he goes on invitation, and . . . people of that community who have invited him will be glad to furnish him with special trains and all other conveniences at their expense and not at his." Let those who invite the president to speak bear the costs of the president's journey.[20]

Next to weigh in was Iowa Republican Walter Smith, a former judge who would return to the federal bench in 1911. For Smith there was no question of travel expenses being an emolument or of the bill being unconstitutional. The president derived no profit from the appropriation since it only covered expenses. The proposed legislation recognized that although "the President is not under a legal obligation to travel, [he] is yet under a duty to travel and meet the people of the country; and the people want him to travel." To loud applause from the Republican side of the aisle, Smith declaimed that the people of the United States "want him to meet them and want to meet him, and they are prepared to pay his expenses for so doing."[21]

Smith's sentiments were seconded by a Democratic congressman from Kentucky, 35-year-old Joseph Sherley, who agreed that "the law defining the duties of the President makes it proper that he should leave Washington and travel among the people." In Sherley's view, presidential travel served the national interest and so should be paid for by the nation. "No President," Sherley declared, "can as well be informed as to the conditions of the country and as to the views of the people by any other method as by traveling among them, meeting them, and learning directly from their viewpoint." Pointing to Roosevelt's recently completed tour of the South, Sherley suggested that not only did the president's speeches have a positive effect on public support for railroad rate legislation, but his traveling also "did [the president] a tremendous amount of good." For it gave the president "a better appreciation of the people of the South, made him understand the actual conditions that confront us, and made him a better President for the whole people of the United States." For Sherley, it was obvious that the president "can not travel as an individual, because the time of the President of the United States is too important. He must have facilities to work as he travels. He must have a special train . . . and that expense ought not to be asked of the President of the United States out of his private purse." Instead the expense "ought to be furnished by the nation at large." Once again applause rang out in the House.[22]

Massachusetts Democrat John Sullivan joined Sherley and Cockran in bolting from their party's position. It "can not be a party question," Sullivan told the chamber. Traveling was an expense of the office just as much as maintenance of the White House. Congress, he pointed out, had already approved "$4,000 for improvements, $35,000 for repairs . . . , $6,000 for fuel, $9,000 for conservatory and greenhouses, $3,000 for repairs of greenhouses, $18,800 for lighting . . . , $20,000 for the contingent fund, $11,000 for the protection of the President, and $66,000 for his clerk hire." Appropriating an additional $25,000 for traveling was no more unconstitutional than were these other items of the budget. Such expenses were necessary "to keep up the dignity of the office." There was no point to "confining [the president] to any log cabin." To fulfill his duties the president must "go out over the United States and discuss questions and get in touch with every section of the country." Loud applause erupted again, followed by a call for the vote.[23]

By an almost three-to-one margin the House approved the bill. All but one of the sixty-six "no" votes were cast by Democrats, and virtually all of these were from the South. No representative from a state west of Texas voted against the measure. On this evidence it appeared the bill would sail through the Senate, particularly since legislators were now eager to put a close to the 59th Congress and escape the capital for the summer. But the bill ran into immediate difficulties when it was introduced on the Senate floor the following day.[24]

THE SENATE DEBATE

Rather than introduce the version that had passed the House, the Republican leadership in the Senate chose to introduce the version of the bill that had been rejected in the House on a point of order. This version not only authorized $25,000 in traveling expenses for the president but allowed the president to use the travel funds for "his attendants and invited guests traveling with him." As a practical matter, the difference mattered little since the House version allowed the president to spend the money at his discretion, but by explicitly including "invited guests" in the language of the bill the Senate Republicans invited more insistent objections.[25]

Among those who took vigorous exception to the bill was Mississippi Democrat Anselm McLaurin. The 58-year-old McLaurin, a former governor and staunch supporter of William Jennings Bryan, objected that the proposed bill violated the sacred American principle of equality before the law. The president, he argued, should not receive special treatment. Since the government did not pay the traveling expenses of ordinary citizens, it should not pay for the president to travel. Moreover, McLaurin could not see why a president needed to travel with attendants. The president, McLaurin insisted, was not "in any danger of harm from anybody." True, three of the last ten presidents had been assassinated, "but a great many other men have been assassinated who were not Presidents." Why didn't those people also deserve protection? Why should the president be set in a class all by himself?[26]

But what really riled McLaurin was the provision allowing the president to take along "invited guests." Who were these handpicked guests of the president? McLaurin suspected that the guests would be newspaper correspondents, selected by the president because they could be counted on to "give out to the press that which the President desires shall be given out and who will conceal that which he desires shall be concealed." By bestowing favors—a free pass—and indulging in favoritism—inviting some correspondents and excluding others—the president would be able to control or manipulate press coverage.

McLaurin was at pains to point out that his comments were aimed not at the current president but at any president; however, his protestations rang hollow. In 1906 Roosevelt was at the height of his popularity, and fear of Roosevelt's power over the press was widespread among Democrats. In January, South Carolina Democrat Ben "Pitchfork" Tillman had complained bitterly on the Senate floor that "the newspapers are the men who have made him what he is . . . the most Popular president the country has ever had." Roosevelt "never had the opportunity in all his journeyings and speeches to meet more than one in a thousand of his fellow-citizens," yet "through the . . . press . . . he has become puffed to such a degree that he 'strides the world like a colussus, and we smaller men . . . crawl around between his legs.'" Although Tillman and McLaurin supported Roosevelt's efforts to get a railroad rate bill, they were in no mood to help Roosevelt become still more popular by "gallivanting over the country."[27]

Senate Democrats were much freer than were House members about expressing their partisan concerns. Presidential travel, they worried openly, would degenerate into "an electioneering tour." Tillman asked whether the bill permitted the president "to use the money in going into States for campaign purposes." Or, Tillman continued sarcastically, did Congress intend it "merely as a donation . . . to let the President travel in any part of the country as a great statesman to enlighten all the people in a nonpartisan way?"[28]

Republicans did not have an easy answer to this query. No Republican was prepared to defend the bill on the grounds that the public should pay for a president to make partisan speeches. Instead Republicans argued that the president should be trusted not to use this money for "political purposes." Tillman and other Democrats were skeptical about the wisdom of leaving this to the discretion of the president. Some presidents might behave honorably, but could all presidents be trusted? Republicans persisted. They had faith that the people would never "elect from either party ... a President who would use this fund for political purposes or for the purpose of making a political campaign."[29]

Not all the questions were coming from the Democratic side of the aisle. Indeed one of the most vocal and persistent voices of opposition was that of the conservative North Dakota Republican Porter McCumber. McCumber disliked Roosevelt and loathed the progressive wing of his party. The progressives, McCumber felt, were overly reliant on executive leadership and were doing permanent damage to the principles and institutions of American government. "There has been too much disposition here," McCumber intoned, "to allow the will of the President to override the will of the Congress and to allow the President to think for Congress." If the president wished to communicate his views on an issue or bill, then "he should do so by message, as was contemplated by the ... makers of the Constitution."[30]

McCumber read into the record an article from the previous day's *Washington Post*, which insisted that "it is better that Congress pass a bad law as the result of its own free will and independent deliberation than to enact a good law at the dictation of the Executive." A bad law could be repealed, but "a wound [to] the independence of Congress makes an ulcer, and it might easily grow to be a cancer." According to the *Post*, the "plain truth" is that "Congress is flat on its back right now with more ulcers than Lazarus had sores." Congress had become "completely overshadowed" by the president.[31]

In McCumber's view, the proposed legislation would exacerbate the tendency to make the president the focal point of the nation's politics. Preserving the framers' original constitutional structure required a president who did not travel from one end of the country to the other, mobilizing public opinion and pressuring Congress to enact his agenda. At stake was not only the Constitution but the principles of democratic equality. For McCumber, the bill before the Senate exalted a "particular man" and thus raised the specter of monarchy. There were lots of qualified Americans who "would be equal to the position [of president and] who would be glad to ... pay their own traveling expenses ... without any retinue ... following [them]." By giving the president special treatment and enabling him to travel with a sycophantic entourage, the bill put the nation on "a course that has been adopted for hundreds of years in the old countries." McCumber saw the bill as symptomatic of "the gradual tendency of the American people ... to ape the manners [and] the customs ... of the monarchies of the old world." The United States, McCumber insisted, must reject "the trappings of royalty": the "great army of underlings" as well as "all their bangles, ... all their spangles, [and] all their ribbons." That required not only defeating this bill but scaling back the presidency so that it was no longer the focus of national attention.[32]

McCumber's fears were greeted with derision by many of his Republican colleagues. Indiana Republican James Hemenway mocked McCumber, from whose remarks "one would think there danger of the President of the United States purchasing royal robes, surrounding himself with royal attendants . . . if the appropriation is granted." For Hemenway the specter of monarchy was a phantom. The president traveled "in order that he may get out and see the people and shake hands with them and mix with them." Such travels were not an indicator of creeping royalism but just the reverse. "The Czar," Hemenway reminded his colleagues, "does not go out among his people. These royal personages of whom the Senator talks do not go out among the people." Traveling among the people was in the thoroughly democratic and American tradition of "shaking hands and getting together." The bill "merely tends to bring the people and the President together by giving the President a proper allowance for traveling expenses."[33]

Moreover, Hemenway argued, the bill promoted equality. If the president was not given a budget for traveling, then only a rich president would be able to travel. And if local communities had to pay for the president's travel, then only wealthy communities would be able to afford to invite the president. "Already," Hemenway observed, "the richer states and richer colleges invite the President to come, and they propose to pay his expenses, while the States far distant and the States that do not care to pay the expenses out of their treasuries . . . can not make these offers." By paying for travel expenses, the government would equalize access to the president.[34]

The opposition was unpersuaded. Even if there was no danger of the president wearing royal robes, there was a very real prospect of the president undermining democratic politics. The issue at hand was traveling expenses but the deeper question was the rise of the president as celebrity. McLaurin denied that the president needed to have newspaper correspondents accompany him. He granted that "a few curious people . . . may like to read, and a good many toadies may like to read what the President is doing, what time of morning he got up, what time of evening he retired, what he ate for breakfast and for dinner and for supper." But true democrats had no interest in this sort of thing. The "vast mass of the people regard the President as a human being. They do not care anything about the diet of the President or the drinking of the President, . . . nor do they think about the President, except that he shall perform the duties that they elected him to perform." The president was just a citizen who had been chosen to discharge temporarily the duties of the office; he should not be made into a celebrity.[35]

Republican defenders of the bill countered that the legislation reflected the people's desire to see the president. The people, Republicans insisted, wanted to know about their president. They wanted to read about the man who represented them and spoke for them. The president traveled not "as a matter of pleasure" but rather because it was "the desire of the people of the United States . . . to see him." The people, Hemenway reiterated, "are anxious to see him, and he goes, following the custom that has grown up now, with his train prepared, with a certain number of newspaper people, with provision for receiving the guests, the committees, the governors, the Senators or Members of Congress, the prominent citizens who go to meet the Presidential train." The people, he believed, "want to pay for it, and they are able to pay for it." It was absurd, added Wisconsin's John Coit Spooner, to imagine that the president, "elected by the people and the servant of the people, should remain a hermit confined to the White House, unless he were a man of fortune and able to travel at his own expense."[36]

Republicans insisted that presidential travel and speaking were essential to the functioning of American democracy. The defining feature of the American form of government, according to Iowa Republican Jonathan Dolliver, is "that everybody is concerned in its administration." One of the greatest challenges is "bringing to the mass of the people a real sense of the Government of the United States." A democratic people must understand how the government works if it is to choose wisely. By appearing among and speaking to the people, the president helped people to identify with and to understand "the administration of national affairs." Moreover, a "familiar intercourse" between people and president promoted a feeling of connection to the nation and "patriotism, in a larger sense than we are possibly aware of." Dolliver warned that "if anything were done to discourage" presidential travel "we would . . . do a very serious wrong to ourselves and especially to our children."[37]

Democrats, however, continued to dig in their heels. The debate spilled over into a second day with no sign that opposition was abating. Georgia Democrat Augustus Bacon had missed the first day of debate and now entered it with gusto. Bacon's objections largely echoed those that had been voiced the previous day: that the legislation was "exalting" the president above his fellow citizens and that it mimicked "the methods and practices of royalty." "Everything that savors of royal distinction, everything that smacks of the special privilege of official rank and class, is justly distasteful to our people." To those who argued that Congress had long approved appropriations for presidential carriages and horses, Bacon responded that he condemned that also. Bacon did not object to all presidential travel, but he insisted that such travel should be paid for by the president, just as George Washington had done. The larger issue was the "growing power of the Executive," which was subverting the original constitutional design that established the legislature and not the executive as "the principal department, the most influential department, the most powerful department."[38]

Tennessee's Edward Carmack reprised a theme that had been pressed forcefully in the House. No senator, insisted Carmack, had been able to demonstrate that the president needed to travel to perform his official duties. Congress was being asked to finance presidential travel so as to "give the people an opportunity to see him and to come in contact with [him]." But why, Carmack asked, should Congress pay "to give the people of the United States a free show"? The people might enjoy such a show but Congress had no more business giving the people such a show than they had providing the people with "roasted peanuts and pink lemonade."[39]

Equally immovable was the veteran senator John Tyler Morgan, who had represented Alabama since 1877. The 82-year-old Morgan wanted to know what was to prevent the president from using the money for frivolous purposes. Knowing Roosevelt's penchant for big game hunting, Morgan suggested that "there will be great hunt gotten up . . . to be conducted in the mountains and on the prairies of the West, and that the scions of royal blood from Europe would be invited over here as guests to see the performance." Morgan imagined that this great presidential hunt "would be attended . . . by retainers in velveteens, red or black or blue, in caps red, black, or white, feathered or otherwise made to fashion, trophies and fanfaronade." Morgan wondered, too, why $25,000 shouldn't be handed out to each of the "overworked and overtaxed" Supreme Court justices. Each of the justices "do more work than [the president] does." Indeed many of these "noble men have gone to early graves" because of their prodigious labors. Morgan asked his colleagues to imagine if these hard-working justices had been given $25,000 a year "to go out with their friends and banquet and attend those great hunts or go to the watering places." Surely "many of them would be living yet."[40]

Morgan assured his colleagues that he did "not wish to be unkind" and that he was "treating this subject seriously." Indeed, behind the humorous barbs lay a serious concern, one that had already been expressed by several Democratic colleagues. What was to stop the president from using the money for partisan purposes? The bill, Morgan feared, invited state and local parties to extend invitations to the president "saying, 'Congress pays your expenses; come to us; we need you; we want you; come to us, enlighten our people; bring your spellbinders along, and in the next Congressional election in November we will roll up a handsome majority for you and your party, or in the next Presidential election we will give you a third term.'"[41]

These fears were not fanciful. Democratic arguments against a presidential traveling allowance were often framed in narrowly constitutional terms—specifically whether traveling expenses constituted an emolument—but the partisan and political implications were never far from Democratic minds. They remembered that Roosevelt had toured the South in October of the previous year with the aim, according to Roosevelt's biographer Edmund Morris, of "generat[ing] favorable publicity before the November elections" and of trying out "some of his centralized rhetoric" in the heartland of states' rights. Many southern Democrats supported Roosevelt's push for railroad rate legislation but they were also concerned that the popular Roosevelt could help the Republicans make political inroads in the solidly Democratic South.[42]

The mix of partisan and constitutional concerns proved a powerful stumbling block. Even several Republicans expressed doubts about the wisdom or constitutionality of appropriating money for the traveling expenses of the president's "invited guests." The protracted and often tedious debate was holding up the rest of the budget, and senators were anxious to finish up their work and return home for the summer. Morgan, however, vowed to keep the Senate in session. "The heat of July," he declared, "does not frighten me." To move the debate forward, the Republican leadership withdrew the bill and substituted the version that had been passed earlier by the House. In exchange, Democrats promised to allow the bill to come to a vote.[43]

The compromise did not mollify everyone. Indeed no Senate Democrat voted in favor of the bill, though a number of Democrats who had spoken against the original version, including Morgan and Tillman, opted not to cast a vote against the bill. The new bill certainly helped to alleviate Republican concerns; McCumber ended up as the only Republican to vote against the measure. As a practical matter, however, there was little or no difference between the two versions of the bill. Both left it to the discretion of the president how to spend the $25,000, and neither required the president to give any accounting of his expenses. McLaurin tried to amend the measure by explicitly forbidding the president from spending the money on anything but the travel expenses of himself, his family, his protective detail, and those "officials necessary for the President's transaction of official business of the Government," but the amendment was easily defeated on a voice vote. Republicans were content to trust their president; Democrats understandably were not.[44]

TAFT'S TRAVELS

During the 1906 debate, a number of legislators suggested that it would be better to give the president a $25,000 pay raise than a $25,000 traveling allowance. In the short run that option was a nonstarter, since the Constitution explicitly forbid Congress from raising or lowering the salary of a sitting president. However, the end of Roosevelt's tenure provided Congress with an opportunity to revisit the issue because it was now free to adjust the salary of the incoming president, William Howard Taft. The Senate proposed to fix the president's income at $100,000, with the understanding that "transportation expenses now otherwise provided for by law" would be paid for out of the president's salary. The House, however, was skeptical that the president needed such a princely sum.[45]

House Democrats noted that Roosevelt had only used $9,000 of his $25,000 traveling allowance. Surely, then, the president did not need $100,000, especially since the government already provided for virtually all of a president's expenses apart from food and clothing. Democrats argued that the amount spent on the president, which by one estimate totaled about $300,000, was already excessive. They worried that these expenditures were creating "practically regal conditions in the White House, imitating the ceremony, imitating the extravagance, imitating the luxury of the courts of the Old World." A monarchy needed such extravagance because "stars, garters, titles and diadems are the secret of its power and the evidence of its glory," but a republic rested upon individual virtue. Presidents should be measured "not by the cost and tinsel of their equipages, but by the nobility of their character and the excellence of their administration." Propelled by such rhetoric, the House decided that $75,000, including travel expenses, would be sufficient for a republican president.[46]

The Senate acquiesced in the House's decision to fix the salary at $75,000 but dropped the provision that a president's traveling expenses should be paid out of this amount. The House accepted this compromise, though many Democrats were deeply unhappy with the change and promised to fight any effort to appropriate additional money for travel expenses. True to their word, House Democrats that spring defeated an appropriation for presidential travel expenses, setting up a conflict with the White House. If Congress would not appropriate money for presidential travel, Taft announced that he would not be able to accept an invitation to tour the southern and western states in the late summer and early fall. Such a trip would be "entirely too expensive to be paid for out of [the president's] own pocket." In a special summer session, Congress was forced to reverse itself and approved a $25,000 appropriation to cover Taft's travel expenses.[47]

The following spring, Congress was again compelled to confront the issue of presidential travel. Taft, it turned out, had spent about $5,000 more than the $25,000 allotted to him for the fiscal year, and he was scheduled to do additional traveling before the fiscal year closed at the end of June. The president's supporters proposed to remedy the shortfall by appropriating an additional $25,000 to cover the president's expenses, but Democrats immediately objected because this additional appropriation would exceed the $25,000 allowed by the 1906 statute.[48]

Animating Democratic objections was the strong feeling that Taft's traveling and speaking were being employed for partisan purposes. Arkansas Democrat Robert Macon, who was the first to object to the additional appropriation, emphasized that "the money appropriated to defray the President's traveling expenses is being used to enable him to address partisan political conventions as well as colleges." As evidence, he pointed to a recent newspaper notice that Taft had accepted an invitation to speak at the end of June to the National Republican League at Carnegie Hall in New York City. That speech, according to the newspaper account, was to "sound the keynote of the league's campaign for the fall elections." Macon reminded his colleagues that they had been assured by the other side that the travel expense account would not be used to enable the president "to address political conventions or gatherings of any kind." Why should the American people pick up the tab for an activity that was intended to advantage one party over another? Macon thundered that he would not support an appropriation that would "enable the President to run around the country and disseminate partisan political views." The president, he insisted, "ought to stay at his post of duty during the session of Congress, just as we ought to stay at ours."[49]

James Tawney, chairman of the House Appropriations Committee, tried to make the administration's case. "No President," Tawney declared to great applause from his fellow Republicans, "ever enjoyed meeting the people more than does the present occupant of the office of Chief Executive." The president had exceeded his allotted $25,000 budget because he had accepted invitations from members of Congress, governors, and civic organizations. These invitations, Tawney emphasized, had come from both Republicans and Democrats. Nine Democratic governors, eleven Democratic senators, and twenty-five Democratic representatives—the great majority of whom were from the South—were among those who had invited the president to visit their states and districts. The president had dutifully complied and was now being punished for his generosity. "Is that southern hospitality?" Tawney taunted his Democratic colleagues. "Is there a meaner man ... than the man who will invite another man to accept his hospitality, and when that man accepts the invitation and becomes the guest of that man, then turns around and kicks him because he accepted the invitation, criticizing him and in effect even charging him for his board?"[50]

Southern Democrats were not amused. An angry Charles Bartlett, a representative from Georgia, rose to challenge Tawney's "sneering attack" on southern hospitality. Bartlett challenged Tawney to name "any instance where [the president] had been charged board." Tawney sidestepped the question, opting instead to reveal that Bartlett was among those Democrats who had traveled as "the guest of the President on this very trip." Bartlett became incensed, insisting that he had paid for his meals and board as well as for the railway fare for the 58 miles he accompanied the president. Tawney did not challenge the veracity of Bartlett's account, but outed two other Democratic representatives—Colorado's Edward Taylor and Thomas Hardwick of Georgia—who had traveled as the president's guests on his tour of the South and West.[51]

Now it was Hardwick's turn to react with outrage at Tawney's charge. Hardwick demanded to know where Tawney had received the list of presidential guests. Following Tawney's admission that the names had come from the president's secretary, Hardwick expressed his dismay that the White House had furnished "ammunition" to embarrass the Democrats. He had accompanied the president for "56 miles in the middle of the day ... through my own district, at [the president's] request, ... so that I might introduce him to an audience in my own district, and thereby render him courtesy and honor as President of the United States." Tawney had violated "every rule of good manners and all canons of courtesy" in suggesting that because members had been "social guests" of the president they were obligated to vote with the president. Moreover, Hardwick, like Bartlett, had paid his own fare. They had not added one cent to the expense of the president's travels. Certainly there were no grounds for impugning the hospitality of the South. "In the South," Hardwick declared proudly, "we entertained [the president] like a lord." And the president "paid for nothing in the South, certainly for nothing in the State of Georgia."[52]

Tawney tried to aid his cause by reading into the record several recent editorials from Georgia newspapers. The *Savannah Press*, for instance, urged Congress to cover the extra expenses the president had incurred in his tour of the South and West. For the *Press* it was clear that "it is in the interest of the South that the President should get out of Washington," and Taft was to be commended for having "done more traveling in the South than all the other Presidents since the civil war." The president should not be "a prisoner in the White House grounds," certainly not when Congress was out of session. Congressmen who voted themselves a generous mileage allowance for their own travels were "not in a position to scrutinize too closely the President's railroad expenses." "Let them ride and let ride," was the *Press*'s advice.[53]

Democrats, however, were in no mood to let the matter drop. New York Democrat John Fitzgerald, who in 1906 had supported giving the president $25,000 for traveling expenses, detailed the Democratic grievances. First, Democrats had supported the increase in the president's salary to $75,000 on the understanding that it would cover traveling expenses. From their point of view, the decision taken the previous summer to vote Taft a $25,000 traveling allowance gave Taft the $100,000 salary that the House had previously rejected. For the president now to ask for even more money was intolerable. Second, the additional appropriation was objectionable because, like the original appropriation, it depended upon the president's certificate alone, without being audited or examined by any other government official. The people had a right to know how their money was spent. They deserved a detailed accounting of how the president had exceeded his budget. Finally, the president's "wanderlust" had gone well beyond the boundaries envisioned by those who originally authorized the appropriation. "No one ever imagined," Fitzgerald maintained, "that the President would spend most of the time when Congress was in session away from Washington." They had been promised, moreover, that such travel would not be used "for the purpose of advocating the election of members of his own party and to make political speeches." It particularly angered Fitzgerald that Taft had come to New York City on Lincoln's birthday—while Congress was still in session—to deliver "a political speech" in which the president defended his party and administration and "ridicule[d] his political opponents." The public, Fitzgerald concluded, should not be forced to foot the bill for the president's partisanship.[54]

The partisan rancor brought Speaker of the House Joseph Cannon into the debate. Cannon tried to redirect the attention of the House to the larger question of the importance of presidential travel. The United States was a nation of 90,000,000 people in an immense territory "reaching 3,500 miles from one ocean to the other." It possessed "the greatest and most prosperous Government on earth," and its president had "more power and more . . . responsibility than any other executive on earth" save the czar of Russia. Unlike in Russia, however, sovereignty in the United States resided in the people, and it was in the interest of "this great people . . . to meet the man who for the time being exercises their power as the Executive." It was equally important that the president have an acquaintance with the diversity of people across this vast nation. Although "not expressly stated in the Constitution," traveling was nonetheless among those duties that were "absolutely necessary for him to perform as Chief Executive." A president should not have to "run into debt" to discharge "the duties of the office." Cannon allowed that each member of Congress "must perform [his] duty as it is given to [him] to see it," but he cautioned members not to forget the views of the public. And he was willing to risk his "soul's salvation that in the State of Georgia or in the State of Missouri, or any other state in the Union you can not find one man, woman, or child out of ten" who would refuse the president the extra appropriation to cover his traveling expenses.[55]

Cannon's cautionary words failed to budge the opposition. Tennessee's Finis Garrett opined that Republicans "fail to understand the real objection that lies on this side of the House." Taft was an "amiable" and "distinguished" man for whom members had great "personal affection." As a result, many members found it "extremely embarrassing" to criticize him. But Democrats felt aggrieved that the president had used "part of this fund . . . to pay his expenses while making partisan political speeches." By Garrett's count, "at least three times upon these public trips the President of the whole people has made purely partisan speeches, assailing the capacity of one of the great political parties of this country." If the president's traveling expenses are to be paid by "taxation upon the whole people" then "the proprieties demand that the President of the whole people . . . should not enter the domain of partisan politics, but should prove himself to be President of the whole people and of the whole country."[56]

Ohio Republican Joseph Keifer agreed that Garrett had "got to the kernel of the objection." But the 74-year-old Keifer questioned whether the Democrats' expectations about presidential behavior were realistic. Should a president who is "elected upon a platform well understood by all of the people" be barred on his travels from saying what he believes? Should he only "be allowed to make . . . speeches in which there is [nothing] but small talk?" Why should a president who believes in "great principles . . . go out and talk little flattering peanut politics all over the West and South just to please and tickle the ear of those who may hear him?" Taft certainly did not do that.

He tried to enlighten the people who turned out to hear him. He . . . uttered the principles upon which he stood and was elected President of the United States. Those who invited him did not expect anything less from him. The people away down in Mississippi, in the Mississippi Valley, or in Texas, or wherever he went, or even in Georgia, knew when he came that he was going to uphold the flag of his party and speak for the great principles that he had been elected upon.

There was nothing improper, Keifer insisted, about the president speaking frankly with the people about his political principles and policies.[57]

Tennessee Democrat Thetus Sims seized on the political impasse to suggest that Congress reconsider its ban on free passes. The law was intended "to prevent the bad influence of the free pass upon public officials as a class." But why apply it to the president? Did anybody seriously believe that allowing the president to ride free enabled the railroads to "exercise a baneful influence" on the president? There had never been a president, nor was there ever likely to be one, "who would be affected by a free pass from here to Beverly, Mass., or to Nashville, Tenn., or to any other city, when he is going as the guest of those cities." When the president visited Nashville or Memphis or Chattanooga, the railroad companies profited from "the fares paid by people who come to these gatherings to greet the President." Since the railroad companies made money on presidential visits, it was reasonable to ask them to pay for the president's fare.[58]

Even if Congress did not have the courage to repeal its ban on free passes for the president, there was no need to tax the people of the entire nation to pay for a visit that benefited a particular locale or party. According to Sims, "There never was a time when people of those cities [who invited the president] would not gladly pay all his expenses." If the president was to visit Chicago, let the people of Chicago pay for the president's room and board. If local Republicans invited the president, let him travel as their guest and at their expense. Sims asked, "Why tax all of the people to benefit, necessarily, a very inconsiderable number?" Eliminate public financing of presidential travel, Sims argued, and the problem that so vexed the House would disappear. Those who wanted to hear the president would pay, and those who chose not to invite the president would not have to pay.[59]

There was a logic to Sims's position, but it was the logic of a past era. Nobody seemed to take his proposal seriously. Macon, however, was very serious about his objection to the additional appropriation. The law allowed Congress to appropriate up to $25,000 per year to cover travel expenses, and Congress had dutifully done that. The law did not, however, permit Congress to appropriate additional monies for presidential travel for the current fiscal year, no matter how much the president might need that additional money. After Macon's objection was sustained by the chair, the additional appropriation appeared dead and buried.[60]

The congressional action drew an immediate response from the White House. In a public letter to Tawney, Taft indicated he was "deeply grieved" over the turn that the debate had taken. Taft chastised Tawney for calling into question the hospitality of the South and for intimating that representatives who accepted Taft's invitation to travel with him should not vote against the appropriation. Those representatives who had traveled with him on the train, Taft clarified, "were not receiving my hospitality—they were only making a little more elaborate the cordial welcome they as Representatives of their districts wished to give." But Taft also used the letter to remind the nation of the administration's case for the additional appropriation. It was "a legitimate argument in favor of such an appropriation," Taft explained, "that Congressmen and many others press acceptance of invitations to visit their sections and districts." The frequency and urgency of these invitations showed that the people felt "that one of the duties of the President is to visit the people in their homes."[61]

The following day's news carried reports of a telegram sent to the president and the Speaker of the House from "the commercial bodies of Augusta, Georgia," including the Chamber of Commerce and the Merchants and Manufacturers' Association. The telegram declared that Augusta "stands indignant and mortified" that "certain Democratic Representatives" had opposed the appropriation. The telegram was a clear slap at Bartlett and especially Hardwick, whose tenth district included Augusta. The business groups of Augusta pledged "to contribute $5,000 to supply any deficiency in the appropriation for the fiscal year 1910." Taft thanked them for their offer but indicated that he could not accept the money. The press reported that Taft's "intention is to pay from his own pocket his traveling expenses until July 1, when the 1911 appropriation will become available."[62]

Public sympathy appeared to be running strongly in favor of the president, and House members scrambled to get on the right side of the issue. Hardwick and Bartlett explained that they would not have opposed the measure but for Tawney's "unfair and unjust" attack on southern hospitality. The Senate passed a compromise that allowed the president to get compensated for his travel expenses and Democratic House members to save face. The president would receive $25,000 for the fiscal year of 1911 but could use some of that money to cover the cost overrun of 1910. House Democrats signaled they would not oppose such a measure, and the plan passed without objection.[63]

The controversy did seem to have a chastening effect on Taft, however, at least for a short while. When he traveled to Maine the following month, he carefully refrained from partisan attacks. To an audience in Rockland, Maine, he explained that "traveling as I am, as President of the United States, I have no right to be other than President of the whole people and to stand only on the platform of patriotism, love of country, and prosperity of all." He confessed, however, that it wasn't always easy for a president to stay away from political or partisan talk. "When you are thinking politics and having a great deal to do with politics," he lamented, "it is a little difficult . . . to make fluent remarks without running up against politics."[64]

Taft's conciliatory words notwithstanding, the president had prevailed. The principle that taxpayers rather than private interests should pay for presidential travel became widely accepted. Political debate over that question largely ceased, though the question of whether taxpayers should pay for avowedly partisan traveling and campaigning would continue to vex American politics. Congress occasionally tinkered with the travel appropriation. In 1922, for instance, the statute was modified to include entertainment as well as travel expenses, and in 1932 Congress reduced the appropriation to $20,000 as a largely symbolic austerity measure. Congress increased the allowable appropriation to $30,000 in 1939, and during the Truman presidency upped it to $40,000. It remained fixed at $40,000 until 1978 when Congress boosted it to its current level of $100,000.[65]

Once a point of fierce partisan and ideological debate, this line item of the budget has become essentially obsolete. One hundred thousand dollars does not even begin to cover the traveling expenses of a modern president. When President Bill Clinton traveled to six African nations for twelve days in 1998, for instance, it cost an estimated $43 million, not including the costs of Secret Service protection (which is classified information and therefore unavailable). A five-day presidential trip to Chile the same year cost over $10 million. The per-hour flying costs aboard Air Force One in the first decade of the twenty-first century are well over $50,000, which means that if George W. Bush had to pay for his traveling expenses out of his appropriated allowance he would use up that amount after less than two hours in the air. So how does a modern president pay for his travel?[66]

The short answer is by having the military pay for it. Eighty eight percent of the expense of Clinton's trip to Africa, for instance, was covered by the Department of Defense. Having the military absorb the cost of presidential travel is not new. Even in the nineteenth century, the military, particularly the navy, often picked up much of the tab for presidential traveling.

Beginning in the 1870s, presidents regularly used a government-owned yacht to travel on the Potomac River and in the Chesapeake Bay. So routine was this usage that it became known as "the presidential yacht," even though it belonged to the navy. During Theodore Roosevelt's term, there were two presidential yachts: the 273-foot *Mayflower* and the smaller *Sylph*, both of which were moored at the naval yard in the capital. The presidential yacht remained a Washington institution for a hundred years, until Jimmy Carter sold the *Sequoia* because he believed the yacht too regal for the image of the presidency he wished to project.

When Roosevelt traveled to Panama in 1906, he traveled on a naval battleship, and was accompanied by an escort of two other battleships. And when President Woodrow Wilson went to Europe in 1918, much the same arrangement was made, though the escort included not only a large battleship but a flotilla of smaller warships. The cost of both of these journeys across the sea was absorbed by the navy.

Even James Monroe, on his early tours of the United States, used naval vessels to traverse segments of his journey. Unlike the post office, the navy did not ask the president for reimbursement.[67]

However, in the nineteenth century the percentage of travel costs absorbed by the navy and army was relatively small. Most nineteenth-century presidential travel did not involve transportation owned by the military. Early nineteenth-century presidents usually used horse and carriage, and generally these were the private possession of the president. Railroads were private corporations. Only when airplanes eclipsed railroads as the preferred mode of long distance domestic presidential travel in the mid-twentieth century were presidents able to travel predominantly on transportation owned and operated by the military. Air Force One, of course, is maintained by the air force just as Marine One, the president's helicopter, is maintained by the Marine Corps. Using military vehicles rather than privately owned railroads helped presidents to hide the real costs of their travel.

Although the military absorbs the bulk of a contemporary president's travel costs, other federal agencies and departments also pick up part of the tab. In the case of Clinton's Africa trip, the Department of State picked up about 8.5 percent of the cost. Other agencies billed for a portion of the cost included the U.S. Information Agency, the Department of Commerce, the Department of Labor, and the Department of Transportation. Only three-tenths of 1 percent of the trip's costs—about $122,000—were covered by the Executive Office of the President.[68]

Domestic travel, too, sometimes gets billed to federal agencies and departments. This practice became particularly common during George W. Bush's presidency. For instance, the Department of Health and Human Services (HHS) paid the White House over half a million dollars in 2001 and 2002 to cover expenses incurred by President Bush during trips in which he promoted administration policies. The Bush White House deflected criticism of such practices by pointing out that the Clinton administration had done the same thing, but an audit by the General Accounting Office (GAO) showed that the Bush administration's practice far outstripped anything the Clinton administration had done. According to the GAO study, HHS was only billed for about $100,000 in traveling expenses associated with Clinton's travel over the final three and a half years of his presidency.[69]

Although the Bush administration has been more aggressive (or creative) in its billing practices than previous administrations, the practice of billing others to cover the costs of presidential travel is at least a century old. As soon as the railroads stopped handing out free passes for presidential travel, the president was forced to confront the yawning gap between the real costs of presidential travel and the actual amount budgeted by Congress. Even in Taft's time the $25,000 budgeted for presidential travel was not nearly enough to cover the expense of hiring a special train for a cross-country rail trip. By some estimates such a trip cost over $200,000. To make ends meet, Taft divided the cost of the special train by the number of people traveling on the train, and each individual passenger was then charged the same amount. Taft's 1911 trip to the West Coast, for instance, worked out to $1,500 per person. Each reporter had to pay $1,500 to accompany the president, the Secret Service was required to come up with $4,500 to cover its three agents, and the military had to contribute $1,500 for each army officer aboard the train.[70]

If such practices were necessary in Taft's time, the skyrocketing costs of presidential travel have made them indispensable today. The presidential travels of Bill Clinton and George W. Bush have each cost well over a billion dollars. Why is it so expensive for a president to travel today? How could a twelve-day presidential sojourn to Africa cost taxpayers $43 million? The GAO estimated that transporting the president to Africa aboard Air Force One, at an hourly rate of $34,400, cost an estimated $1.3 million. What accounts, then, for the remaining $42 million?[71]

Part of the answer lies in the large number of people traveling with or in support of the president. When Theodore Roosevelt went to Panama in 1906 he was accompanied by his wife, a naval doctor, a junior White House staffer, a military officer, and a small Secret Service detail. In contrast, when Clinton went to Africa, the official delegation totaled 1,300 people (not counting Secret Service agents), including over 200 individuals from the Executive Office of the President, as well as 900 military personnel whose travel expenses were paid by the Department of Defense.[72]

Modern presidential travel is also expensive because for every trip the president makes there may be several advance trips by administration officials. Foreign travel generally begins with a preliminary "site survey" followed by a "preadvance visit" in which officials make plans for the events and select the locations of the events. There is also typically an official advance trip, usually a week before the president's visit. During this final advance trip, officials ensure that the president has the required equipment and they iron out any logistical problems that may remain. Between January 1997 and March 2000, Clinton made twenty-seven foreign trips, the First Lady twenty, and the vice president eight. But during that same period there were over one hundred "White House-directed" foreign trips, most of which were advance trips ahead of the president's travel. In preparation for Clinton's visit to the African continent, ten separate advance teams journeyed there.[73]

Although advance trips and large delegations explain much of the high cost of presidential travel, they are not the major reason. The 104 White House–directed foreign trips between January 1997 and March 2000 cost a little over $20 million, and the 28 trips by the First Lady and Vice President totaled about $25 million. The 27 presidential trips during this time period, in contrast, cost almost $250 million. If it's not the cost of flying Air Force One and not the advance teams and large delegations, then what accounts for the extraordinarily high cost of modern presidential travel?[74]

The answer is the transportation of vehicles and equipment and the deployment of military troops. In 1999, the Department of Defense spent over 85 percent of the $37.7 million it expended on Clinton's trip to Africa on the transportation of equipment and troops from the United States and Europe. Included in the cost of the airlift were the transporting of thirteen military helicopters, the establishment of maintenance support teams and medical evacuation units, as well as nearly 110 aerial refueling missions.[75]

Clinton's brief trip to Chile in April 1999 was less expensive, but still required twenty-four airlifts of vehicles and other equipment, at a cost of nearly $7 million, or about two-thirds of the total cost of the trip. The same pattern is evident in Clinton's trip to China at the end of June. The transportation of troops, equipment, and vehicles—including a fleet of helicopters that was never used—cost the Department of Defense over $12 million, which was again two-thirds of the total cost of the trip.[76]

Domestic travel is logistically less complex than foreign travel, but the costs of transporting the president within the United States are still substantial, particularly because the president spends much more time traveling domestically than he does traveling abroad. Few presidents enjoyed foreign travel more than George H. W. Bush, yet he spent less than one month a year in international travel and close to three months a year traveling domestically. Clinton traveled abroad more than any other president, spending more than 230 days in foreign travel, yet that figure pales behind the roughly 700 days he spent traveling within the United States.[77]

Much of a president's hectic domestic traveling schedule is fueled by his need to raise money, particularly for his own reelection effort but also for the campaigns of congressional and state level candidates. Since federal regulations forbid "campaign activity" from being paid for by the government, one might think that this type of travel would not be added to the taxpayers' tab. But one would be wrong. Despite the law's seemingly sharp distinction between campaign- and non-campaign-related travel (campaign travel, according to the Federal Election Commission [FEC], "includes soliciting, making, or accepting contributions, and expressly advocating the election or defeat of the candidate"), the amount that the government is reimbursed for the president's campaign-related travel is relatively small. One study estimated that the government was reimbursed for only about 2 percent of the flight costs associated with the 46 campaign-related trips taken by President George W. Bush in 2002. The Bush administration did not break the law but instead, like previous presidencies, took advantage of the law to bill taxpayers for much of the administration's campaign-related travel.[78]

When campaigning, the president is not required to pay the actual costs of flying Air Force One. Instead the FEC requires that any "campaign traveler"—including the president—reimburse the government for what it would have cost that person to fly first class on a commercial airline. Moreover, the law does not require that the campaign reimburse the government for the costs of the cargo planes that transport the presidential motorcade and helicopters. And, of course, none of the security costs need to be reimbursed. Nor does the campaign pick up the costs for travelers aboard Air Force One who are not deemed by the White House to be connected to the campaign. The travel of the president's doctors and the flight stewards, for instance, is never considered campaign-related. The White House, moreover, has substantial discretion in deciding how to count the travel of White House aides. For instance, when President George W. Bush visited Louisville, Kentucky, in February 2004 for a fund-raising event that netted over $1 million for Bush's reelection campaign, the White House designated only two of the staffers accompanying the president as campaign travelers. To take another example, a June 2004 fund-raising trip by the president to Spokane, Washington, netted around $1 million for the campaign of Republican House member George Nethercutt, yet only three staffers aboard the plane were considered campaign-related travelers. The Nethercutt campaign was billed $10,000 ($2,000 per political traveler: the president, Nethercutt, and three political aides) for a flight that cost taxpayers roughly $500,000.[79]

Federal election rules require that if a trip is "entirely campaign-related" then the costs associated with the trip must be counted as a campaign expense, but the rules also permit some costs to be shared if the trip has purposes that are not campaign-related. So if a presidential trip includes both a campaign event and a noncampaign event (that is, an event in which money is not being raised and there is not an explicit appeal to vote for a particular candidate) then some of the costs associated with the trip can be split between the campaign treasury and the government treasury.[80] The Bush White House took full advantage of this provision in 2004 by combining scores of fund-raising events with official events. So, for instance, when the president went to Louisville in February for a mid-day fund-raiser he first stopped by a local plastic pipe company to participate in what the White House billed as a "conversation on the economy." That "conversation" enabled the Bush campaign to reduce significantly the amount it had to pay in reimbursements.[81]

When its practice of pairing a campaign event with a "policy event" attracted criticism, the Bush administration insisted that the policy events were "scheduled first, and . . . the fundraisers added" later. But more often, as other White House officials conceded, "fundraising plans drove the schedules." The policy event was typically added only after the fund-raising event had been arranged. Adding a public event to the travel itinerary has the advantage not only of defraying some on-the-ground costs but also of providing the press a story line that focuses on the president as policy-maker rather than the president as fund-raiser. Better to have the media depict the president having a conversation with American workers about pressing economic issues than to show the president trolling for money at a $1,000-a-plate dinner at an exclusive hotel. Moreover, fund-raisers are typically private affairs, whereas the carefully staged public events provide the kind of appealing photo opportunities that every White House craves.[82]

Not all events are easily categorized as either campaign-related travel or non-campaign-related travel. In June 1980, for instance, feeling the heat from a stiff primary challenge by Senator Edward Kennedy, President Jimmy Carter traveled to Indiana to visit a hospitalized African American leader who had been shot. The president's visit was not classified as campaign-related, but it clearly had political overtones since voters in eight states, including several key states with large African American populations, were only two days away from going to the polls. The following month Carter flew to Detroit, where Republicans were preparing to hold their national nominating convention, and announced a plan to help struggling automakers. In other speeches to the National Education Association in California and the National Association for the Advancement of Colored People, Carter trumpeted his administration's accomplishments and issued "veiled warnings" about what would happen if the Republicans won the White House. Each of these events, though saturated with electoral ramifications, were designated by the White House as official, nonpolitical events and thus paid for entirely by the government.[83]

Complaints about taxpayer monies subsidizing presidential campaigning have been commonplace ever since the government got into the business of financing presidential travel in the early twentieth century. Just as Democrats cried foul at Taft's taxpayer-financed partisan travels, so Republicans howled with justifiable outrage when Truman embarked on an ostensibly "nonpolitical" cross-country railroad tour in June 1948, shortly before the Democratic National Convention was scheduled to meet to anoint him as the party's presidential nominee. Had the White House designated the trip as "political," the *New York Times* reported, the expense of the trip would have been "transferred . . . to the Democratic National Committee, whose treasury is at low ebb." In addition, "radio and television stations en route [would have been required] to give opponents of the President equal time for each of many local appearances he [made] on the air waves." The Truman administration justified the designation of the trip as "nonpolitical" on the grounds that "none of the sponsors for the President's scheduled appearances [were] political organizations," but the designation was an obvious fiction. In reality, as Truman's aide Charles Murphy later admitted, the trip—which Truman punctuated with harsh condemnations of the Republican-controlled Congress—was "a practice trip or shakedown cruise" for the fall campaign. From the start, Truman made few efforts to disguise the trip's partisan aims. Indeed on the first day of the tour, at an early morning stop in Crestline, Ohio, Truman "laughingly" described his trip as "nonpartisan, bipartisan," drawing loud guffaws from the friendly crowd. The next day the *Times* reported: "It is the belief aboard the Truman special that the fiction of a nonpolitical tour may be considered ended." But the legal fiction remained, and the administration, despite Republican protests, made the entire trip at government expense.[84]

Presidents today are perhaps less brazen than Truman was in 1948, but presidential political travel is far more heavily subsidized today than it was in Truman's day. Prior to the 1970s, campaigns and political parties were required to reimburse the government for the actual cost of flying Air Force One when the president used it to campaign. The Pentagon, for instance, billed the Democratic National Committee for Lyndon Johnson's 1964 campaign-related travel using the actual flight costs of Air Force One, which they estimated at $2,350 an hour. The air force even added a 5 percent tax, leaving the DNC with a $150,000 bill. According to newspaper reports, the DNC "paid the bill most unhappily."[85]

This reimbursement policy created an incentive for presidents to look for ways to save their party money. In June 1964, President Johnson flew to a party fund-raiser in Detroit aboard a ten-passenger Jetstar, which cost about $500 an hour to operate, and ordered that the backup plane be left behind. The trip reportedly annoyed high-level aides, who worried that the smaller plane did not have the kind of communications equipment that the president might require in case of an emergency. In September, however, Johnson again flew to Detroit for a campaign visit aboard a small Jetstar, and again he caught public flak, this time because there was no room aboard the plane for the president's doctor or for the military officer charged with carrying the top secret codes needed in case of a nuclear attack. Both men were required to travel on a separate plane. Johnson's cost-cutting measures struck many observers as decidedly unwise.[86]

In the mid-1970s, FEC rules were amended so that presidents would not be tempted to do what Johnson had done. In the fall of 1975, the Ford administration worked out a formula with the FEC whereby the flight costs of Air Force One were divided by the number of people (including flights stewards and military personnel) traveling on the plane. Each political traveler was charged a pro rata fee that was then reimbursed by the Ford campaign. During the Carter administration, the rules were changed again so that the president and any other political travelers aboard Air Force One reimbursed the government for the equivalent of a first-class commercial ticket. Michael Berman, who had advocated for the change in reimbursement rates as an insider in the Carter administration, explained that the change was intended to "reimburse the government the least amount and still be within the law." Berman had cause to regret the change in 1984 when he tried to help Walter Mondale unseat Ronald Reagan. Mondale's failed campaign prompted Berman to wonder whether the rules had shifted too far in favor of the president. "There's no sense in penalizing an incumbent president by charging so much it keeps him in the White House," Berman conceded. But perhaps, he wondered, "there ought to be some way to create a level playing field," perhaps by billing the White House at the charter rate that a challenger often had to pay.[87]

Although the change in the way presidential campaign travel was reimbursed had been a boon to the Carter administration, the gap between the costs of operating Air Force One and the reimbursement charge for campaign trips was still relatively modest by today's standards. Costs on Air Force One in the 1960s and 1970s generally ranged between $1,000 and $2,500 an hour. In the first year of Carter's presidency, the cost was estimated to be $2,337 an hour. Increasing fuel prices contributed to a steep increase in flight costs in the late 1970s but at the end of the Reagan administration flight costs for Air Force One were still estimated to be only about $8,000 an hour. The per-hour flight cost of Air Force One soared dramatically, however, after the acquisition of a new presidential aircraft in 1990. Overnight, the per-hour flight cost climbed to $40,000. As the gap between what it cost to operate Air Force One and the amount paid in reimbursements for campaign travel widened, the size of the taxpayer subsidy for presidential campaigning ballooned.[88]

The massive taxpayer subsidy for the increasingly frequent campaign activities of incumbent presidents has invited sharp criticism in recent years. In 1998, the Republican-controlled House of Representatives even passed a bill requiring that a campaign committee or political party reimburse the government for the actual costs of Air Force One whenever the president, vice president, or head of an executive department uses the plane to attend a fund-raising event. Those who oppose taxpayer subsidies for a president's campaign-related travel contend that they give the president an unfair advantage. For not only does the president benefit from ostensibly official travel that is clearly calculated to advance his candidacy, but he also pays only a minuscule fraction of the costs associated with political or campaign-related travel. In contrast, all of a challenger's travel is typically campaign-related and must be reported as a campaign expenditure.[89]

Those who oppose efforts to end or reduce the taxpayer subsidy for presidential travel argue that it is unfair to bill the president for costs he can't avoid. The need for security and secure communications, they point out, means that the president does not have the option to find a cheap flight on a commercial airline, ground his backup plane, or dispense with his Secret Service detail. Moreover, requiring the president to pay the actual costs of flying Air Force One would make the president "a prisoner of the White House," as Republican Congressman Dan Burton expressed it in 1992 when defending George H. W. Bush's election-year traveling. Subsidizing presidential travel, explains one member of Congress who benefited from President George W. Bush's campaigning-related travel in 2002, is "what we as taxpayers must do if we don't want the president to live in a glass bubble in the White House."[90]

Fears that the president will become imprisoned in the White House if the political beneficiaries of presidential travel have to pay the full flight costs of Air Force One are exaggerated. To be sure, flight costs of over $50,000 an hour would mean that if the president attended a fund-raiser on the West Coast the event might cost nearly as much as it would raise. But that could create an incentive not for the president to stay in Washington, D.C., but to stay on the road, so that the president could attend multiple fund-raisers on the same trip. Reducing the subsidy for travel could also mean presidents would schedule fewer fund-raisers on the West Coast but more on the East Coast. But perhaps the most likely outcome would be a redoubling of efforts to find or create regulatory loopholes to exploit. Presidents would have an increased incentive to disguise political events as official events—as Truman did in 1948. Federal election law would constrain what a president could get away with, but the administration could also rewrite the federal regulations that govern reimbursement of political travel by executive branch officials.

Probably the most valuable step that Congress could take would be to insist on greater transparency with respect to the costs of presidential travel. In the early twentieth century, Congress took the important step of requiring presidential travel to be paid for by the government, but the amount budgeted has always been unrealistically low. Presidents had little choice but to diffuse and obscure the real costs of traveling. Congress compounded the problem by allowing the president to spend his travel allowance without any congressional oversight. In 1978 Congress took a modest step in the direction of a more realistic and transparent presidential travel budget. That step was not the increase in the presidential travel allowance from $40,000 to $100,000—the latter figure was as fictional as the former. But the 1978 law (the White House Personnel Authorization Act of 1978) also authorized the appropriation of "such sums as may be necessary" for "the subsistence expenses of persons in the Government service while traveling on official business in connection with the travel of the President." Although the statute provided no limit on what Congress could authorize for such travel, the Comptroller General (who heads the GAO) was empowered by the law to "inspect all necessary books, documents, papers, and records relating to any such expenditures" in order to verify that the money was spent consistent with the statute. With this act, Congress could essentially audit presidential travel expenses.[91]

But while the 1978 law has generated the occasional GAO report on presidential travel expenses, the nation remains largely in the dark about what it actually costs for the president to travel. When the media ask about such costs, the White House refuses to divulge specific numbers. Neither the press nor the general public has the power to compel the White House to turn over such information. Even the GAO finds it difficult to provide precise numbers relating to presidential travel. When Congressional Republicans asked the GAO to calculate President Clinton's foreign travel costs, the GAO found its efforts frustrated because there was no "centralized database for White House travel costs." Making life more difficult still for the GAO, the different agencies and departments used "various methods to account for expenses." Comparisons across time were even more difficult. The GAO looked at Clinton's travels in his second term, but could not provide comparative data because the travel records of previous presidents "were not readily available."[92]

There have been occasional congressional efforts to remedy this situation. In 1992, Pennsylvania Democrat Paul Kanjorski held hearings to consider the reauthorization of the 1978 White House Personnel Authorization Act, focusing in particular on travel expenditures. Kanjorski found it "ludicrous" that in 1990 President Bush had spent only $29,000 of his $100,000 travel appropriation when the cost of the president's 108 days of travel that year had clearly been many millions. Kanjorski did not suggest that the president should travel less, but insisted that the president should be required to make a "full disclosure" of travel expenses and be subject to "an accounting system which makes information available to the press and to the American people." Once the president's travel costs were publicly available, citizens could make their own "judgment on the frugality, effectiveness, and efficiency" of presidential travel. Kanjorski proposed to increase the authorization from $100,000 to $185 million—which was his best estimate of the actual costs of presidential travel.[93]

The White House, however, showed no interest in Kanjorski's proposal. The Bush administration refused to send witnesses to testify and largely stonewalled the committee's inquiries into the costs of presidential travel. Kanjorski's quixotic effort to bring greater transparency to presidential travel was caught in a hail of partisan sniping. The ranking Republican on the subcommittee, Dan Burton, continuously assailed the hearings as an attempt to deflect attention from congressional scandals and to embarrass the president in an election year. Election year or not, the administration had no interest in advertising to the American people how much it cost the president to travel. Like every other modern president, Bush preferred to keep the costs concealed in a baffling array of department and agency budgets.

The decision in the early twentieth century to publicly fund presidential travel was an important step in democratizing the office. A democracy should not rely on powerful private interests to transport the president, and only a president possessed of phenomenal wealth could afford today to pay for his own travel. However, public financing of presidential travel has not been accompanied by an open and honest accounting of those costs. Americans know they pick up the tab for presidential travel, but they have no way of determining precisely what that tab is. If openness is a hallmark of democracy then presidential travel falls a long way short of democratic ideals.

CHAPTER SIX

Going Abroad: Breaking the "Ironclad Custom"

On August 6, 1906, Theodore Roosevelt wrote to Andrew Carnegie from his summer residence in Oyster Bay, New York. "Do you know," Roosevelt began, "I sometimes wish that we did not have the ironclad custom which forbids a President ever to go abroad." Roosevelt felt that if he could go to Europe and meet the leaders of France, Germany, and England, he could help them to resolve their conflicts. But for that "ironclad custom," Roosevelt would have been on the next boat out of New York harbor.[1]

Nearly 120 years had elapsed since George Washington first took the oath of office, yet no president had ever left the country. Why had Americans created this "ironclad custom"? What purposes did it serve, and how was it enforced? How and when was it ultimately broken, and what difference has its breakdown made to American politics?

EXPLAINING THE IRONCLAD CUSTOM

It is tempting to reduce the taboo against foreign travel to a question of technology. After all, when Washington was president the passage across the Atlantic Ocean was dangerous and uncertain. Sailing ships could take anywhere from four to eight weeks to reach England. Had Washington decided to visit Europe he would have expected to be away from the capital for at least three or four months. Moreover, in an age in which communications across the Atlantic could only travel as fast as the swiftest ship, the president would have been dangerously out of touch with events in the United States.

The invention of steamships substantially decreased the time it took to cross the Atlantic. What had typically been a five- or six-week journey was shortened to only two to three weeks. Reducing the amount of time that a ship was on the ocean also made the trip safer because the ship was less likely to get caught in a storm. The journey also became more predictable since there was less reliance on favorable winds. The *Savannah* is credited as the first steamship to cross the Atlantic, though only about three and a half days of its monthlong journey in 1819 were achieved with the aid of steam; the rest of the time the ship traveled under sail. The first crossing of the Atlantic using steam exclusively occurred in 1838, a journey that took just over two weeks. Steamship technology continued to improve in the latter half of the nineteenth century, and by 1890 a traveler could expect to get from the United States to Europe in a week. And in some comfort.

Equally important was the change in communications technology. The first electric telegraph line, connecting Washington, D.C., and Baltimore, was finished in 1844. But not until 1866, when the last of the transatlantic cable was laid across the floor of the Atlantic Ocean, was it possible to communicate instantaneously between Europe and the United States, using Morse Code. At the dawn of the twentieth century, a new technology emerged that dramatically improved the ability to communicate while traveling: the wireless telegraph. For the first time, travelers aboard a ship in the middle of the Atlantic Ocean could now communicate directly with those on land.

Although technology helps to explain why the nation's first presidents did not dash off to London or Paris, it is of less use in understanding why no president prior to the outbreak of World War I made such a journey. Nor can technology explain why no eighteenth- or nineteenth-century president visited the neighboring countries of Mexico or Canada. Several nineteenth-century presidents, including Martin Van Buren and Andrew Johnson, visited Niagara Falls, yet each chose not to venture into Canada. In Johnson's case, his entire traveling party crossed over to the Canadian side; only the president and secretary of state remained behind. Johnson "had his carriage driven as far as the center of the Suspension Bridge" that connected Canada and the United States, but refused to go any further. President Ulysses S. Grant was invited to visit New Brunswick for the opening of the European and North American Railway, but declined the invitation on the grounds that "it has never been the custom for the President to leave the United States during his term of office." Grant thought there was "a Statute, or some provision, against the President leaving the territory of the U.S.," but even if there was no legal prohibition, he explained, he did not want to "be the one to establish the precedent of an Executive going beyond the limits of his country." Clearly, then, technology did not prevent nineteenth-century presidents from leaving the country. Instead presidents were constrained by norms and expectations that were rooted in the nation's understanding of its role in the world.[2]

In the nineteenth century, most citizens of the United States saw their country as a beacon of liberty, a shining example to a world largely shrouded in darkness. Americans also viewed their nation as a refuge for Europe's oppressed and persecuted. It was the promised land, a land of liberty. This was what made the United States exceptional. It could only remain this way, however, by avoiding what Washington famously called "entangling alliances."

To be sure, Washington's doctrine did not apply to the Americas. The Monroe Doctrine, however, was conceived largely as a defensive measure, aimed particularly against colonial European nation-states. Allowing European powers to establish client states along America's borders endangered the new republic's safety and would impel the United States to establish a standing army, which, according to republican ideology, would threaten the nation's liberty. Only by keeping European powers at a safe distance could the United States afford to maintain a relatively small, decentralized, and unintrusive government. American exceptionalism required the Monroe Doctrine.

Entangling alliances and power politics were the instruments of European monarchy and autocracy. They set nations on the path of war, conquest, taxation, and empire. Republicanism, in contrast, entailed a rejection of the decadence of European courts, the flattery and scheming of courtiers, and the executive's corrupting influence on politics. A republican president was to exhibit simplicity of manners; he was to be the nation's "first citizen"—distinguished and admired but a fellow citizen nonetheless.

The taboo against foreign travel by a president owed its staying power to the continuing hold that the republican fear of monarchical pomp and power had on the American imagination. A president who traveled abroad, Americans feared, would be invited to visit palaces and courts, to exchange pleasantries and genuflections with kings and queens. Such a president might even be seduced by the ways of the court: the pomp and ceremony, the fine dinners and expensive silverware, the flirting and drinking to excess. Certainly, presidential travel to foreign countries threatened to draw the nation into those "entangling alliances" that Washington had warned against. Republican simplicity and American exceptionalism were best preserved if presidents stayed at home.

BENDING THE IRONCLAD CUSTOM:

MCKINLEY, ROOSEVELT, AND TAFT

If the taboo against presidents traveling abroad was rooted in fears of monarchy, empire, and entangling alliances, then it is not surprising that the taboo was challenged only after ideas about America's place in the world began to change. In the 1890s, an alternative understanding of the role of the United States in world affairs took hold. Empire and even imperialism no longer seemed a perversion of America's mission but its fulfillment. The United States had been called by God to spread liberty, civilization, and Christianity throughout the world. The "promised land," as historian Walter McDougall has argued, became a "crusader state."[3]

William McKinley

The Spanish-American War in 1898 was a critical turning point in the emergence of America as a crusader state. As a result of the short-lived war, the United States acquired what remained of the crumbling Spanish empire: Cuba, the Philippines, Puerto Rico, and Guam. An Anti-Imperialist League emerged almost immediately in protest. The venerable Republican senator George Frisbie Hoar, whose grandfather Roger Sherman had affixed his signature to the Declaration of Independence and the Constitution, declared that the Founding Fathers would be horrified to find Americans "strut[ting] about in the cast-off clothing of pinchbeck emperors and pewter kings." In the 1900 election, William Jennings Bryan tried to play on these fears of the corrupting effects of empire, but his appeals fell flat with voters, most of whom did not appear to be particularly bothered by the nation's "little empire." Instead Americans seemed to share President McKinley's confidence that "It is not possible that 75 millions of American freemen are unable to establish liberty and justice and good government in our new possessions." American institutions, McKinley promised, "will not deteriorate by extension, and our sense of justice will not abate under tropic suns in distant seas." The United States was doing righteous work in these far-flung lands: spreading democracy and liberty, fighting disease, promoting economic development, and freeing people from the superstitions and dogmas of Spanish Catholicism.[4]

McKinley was the United States' first avowedly imperialist president and, not coincidentally, also the first president to express a strong desire to travel beyond the nation's borders. Several months after being sworn in for a second term, McKinley met with the French ambassador, who wanted to know "if it would be really impossible for a president of the United States to go to Europe." The ambassador, accustomed to European heads of state routinely traveling outside the nation, found it hard to believe that the president would be forbidden from traveling outside of the country. McKinley explained that "there was no constitutional reason against such a voyage." If "a sort of tradition had been established," McKinley continued, it was because the nation did not "have the foreign affairs that it has today." Such a tradition, in the president's view, was an archaic residue from an era that lacked the telegraph and modern shipping. McKinley informed the ambassador that he planned to travel to Hawaii, Puerto Rico, and Cuba during his second term. Because Cuba had a "slightly mixed character"—that is, it was essentially an American protectorate—McKinley thought a visit there would "be a step made on the path which would allow the President to leave the soil of the United States." However, he never had the opportunity to carry out these plans, as he was assassinated a few months after his conversation with the ambassador.[5]

The closest that President McKinley ever came to leaving the nation was a trip to the border town of El Paso, Texas, which he visited as part of a 12,000-mile journey across the United States in the spring of 1901. In the town's main plaza, beneath "intertwined . . . American and Mexican flags," McKinley exchanged formal greetings with representatives from the Mexican government and then spoke to a "vast concourse of people" that included "thousands of Mexicans." McKinley thanked the Mexican officials for crossing the border to greet him. "I cannot go over there," he explained, for "there is something in the traditions of this Republic, something in its precedents that does not permit the President to go outside the United States during his term of office." Many of the Americans in the audience applauded. The president then drew laughter by adding that he could, however, "look over there."[6]

After the speech-making had finished, the president "expressed a desire to take a look into Mexico" and so was driven, along with the Mexican officials, to "the international bridge" that connected El Paso with Juarez, Mexico. From the Texas side of the border, officials pointed out noteworthy sights visible on the other side of the Rio Grande, including a 300-year-old church and a Spanish prison. Although it would have taken only a few minutes to walk across the bridge, McKinley kept his feet firmly planted on American ground. Meanwhile, the wives of the Cabinet officials who were traveling with the president crossed over the border to have breakfast with their Mexican hosts.[7]

McKinley was not the first president to visit El Paso. A decade earlier, in the spring of 1891, Benjamin Harrison had made the same trip and been welcomed in much the same fashion. Harrison actually got somewhat closer to treading on Mexican soil than McKinley, journeying halfway across the international bridge, whereas McKinley had refused even to step upon it. Although both Harrison and McKinley used their visits to the border to underscore Mexican-American friendship, they felt that a deeply held tradition prevented them from entering Mexico.[8]

Theodore Roosevelt

Theodore Roosevelt was not one to be constrained by conventions. In many ways he remade the presidency in his image, insisting that the office should be a bully pulpit and the president a leader of public opinion. Moreover, Roosevelt loved adventure and travel. When the United States declared war on Spain in 1898, he promptly quit his desk job as assistant secretary of the navy to lead his famous charge up San Juan Hill in Cuba. After Roosevelt retired from the presidency, he immediately left for Africa, and several years later he traveled extensively in South America, including a harrowing journey down the Amazon River that almost killed him. But even Roosevelt, as adventurous and sometimes reckless as he was, stayed on U.S. soil throughout his two terms as president, with one exception: Panama.

When Roosevelt became president, the region that is now Panama still belonged to Colombia, and the Colombian government was continuing to frustrate American attempts to build a canal across the Panamanian isthmus. With American encouragement and aid, both financial and military, Panama declared its independence from Colombia in November 1903. In exchange for American support (as well as a payment of $10 million and a pledge of $250,000 annually), the Panamanians signed a treaty granting the U.S. government control in perpetuity over a 10-mile-wide strip of land through which the canal was to be built. Within this territory, the United States was given "all the rights, power, and authority . . . which the United States would possess and exercise if it were the sovereign . . . to the entire exclusion" of Panama. The United States also promised to protect Panamanian independence (and implicitly American commercial interests), rendering Panama virtually an American protectorate.[9]

Roosevelt regarded the acquisition of the Panamanian isthmus and construction of the Panama Canal as among his greatest achievements. Perhaps it was not quite on a par with Jefferson's Louisiana Purchase, but Roosevelt believed its importance to the nation was not far behind. The Panama Canal, he excitedly told his son Kermit, was "the greatest engineering feat of the ages" and was "changing the face of the continent." Its effect, he predicted, "will be felt while our civilization lasts."[10]

On November 8, 1906, with Congress not due back in session until the beginning of December, Roosevelt embarked for Panama aboard a government yacht, which would then transfer him the following day to a naval battleship. The president's departure made the front page of the New York Times, which noted that the president's trip "will violate the traditions of the United States for 117 years by taking the President outside the jurisdiction of the Government at Washington." But nothing in the story or in any subsequent Times coverage expressed disapproval of the president's trip.[11]

The administration was anxious, however, that Roosevelt's journey might draw criticism for violating a venerable precedent. The White House was at pains to reassure the country that, as the Times reported, "arrangements have been made to keep constantly in touch with the President by means of wireless telegraphy during the voyage to and from the Isthmus." Moreover, as soon as the president docked in Panama, "the regular cable [could] be relied upon to keep the President in close touch with his office work" in Washington. Moreover, the itinerary that the White House released to the press was notable for its omission of any mention of a meeting between Roosevelt and the Panamanian president, except for an oblique mention that the afternoon and evening of the first day would be "at the disposal of the Panama government." There was no mention of the president going to Panama City. Indeed nothing in the announced itinerary suggested that the president would set foot in Panama proper. Every town mentioned on the itinerary was within the American controlled "Canal Zone," which extended 5 miles on each side of the canal. The administration could not disguise that the president would be leaving the United States, but it left the nation guessing whether the president would actually "put his foot on foreign territory."[12]

As the president pulled away from the dock in the naval harbor, he shouted out his parting words: "Goodbye; I am going down to see how the ditch is getting along." The president's farewell greeting—which formed the basis for the headline in the next day's New York Times—was a public reminder that he was embarking on a tour of inspection, not engaging in foreign diplomacy. Roosevelt could believe, with some justification, that his tour was not dissimilar to the early tours of James Monroe, who had traveled to inspect American harbors and forts. Although Roosevelt had to leave the country to carry out his inspection of an American installation, his aims were still in keeping with the spirit of the nation's "ironclad custom." Or at least that is what he appeared to hope his fellow Americans would believe.[13]

At the close of his inspection of the Panama Canal, however, Roosevelt struck a less deprecating note. Speaking before a crowd of some eight hundred people, largely canal workers, Roosevelt stressed that "it was without precedent for a President to leave the United States." But he justified the departure from precedent on that ground that "this work is without precedent." He likened the work of the canal diggers to the noble work their fathers had performed in the Civil War. There would be critics and doubters, he warned. "They will have their say, and they will go down stream like bubbles, they will vanish; but the work you have done will remain for ages." Sounding a typical Roosevelt theme, he counseled the laborers that "it is the man who does the job who counts, not the little scolding critic who thinks how it ought to have been done." Roosevelt's words were a vindication not only of their work but of his own.[14]

Most of Roosevelt's time in Panama was spent, as advertised, in the American Canal Zone. Roosevelt liked nothing better than clambering onto cranes, braving the torrential rain, and wading through knee-high mud, particularly when he knew cameras were present. Those were the images of his trip that he wanted the American people back home to see. However, he also engaged in some of the diplomatic niceties that had been glossed over in the administration's published itinerary. The 73-year-old Panamanian president, Manuel Amador, greeted Roosevelt upon his arrival and Roosevelt reciprocated by visiting Panama City, where the two leaders exchanged public greetings and speeches. In the evening Roosevelt and Amador, along with their wives, watched a fireworks display from the balcony of the presidential palace and then attended a glittering reception at the Commercial Club. Roosevelt, in short, behaved much as heads of state the world over do when visiting other nations.[15]

For all its novelty, Roosevelt's trip to Panama attracted little criticism in the United States. If few Americans seemed particularly concerned that the popular president had violated a 117-year-old custom, that was perhaps because most Americans regarded the Panama Canal as their property. To be sure, some Americans felt that the United States' intervention in Panama was sordid and shameful and that the deal the Roosevelt administration had struck with Panama was state-sanctioned larceny. But their objection was not to the traveling but to the policy.[16]

William Howard Taft

Roosevelt's successor, William Howard Taft, was a genial, cautious man, not the sort to defy convention or trample upon traditions. Once as president-elect (in February 1909) and twice as president (in November 1910 and December 1912) he followed Roosevelt's example in journeying to Panama to inspect the canal. On each of these visits Taft crossed over the "invisible lines" separating the Panamanian Re-

Theodore Roosevelt as he wished the public to see him: at the controls of a crane in the Panama Canal. (Theodore Roosevelt Collection, Harvard College Library)

public from the American Canal Zone. Like Roosevelt, Taft visited the Panamanian president at the presidential palace in Panama City. And like Roosevelt, who visited Puerto Rico on the return leg, Taft used the return journey to visit an American possession, Cuba.[17]

More significant, however, was the trip Taft made in the fall of 1909. Like Harrison and McKinley before him, Taft traveled on the Southern Pacific Railroad line to El Paso as part of an ambitious coast-to-coast railroad journey. But unlike his predecessors, Taft agreed to meet personally with the Mexican leader Porfirio Díaz. Although styled a "president," Díaz had ruled Mexico for nearly thirty-five years and was more dictator than democrat. Taft was particularly anxious about several billion dollars of U.S. capital investments in Mexico, and he wanted to help shore up the aging autocrat who, he insisted, "had done more for the people of Mexico than any other Latin American had done for any of his people."[18]

When Díaz crossed over the international bridge he was greeted by Secretary of War Jacob Dickinson, who hailed the Mexican leader as "the first Chief Executive of a nation to cross our border." Attired in military dress, including a bulging chestful of medals and decorations, the nearly 80-year-old Díaz was driven by carriage into El Paso for an exchange of greetings and a brief private meeting with Taft. Díaz then returned to Mexico, and an hour later Taft, wearing a "frock coat and silk hat," set off to return the call. Taft crossed over the international bridge and, through streets lined with cheering crowds, garlands of flowers, and a "veritable cloud of waving" Mexican and U.S. flags, he made his way to the customs house in Juarez to meet the aging Mexican ruler. Taft greeted Díaz by drawing attention to the historic nature of the occasion: "This is the first time so far as I know," he began, "that a President of the United States has stepped beyond the border of the United States, either on the north or the south." Advances in transportation and communications technology, Taft added, had "brought us closer to each other," and enabled there to be a "closer union of feeling" between the people of Mexico and the people of the United States, as well as between the leaders of the two nations.[19]

After an exchange of greetings, Taft turned around and headed back to the U.S. side of the border. Later that afternoon he spoke to a large crowd in El Paso. Again he drew attention to the importance of his trip across the international bridge into Mexico. His visit, he said, was "the first time in history, except one [that] a President of the United States has stepped on foreign soil and enjoyed the hospitality of a foreign Government." That one exception, he noted, "was when Theodore Roosevelt stepped over the border in Panama," but American control of the Panamanian isthmus meant "that it did not seem to be quite stepping out of the country." Mexico was different for it was an unambiguously sovereign nation.[20]

In the evening Taft crossed back over the border, this time for a splendid banquet given by the Mexican president in Taft's honor. Three trainloads of flowers were used for decorations, and gold and silverware valued at a million dollars adorned the table. Taft sat next to Díaz throughout the dinner, chatting amiably with his host. The American president did not seem bothered in the least that he was conversing with a dictator. Nor did he seem disturbed by the discrepancy between the wealth on display and the poverty of the people. He was oblivious to the mounting sense of injustice that in less than two years would boil over into a revolution that would force Díaz to flee the country.[21]

Press reactions to Taft's brief foray into Mexico suggest the taboo against foreign

Presidents Taft and Díaz pose for the cameras on the steps of the customs house in Juarez, Mexico. Between and behind the two presidents is Secretary of War Jacob Dickinson. (Aultman Collection, El Paso Public Library)

travel had been seriously weakened. On September 14, the day the president began his cross-country journey, the *New York Times* drew attention to Taft's plan to visit President Díaz in Mexico. "For the first time in American history a President of the United States is to set foot in foreign territory during the period of his incumbency," noted the *Times*, evidently forgetting Roosevelt's visit to Panama three years before. "Mr. Taft," continued the *Times*, "may violate this precedent cheerfully and with impunity. The immediate effect . . . will be to strengthen our friendly relations

Taft, at the back of the front carriage, doffs his hat as he is driven through the streets of El Paso, Texas. (The Centennial Museum, University of Texas at El Paso)

with the Mexican Republic. Its remote effects can by no stretch of the imagination be considered harmful."[22]

Still, the departure from the precedent was modest at best. Taft spent no more than three or four hours in Mexico and was never further than a couple of hundred yards from the U.S. border. Moreover, apart from a couple of short visits to Panama City, Taft's foray into Mexico was the only time he ventured outside the nation. If the custom was no longer ironclad, it was still sufficiently strong to constrain presidential behavior. Taft's successor, Woodrow Wilson, never left the United States during his first term, despite several invitations to do so. In July 1913, for instance, the U.S. ambassador to England pressed Wilson to visit England and "smash a precedent," but the president resisted the ambassador's overtures. "The case against the President's leaving the country," he explained, "is very strong and I am afraid overwhelming, . . . particularly now that he is expected to exercise a constant leadership in all parts of the business of government." Wilson cautioned that "it might be the beginning of a practice of visiting foreign countries which would lead Presidents rather far afield." In short, from 1789 until World War I, foreign presidential travel amounted only to Taft's handful of hours in a Mexican border town and Roosevelt's and Taft's errands to Panama. The custom was dented but not yet broken.[23]

BREAKING THE IRONCLAD CUSTOM:
WOODROW WILSON GOES TO EUROPE

The muted reactions to Roosevelt's and Taft's modest foreign travel indicate that the taboo against presidents traveling abroad had weakened considerably, at least with respect to America's closest neighbors, possessions, and protectorates. Traveling to Europe, however, posed a more direct challenge to received tradition. It was one thing for the president to visit client states in America's hemisphere; it was quite another for him to cross the Atlantic and become drawn into the power politics of the Old World that Washington had warned against. Before a president could travel to Europe, he would first have to persuade his fellow citizens to reject the vision of America's place in the world embodied in Washington's Farewell Address.

When war broke out in 1914, the United States initially reacted with characteristic aversion to European wars and diplomacy. The outbreak of yet another war on the European continent seemed to confirm the wisdom of Washington's warning against getting involved in the affairs of Europe. For the first two years of the war, the president and the nation did their best to ignore it. Wilson kept the nation's attention focused on his ambitious domestic agenda and assured the country that no American boys would be sent to settle European quarrels.

However, toward the end of his first term, and especially after his reelection, Wilson began to prepare the nation for international engagement if not war. Speaking on May 27, 1916, Wilson articulated a vision of the United States' role in the world that repudiated the central tenet of Washington's Farewell Address. "We are participants," Wilson emphasized, "whether we would or not, in the life of the world. The interests of all nations are our own also. We are partners with the rest." The world was characterized by an interdependency of interests from which the United States could not withdraw. Following his reelection, Wilson increasingly stressed that the United States was not just one partner among many but instead was burdened with the responsibility of leadership. The United States was the only nation with the political power and idealism to ensure that "peace assume an aspect of permanence." Only the United States could redeem the war by making it a war to end all wars. In the service of such a righteous cause, a president could be forgiven for entangling the nation in world politics. The European world that Washington had warned against—the world of shifting alliances, devious diplomats, territorial disputes, and authoritarian governments—could be transformed by the United States into a peaceful, democratic family of nations. A goal so glorious justified jettisoning archaic traditions and outdated modes of thinking.[24]

Among the traditions that Wilson believed stood in the way of constructing a more peaceful world was the prohibition against foreign travel by presidents. According to Wilson, permanent peace required a League of Nations, and only the United States had the moral authority to ensure that Europe accept the League. If the United States was the indispensable nation, Wilson was the indispensable man. Only he had the moral authority to make European leaders put aside their immediate interests and grievances, and think instead of the long-term good of the human race. Or so at least Wilson believed.

Wilson's argument that the president was needed in Paris cleverly capitalized on the nation's longstanding distrust of entangling alliances in Europe. Wilson argued, as did his defenders, that the presence of the president was required to ensure that the peace process was not diplomacy as usual. As the *New Republic* expressed it in a full page advertisement in the *New York Times*, "If the diplomats should begin once more their ancient game of cheat with peoples as pawns, the game of military supremacies, selfish alliance, balances of power, strategic frontiers and economic barriers—it would be the supreme tragedy of history." Wilson's presence at the peace negotiations would ensure that diplomats did not play their "ancient game of cheat." Wilson was no diplomat; he spoke the language of right and justice, not state interests and territorial gain. The president's international travel, from this perspective, was in keeping with the spirit of Washington's warning against the corruption and entangling alliances of the Old World.[25]

On November 18, 1918, one week after the Germans signed the armistice agreement that brought World War I to an end, the White House announced that the president would travel to France "for the purpose of taking part in the discussion and settlement of the main features of the treaty of peace." The White House statement indicated that the president would depart "immediately after the opening of the regular session of Congress," but was vague about when the president would return. It was "not likely" that the president would be able to remain for the entire Paris Peace Conference, but "his presence at the outset" was necessary because of "the manifest disadvantages" in relying on cable communications to shape the "greater outlines of the final treaty, about which he must necessarily be consulted."[26]

A number of individuals within the administration were skeptical about the wisdom of Wilson's travel plans. Secretary of State Robert Lansing met with the president following the signing of the armistice and told him that "the plan for him to attend was unwise." Lansing believed that the president "would be criticized severely ... for leaving at a time when Congress particularly needed his guidance, and that he would be greatly embarrassed in directing domestic affairs from overseas." Wilson, however, was unreceptive. "His face," Lansing reported, "assumed that harsh, obstinate expression which indicates resentment at unacceptable advice."[27]

In Lansing's view, the president was "making one of the greatest mistakes of his career and imperiling his reputation." Lansing prophesied that there would be "trouble in Paris and worse than trouble here." By going to Paris, Wilson would "lose the unique position which he now holds in world affairs. He will have to sit there on an equality with the Premiers of the Allies. That is, he will have to step down from his pedestal, thereby running the risk of weakening his great influence with foreign governments and the popular reverence in which he is held everywhere." Wilson took an even bigger risk on the domestic front, Lansing predicted, for "Congress will resent [the president's] leaving and without a guiding hand will act very badly." Lansing's concerns were couched largely in terms of political and strategic calculations, but underneath was a sense that the president was violating an important American tradition. "The President's place," Lansing concluded, "is here in America."[28]

Other allies of the president communicated misgivings about the idea of Wilson traveling to Europe. On November 14 Wilson had met with Senate Democrat Key Pittman, who assured the president that a majority of the Senate recognized the necessity of Wilson attending the Paris Peace Conference. But the following day, Pittman hurriedly wrote to alert the president that there was far more opposition to the idea than he had initially realized. Pittman had invited thirty of Wilson's "closest and strongest political supporters" to dinner in order to sound them out about the desirability of the president's plan and found that many were strongly opposed. Among their reasons, Pittman reported, was that at this critical juncture the nation could not afford to be without Wilson's "guiding hand upon the rudder at all times." In the president's absence, they feared, "our government may be shipwrecked." In addition, they emphasized that Congress would be in session while the president was gone and that his "advice and . . . executive action may be required at any minute."[29]

Similar concerns were communicated to Wilson by another Democratic stalwart, Rhode Island senator Peter Gerry. Writing on November 16, Gerry noted that a looming dispute over the administration's tax bill meant that Democrats felt "some doubt of the advisability of your leaving to attend the Peace Conference." Specifically they worried that "when the bill goes to conference, . . . your leadership will be necessary to bring about a speedy adjustment of the divergent views." It was not only the tax bill, however, that made the president's presence in Washington desirable. There were many other "very important matters that will undoubtedly arise this session" and "if a division or serious difficulty in our party is to be avoided, our Senate and House leaders must often secure your counsel and advice." Wilson was the party's leader, and his absence, Democrats worried, could seriously weaken a party that had already suffered heavy losses in the recently concluded midterm election. Democrats had lost control of both the House and the Senate, and now their president was proposing to leave the country. No wonder they were nervous.[30]

Doubts about the wisdom and propriety of the president's trip were not limited to anxious Democrats. On November 14, four days before the White House formally announced the presidential trip, the *New York Times* canvassed thirty-five major newspapers as to whether Wilson should attend the peace conference. The following day the *Times* published the results on the front page: only ten of the thirty-five papers endorsed the idea of the president going to Paris.[31]

Some of the newspapers that opposed the plan were not concerned that the president would be breaking with tradition. The *Syracuse Post-Standard*, for instance, pronounced the "precedent that forbids a President from stepping on foreign soil" to be "foolish." But the *Post-Standard* still opposed the trip because the president had "urgent and important work in Washington." Other opponents of the president's trip did insist on the importance of upholding the tradition against presidential travel. The *Boston Herald*, for instance, affirmed that "the unwritten law of the Republic which forbids the President to go outside of its territory while holding office is essentially wise and desirable." Moreover, advances in communications technologies made it unnecessary for a president to violate this "unwritten law" since the president could now "remain in . . . close touch with the peace conference without being in actual presence." The *Chattanooga Times* agreed that the trip "would be breaking a highly regarded precedent without warrant" since the president could readily use cable and wireless communication to "impress his opinions upon the proceedings." It was "essential," the *Times* argued, for the president to remain at home "where he can keep his hand on the pulse of his own people." By traveling abroad for an extended period of time, the *Times* intimated, the president risked losing touch with the sentiments of his fellow citizens.[32]

Although opposition to the trip was widespread, Wilson also heard from those who were supportive. On November 18, Supreme Court Justice John Hessin Clarke—a Wilson appointee—implored the president "not [to] heed the opposition, developing in the newspapers, to your attending in person the peace conference." Nobody else, Clarke assured Wilson, has "your power of stating the case." Moreover, "the personal prestige you have at home and abroad, and the weight of your great office will give many fold greater influence to your advocacy of any measures than would be given to . . . any representatives you may send, however able they may be." The president should pay little heed to outdated traditions. "The unfortunate results of the management of international affairs in the past," the justice maintained, were enough to discredit "the protest based on the novelty of the course proposed." Clarke, who in 1922 would resign his position on the Supreme Court in order to campaign for United States' membership in the League of Nations, closed with an impassioned plea: "I believe the League of Nations to Enforce the Peace of the World will fail if you do not go, and this, if obtained, will prove the most important result of the war. If it is not obtained, the sacrifices of the great war will have been, in large measure, made in vain." The new world order required bold and visionary leadership, not timid adherence to convention and custom.[33]

Clarke expressed Wilson's sentiments exactly. Upon reading the letter Wilson immediately penned an appreciative response. "My judgment," Wilson assured Clarke, "is your own." Wilson had made up his mind, and later that evening the announcement of the president's trip was issued by the White House. Wilson was willing to admit that there were "undoubtedly cogent arguments why I should not go abroad," as he told Democratic Party politician Gavin McNab in a letter on the same day, but he did "not see how [he could] escape going." The "whole matter," he confided, "has caused me a great deal of anxious arguing with myself," but too much was at stake for him not to risk his reputation, even if it did mean transgressing tradition.[34]

The official White House announcement on November 18 met with a wide range of responses. Many supported the president's decision, some were sharply critical, and still others offered mixed signals. Typical of the critical commentary was the opinion page of the *Detroit Free Press*, which called Wilson's decision to go to Europe a "grave error." The president had no business leaving the country at a time when its own needs were so pressing. By traveling across the ocean the president irresponsibly placed his own life at risk "at a time when . . . his life belongs to the nation." Although the president might have a "legal right" to leave the country he had no "moral right" to do so under these circumstances. If it was true, as the president claimed, that his presence was required in France because he could not conduct diplomacy by cable, then how, once he was on the other side of the Atlantic, could he expect to remain "in close enough touch with Washington . . . to perform his home duties as president?" Wilson's "projected jaunt," the *Free Press* concluded, placed the interests of Europe above those of the United States.[35]

The feeling that the president's trip was "neither wise nor proper" was shared by the *St. Louis Daily Globe-Democrat*. The *Globe-Democrat* conceded that Americans were not likely to object to the trip "merely because no president has ever done such a thing before." Americans were a forward-looking people, not the sort to be unthinkingly shackled to precedents. However, by attending the peace conference the president degraded "the dignity of the office," since he would be sitting down at the negotiating table not with other heads of state but with premiers and party leaders. The president, to be sure, "has the functions of a premier, but he is more than a premier." But it was not only the dignity of the presidency that was at stake, it was also the interests of the nation. Given the "grave situation of the present" the nation could not afford "the president absenting himself from the country, from his office and its continuous and pressing duties," and particularly not while Congress was in session.[36]

The *Louisville Courier Journal* was among the trip's enthusiastic backers. Wilson's journey was perfectly proper since the Constitution "expressly empowered [the president] to deal with foreign affairs." Precedents were "useful" but only "so long as circumstances do not become extraordinary." In the view of the *Courier Journal*, the circumstances that had rendered the precedent meaningful had changed dramatically. "The isolated nation of our fathers separated by 3,000 square miles from the quarreling Europe has become a world power, has proved the decisive factor in the greatest war, and now is to cast the deciding vote at the peace table. The ocean gap is closed; the isolation is ended; and ended are the insular precedents that accompanied it."[37]

The *Outlook*, a New York weekly, took a similar view, noting that the United States was "entering upon a new political era" in which the nation would necessarily play a leading role in international politics. The "unreasonable and parrot-like repetition of Washington's phrase 'entangling alliances' " had created "a foolish tradition that we must have 'nothing to do with abroad.' " World War I had taught Americans that "our National life is bound up with the national lives of Europe, Asia, Africa, and South America." However, the *Outlook* also expressed reservations about the trip. Its support for Wilson's trip was "predicated upon the assumption that the President's visit will be a brief and personal one, and that he will leave the detailed discussions to the official delegates whom he may appoint for the purpose." It was one thing for the president to visit Paris but it was quite another for him "to transfer the seat of Government of the United States from Washington to the American Embassy in Paris, and to transact his business as Chief Executive by couriers, dispatch boats, and cabled vetoes." If the president tried anything like that, he would find that "the country will strongly and seriously object."[38]

The *Philadelphia Record* vigorously defended Wilson, noting that the president's decision to go to Paris corresponded with his republican understanding of the presidency. Wilson rightly regarded himself not "as an elected King, but as a party leader corresponding to Lloyd George and M. Clemenceau," the prime ministers of Great Britain and France, respectively. If it was proper for democratically elected leaders like George and Clemenceau to attend, then it was proper for the democratically elected leader of the United States to attend as well. Kings and queens should stay away from negotiating the peace, but the president was no monarch. And so it was not only proper for Wilson to attend the Paris Peace Conference, it was an affirmation of the democratic character of the presidency.[39]

Fears persisted, however, that the president, whatever his own understanding of the presidency, would be treated more like a monarch than a party leader when he arrived in Europe. Such fears could only have been intensified by reports that in Paris "popular demonstrations will mark the visits of the President and the sovereigns of Great Britain and Belgium, who will also be entertained at a series of fetes and official functions." Nor would republican anxieties have been eased by the announcement that Wilson and his wife would be staying at the splendid Parisian "mansion" of the Prince and Princess Joachim Murat.[40]

The *New York Post*'s David Lawrence, one of the nation's first syndicated columnists, reported on November 25 that the president was "face to face with a crisis" brought on by a "revolt inside the Democratic party." Lawrence relayed that "there is dissatisfaction and discontent inside the Democratic party of which the public has hitherto had no hint." The dissatisfaction communicated to Lawrence came from Democrats who "are not officeholders but unselfish friends of the President." Their criticisms were many, but Lawrence related that "perhaps the most severe criticism heard is of Mr. Wilson's decision to go to Europe at this critical time." The journey was symptomatic of a larger problem: "the President in his absorption in foreign questions, has gotten out of touch with the true spirit of America on domestic questions." Having been lured onto the world stage, Wilson was not only forgetting to tend to domestic policy and politics, but he was becoming less accessible. Although he "preached [democracy] at the outset of his Administration" he had substituted for that "seclusiveness" and "distinctly autocratic and bureaucratic advisers."[41]

The following day the *New York Times* published Lawrence's column as well as a lengthy critique of Wilson's trip by an unidentified "eminent jurist." Arguing his case before "the Supreme Court of Public Opinion," the author scored the president's "absenteeism" as an abrogation of his constitutional duties as chief executive. By leaving the United States for an indefinite period, the president essentially suspended Congress's lawmaking power. And that, the eminent jurist insisted, the president could not constitutionally do. Moreover, he suggested that Wilson's prolonged absence was "a practical denial" of the "right of the people . . . to communicate [with the president] by mail, wire, or personal presence." Putting aside the propriety of disregarding an "unwritten law of the nation which time has graven on its national conscience" and the wisdom of leaving the United States at a time when the nation faced massive problems of its own, the president had a constitutional duty to stay at the seat of government while Congress was in session.[42]

A New York attorney named Archibald Watson bolstered the legal case against the president's trip by digging up an obscure 1790 statute, which required that "all offices attached to the seat of Government shall be exercised in the District of Columbia, and not elsewhere, except as otherwise expressly provided for by law." According to Watson, this statute meant not simply that the District of Columbia was designated as the capital city, but that should the president leave the capital the vice president would assume the powers and responsibilities of the office during the president's absence. Watson's argument was dubious. For starters, virtually every president had exercised his presidential duties while away from the seat of government. During the summer months, for instance, Taft had set up shop in Beverly, Massachusetts, and Roosevelt in Oyster Bay. And, of course, countless presidents had toured the country since Washington, without giving up the powers and duties of their office. It was a measure of the discontent with Wilson's plans that even such far-fetched legal theories were given prominent attention. People were desperately seeking legal and constitutional arguments to bolster a political norm that the president was preparing to cast aside.[43]

Although many Democrats in Congress were unhappy with Wilson's decision, they tended to keep their discontent hidden from public view after the decision had been announced. Party loyalty rallied most Democrats to the president's side. Republicans, however, had no such reservations, and they became increasingly vocal in their criticisms as they sensed the president's vulnerability. On November 21, the *New York Times* reported growing opposition to the president's plan in Congress, especially among Republicans who "doubt the wisdom of the Chief Executive of the nation going abroad for an extended stay."[44]

If Wilson had any illusions about the depth of dissatisfaction in Congress, they should have been dispelled by the tepid reception of his State of the Union address on December 2. When, toward the end of the speech, he announced his intention to travel to Paris to discuss a peace treaty with the leaders of Europe, only "a few hand-claps" echoed through the packed chamber. What little applause there was came from House Democrats. House and Senate Republicans remained seated and silent, as did "nearly every Democratic Senator." Wilson said that he recognized "the great inconveniences" that would attend his absence from the United States, but insisted that it was his "paramount duty" to go to Paris. He vowed that he would remain "in close touch" with Congress and "with affairs on this side of the water." Modern communications technologies, he reassured the Congressmen, would "render him available for any counsel or service" that they might desire. In addition, members of Congress would be kept constantly abreast of what the president was doing. "You will know all that I do," he promised. Nothing would be censored or withheld from them. In closing, he pledged to make his absence "as brief as possible" as he strove "to translate into action the great ideals for which America has striven."[45]

The day after Wilson's address, Republican Senator Lawrence Sherman introduced a joint resolution calling upon Congress to declare that Wilson's absence from the country would constitute "an inability to discharge the powers and duties" of the presidency and that therefore the powers of the office should, as Article 2, section 1 of the Constitution required, "devolve on the Vice President." Nor was this to be a temporary devolution of power. The power of the presidency, under the terms of Sherman's resolution, would be exercised by the vice president until the next presidential election.[46]

Sherman conceded that the Constitution did not explicitly proscribe foreign travel by a president, but he argued that "common sense" suggested that such a prohibition was implied by the founders' decision to make the president an "essential element" of the lawmaking process. Requiring that every bill be presented to the president for his signature and giving the president ten days to sign or veto a bill indicated that the framers presupposed that the president would be at the seat of government, at least while Congress was in session. And so it fell to Congress to codify the norm—"an unwritten law of unbroken tradition," Sherman called it—that had governed presidents for over a century.[47]

Such a law would reflect the original intent of the framers. "The intention of those who wrote, and the American people who adopted, the Constitution," Sherman insisted, "was to guard the President against the insidious influences and flattery incident to the servile adulation and absurd pomp of the kings and council chambers of the Old World. Amid crowns and reminiscences of ancient thrones [and] diplomats grown gray in Europe's quarrels, . . . the whole American atmosphere that ought to surround the President is lost." The taboo against presidents traveling was as relevant today as it was in the eighteenth and nineteenth centuries, when it had served the United States so well. "A courtier's smile and the bending knee of a sycophant," Sherman warned, "have often in history entangled a nation in fatal alliances." And the "kiss of a sensuous woman has changed the course of empire." By sending the president to Europe he was being put in the way of "temptation." Not sexual temptation, but the temptation of power. "The savory fragrance of incense offered by alien satellites may mount with intoxicating power to a head already strangely obsessed with the phantasy that he has become the State." Americans were mistaken if they thought it could not happen here. Kings, cautioned Sherman, "may be bred on American soil."[48]

Kansas Republican Charles Curtis, who would become vice president of the United States in 1929, added legal weight to Sherman's resolution. Curtis drew the Senate's attention to a 1900 Oklahoma state court decision, in which the court affirmed that the governor could not exercise his executive powers while he was outside of the state "any more than . . . a judicial officer of Oklahoma could open court and try cases . . . in another state, or upon foreign territory." For the court this was a self-evident truth—"no one," the court said, would contend differently. A governor was free to travel to other states or other nations "without forfeiting his office, and may carry his title with him." But his "powers as Governor become dormant the very moment he crosses the state line, and they revive again as soon as he returns and is within the borders of the state." While the governor is outside of the state, he cannot discharge the executive powers and duties and therefore, under the relevant provision of the state constitution (which was almost identical to that in the federal constitution), the powers of the governor devolve upon the lieutenant governor until the governor's return.[49]

Mississippi Democrat John Williams sprang to the president's defense. He began by citing the recent occasions when past presidents had traveled abroad. Williams noted, correctly, that Roosevelt had visited Panama for a short time. He maintained, with decidedly less accuracy, that President Taft had spent "a week or two" in Canada, and had traveled "about 2,000 miles . . . into Mexico," which would have been difficult since at a little less than 1,500 miles Taft would have hit the Guatemalan border. Although Williams's history was weak and his geography woeful, the basic thrust of his argument was sound. Should Taft have been deemed to have vacated the presidency at the moment he crossed over the international bridge? Should Vice President Charles Fairbanks have been made president just because Roosevelt stepped onto Panamanian soil?[50]

Anxious to demonstrate that he was not motivated by a narrow partisanship, Sherman insisted that had he been in the Senate during these previous administrations he would have also condemned the transgressions of those Republican presidents. Sherman was so concerned to defend himself against charges of partisanship that he missed a chance to articulate the ways in which Wilson's trip was different in kind from the foreign travels of Taft and Roosevelt. First, Wilson was out of the country for far longer than either Taft or Roosevelt. Wilson intended to be gone for the duration of the peace conference, which he estimated would take at least six weeks; in the end it kept him out of the country for closer to six months. Moreover, Roosevelt and Taft traveled to Mexico and Panama while Congress was not in session, and both were careful to be back in the capital by the beginning of the next legislative session. Wilson, in contrast, planned to leave two days after Congress had *begun* its session. The way to attack Wilson was not to adopt a literalist reading of the presidential disability clause but to differentiate between the cautious amending of tradition by Taft and Roosevelt and the radical repudiation of tradition by Wilson.

Sherman's resolution went nowhere, but not because members of Congress approved of the president's trip. Democratic Senator Henry Ashurst called on the president on the day the joint resolution was introduced, and informed the president that Congress "opposes your going to Europe." The House of Representatives, Ashurst reported, "would impeach you and the Senate convict you if they had the courage. Their lack of nerve is all that saves your removal from office." Wilson was in no mood to be conciliatory and brushed aside such sentiments as little more than a congressional "brain-storm" from which it would "recover . . . as soon as [he was] on the high seas."[51]

After Wilson departed for Europe on December 4, questions about the trip persisted but the criticisms became more muted, at least initially. Partisans were wary of criticizing the president while he was out of the country representing the nation. Republicans feared, as the *New York Tribune* expressed it, that continuing criticism of the president would "seem petty." Newspapers from across the political spectrum warned that continuing the "barrage of political criticism" would undercut the president's bargaining position in Paris and thereby undermine the interests of the United States. The nation, lectured the *New York Evening Post*, could not afford the spectacle of "a squabbling people" but needed instead to project to the world the "calm and dignified attitude" of a united populace. A nation divided was a weakened nation. Whether Wilson's decision to go to Europe was right or wrong, the *Brooklyn Eagle* concluded, the president was "entitled to the reinforcement of the American people" as he attempted to negotiate a peace settlement. Partisanship should stop at the water's edge.[52]

The contention that a president should not be criticized while out of the country confirmed the worst fears of those who had warned that foreign travel would turn the president into a kingly figure. Monarchies worked on the principle that ministers and advisers might properly be criticized but not the head of state. And now, ominously, Americans were being instructed that finding fault with the president was a sign of national weakness. One did not have to embrace Sherman's alarmism to worry that the path on which Wilson had embarked might lead in the direction of the regal presidency.

Former president Taft quickly came to the president's defense. On the day that Wilson set sail for Paris, Taft told reporters that he believed that the president's presence at the peace conference would "stamp upon it a democratic character." Taft rejected the argument that the president had no constitutional authority to leave the country. Nowhere in the Constitution, he pointed out, was there an implicit or explicit prohibition against a president leaving the country to fulfill his constitutional duties. Taft acknowledged that Wilson's actions—particularly his refusal to appoint a Republican senator to accompany him on the trip—had created a "resentful feeling," but he urged Congress not to engage in spiteful actions designed to embarrass or "nag the president" during this critically important period. The voters, he warned, would not look kindly on such efforts while the president was abroad representing the nation in world affairs. "If the fact or the manner of the President's going is a mistake, and it is unpopular with the American people," Taft advised, "that may be made a legitimate ground for criticism in a political campaign." But it would be bad for the country and bad politics for the Republicans to seem to undermine the president while he was abroad.[53]

Taft's views echoed those of the House floor leader, Republican James Mann, who promised that there would "be no concerted effort on the part of the Republicans of the House to embarrass the President in any way while he is abroad." Mann made it clear that he had no "sympathy with any attempt to pin-prick the President while he is abroad on so important a mission." While the president was abroad, Mann insisted, the president "should have the support of Congress" and that "factional strife ought not to be permitted to interfere with his mission, or to give the rest of the world the impression that the American people are divided on issues involving the peace of the world."[54]

Behind the scenes, however, leading Republicans, particularly in the Senate, were plotting to undermine the president. Henry Cabot Lodge, the influential chair of the Senate Foreign Relations Committee, confided to Theodore Roosevelt:

The sympathy of the country is with Congress to a degree I have never seen before. . . . Now with the situation so good, we do not want to make any mistakes which will cause a reaction of sympathy toward the President. Everything, so far as I see, is working our way. . . . The country as a whole is absolutely adverse to his going. . . . [N]o matter what kind of a reception he has [in Europe, his trip] is going to do him no good here, but it would be a very serious error for us to attack him for going and to make it seem as if it was a party assault. When a political situation is entirely favorable it is not wise to meddle with it. Wilson is on the downgrade.

The Republican leadership's strategy was to give Wilson the rope to hang himself.[55]

Not every Republican senator was reading from Lodge's playbook, however. On January 3, 1919, Sherman was again on the floor of the Senate sharply criticizing the president's trip. Sherman drew his colleagues' attention to a number of press reports describing the president's royal welcome in Europe. The opulent French palace in which Wilson was residing included a "ballroom, grand salon, huge state dining room and kitchens," each of which were of "regal proportions." He was to dine at "an inlaid mahogany table large enough to accommodate 35 guests." The pantries included three thousand glasses, and the presidential party had at its disposal the princess's "celebrated gold dinner service." The parlors had "great candelabras with myriads of crystals dangling from them." An impressive library was "decorated in crimson damask" and contained "many paintings and busts of Napoleon." Wilson's bedroom was filled with "innumerable relics, engravings and paintings of the famous Emperor," and all of the pieces of furniture in the room were "exquisite examples of the empire period," including a "beautiful gondola-shaped bed." Mrs. Wilson's rooms were equally splendid, adorned with "soft, French gray walls, gray satin hangings, brocaded cupids and garlands of golden hue." In short, the president and first lady would be "surrounded by magnificent surroundings of the days of the Louis—with the added attractions of open plumbing."[56]

Such luxuriousness was not limited to the president's palace in France. In London the press reported on the "gorgeous scene" of the dinner that the King of England hosted in Wilson's honor. "No more regal setting," the *Times* reported,

> had ever been arranged in Buckingham Palace than that which greeted President Wilson and Mrs. Wilson when they were escorted into the banquet hall. . . . Every royal formality which has attended epochal occasions at the palace for two or three hundred years was carried out before and during the banquet. President Wilson with Queen Mary led the procession into the dining hall, preceded by officials of the palace, splendidly costumed, bearing wands and walking backwards and making obeisance to the guests.

This "scene of splendor" included a throne at one end of the room, "a crimson carpet," "128 candles in gold candelabra, each surrounded by a pink silk shade," and "a great collection of solid gold plate and huge gold ornaments valued at $15,000,000."[57]

Sherman contrasted the president's luxurious living arrangements with reports of the wretched living conditions in the "mud swamps" of Camp Pontanezen in Brest, where seventy thousand American military personnel awaited transportation home. According to the *Washington Post*, the soldiers were living in the camp in "conditions of . . . intolerable wretchedness and misery." It was, lamented the camp

President Woodrow Wilson at Buckingham Palace, flanked on his left by King George V and Princess Mary, and on his right by Queen Mary and First Lady Edith Bolling Wilson. (Prints and Photographs Division, Library of Congress)

commander, "the worst place I have ever seen anywhere on earth." The *Post*'s reporter had "seen mud in the front-line trenches" but realized now that he "had never known what mud was until [he] visited this miserable place of suffering. . . . Every company street is a river of mud, which flows over into the tents, covering the men and the rude bed rolls in which they sleep with greasy black slime." Soldiers were fed meager and virtually inedible rations from "large zinc garbage cans." Was it right, the outraged Sherman asked his colleagues, that America's soldiers were eating out of garbage cans, while the president is feasting at an "inlaid mahogany table" with "$15,000,000 solid-gold plate service?"[58]

Sherman continued to turn the screw. "Sleepless mothers" and "despairing fathers" anxiously await news of their "long absent" sons in Europe, but they are "told the cables are overworked" and that they must be patient. And so they wait, but while they wait they read column after column of "useless" news describing in detail the fancy "gowns and headgear of queens, princesses, and Mrs. President" and the extravagant receptions of the president "in the various capitals of Europe." Anxious parents "have been crowded off the wires in this foolish and cruel display of un-American adulation abroad." The nation, Sherman thundered, needed "less obeisance and more information about the absent soldiers."[59]

While Sherman railed against Wilson's foreign junket, the Republican leadership slowed down the work of the Senate in order to force the president to call a special session. When Wilson departed for Europe he had assured the nation that the government would continue to function smoothly in his absence. Republicans made sure that did not happen. Still reeling from their crushing defeat in November, Democrats were too demoralized and disorganized to act effectively in Wilson's absence. The president continued to insist that he would not be blackmailed into calling a special session but would instead wait until the following December when the new Congress was scheduled to convene. But by filibustering and stalling critical appropriation bills, the Republican leadership in the Senate left Wilson no choice but to call Congress back into session in early May. As a result, when Wilson finally returned to the United States with the treaty in hand in early July, he came home to a Republican-controlled House and Senate open for business and prepared for political battle. Wilson had hoped to have the political stage to himself throughout the summer and fall of 1919, but by leaving the country for an extended period he allowed Republicans to maneuver him into sharing the spotlight.[60]

As John Pyne has documented, Wilson's prolonged absence from the country (he was gone from December 4, 1918, until February 24, 1919, and from March 5, 1919 until July 9, 1919) had serious repercussions for governance. The president was, as Wilson so often stressed, a party leader, not just a head of state. And as many Democrats had realized from the outset, the prolonged absence of the party head left the party adrift. Robert Woolley, an architect of Wilson's reelection in 1916, deplored the "utter lack of organization or of team work" that had resulted from the president's absence. "Only occasionally," lamented Woolley, "does anyone speak in defense of the Administration or its measures." In a strongly worded letter to his mentor and ally Colonel Edward House, Woolley advised, "There should be some one here who would spend 365 days every year looking after conditions on Capitol Hill," and that someone was obviously Wilson. "Without [Wilson's] personal leadership," as Secretary of State Lansing noted, "the Democrats in Congress . . . simply went to pieces."[61]

Feuding Democrats cabled Wilson, asking him to intervene and resolve conflicts between contending factions within the administration and the party. But the president had neither the inclination nor the information to intervene constructively. Writing from Paris on February 20, Vance McCormick confided that the president's "time in Paris is so fully occupied with Peace matters that it is most difficult for him to do anything but devote his entire time and energy to the work at hand." Harsher was the judgment of the *Evening Post*'s David Lawrence, who reported in early March that "those who know the President best consider that he is solely interested in the success of his peace mission and not concerned with domestic politics anymore." To the extent that Wilson did show interest in domestic politics it was almost exclusively in terms of how public opinion would affect the debate over ratification of the peace treaty, and especially the League of Nations.[62]

Before departing for Paris, Wilson had requested that his aide Joseph Tumulty keep him informed of "the state of public opinion on this side of the water." Tumulty did his best, feeding the president and Wilson's personal physician and confidant, Cary Grayson, a steady diet of cables about press coverage of the president's trip. Shortly after Wilson's arrival in France, Tumulty cabled Grayson to communicate his concern that the president's stay in Paris was creating an overly regal impression. "Can't you have the President do more mixing with people, if it can be done with safety? Stories that come over only show tribute to President as an official living in a palace and guarded by soldiery [which] makes [a] bad impression here." However, most of Tumulty's cables to the president, at least initially, provided upbeat assessments of media coverage and public opinion. In early January, for instance, Tumulty told Wilson that "the attitude of the whole country toward [the] trip has changed." The "criticisms of the cloak room statesmen have lost their force" and the president's "prestige and influence [have been] greatly enhanced here and abroad." A month later, Tumulty informed Wilson that despite stepped-up partisan attacks in Congress most newspapers still backed the League. Moreover, he assured Wilson that the "plain people throughout America [are] for you. You have but to ask their support and all opposition will melt away."[63]

Tumulty, however, was becoming increasingly worried about press coverage. In March, for instance, he cabled Wilson a terse message: "Publicity from European end doing great damage here." Tumulty was particularly concerned that the secrecy surrounding the peace conference deliberations was turning the press against Wilson. Shrouding the negotiations in secrecy was particularly damaging because Wilson had vowed that by traveling to Paris he would transform the way diplomacy was conducted. He had promised "open covenants of peace, openly arrived at." That was the first of Wilson's famous Fourteen Points: that "diplomacy shall proceed always frankly and in the public view." However, now instead of shaping new rules the president was playing by the old ones. Tumulty and others urged the president to be more forthcoming with the press, but Wilson only became defensive. Writing to the New York *World* correspondent Herbert Bayard Swope, Wilson explained his unwillingness to grant interviews, even to those—like Swope—who were favorably disposed to the administration: "I am surrounded by intrigue here, and the only way I can succeed is by working silently, saying nothing in public unless it becomes necessary to bring about an open [covenant]."[64]

As the press turned increasingly negative, unhappy both with the lack of openness in Europe and the lack of direction at home, Tumulty worked desperately to reassure the public that the president's continued absence from the capital was not affecting the functioning of the government. On Sunday, March 23, the *World*, the newspaper most closely allied with the administration, devoted virtually its entire front page to blunting the growing perception that there was "nobody home" in Washington. "The absence of the President," declared the *World*, "causes no inconvenience or delay." Communicating with Wilson in Paris was "to all intents and purposes as easy as when he [was] in the White House." Cables could be sent at any hour, day or night. Furthermore, Tumulty faithfully "handled and looked after . . . all routine matters" at the White House "in just the same fashion as if the President were at hand." Other White House officials "follow the example of Mr. Tumulty, going about their daily tasks in precisely the same manner as if the President was expected to drop in on a reviewing and inspection expedition [at any] minute." In sum, the *World* concluded reassuringly, "the Government runs along on an even keel without the President."[65]

Even the *World*'s spirited defense of the administration betrayed signs that all was not well, contrary to the administration's public professions. One clue was that "the most impressive and understandable illustration" offered in support of the contention that the government was running on "an even keel" was that "preliminary preparations" had begun "to paint the White House and executive offices." The *World* boasted that last week "workmen in spotted overalls gayly began taking measurements for scaffolding and leaders" and "soon the work of daubing oil and white lead will be going on under union rules." If this was the best the administration could offer up as evidence of a smoothly functioning White House, then readers might be pardoned for fearing that the president's critics were right.[66]

Tumulty made sure that Wilson was aware of the criticism being leveled at the administration, but the president was unsure what to make of what he read in cables. "It is hard to tell from this distance," Wilson confided to Secretary of the Navy Josephus Daniels, "how far the malicious partisan attacks that are constantly being made reflect any considerable volume of public opinion." He suspected, as one of his wife's confidants reported, that the newspapers "were controlled by the large moneyed interests and [therefore were] not in touch with the people." Wilson appeared confident that when he returned home the people would instinctively rally around him and the League, and that the criticisms in Congress and the press would melt away or at least be rendered inconsequential.[67]

Wilson, of course, miscalculated. Most accounts of Wilson's failure to secure support for the League of Nations focus on his actions when he returned to the United States in July, and they particularly zero in on his ambitious speaking tour that ended dramatically with Wilson's physical collapse. But his prolonged European journey played a critical and underappreciated role in Wilson's political defeat. It not only demoralized his political allies and galvanized his opponents, but it pulled the president out of the country when he most needed his ear to the ground. Absent from the United States for more than six months, Wilson, as Pyne points out, "lost touch" with the state of public opinion and "failed to gauge the depths of Democratic weakness." To be sure, even if Wilson had remained in the country he would have retained his conviction that foreign policy was properly a presidential domain and he would not have readily relinquished his belief that he could go over the heads of Congress and the press and win the people to his side. However, his extended absence made it easier for him to journey down the disastrous path to which he stubbornly clung. Fears of the corrupting influence of Europe proved to be wide of the mark, but the concern that a president who ventured abroad would lose touch with the people he represented proved prescient.[68]

A "RETURN TO NORMALCY"

Wilson's European sojourn provoked a strong Republican reaction after the war. Warren Harding campaigned for president in 1920 on the promise to return the nation to "normalcy." Normalcy meant pulling back from Europe. It meant an end to heroic crusades and sharp partisan divisions. "Tranquility at home," Harding intoned on the campaign trail, "is more precious than peace abroad." It meant scaling back the scope of government and reining in presidential power. And it meant presidents sticking close to home, remaining at their post of duty while Congress was in session.[69]

Although Wilson was not on the Democratic ticket in 1920, Republicans continued to pound away at Wilson for his European travels. A campaign pamphlet produced by the Republican National Committee, titled "Mr. Wilson at Court," reminded voters of the adulation and extravagance that accompanied Wilson's excursion to Paris, "where the League of Nations was born in all the pomp of imperialism." The naval vessel on which Wilson had traveled "was fitted up with extraordinary sumptuousness. . . . Glass canopies were built under which the President could promenade [and] the most celebrated chefs from New York hotels were engaged to prepare the coffee and rolls for the world-savers." When the host of "administration favorites" arrived in Paris the extravagance became even more obscene and wasteful. Occupying an entire, exclusive Parisian hotel, the peace delegates consumed $1.5 million in taxpayer money. Everywhere the president went he was surrounded with grandeur that "would have stupefied, if not altogether bewildered, an average American farmer." Wilson was seduced by the royal receptions and magnificent dinners, the splendid costumes and "brilliant uniforms," the "royally bedecked footmen" and the fancy coaches.

> Is it any wonder that in this fantastic pageant the United States gradually became to him a mere speck on the earth, and the President came to believe he was specially ordained by Providence to sit on Mount Olympus and rule the world? . . . Is it any wonder he returned home to the plain American people with the arrogance of an autocrat, assuming to set up a one-man government? . . .

Was this spectacle just the hypnosis that Washington, Jefferson, Adams and Monroe and their associates foresaw when they adjured their countrymen, with the fervency of a prayer to High Heaven, to beware forever of European entanglements and European blandishments?

Wilson's course vindicated the enduring wisdom of the founders and of the ironclad custom. And voters could thank "the solid patriotism" of the Republican-controlled Senate for preventing Wilson from bringing the forms and habits of European royalty to America's shores.[70]

Nor was this indictment merely a matter of overheated campaign rhetoric, for the backlash against Wilson's trip inhibited his Republican successors from traveling abroad. Neither Harding, Calvin Coolidge, nor Herbert Hoover embarked on any significant foreign travel while president. Harding only visited Canada for a day on his way back from Alaska, and Coolidge just left the country once, to attend a conference in Cuba in the final year of his presidency. As Coolidge's Secretary of Commerce, Hoover had traversed the globe, but apart from a brief trip to Puerto Rico and the Virgin Islands he never left the United States while he was president.

While serving in the U.S. Senate, Harding had been among those Republicans who were sharply critical of Wilson for traveling to Europe. Although not as vituperative as Sherman, the genial Harding made his disapproval clear. For Harding, the trip was a symptom of the larger problem that Wilson put the interests of other nations above those of the United States. In Harding's view, Wilson's decision to leave the United States at a time that the nation faced severe social and economic dislocations was negligent and a betrayal of the national interest. For six years, Harding lamented in January 1919, Wilson had dictated to a Democratic Congress, so that "it can't do anything except as he orders, and then he runs away at a difficult time and leaves no one to teach and direct in his stead." In his campaign for president, Harding made it clear that he would put the interests of the United States above the interests of the world. He would be a different sort of president from Wilson by staying at his desk and respecting the will of Congress.[71]

When President Harding made what he called a "passing call" to Canada on his way back from Alaska, he reflected upon the tradition against foreign travel by a president. "I may as well confess to you at the outset a certain perplexity as to how I should address you," he began.

> The truth of the matter is that this is the first time I have ever spoken as President in any country other than my own. Indeed, so far as I can recall, I am, with the single exception of my immediate predecessor, the first President in office even to set foot on politically foreign soil. . . . True, there is no definite inhibition upon one doing so, such as prevents any but a natural born from becoming President, but an early prepossession soon developed into a tradition and for more than a hundred years held the effect of unwritten law. I am not

prepared to say that the custom was not desirable, perhaps even needful, in the early days, when time was the chief requisite of travel. Assuredly, too, at present, the Chief Magistrate of a great Republic ought not to cultivate the habit or make a hobby of wandering over all the continents of the earth. . . . But exceptions are required to prove rules. And Canada is an exception, a most notable exception, from every viewpoint of the United States. You are not only our neighbor, but a very good neighbor.

Canada was a close neighbor and so Harding's transgression of the tradition could be forgiven. Since he was only there for a day he could not be charged with "wandering over all the continents of the earth," as his predecessor had.[72]

THE GLOBETROTTING PRESIDENCY

Not until Franklin Roosevelt's presidency did the proscription against foreign travel finally crumble. At first the change was gradual. In his initial year in office, Roosevelt's only trip out of the country was a brief visit to the family's summer home on the Canadian island of Campobello. The following year, after Congress adjourned, he set sail for Hawaii, becoming the first president to visit the Hawaiian islands. En route he visited Haiti, Colombia, and Panama. In 1936 he combined a short summer trip to Campobello with a quick official visit to Quebec. Immediately after his reelection in 1936, FDR traveled to South America, visiting Brazil, where he addressed the legislature; Uruguay, where he met the president; and Argentina, where he attended the Inter-American Conference for the Maintenance of Peace. In addition, in 1934, 1935, and 1936, FDR sailed to the British-owned Bahamas for a two-week spring vacation.

In four years FDR had undertaken more foreign travel than his three Republican predecessors had in twelve. It was not, however, until the outbreak of World War II that Roosevelt shattered the ironclad custom that had so vexed his cousin. President Wilson did not feel he could leave the country while the war was still ongoing, but Roosevelt had no such reservations. With the exception of his fishing trips to the Bahamas, FDR had refrained from leaving the country while Congress was in session. But with the outbreak of war in Europe, Congress was in session almost perpetually, particularly in the first few years of the war. If Roosevelt was going to meet with Allied leaders—which he believed was essential to the war effort—it would have to be while Congress was in session. Sometimes the meetings took place in Washington, D.C., but often they required FDR to travel abroad. In 1941 he met with Churchill in Argentina, and in January 1943 he traveled to Casablanca in North Africa to meet Churchill again. At the end of 1943 FDR traveled to Cairo and Tehran to confer with Churchill, Stalin, and Chiang Kai-shek, and then visited General Dwight Eisenhower in North Africa. Finally, and most famously, in February 1945, he traveled to Yalta (as well as to Malta, Egypt, and Algiers).[73]

After World War II, the ironclad custom no longer applied. The war's enduring lesson, according to conventional Cold War wisdom, was that the United States could not retreat from entangling alliances or run from the Old World's problems. The United States was now the "leader of the free world," and the president could no longer shrink from his world leadership role or the traveling that went with that role. Indeed the phrase "leader of the free world," which was used in the late 1940s to describe the nation's indispensable place in the new world order, quickly mutated into a presidential job title. The American president himself became the leader of the free world, even if the free people of that world had no say in his selection.[74]

Over the last sixty years, foreign presidential travel has increased steadily and inexorably. Between 1945 and 1968 presidents averaged about nine days of international travel per year, between 1969 and 1988 fifteen days, and between 1989 and 2006 almost twenty-seven days. The most adventurous was Bill Clinton, who spent an average of twenty-nine days a year traveling abroad during his eight years in office, and about thirty-eight days a year during his second term. Even George W. Bush, who reportedly shares neither his father's nor Clinton's appetite for world travel, has averaged almost twenty-five days a year, essentially the same as his father's total and well above Clinton's first-term average.[75]

On occasion, the old anxieties reassert themselves and presidents find themselves under attack for spending too much time strutting across the world's stage. Democrats vying for the party's nomination in 1992, for instance, pounded George H. W. Bush for his foreign travel, complaining that he spent too much time attending to the world's problems and not enough time tending to domestic ones. Sounding strangely like Warren Harding, Bill Clinton campaigned in New Hampshire by insisting that "it is time for us to have a president who cares more about Littleton, N.H., than about Liechtenstein; more about Manchester than Micronesia." Bush felt the sting of such criticism. Asked at a press conference whether he would attend an arms control summit, Bush replied, "Well, I've got to watch foreign travel. I don't want to have it leveled against me that I'm interested in only one area." Bush changed more than just his rhetoric; he changed his behavior, canceling a scheduled trip to Asia and then putting it back on the calendar only after it was recast as a trip designed to boost American exports and protect American jobs. In the nine months prior to his defeat in 1992, Bush was out of the country for only nine days.[76]

Generally, however, modern presidents have seen foreign travel as an opportunity to project an aura of glamour and command. Perhaps the most famous instance was Nixon's historic trip to China in February 1972, a carefully staged pageant that provided the nation with a captivating week of live televised theater. Determined to maximize the trip's impact at home, the White House arranged for Air Force One to touch down in Beijing during prime time. On the return leg the president waited on the tarmac for nine hours in Anchorage, Alaska, so that his arrival could be again covered live on prime time. Prior to the trip Nixon's popularity had been mired at around 50 percent, but immediately afterward his job approval jumped to 56 percent, a level of support he had not seen since March of the previous year.[77]

Few presidential trips, of course, can match the drama of Nixon going to China. Indeed, as foreign travel has become an increasingly routine part of their job, it is more difficult for presidents to command the intensive media coverage that accompanied the foreign travel of Eisenhower, Kennedy, or Nixon. Nixon's one trip to China netted forty-one hours of coverage on network television, whereas George W. Bush's three visits to China produced only a tiny fraction of that amount. Paradoxically, the more presidents travel abroad the less political mileage they may be able to extract from a trip.[78]

Political scientists have found little evidence that foreign travel per se boosts presidential job approval, but they have found that presidents are more likely to undertake such travel when their approval rating is low and when the economy is weak. Presidents act as if they believe foreign travel will help them, either because it will change the subject or because it will make them appear presidential. Perhaps presidents are behaving irrationally, or perhaps the measures of public evaluation that political scientists use are too crude. Or perhaps struggling presidents look to travel for a psychic boost. As Bush's press secretary, Marlin Fitzwater, has observed: "Foreign travel does a lot for the President under siege in terms of his own psyche. . . . Every president enjoys traveling in foreign countries because it makes him feel like a President again." That may explain why Nixon spent so much time traveling abroad in the final months before his resignation in 1974, and why in 1998, as Republicans were pressing the case for impeachment, Clinton racked up a record forty-two days of foreign travel in four continents.[79]

Is all this foreign travel necessary or desirable? Many believe it is. Political scientist Charles Jones suggests that it gives presidents a valuable chance to take the measure of their opposite numbers, "how they talk, how they laugh, . . . if they laugh." Direct personal communication provides presidents an opportunity to forge ties of friendships or at least bonds of trust that will help facilitate compromise or avert conflict. Others are more skeptical. George Ball, who served in the 1960s as Under Secretary of State and as the U.S. Ambassador to the United Nations, sees it as a throwback to "the palmy days of the European dynasties [when] kings and emperors, sovereigns of all titles and descriptions, were accustomed to visit one another's courts." It took centuries, Ball contends, to create a diplomatic system built upon "impersonal diplomacy practiced through career ambassadors, acting on instructions from professional foreign offices." By making the president diplomat-in-chief and by centralizing control over foreign policy in the White House, the United States was "moving back toward the medieval dynastic practice" in which "a king could dispose of the affairs of his kingdom as he saw fit."[80]

Whether one applauds or deplores the globetrotting presidency, there is little prospect of its being rolled back. Both Clinton and George W. Bush came to power pledging to focus on domestic politics, yet each has succumbed to the attractions of the world stage, traveling abroad more days and more miles than any other presidents in American history. Much of this travel is now dictated by annual summit meetings, most notably the G-8 Summit, which dates from the mid-1970s, and the APEC (Asia-Pacific Economic Cooperation) Summit, which dates from 1993. In his first six years in office, George Bush never missed a G-8 or APEC meeting and attended an average of four summit meetings a year. Even if attendance at such summits doesn't boost a president's popularity, it certainly shapes how people understand the president's role, cementing in place the belief that the president should run the nation's foreign policy.

The increase in presidential summitry and foreign travel is particularly notable since 1989. Prior to 1989, no president averaged more than fifteen days of foreign travel a year; since 1989 no president has averaged less than twenty-five days abroad. The two Bushes and Clinton have each averaged about four international summits a year, whereas Reagan attended less than half that number, and Carter, Ford, and Nixon fewer still. Why did presidents' wanderlust increase so markedly after 1989? Why did George W. Bush and Clinton, two presidents who began with little experience or interest in foreign policy, travel abroad so much more frequently than a president like Nixon, a seasoned foreign policy expert who relished the international stage? The simplest explanation is transportation technology: in 1989 the president was given a new, far more luxurious, and faster Air Force One.

The old norm against traveling abroad had been remarkably resilient in the face of changing transportation technologies. Faster and safer ships had not led nineteenth-century presidents to head for Europe. Isolationism tethered the nineteenth- and early-twentieth-century presidencies. However, as the nation's conception of its place in the world changed, the ironclad custom against a president traveling abroad was reduced to an archaic remnant of a bygone age. An isolationist nation could afford a tethered presidency, an internationalist one could not. Once the norm had been kicked away, there was nothing to prevent technological change from reshaping the bounds of presidential travel. Those transformations in transportation technology profoundly shaped not only the presidents' emergence as a leader on the world stage but, as we shall see in the next chapter, the way presidents interacted with their own people.

CHAPTER SEVEN

Trains, Planes, and the Paradox of the Transportation Revolution

"Aviation is demanding and unforgiving," wrote a columnist in the Washington *Evening Star* after news leaked out of Franklin Roosevelt's secret trip to Casablanca. "It is still not clear," the journalist clucked, "that the obvious advantages of air travel carry greater weight than the peril incurred by risking the life of a president on a journey through the sky." The columnist's concern was understandable. Prior to FDR's flight, no American president had ever traveled by air, not even for a short domestic flight. And Roosevelt's daring trip across the Atlantic Ocean was anything but short. It took five grueling days to get from Washington, D.C., to Casablanca.[1]

Roosevelt's 17,000-mile round trip journey commenced on the evening of January 9, 1943, with a secret train trip to Miami, where the president and his party boarded the *Dixie Clipper* in the predawn darkness. The "flying boat" traversed the first 1,600 miles to Trinidad in about eleven hours. After staying overnight in Trinidad, the president then flew an eight-hour, 1,200-mile leg to Belem, Brazil, where the plane was refueled and serviced (and almost rammed accidentally by a naval scow). After a three-hour stopover in Brazil, the *Dixie Clipper* then made the eighteen-hour ocean crossing to British Gambia in West Africa. From there the president changed to a propeller plane, in which he flew another nine hours before touching down at his destination in Casablanca on January 14. By the time the president got back to Washington on the final day of January, he had spent a total of nearly ninety hours in the air.[2]

Adding to the drama of the flight was the secrecy shrouding the trip. Although Roosevelt left the White House on January 9, it was not until the 27th—after the conference had finished—that the trip was made public. The press corps had been notified on the evening of January 9 that the president was "taking another trip," but they were not told where he was going. Reporters were "forcefully" reminded by the Office of Censorship that "the code of voluntary censorship . . . forbids publication of any hints or speculation about the President's movements." Although rumors abounded about the president's destination, the press remained mum. The secrecy that enveloped the trip fooled even the Axis powers, who suspected Roosevelt was meeting Churchill in Washington. The Germans came close to discovering the truth when they intercepted a cable that identified the meeting place, but they thought Casablanca referred literally to the "white house." Truth sometimes is stranger than fiction.[3]

As soon as the president's trip became public knowledge, letters poured into the White House, expressing a mix of anxiousness, amazement, and admiration at the president's audacity. Many applauded FDR's courage. Harold Tabor, an insurance company executive, wrote to FDR to pay his "humble respects to a courageous president who when duty called made a hazardous trip. . . . to defend democracy and us all." Roosevelt's perilous journey "was an act of heroism beyond the call of duty" and he deserved the nation's "highest medal" for having made it. Mr. Tabor conceded that he had "not always seen eye to eye with all of [FDR's] policies," yet he could not but "admire intestinal fortitude when it is displayed for the benefit of us all." A Rhode Island woman with a son in the military also wrote to the president to express her "gratitude . . . for the courage and inspiration you gave those brave men there and making them feel nearer home." The president even received encouragement from a fourth grade class in Shidler, Oklahoma, which declared that his "braveness in crossing the Atlantic Ocean was very, very fine."[4]

Most of the letter writers combined admiration for Roosevelt's courage with admonitions to be more careful in the future. Typical was a druggist and World War I veteran from LaGrange, Georgia, who wrote to tell the president that he had "done a great job" but also to warn him against taking "too many hazardous chances." If "something might happen to you," the man explained, "then we people who love you so much would be lost ourselves" because only "you can steer us clear and out into a new world order." In a similar vein, an Oakland, California, woman wrote, "It was so like you, so courageous to take that dangerous trip to Africa, but it makes me weak all over to think of it because if anything should have happened to you, what would we, all the people do. . . . We would be lost without you. Please do not endanger yourself again." A woman with three sons in the army was still more insistent: "Please Mr President don't ever leave the USA again while this war is going on. What would we do if you should be on a plane that would be lost. No one could fill your place." A pleading telegram from a resident of Washington, D.C., summed up the feelings of the many admirers who wrote to FDR: "Please Mr. President don't do it again not just for your sake but for the sake of millions all over the world."[5]

Other letter writers tried communicating their concern to Steve Early, the president's secretary. For instance, a Connecticut man wrote to Early urging him to "bring home" to Roosevelt "the danger of air travel, especially over the ocean." "The body of the President of the United States," he explained, "is the property of all of its citizens, and neither he nor anyone should be allowed to endanger it in even the slightest degree." The nation had waited "a long time . . . to get a man in the White

House who would inaugurate such social reforms as Social Security, Unemployment Compensation, [and] bank insurance." The "common people" could not afford to lose their champion. "Where would we find a humanitarian and a statesman capable of replacing him?" The correspondent confessed that he had "no organizing ability" and he did not "ordinarily favor pressure groups," but he felt "so strongly on this matter" that he would "gladly contribute out of a modest salary toward any 'Ground the President' movement."[6]

Judging by the letters written to Roosevelt, many Americans would have gladly joined a movement to keep the president out of the sky. Joseph Kramer, a New York lawyer and loyal Democrat, scolded the president for the risks he had taken in flying to Casablanca. Describing himself as "an ardent, unwavering admirer of your leadership . . . ever since the first day that you became Governor of the State of New York," Kramer announced that this was "the first occasion that I have to disapprove of what you did. . . . It's just plain luck that the plane which crashed a few days ago containing some of our military leaders was not yours. . . . I therefore respectfully implore you to avoid hereafter such great risks to your person as come from taking airplane trips regardless of how important the purpose may be." The president received the same advice from a 75-year-old man who reminded FDR of the "many fatal disasters in traveling by air" and asked if the president "could not get someone else to take these dangerous air voyages, and save the American people from having to meet such a *terrible Disaster*."[7]

The president, who never liked flying, would have been happy to accommodate his fellow citizens' request that he avoid air travel. Had the Secret Service not ruled out ocean travel as too dangerous, FDR would almost certainly have opted for a more leisurely trip aboard a naval vessel. For Roosevelt the problem with air travel was not that it was dangerous but rather that it did not allow him to relax and enjoy himself in the way he could when traveling by ship or on the presidential rail car, the *Magellan*. However, Roosevelt clearly relished the daring of the secret rendezvous with Churchill. "The more the president's aides fretted over the risk he was taking," historian Doris Kearns Goodwin observes, "the more excited Roosevelt became, his enthusiasm like that of a young child escaping the control of his parents." But the trip was about more than Roosevelt's love of adventure and intrigue. The wily president understood the strategic value of the Allied leaders meeting "right under the nose of the Axis powers"—and at a site which until just two months before had been under Axis control. Traveling by air, which no president had ever done, was guaranteed to enhance the dramatic effect of the meeting.[8]

Roosevelt calculated correctly. Although the risks of the trip made many of his advisers and much of the public nervous, the audacity of the trip captured the nation's imagination. Indeed, according to the *Detroit Free Press*, the meeting had "electrified the world." The *Louisville Courier-Journal* trumpeted the trip as "a bold and spectacular stroke in the war of nerves" that showed "the spirit of offense, daring and resolute." The *Boston Post* declared that "America stands today mute in awed admiration of [the president's] bravery . . . and valor," and proposed that the nation recognize Roosevelt's "courage on his historic voyage" by bestowing on him a Congressional Medal of Honor. The historic trip was described by the *Philadelphia Record* as a testament to the "heroic boldness" and "magnificent stamina" of the president. "Our children's children, and their children's children," the *Record* gushed, "will read with awe and excitement of the famous journey of Franklin Roosevelt— to win their peace and security along with victory for their fathers."[9]

Many commentators sensed that Roosevelt's "epoch-making and tradition-shattering" journey was a momentous event, but few appreciated how profoundly air travel would change the presidency. Those who paid attention to the larger significance of the event focused on the ways in which the trip signaled a new willingness on the part of the United States to assume a leadership role in the world of nations. The *New York Times*, for instance, which labeled Roosevelt's trip a "bold and brilliant stroke of leadership," believed its lasting importance was that it "foreshadow[ed] . . . the United States accepting its proper share of responsibility . . . in world affairs." A nation whose president was able and willing to fly across the world was a nation ready to take its rightful place as a world power. Similar lessons from the historic journey were drawn by the Washington *Evening Star*. In breaking the barriers that had constrained previous presidents and shattering "every tradition regarding the safety of the President," the *Evening Star* reasoned, Roosevelt had "made a journey that symbolizes the new part we have come to play, as a nation, in the new and smaller world that is being forged by the war; a world where distances and modes of travel no longer mean what they once meant and where territorial boundaries no longer stand as rigid walls." In the age of air travel, isolationism was no longer an option for the United States.[10]

The huge oceans that separated the United States from other powerful nation-states were losing their significance as natural barriers. Columbia University president Nicholas Murray Butler was among those who celebrated Roosevelt's trip as a harbinger of a new world order. The president's journey to Casablanca, Butler insisted, was "one of the greatest happenings in the history of the modern world" because it demonstrated that "the great oceans and the limitless skies are not barriers but pathways in order to meet for consultation and common interest." Butler's euphoria, however, missed the broader significance of the event. Tearing down the natural barriers that had protected the United States for so long brought with it a need to create new barriers and protections. It meant not just more cooperation and consultation but the emergence of a national security state. Throughout the nineteenth and early twentieth century, the protection afforded by the Atlantic Ocean had enabled the United States to avoid the state-building pattern—specifically, a standing army, centralization, and strong executive power—characteristic of leading European nation-states.[11]

If presidential air travel was the death knell of isolationism, the demise of isolationism also guaranteed the fall of congressional government and the rise of presidential government. The same forces that pulled the United States onto the world stage pushed the presidency to the center of the American political stage. In previous wars, the wartime powers exercised by the American presidency were short-lived; when the war ended, Congress and the states quickly reasserted their powers. World War II was different. Wartime powers became institutionalized and woven into the fabric of political life. The Cold War had no discernible end point, and dangers appeared to be everywhere. The task of protecting a vulnerable nation fell to the federal government and especially to the president.

Roosevelt's flight to Casablanca had dazzled the nation and induced a kaleidoscope of conflicting emotions, of wonder, admiration, concern, and condemnation. But the exceptional quickly became the expected. Presidential globetrotting rapidly became routine. Indeed even FDR's journey to Tehran and Cairo at the end of 1943 and to Yalta in February 1945 invited little public commentary. These important meetings were, of course, closely attended to in the press, but people had evidently already accustomed themselves to the notion that in the new world order presidents needed to travel across the globe to meet the leaders of other nations.

TOURING THE COUNTRY BY RAIL

That airplanes made it easier for presidents to travel abroad and to engage in face-to-face negotiations with foreign leaders is obvious. Less self-evident is the effect that air travel had on the president's interaction with the American public. One might expect that the capability to travel greater distances much more quickly would draw the president closer to the people. In the late nineteenth century, after all, it took a president nearly two weeks to reach the West Coast. Today the president can leave Washington after breakfast and be in California by lunch. The ability to traverse thousands of miles in several hours rather than several weeks made distant regions of the country more accessible. But planes also allowed presidents to be more selective and strategic about where they visited. Trains took presidents through scores of small towns that they might otherwise choose not to visit, whereas planes enabled presidents to pass over those smaller or less strategic locales and head directly for the large population center, the swing state, or the desired photo opportunity. The paradox at the heart of the transportation revolution, then, is that while air travel has enabled presidents to travel further and faster than ever before, many communities now see the president less frequently than they had in the era of rail travel.

Consider, for example, my hometown of Salem, Oregon. Although it is the state capital, with a population of nearly 150,000 people, Salem has not had a presidential visit in nearly sixty years. The last president to visit Salem was Harry Truman in 1948. This might not seem so surprising; after all, it's a big country and the president can hardly be expected to visit every small and medium-sized town in the nation. Yet between 1880 and 1923, Salem received visits from six presidents: Rutherford Hayes, Benjamin Harrison, Theodore Roosevelt, William Howard Taft, Woodrow Wilson, and Warren Harding. During that forty-three-year span, only James Garfield, Chester Arthur, Grover Cleveland, and William McKinley failed to pay a presidential visit to the capital city of Oregon. And McKinley would have visited Salem in 1901 but for his wife's illness, which forced him to cancel the northwestern leg of his cross-county tour.[12]

To be sure, some of these were visits in name only. The trains that carried both Wilson and Harding stopped in Salem for only a few minutes in the middle of the night. Harding was ill and so the town was asked not to make arrangements to welcome the president, and Wilson was rushing to San Francisco to mount his defense of the League of Nations. But the other four visits were substantial ones. In 1880, followed by a "large number of patriotic and enthusiastic citizens," Hayes was escorted to the state capitol where he was introduced to members of the legislature. After a brief exchange of greetings, the president went outdoors where he addressed an appreciative crowd of some 5,000 people; not a bad turnout for a town of only about 2,500. Salem wasn't a lot bigger when Harrison arrived a decade later, yet a reported 20,000 people came from the surrounding areas and braved steady rain to greet the president and hear him speak. Schoolchildren in Salem were even given the day off so they could cheer the president. When Roosevelt visited in 1903 an estimated 50,000 people gathered at the steps of the capitol to listen to the president in what was hailed as "the grandest occasion the city has ever known." Taft's visit in 1911 was also a grand event. Children were again given the day off from school, and thousands of people lined the streets to see the president. After eating "the most elegant breakfast ever served" in Salem, Taft participated in a colorful parade through the downtown area. Along the way the president answered questions from schoolchildren and spoke extemporaneously to an enthusiastic "mob of Willamette University students" on the virtues of studying "the science of government." When he reached the courthouse Taft delivered a formal address to an audience of more than 5,000 people.[13]

It might be thought that the presidential attention lavished on Salem during this period was due to the state's electoral competitiveness. But throughout the late nineteenth and early twentieth centuries Oregon was a reasonably safe Republican seat; the only time the state went Democratic between 1876 and 1924 was when Roosevelt ran as a third-party candidate in 1912, splitting the Republican vote and allowing Wilson to carry the state. The year after Roosevelt's 1903 visit to Salem, he crushed his Democratic opponent in Oregon by almost 50 percentage points. And Harrison carried Oregon by better than 10 percentage points in both 1888 and 1892. In fact the average presidential margin of victory in Oregon between 1876 and 1924 was about 14 percentage points, nearly triple the margin of victory in Oregon between 1988

A beaming President Theodore Roosevelt walks away from the Oregon state capitol in Salem. To his right is Oregon's Democratic governor, George Chamberlain. (Marion County Historical Society)

and 2004. So presidential presence (and absence) in Salem cannot be reduced to a matter of electoral incentives.[14]

Salem was visited by late-nineteenth- and early-twentieth-century presidents not for its strategic value but largely because the main rail line went through Salem. Presidents traveling up and down the West Coast had to pass through Salem. And if a president was passing through town, residents expected him to stop, even if only briefly, to address them and to allow them to pay homage to the nation's chief executive.[15]

When President Hayes visited Salem on September 30, 1880, it was part of a ten-week, cross-country rail journey traversing more than ten thousand miles and some twenty states and territories. Hayes left the capital in late August and did not return until early November. Along the way he exchanged greetings with the residents of hundreds of small and medium-sized towns across the nation. At some spots the president would do little more than wave to the crowd from the back of the train, and at others he and his traveling companions would briefly address the crowd before moving on.

A teacher in Salem, Oregon, conducts her pupils through a song of welcome for President Taft. (Marion County Historical Society)

By the time Hayes reached Salem, for instance, he had already greeted or spoken to crowds at several stops along the route that day. Hayes had spent the previous night in the southern Oregon town of Roseburg (population 822). Departing early in the morning the traveling party stopped first in Oakland (population 369), where they breakfasted. Later that morning the train stopped in Eugene City (population 1,117), where Hayes addressed a large crowd from the train's back platform after being formally greeted by a welcoming committee. The president's train also stopped at Junction City (population 428) to allow the president to acknowledge the cheers of the crowd that had gathered at the station as well as to enable a representative from the city to board the train and formally welcome the president on behalf of the town's residents. Further up the line, the train stopped again at Albany (population 1,867), where an "immense concourse of people" had gathered. The mayor of the city was on hand to welcome the president, who offered "a few fitting remarks" in return. After leaving Salem in the afternoon the president's train made its way to Portland, but before reaching its destination it stopped briefly at Aurora (population 291) and Oregon City (population 1,263) to enable the "large crowds" to greet their president and the president to acknowledge their cheers. Even where the train did not stop, "the people congregated in large numbers . . . at every station" to get "a glimpse of the party" and to "cheer . . . lustily as the train passed." The entire day's

Beneath a patriotically decorated bower, President Benjamin Harrison addresses a crowd at a whistle-stop in Santa Ana, California, April 23, 1891. (Santa Ana History Room)

trip from Roseburg to Portland, according to one newspaper account, "was a series of ovations." It was, in short, a typical day in the life of a nineteenth-century president on tour.[16]

The next president to make it out to the Pacific coast was Benjamin Harrison in 1891. Harrison's cross-country trip was done at a considerably faster pace than Hayes's tour. Whereas Hayes had taken ten weeks to complete his journey, Harrison did a comparable distance in about five weeks. In part that was due to improved transportation, but most of it was down to Harrison's preference for a more tightly scheduled tour; at trip's end the punctilious Harrison celebrated that the trip had occurred "without one minute's variation from the pre-arranged schedule." Despite Harrison's haste, he delivered at least 140 speeches in thirty-five days, an average of about 4 speeches a day. Toward the end of the trip, he delivered 11 speeches in a single day.[17]

Roosevelt's cross-country tour in 1903 was even more impressive. Roosevelt was absent from Washington for over nine weeks, traveled 14,000 miles, and delivered 265 speeches in over 150 towns and cities in 25 states and territories. Sixteen of those days were spent in the solitude of Yellowstone Park; no crowds, no speeches, and no reporters. But for most of the remainder of the tour Roosevelt was in almost perpetual motion, delivering speeches, shaking hands, patting heads, waving at crowds, and brandishing his trademark grin in villages and towns that today rarely if ever warrant a presidential visit.[18]

Roosevelt spent an entire Sunday, for instance, in Sharon Springs, an isolated "little ranch town" on the west Kansas plains with a population of fewer than 200 people. The tiny town buzzed with excitement at Roosevelt's presence. "Every ranch within a radius of forty or fifty miles," Roosevelt observed, had "sent its occupants to church that day," and every pew but the president's "bulge[d] with occupants." The village was crowded with "buggies, ranch wagons, and dispirited-looking saddle ponies [that] were tied to everything available." Estimates put the number in the town at 1,000 people. A preacher from Kansas City was even brought in for the great occasion. After the service was over, the Secret Service formed a greeting line and the president "had a firm handshake and a pleasant word" for each and every person in the congregation. Roosevelt estimated that he shook as many as 700 hands. After an afternoon horseback ride, Roosevelt returned to find that "all the population that had not left was gathered solemnly around the train." Among the crowd was a small girl who offered the president a young badger that she and her brother had caught. The president accepted and when the presidential party resumed the journey the following day they did so with the badger on board.[19]

Sundays provided a good excuse for a day of rest, but most days on the train followed a punishing schedule. Before arriving in Sharon Springs on Saturday evening, Roosevelt had covered more than 350 miles, beginning that morning in the state capital of Topeka. The train made nine scheduled stops of between ten and fifteen minutes each in towns ranging in size from Salina, which had a population of about 6,000 people, to WaKeeney, which counted only about 400 residents. Even in the smallest towns Roosevelt was received by "large and cheering crowds." At WaKeeney, for instance, the crowd was estimated at between 1,500 and 2,000 people. At Junction City, a relative metropolis of nearly 5,000 people, an estimated 12,000 people gathered to hear the president speak.[20]

Even where Roosevelt was not scheduled to stop and speak, the train would often halt for a brief time and the president would greet the crowd. Wamego, for instance, was not on the announced itinerary, but the president stopped there to speak a "few words" to the "large crowd" that had gathered at the depot. At Ellis, a town of fewer than 1,000 people, "the train stopped for ice and to change engines," and while the train was stopped Roosevelt "held a reception and invited the people to walk thro. & inspect his train." The president's train also made an unexpected stop in the small town of Collyer to allow the "iron horses" pulling the president's train to "have a drink." Most of the town's citizens had traveled to nearby WaKeeney for the day to see and hear Roosevelt but those who stayed behind gathered round the president's train as it came to a stop at the water tank. Roosevelt emerged from his car, greeted a crowd of some 100 people, and shook hands with everybody, "both large and small." By the end of the day, according to one estimate, Roosevelt had addressed crowds in twenty different towns in a twelve-hour period.[21]

Moreover, even when Roosevelt did not stop in a town, his train would often slow to a crawl as it passed a crowd that had gathered to pay tribute to the president. In Wilson, for instance, a town of about 1,000 people, the president's train rolled slowly through the town in order to give the crowd a "good look" at the president, who

Expectant young faces greet the arrival of Theodore Roosevelt in Salina, Kansas. (Prints and Photographs Division, Library of Congress)

stood on the rear platform of the train, "bowing right and left and smiling that inimitable smile of his." This was repeated at countless other small towns along the rail line until, finally, Roosevelt arrived in Sharon Springs at 8:30 that night, bringing the "continuous ovation" to a merciful end.[22]

Roosevelt loved a crowd and relished public speaking, but even he found the pace grueling. Barely an hour would go by before the train would pull into another station where another enthusiastic crowd awaited, expecting their president to appear, wave, smile, and speak. Toward the end he confided to Henry Cabot Lodge that the trip had been "very severe" and had him "feeling jaded and tired.... Now, thank heavens, I have little more than a week left." Writing several months later, Roosevelt told a friend that as much as he "liked and respected ... [the] many thousands of

In Lincoln, Nebraska, the crowd that came to see Roosevelt was decidedly more venerable. (Prints and Photographs Division, Library of Congress)

most friendly and often enthusiastic citizens, . . . I could not to save my neck differ-entiate one town from another or one crowd from another." The constant appear-ances and public speaking, he continued, were "very hard and rather monotonous." "Much though I liked them and glad though I was to see them," Roosevelt wrote, "it was inevitable that I should begin repeating myself unless I wished to become merely fatuous."[23]

One day blended into another, one crowd resembled another. Recounting his first day in Colorado, Roosevelt sounded a detached, almost bored tone: "The rest of the day was of the ordinary type . . . [with] the usual features—enormous crowds, processions, masses of school children, local Grand Army posts; sweating, bustling, self-conscious local committees; universal kindliness and friendliness; little girls dressed up as Goddesses of Liberty; misguided enthusiasts who ... endeavored ... to shake my hand and felt deeply injured when repulsed by the secret service men and local policemen, etc., etc., etc." Recounting his journey through South Dakota, the same jaded tone crept into his writing:

> Next day I went north through South Dakota, stopping at place after place, sometimes speaking from the end of the train, sometimes going in solemn procession with the local notables to a stand specially erected for the occasion, the procession being headed by the town brass band, which usually played "Hail to the Chief" as a brilliant novelty when I stepped off the train. ... At each stop there were the usual audiences of grizzled, bearded, elderly men; of smooth-faced, shy, hulking young men; of older women either faded and dragged or exceedingly brisk and capable; and of robust, healthy, high-spirited young girls. Most of these people habitually led rather gray lives, and they came in to see the President much as they would have come in to see a circus. It was something to talk over and remember and tell their children about. But I think that besides the mere curiosity there was a good feeling behind it all, a feeling that the President was their man and symbolized their government, and that they had a proprietary interest in him and wished to see him, and that they hoped he embodied their aspirations and their best thought.[24]

But the endless meeting and greeting was not limited to the places where the presidential train stopped. The president's train was constantly taking on welcoming committees that expected to be introduced to the president. Prior to President McKinley's journey to the West Coast in 1901, the *New York Times* commented caustically on this practice:

> About the most annoying incidents of such trips as this the President will soon begin are those marking the arrival of reception delegations. These committees, always larger than they should be, and rarely of any use whatever, meet the train they are imposed upon a long way out. They swarm into it and into the seats of those already entitled to travel by that train; they tumble over each other; they blunder into the car of the principal man on the train, and then do a great deal of gawking and obstructing. ... When the town is reached from which this sort of reception committee was dispatched, it will have a new committee ready from the next town beyond, with more men whose curiosity and appetites must be satisfied before they alight and join in turn the shouters on foot and in carriages. ... [In short] it does not give any convincing impression of welcome; it creates a very unpleasant and uncomfortable notion

of a beastly and unnecessary crush. The idea of traveling 12,000 miles with a reception committee is enough in itself to make the most suave and patient of men pause.

Still, the *Times* reflected, the train, even with its irksome welcoming committees and its "constant motion and vibration," was probably still preferable to having the President stay in Washington, D.C., and suffering "the hand-to-hand conflicts with the midsummer office hunter."[25]

Hayes, Harrison, McKinley, and Roosevelt all traveled extensively, despite the trials. Each made it to the West Coast, each made extensive speaking tours of the southern states, and each traveled along the eastern seaboard as well as in the midwestern states. But the most traveled president from this period was William Howard Taft. Although Taft did not have his predecessor's energy levels or his gift for public speaking, he smashed the travel record established by Roosevelt, perhaps the only area where Taft could boast of having bested his political mentor. North Dakota was the sole state that did not receive a visit from Taft, who made not one but two pilgrimages to the West Coast. The first, in 1909, lasted sixty days, traversed thirty-three states and territories, and resulted in 260 presidential speeches. The second cross-county tour, in the fall of 1911, lasted fifty-seven days during which Taft traveled more than 15,000 miles and made nearly 350 speeches, many in tiny communities like Three Forks, Montana, and Baldwin, Kansas.[26]

TRAVELING THE COUNTRY BY AIR

How different these trips are from those taken by presidents today. The typical twenty-first-century domestic presidential trip entails a flight aboard Air Force One. The president takes off in the morning from Andrews Air Force Base and flies to a selected city, returning to the White House later that same day. On February 8, 2005, for instance, President George W. Bush began his day in the capital with his usual morning briefings, then flew to Detroit where he spoke to the Detroit Economic Club about the economy, the budget, and Social Security. After a forty-five-minute speech, Bush hopped back into Air Force One, returning to the White House that afternoon to participate in a celebration of Black History Month and to meet with Republican House members about Social Security reform.[27]

When a president travels further afield or visits more than one location, he will sometimes spend a night on the road. In November 2005, for instance, Bush flew to Arizona to promote his plan for immigration reform. He arrived at Davis-Monthan Air Force Base in Tucson, where he spoke for twenty-five minutes about the need for greater border security. He then flew to Phoenix to attend a $1,000-a-plate fund-raising dinner, the proceeds going to the reelection campaign of Republican Senator Jon Kyl. After staying overnight in Phoenix, Bush flew out to El Paso, Texas, in the

Taft appears at the back of a train at Three Forks, Montana, during his 1911 tour. (Prints and Photographs Division, Library of Congress)

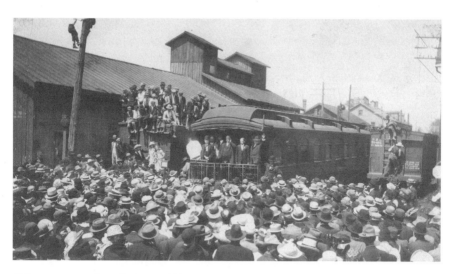

Taft greets an audience in Eaton, Ohio, in 1911. (Preble County Historical Society)

morning to tour the border and tout his proposals for reforming immigration. After talking for fifteen minutes, and having secured a suitable photo opportunity for his immigration pitch, Bush jetted off to Denver where he spoke at a luncheon at the Brown Palace Hotel, helping Republican House member Marilyn Musgrave raise $450,000 for her campaign. Afterwards Bush met privately with the family of a dead soldier, and then he returned to Washington.

A president in the late nineteenth and early twentieth centuries was lucky to get to Arizona once, but Bush's November 2005 visit to Arizona marked the third time that year that he had been there. Yet none of Bush's three visits to Arizona took him outside of the two largest cities in the state: Phoenix and Tucson. In August 2005, Bush touched down at Luke Air Force Base just outside of Phoenix and then was hurried to the nearby El Mirage RV Resort and Country Club, where he promoted the virtues of the new Medicare Prescription Drug plan before four hundred carefully selected guests. After a forty-five-minute "conversation" with the audience, Bush scurried back to the airport and headed for Southern California. And in March 2005, Bush flew to Tucson where he talked about Social Security, first for a few minutes to some seniors in a recreational center and then again at the downtown convention center. Immediately after that event, Bush was whisked off to Air Force One to fly to Denver.

Bush's visit to Tucson in March 2005 to talk about Social Security was part of a concerted White House effort after the 2004 election to sell the American people on the president's plan for Social Security reform. Between January and July of 2005 the president talked about Social Security reform in twenty-nine states as well as the District of Columbia. Almost all of the forty speeches and conversations took place in large cities. In Alabama the president spoke in Montgomery, in Arkansas the White House chose Little Rock, in Colorado it was Denver, in Georgia the site was Atlanta, and so on. Occasionally the president did get off the beaten path: in Montana, for instance, he spoke at Great Falls, but almost all the speeches were in close proximity to large metropolitan areas. And none of these visits involved the president traveling through these states or inadvertently mixing with the population; rather, the White House strategically identified each destination with surgical precision, selected the audience, and scripted the event.[28]

The distinctive rhythm and pattern of modern presidential travel is illustrated by the tour "around the country" Bush embarked upon immediately after his 2006 State of the Union address. The tour was designed to publicize and rally support for some of the key ideas of the speech. The day following the speech the president flew to Nashville, Tennessee, where he defended the Iraq war and attacked isolationism before an audience of several thousand people at the Grand Ole Opry. He arrived just before noon, finished just after one, and was back in the capital in time to attend the swearing-in ceremony of the new Supreme Court justice, Samuel Alito. The next day, after attending the annual National Prayer Breakfast, Bush jetted off to Minneapolis to visit the corporate headquarters of 3M. There he quickly toured part of the plant, before touting his American Competitiveness Institute in a forty-minute speech to eight hundred company employees. The aim of the trip was to garner publicity for the initiative and to provide a suitable backdrop for the nightly news, not to meet the people of Minnesota. After the stop in Minneapolis, he took to the air again, descending in Albuquerque, where he stayed the night. The next morning he talked about competitiveness before a select audience of two hundred at Intel Corporation, and then he flew to Dallas where he appeared at an elementary school and talked for a few minutes about the need for more advanced science and math education. The president then boarded Air Force One and returned to the White House.

Although touted by the White House as a trip "around the country," the president's four-city tour exposed him to precious few of his fellow Americans. He was seen in person by at most several thousand people, virtually all of whom had been invited by the White House to see the president. Even when Bush stayed overnight at Albuquerque he never appeared before the people. The purpose of the travel was not to be seen by the people of these four cities; it was to get on the nightly news promoting the story of the day—competitiveness—before a television audience of millions. The president had given four talks in forty-eight hours, but he had visited only four places—each of them large cities or suburbs of large cities. He had not once strayed more than a thirty-minute drive from a major metropolitan airport.

In sum, an enormous gulf separates the cross-country flights of President Bush and the cross-country rail tours of a President Hayes or Harrison. Whereas the nineteenth-century president rode through America's small towns and village hamlets, the modern president flies far above them. In the late nineteenth century, the entire town and the surrounding area for miles around would come to see and greet the president; today the audience for a presidential visit is generally small and carefully screened. Nineteenth-century welcoming committees were, of course, also screened, but by the town's leading citizens, not by White House operatives.

THE WHISTLE-STOP CAMPAIGN

For a brief period in the middle of the twentieth century, plane and train co-existed as viable travel options for the president. In fact, when President Truman visited Salem, Oregon, in 1948, he arrived twice in a single day, once by plane and the other time by train. Whereas Franklin Roosevelt never took a domestic flight as president, preferring instead to travel the country by train or automobile, Truman immediately seized the opportunity to tour the nation by plane. On June 19, 1945, a little over two months after being sworn in as president, Truman flew to Olympia, Washington—the journey took "12½ hours continuous flying," Truman reported—where he stayed for a week before flying to San Francisco to address a United Nations conference and then flying to a "homecoming" in Kansas City and Independence. Truman also used the presidential plane in ways that today's presidents would have found familiar. In August 1949, for instance, Truman departed from National Airport in the morning, touched down in Miami just before midday, commenced speaking to a Veterans of Foreign War convention at 12:30, and less than an hour later was back in his plane, arriving at the capital in time for dinner. During his more than seven years as president, Truman flew sixty-one times and over 135,000 miles.[29]

Truman also made extensive use of train travel, most famously in the 1948 campaign when he lambasted the "do-nothing" Republican Congress from the rear platform of a train at every "whistle-stop" in the nation. Truman's whistle-stop campaign began innocently enough with an invitation for the president to deliver the commencement address at the University of California at Berkeley and an entreaty for him to visit flood damaged areas in the Pacific Northwest. Truman could have easily flown to the West Coast, as he had done on his previous visit there in 1945, but he chose instead to make the journey by train because it enabled him to see and be seen with the American people. Although Truman originally contemplated making only the westward trip by train and returning to Washington by plane, the trip's success prompted him to change his plans and instead "talk his way back to Washington." In the end, almost the entire 9,500-mile journey was made by rail.[30]

Truman's sharp attacks on the Republican Congress in what the White House had announced would be a nonpolitical trip sparked strong protests from Republicans. The opposition was particularly upset by Truman's infamous comment—made in Spokane, Washington, where he was surveying the devastation wrought by the Columbia River's worst flood in half a century—that the Eightieth Congress was the "worst Congress" in the nation's long history. Ohio Senator Robert Taft, considered a frontrunner for the Republican presidential nomination, took the bait and launched a blistering counterattack on Truman's record and his trip. Truman, Taft charged, was "gallivanting" across the country in "a fifteen-car train" at taxpayer expense, "blackguarding Congress at every whistle station in the West."[31]

The Democrats immediately seized upon the opportunity presented by Taft's comment. Strictly speaking, a "whistle station" or "whistle-stop" denoted a place so small that trains did not make scheduled stops; the train only stopped if the whistle signaled to the engineer that there was a passenger who needed to be picked up or dropped off. The Democratic National Committee contacted the mayors and chambers of commerce of thirty-five towns and cities that the president had visited, inquiring whether they agreed with Taft's disparaging remark that their town was "a whistle-stop." Democrats brandished the results of their poll: three-quarters of the respondents condemned Taft's remark and bristled with indignation at the insult to their civic pride. The mayor of Crestline, Ohio, wired back: "Forty-two passenger trains make regular scheduled stops here daily. . . . Suggest that Senator Taft consult timetables." Similar responses came from Pocatello, Idaho; Laramie, Wyoming; Gary, Indiana; and Eugene, Oregon. The Los Angeles mayor replied that

President Truman speaks from the back of the train in Newton, Kansas, on June 16, 1948. (Harry S. Truman Library)

"anyone who could have been in Los Angeles . . . and witnessed nearly 1,000,000 good American citizens lining the streets to welcome their President would have both whistled and stopped."[32]

Truman recognized a good thing when it was handed to him and made the whistle-stop his campaign signature. When the presidential campaign began in earnest in September, Truman vowed to "visit every whistle stop in the United States." The following month, speaking from the rear platform of a train, he told the residents of the small town of Fostoria, Ohio: "thank God for the whistlestops of our country." By embracing the whistle-stop, Truman attempted to forge a populist connection with small-town America, middle America, and the far West, while implicitly portraying the Republicans as the party of out-of-touch eastern elites. It helped, too, that the Republicans chose as their nominee the urbane and debonair New York governor Thomas Dewey.[33]

Truman, of course, did not visit every whistle-stop in America but he certainly campaigned aggressively and he relied almost exclusively on trains. Between Labor Day and Election Day, Truman delivered around 250 speeches from the back of a train. Many of these were delivered during a cross-country rail trip he took during the last two weeks of September, a trip that took him all the way to California. Truman also spent much of October traveling the country by train; in fact, during that month he was on a train more than he was in the White House. Only once during the campaign did he travel by plane, for a flight to Miami on October 18.[34]

Truman's shock victory in 1948 made the whistle-stop campaign the stuff of American political legend. The "whistle-stop" became an enduring shorthand for a barnstorming populist campaign through the heartland of America. But, ironically, at the very moment the term entered the American political lexicon it was fading from the American political landscape. The whistle-stop technique was not invented by Truman; for at least the previous half century, presidents had been speaking from the rear of the train at small towns across America. Some of these stops were political, some nonpolitical, most a mix of the two. Truman's presidency marked not the beginning of the whistle-stop but its terminus.

Truman continued to rely on the whistle-stop technique, particularly at election time. In 1952, the president campaigned vigorously for the Democratic nominee Adlai Stevenson, making over two hundred speeches in five train trips that covered nearly 20,000 miles. Truman reveled in denouncing the Republicans' record at railway stations across America. On September 29, for instance, the presidential train stopped at nearly a dozen towns in North Dakota, including Berthold, Larimore, Stanley, and Tioga, tiny towns even by North Dakota's demographically challenged standards. But Stevenson, tellingly, did most of his 32,000 miles of traveling by air, as did the Republican nominee Dwight D. Eisenhower, who covered around 50,000 miles.[35]

Eisenhower signaled early on that he regarded Truman's whistle-stop campaigning as lacking in the requisite presidential dignity. Eisenhower preferred formal, prepared speeches to impromptu remarks from the back of a train. In the spring of 1956, spokesmen for the president announced that "Ike will make absolutely no whistle-stop train trips." Instead the campaign would consist of "mass communications" supplemented by "certain flying trips"—what was called "area stopping," which, as a *Times* reporter opined, "isn't at all the same thing as a train grinding to a halt in Bozeman, Mont." But the bigger problem with train travel was not that it was unseemly but that it was inefficient. As Representative Hugh Scott, a former national chairman of the Republican Party, explained, "If a candidate goes through three states. Suppose even a million see him—most will not hear what he says. What's that compared to getting into every voter's living room."[36]

Some old political hands groused about candidates avoiding the train in favor of television and air travel. Jim Farley, who had been postmaster general under Franklin Roosevelt, insisted that a "presidential candidate . . . must get out in the hinterland and be seen. The older people like to see him, they like to bring the kids to see him. It's a great occasion, a campaign train." Another Democratic operative, Clayton Fritchey, pointed out that "It isn't just the 200 or 300 people who see a candidate at a series of small-town whistle stops; it's the copy that is made day after day, copy that keeps the candidate continuously before the voters." Vic Johnston, a veteran Republican hand, agreed: "We just can't conceive here in Washington what an effect a campaign train has with its carnival atmosphere, the reporters hopping off the train . . . the flash-bulbs popping. This is big stuff in a small town." Johnston still remembered his father telling him about Taft's visit to Grand Forks, North Dakota, in 1908, just as Farley still remembered seeing William Jennings Bryan at a rail station in Haverstraw, New York, in 1900. But by 1956, such sentiments seemed more like nostalgia than hard-headed political analysis.[37]

According to Leonard Hall, the savvy Republican national chairman, "being there" was no longer important. As evidence he pointed to the "Salute to Eisenhower" dinners, in which the president spoke to the attendees over closed-circuit television. "Fifty-three dinners attended by 53,000 people [and] the full impact was there—the same emotion, the same tears—just as if the President had been there in person." Rushing around the nation in a train traveling thirty or forty miles an hour, stopping along the way at innumerable small towns, was a luxury the modern president could no longer afford and an inconvenience he no longer needed. People didn't require or even want to see their president in person; having him appear on television was just as good. And when the president did need to travel, airplanes were ready to take him.[38]

By 1960, the campaign train that Truman had made famous was already ancient history. Some commentators lamented its demise, like the New York Times's Cabell Phillips, who complained that air travel had taken "a lot of the fun and drama out of campaigning." "An airborne campaign," Phillips complained, "has to operate on a tighter, more businesslike schedule; its whole mood is geared to speed and efficiency." The crowds weren't the same either. "There is little comparison," Phillips observed, "in either the size or the spirit of the crowds who will drive miles out of town to the airport and those who would flock to the near-by railroad station to see the candidate and his party come in." In the era of the railroad, "people for miles around closed their shops or quit their farms to be on hand for the great event." Not that people had stopped coming to see the president. "Sizeable crowds" would still appear for presidential speeches at "halls and stadiums," but "all you look for in a turnout of that kind today . . . is a window dressing for the candidate; enough bodies to cheer and make a lot of noise so it goes out over the radio and television like a stampede." The modern presidential campaign and the modern presidential celebrity had arrived. Television was, of course, critical to the emergence of the president as celebrity, but so, too, was the mode of presidential transportation, particularly the drama of Air Force One.[39]

The plane that Franklin Roosevelt flew in 1943 had nothing to mark it as the plane of the president. Indeed it was not the president's plane but rather an ordinary military aircraft that the White House had chartered for the occasion. The plane in which Roosevelt flew to Yalta in 1945, dubbed the "Sacred Cow," had a wheelchair lift specially installed for the president, but from the outside it looked the same as any other Douglas C-54 Skymaster propeller plane. Roosevelt and his security detail preferred it this way so that those who might wish the president harm could not identify the plane.[40]

With the end of World War II, concerns about security abated and thoughts turned instead to the political uses of the presidential plane. The idea quickly emerged of providing the president's plane with a distinctive insignia. Walt Disney proposed "the face of a smiling cow with a halo over one horn and an Uncle Sam top hat over the other." Another suggested a "bemedaled and haloed cow flying over a globe." In the end, a more understated design was selected: forty-four small flags painted on the plane's front left side, one for each country the plane had visited. Even with the flags affixed to the plane there was little about the aircraft that suggested presidential dignity let alone grandeur.[41]

In 1947 President Truman was given a more modern and comfortable plane, a Douglas DC-6. The first order of business was to find a name befitting a presidential transport. Nobody in the Truman administration had been fond of the C-54's "Sacred Cow" nickname; in fact criticism of the nickname, emanating from "church people" especially, became serious enough that on several occasions the White House issued public statements distancing the president from the name. The president's press secretary, Charlie Ross, explained that the president "had no responsibility" for "the nickname" and assured citizens that the president referred to the plane simply as "The C-54." The new plane was christened the "Independence," a name that brought the Independence-born Truman's hearty approval.[42]

Although a Douglas DC-6 looked a lot like a Douglas C-54, nobody would mistake the *Independence* for the Sacred Cow. Whereas the latter had only a few small postcard-size flags discreetly placed on one side of the plane, the *Independence* was gaudily dressed up to look like a flying eagle. "Stylized feathers, in two shades of blue, swept back along both sides of the fuselage. On the tail section, three blue feathers outlined in yellow, fanned up on the vertical stabilizer. . . . The cockpit windows looked for all the world like the eyes of this man-made eagle. They peered over a broad [golden yellow] beak and a mouth, also outlined in pin stripes."

And the plane's name, the *Independence*, was blazoned prominently on the side of the window. Although the design was garish—"more likely to be mistaken for a flying circus than a 'Flying White House,'" quipped a former presidential pilot— Truman loved it. When he arrived at an airport there would be no doubt that it was the president arriving. And for a president a little short on stature (physical as well as political), this was not a bad way to grab attention and get out from under FDR's shadow.[43]

Eisenhower didn't like much about Truman and that dislike extended to the Democrat's taste in planes. The gaudily painted *Independence* was one of the first casualties of the changeover in administrations. Eisenhower opted instead to use a Lockheed plane that closely resembled the one he had flown while serving as the head of the North Atlantic Treaty Organization (NATO) between 1950 and 1952. He also dumped Truman's pilot in favor of the pilot who had flown Eisenhower while he was NATO chief. The new plane was christened *Columbine II*—the same nickname Eisenhower had given the NATO plane—and "the name was painted across the plane's nose in a flowing script, together with a painting of a blue columbine." Two years into the Eisenhower presidency, the White House upgraded to a new propeller plane, the *Columbine III*, with much the same floral design.[44]

Although Eisenhower replaced Truman's plane, he generally used the presidential aircraft in much the same way that Truman had. To be sure, Eisenhower flew more than Truman; Eisenhower's 300,000-plus miles were more than twice the number flown by his predecessor. But a significant chunk of that mileage—nearly 80,000 miles—came in the final year of his presidency when he was able to use a Boeing 707 jet. Prior to that final year, Eisenhower had averaged about 30,000 miles each year, about 50 percent more than the average number of miles that President Truman flew in a year. But for both Eisenhower and Truman, the presidential plane was, first and foremost, an efficient means of getting somewhere. It was not yet the symbol of presidential power and American democracy that it would become during the Kennedy years.[45]

The term "Air Force One" entered the public lexicon for the first time during Kennedy's presidency, though it was coined during Eisenhower's tenure as a radio call sign that would identify the plane on which the president was traveling. Initially the system used to identify the president's plane while in flight was essentially the same as for any other plane. A plane, whether military or commercial, was identified by the numbers on the tail of the plane, preceded by the name of the organization that owned the plane. *Columbine II*, for instance, was identified as Air Force 610, no matter who was on board the plane; the aerial license plate of the Sacred Cow was Army 7451. Some worried that this system was deficient because it failed to identify the president's plane quickly and unambiguously, so the president's plane was given the radio call sign "Air Force One." Unlike other radio call signs, which are attached to specific planes (just as license plates are attached to particular cars), Air Force One is the call sign for whatever plane the president boards. During Eisenhower's presidency, the term "Air Force One" was used only by pilots and air traffic controllers. Not until 1961 did the press begin to identify the president's plane as Air Force One.[46]

Endowing the president's plane with the title "Air Force One" helped to enhance its symbolic visibility. Under Truman and Eisenhower, the plane had been self-consciously personalized in an almost whimsical way—the *Independence* referenced Truman's hometown in Missouri and the *Columbine* referred to the state flower of Mamie Eisenhower's home state of Colorado. Neither name was as irreverent as the "Sacred Cow," but neither name was calculated to induce feelings of reverence for the institution of the presidency. Because the designation "Air Force One" would not change with each president, it could represent the enduring majesty of the office rather than the passing idiosyncrasies of an individual man.

But more than a new name was needed to endow the president's plane with the proper dignity. A redesign of the plane's exterior was also required, or so President Kennedy believed. Apart from the incongruous floral decoration on its nose, Eisenhower's plane looked just like any other "simple gray, utilitarian, military-style aircraft," complete with the words "United States Air Force" prominently displayed across the upper body of both sides of the plane. One of Kennedy's first acts was to remove the words "United States Air Force" and to replace them with "United States of America." He also directed that a conspicuous American flag be painted on both sides of the plane's tail; prior to Kennedy no presidential plane had a representation of an American flag affixed to its exterior. Kennedy's aim, as Kenneth Walsh points out, was to ensure the plane was viewed "not just as a military aircraft but as a symbol of the presidency as an institution and of the nation as a whole."[47]

The aura surrounding the presidential plane was greatly enhanced by the new Boeing 707 Kennedy received in 1962. In the past, presidents generally had to settle for military hand-me-downs. President Eisenhower's first plane, *Columbine II*, had logged 650,000 miles and 3,000 flying hours before Eisenhower set foot in it. The Sacred Cow had visited forty-four nations prior to its becoming Truman's presidential plane. Each of these planes was retrofitted to suit the president's needs, but no president before Kennedy received a plane that had been designed with the president in mind. The new jet was impressive. It could travel 620 miles an hour; the top speed of Truman's *Independence*, by contrast, was around 350 miles an hour. Moreover, the new Boeing was capable of flying 7,000 miles without refueling, which was about 2,500 miles further than previous presidential planes. The price of the plane was also unprecedented: $8.5 million.[48]

Kennedy wanted the new plane to have a distinctive, stylish look and so turned to the legendary industrial designer Raymond Loewy for help. Loewy was well known for his sleek, curvaceous designs for automobiles (the Studebaker), buses (Greyhound), trains, and luxury liners, as well as for his fashionable designs of consumer goods packaging, like Lucky Strikes cigarette packs, the Coca-Cola bottle, and Nabisco's trademark triangular seal. Loewy's blue and white design for the president's new jet—which included a presidential seal prominently affixed to both sides of the front of the plane—was unveiled to widespread acclaim and remains the signature design of Air Force One to this day.

Loewy's design helped to make Air Force One among the most recognizable symbols of the American presidency and indeed of American democracy. Four out of five Americans today can identify Air Force One as the president's plane, which is more than twice the number of people who can identify their member of Congress. Beginning in the 1960s, Air Force One emerged as a patriotic icon that evoked feelings of national pride. President Reagan compared seeing Air Force One to "hearing the national anthem," while President George W. Bush likened it to the bald eagle. "It's just a powerful look," Bush explained. "Every time I see it, I'm proud of our country."[49]

Air Force One is the modern presidency at its most glamorous and seductive. The redesigned plane, as Von Hardesty points out, offered "a stylish winged expression of Camelot," but after Camelot had vanished the glamour of Air Force One remained. "The aura of *Air Force One*," as Jimmy Carter observes, is "an overwhelming factor of power and prestige." Even generally sensible people find themselves starstruck by Air Force One. *New York Times* reporter Hedrick Smith, who flew on Air Force One to interview President Reagan, remembers "being impressed by the high-backed luxury-style seats and a signal corps operator asking, 'Where would you like to call, sir?'" Smith found himself acting like "an overawed tourist, . . . scoop[ing] up souvenirs: matchboxes, napkins, swizzle sticks, any item embossed with the presidential seal." The presidential historian Douglas Brinkley reported that flying on Air Force One was "awe inspiring," and the political scientist (and Clinton advisor) William Galston confessed that boarding Air Force One was an almost "existential experience. . . . You walk on Air Force One for the first time and you have to pinch yourself" lest you think it merely a dream.[50]

Every president since Kennedy has capitalized on the mesmerizing effect of Air Force One to project presidential power, to impress and intimidate, to reward friends and court wavering votes. As Lyndon Johnson's loyal aide Jack Valenti put it: "there are two places where the [president's] illumination shines the most. The first is the White House itself. The second is Air Force One." In some ways, the illumination is even more intense aboard Air Force One. Whereas "hordes of people are turnstiling through" the White House, a flight on Air Force One bestows a sense of privilege and perhaps, as a result, feelings of obligation. Air Force One's powerful symbolism makes it a potent political tool.[51]

Although Air Force One has proved to be an enduring symbol of American democracy, it has also, at times, served as a lightning rod for critics of the "imperial presidency." In 1973, columnist William Safire wrote of the need for the "deroyalization" of the presidency. Safire suggested that "President Nixon, in a grand gesture of fuel frugality, could mothball Air Force One for the duration of the [gasoline] shortage with the exception of overseas visits" and travel to San Clemente on "a regularly scheduled commercial jet." If the suggestion sounded "ridiculous," Safire continued, it was only "because we now surround the citizen we elect with royal trappings, against all propriety and American tradition." And nothing was more royal in its trappings than Air Force One. "In the fell clutch of pomp and circumstance," Safire lamented, "we turn [presidents'] heads and wonder why they lose touch with 'the people.'"[52]

Nixon was evidently listening to his former speech writer. Six weeks later, he surprised his staff and the country by boarding a regularly scheduled commercial flight for a holiday trip to San Clemente. The next morning's papers featured pictures of a smiling Nixon casually "shaking hands [and] exchanging pleasantries with passengers." The flight, one aide claimed, "scored points" with the public by showing that the president was fuel conscious and that he was "a man of the people, not afraid to mingle with ordinary travelers." The White House estimated that Nixon "saved at least 60,000 gallons of jet fuel" since a trip to San Clemente would usually require not only sending Air Force One, but also "a back-up plane, a press plane, three helicopters and a steady stream of White House courier aircraft." But while the administration worked to spin the flight as "a public relations coup," many viewed the trip as a foolish stunt. The Secret Service took the unusual step of issuing a statement that it "would prefer the President to use military aircraft for security reasons," while the head of the Federal Aviation Agency told reporters he was "dismayed" that the agency had been given almost no prior notice of the president's plans. Complaints also came from low-level White House staffers and especially members of the press corps, who found themselves scrambling to book flights to San Clemente.[53]

Press reaction to Nixon's trip was sharply negative. The *Washington Post* pronounced the trip a "penny-wise, pound-foolish venture." Most viewed the trip through the lens of Watergate and Nixon's plummeting popularity. On the same day that Nixon was flying to San Clemente, William Shannon of the *New York Times* wrote that Nixon's resignation was "only a matter of time." Boarding a commercial flight was seen as the desperate act of a failed president. Not surprisingly, none of Nixon's successors have tried repeating the feat.[54]

Flying on a commercial airline may be out of the question for a modern president, but Air Force One still periodically attracts criticism for its regal connotations. Writing in 1977, at the close of Carter's first year as president and four years after Nixon's labored effort to fly commercial, the *New York Times* reporter Marjorie Hunter likened Air Force One to "the ultimate magic carpet. . . . Not even Solomon's legendary green silk carpet, which bore his throne and entourage aloft, could compare to the luxury of its modern counterpart." Hunter contrasted the "luxurious" comforts of Air Force One with the "no-frills, no-reservation, no-food, no-drinks economy flights" being introduced on commercial airlines. And Hunter could not resist drawing attention to the plane's sticker price of $12.5 million, including $3.8 million for "interior . . . furnishings and electronic and communications equipment."[55]

Days after Carter's election, columnist Tom Wicker reacted with alarm at reports that on boarding the "flying palace," the president-elect reportedly said: "This is the one I've been waiting for." Wicker feared that the populist Carter might already be backsliding, seduced by the lure of Air Force One. Next, Carter would be emulating the high-handed tactics of Nixon or the egotism of Lyndon Johnson, who installed an imposing armchair—dubbed "the throne" by staffers—on Air Force One that he could "raise at the push of a button so he could ascend to a higher, more regal elevation than everyone else." Wicker offered Carter advice on how to fulfill his campaign vow to make the presidency "more democratic with a little 'd.' " The newly elected president could "give the commercial airlines a try" ("the rest of us . . . have to stand in line for luggage and sit three abreast and that's really life with a little 'd' ") and rename Air Force One "The Peanut" ("what was good enough for you when you wanted our votes ought to be good enough when you've got them"). Carter paid little heed to Wicker's counsel, though he did follow another of Wicker's suggestions by walking down Pennsylvania Avenue after taking the oath of office.[56]

Concerns about a regal presidency were amplified when a new Air Force One was rolled out in 1990. Its sticker price dwarfed that of any previous presidential aircraft. Some estimates put the cost as high as $325 million. And that was just for the first plane. The identical back-up plane, built at the same time, brought the total cost to a reported $650 million. Writing in *Time* magazine, Hugh Sidey lamented not only the cost but the symbolism of a "$650 Million Flying Palace." In a time of economic uncertainty and cutbacks in government spending, this "item of conspicuous consumption," Sidey wrote, "crossed the line of common political sense." The "behemoth" six-story jet offended against the "Jeffersonian image of a citizen Executive going modestly among his people." The plane was undoubtedly a technological wonder but it was a democratic "monster."[57]

This wasn't the first time Sidey had expressed such concerns. Four years earlier, when plans for a new Air Force One were announced, Sidey wrote another column in which he raised the alarm for the future of the republic. Whereas Hunter compared Air Force One to a luxurious magic carpet, evoking the "throne and entourage" of a Middle Eastern despot, Sidey thought the apt comparison was to "the final days of Rome" in which—according to Ammianus Marcellinus—"the modern nobles measure[d] their rank and consequence according to the loftiness of their chariots." "If old Marcellinus were around today," Sidey suggested, "he might be fretting about the future of the U.S., because we are about to put the President in the loftiest chariot that man has yet devised." Sidey was outraged not only by the "mind-boggling" cost of the plane but by its many luxuries—the "spacious bedroom, . . . complete with vanity closets, lavatory, and shower-tub" and the kitchens where "lobster souffle can be created"—and the myriad electronic gadgets—including a monitor that allows the "president . . . to scan his welcoming crowds on the TV screen as the plane taxis up." Worst of all, the president "will exit on special stairs from the forward door, an elegant pulpit high above his waiting subjects." For Sidey, Air Force One was not a symbol of democracy but of its opposite: imperial rule and the ostentatious display of power.[58]

Sidey was not the only member of the press to raise concerns about the new Air Force One. The plane was a "Flying Taj Mahal," sneered one. The *St. Petersburg Times* referred to the plane as "a mansion in the sky" and derided President Bush's "boarding pass to luxury." The editors found it almost obscene that Bush needed a plane with "85 telephones, seven bathrooms, . . . and presidential suite," while "37 million Americans . . . lack access to primary medical care." The plane's "lavish trappings" symbolized just how out of touch the president was from the needs of ordinary people.[59]

Bush was sensitive about such criticisms. In January 1990, unidentified aides told reporters that the president was "somewhat embarrassed and irritated" to inherit such a high-priced and luxurious plane. When the plane was delivered in the late summer of 1990, some reporters were given a tour of the plane and Bush "twice asked [them] whether they were aware that Congress approved the purchase, and he made sure they wrote down that it was done under the previous Administration." But Bush, who loved traveling, found it difficult to disguise his excitement at the plane's many gadgets and comforts. The plane, he admitted, was "marvelous in every way."[60]

The new Air Force One had its defenders, especially in Washington State where the Boeing planes were built. The *Seattle Times* dismissed the "nitpicky quibblers" who complained about the plane's cost. Did these "petty, partisan critics really want the president of the U.S. flying around in . . . old and outmoded" planes? A letter writer to the *Seattle Times* agreed that we did not want "the president running around the world in an obsolete, 18-year-old plane." Others felt no need for apologies. They professed their desire "to see our President land around the world in the biggest and best America has." Air Force One's splendors suited the most powerful office in the world.[61]

Criticisms of the "lavish trappings" of Air Force One speak to the continuing distrust of the regal presidency in American political culture. But while presidents remain sensitive to such appearances, particularly during economic hard times, the more remarkable feature of contemporary American political discourse is how comfortable we have become with a regal presidency. We have not only reconciled ourselves to Air Force One but have embraced it. We take pride in seeing the president fly in the "biggest and best" aircraft. We imagine Air Force One not as an undemocratic symbol of power or privilege, but as a magnificent symbol of a great nation and an enduring democracy. Air Force One, in the words of President George W. Bush, is seen as a "majestic symbol of our country."[62]

And yet Air Force One is more than just a symbol. It is also an instrument of personal power. Moreover, its symbolism is as much regal as it is democratic. The omnipresent presidential seal—affixed to everything from seat belt buckles to coffee cups—is a constant reminder of the majesty of the office. In *The Flying White House*, written more than a decade before the new Air Force One was introduced in 1990, J. F. terHorst (President Gerald Ford's first press secretary) and Ralph Albertazzie (Nixon's presidential pilot) noted that one of "the contradictions of the presidency" is "that the elected head of a democratic nation could have—or even desire— an airplane as magnificent as Air Force One." The contradiction is, of course, not a new one. John Adams tried to give the presidency a regal title and George Washington rode around the capital in a fine, liveried carriage. The president is a democratically elected representative but he is also the symbolic head of state. He is the prime minister and monarch rolled into one. And aboard Air Force One the president looks a lot more like a monarch than he does a prime minister. Little wonder that presidents are so fond of flying aboard Air Force One, thousands of miles above their admiring subjects.[63]

Conclusion: The Rise of the Regal Presidency

How, wonders James Mann, did a nation "founded in . . . mistrust of a king . . . end up with [a presidency that] looks so . . . royal?" It is a question that has been asked often in American history. From the outset many Americans worried that the nation was creating a monarch in republican clothing. At the federal constitutional convention in 1787, Virginia's governor, Edmund Randolph, refused to sign the new constitution because he worried that the presidency was "the foetus of monarchy." At the Virginia ratifying convention Patrick Henry thundered against the new constitution, which had among its many "deformities" an "awful . . . squinting towards monarchy."[1]

Supporters of the new constitution dismissed these concerns as paranoid imaginings. The president of the United States, wrote Alexander Hamilton, bore as much resemblance to the king of Great Britain as he did to "the Man of the Seven Mountains." Hamilton detailed the powers that the British monarch possessed that the president did not, including the power to declare war, dissolve Parliament, and create offices. In addition Hamilton pointed to the powers that a monarch exercised alone but that the president shared with the legislature. Whereas the king had an absolute veto the legislature could override a presidential veto; the king could appoint all the realm's officers whereas the president needed the "advice and consent" of the Senate; and unlike the king, who possessed the sole power to make treaties, the president shared that power with the Senate. And, of course, the president was elected by the people every four years whereas the king of England was a hereditary and lifelong position. Moreover, unlike the king, a president could be impeached and removed from office. Only a crank or a malicious partisan could not see the silliness of the comparison.[2]

Hamilton and his political allies helped to persuade the nation to adopt the new constitution but they did not succeed in exorcizing the country's fear of monarchy. Hamilton's nemesis, Thomas Jefferson, came to power in 1800 by exploiting fears about the monarchical aspirations of the Federalists. Republicans believed that the pomp and ceremony as well as the adulation and "extravagant flattery" that at times characterized Washington's presidency were inconsistent with true republicanism. The elaborate celebrations of Washington's birthday, for instance, were a "monarchical farce." A proper respect for the nation's elected chief executive was certainly a republican virtue but "blind servility" was the mark of monarchy. Jefferson attributed Washington's regal presidency to the "satellites and sycophants which surrounded him" and "inveloped [him] in the rags of royalty." The person Jefferson blamed most was Hamilton, whom Jefferson regarded as a "monarchist"—not without reason since at the constitutional convention Hamilton had pushed for a president who would serve for life and be empowered to nullify any law enacted by Congress.[3]

The Federalist Party never recovered from being tagged as the party of monarchy and aristocracy. Washington's towering popularity shielded the party for a short time but when he stepped down after two terms the party quickly disintegrated. Although a regional force in New England into the 1820s, the Federalist Party was unable to mount a serious campaign for the presidency after John Adams's defeat in 1800. Jefferson, James Madison, and James Monroe each clobbered their Federalist or Federalist-backed opponents. By 1820 the Federalist Party was unable even to offer up a sacrificial candidate to run against Monroe.

Neither the total eclipse of the Federalist Party nor the unchallenged ascendancy of the Republican Party banished fears of an American monarchy. The fright of monarchy was rekindled by President Andrew Jackson's assertion of unilateral executive power. His opponents called him "King Andrew." In a famous drawing from the bitterly contested 1832 election, "King Andrew the First" was dressed in royal robes, crown upon his head and scepter in hand, standing in front of his throne with torn pieces of the Constitution underfoot. Underneath the picture was posed the question: "Shall he reign over us, Or shall the People Rule?" So resonant was this rhetoric that the president's disparate enemies banded together under the unlikely label of "Whig." In eighteenth-century England the Whigs were the enemies of King George III and the proponents of a strong Parliament. By calling themselves Whigs, Jackson's opponents cast themselves as the defenders of the legislature against arbitrary, regal executive power.[4]

The English Whigs were determined foes not only of the unilateral exercise of monarchical power but also of the luxury of the king's court. Worries about the corrupting effects of the court's opulence had long haunted the republican imagination in America as well. The Republican Party had capitalized on those anxieties in unseating Adams in 1800, and the Whigs employed the same stratagem in defeating Jackson's successor, Martin Van Buren. A major theme in the 1840 "log-cabin campaign" was the alleged extravagance of the Van Buren White House. A Pennsylvania Whig named Charles Ogle famously spoke for three days on the House floor on the subject of "The Regal Splendor of the Presidential Palace." Ogle spotlighted the $2,400 that Van Buren had spent on four mirrors for the White House: "What would frugal and honest 'Hoosiers' think were they to behold a democratic peacock, in full court costume, strutting by the hour before golden-framed mirrors, nine feet high and four feet and a half wide?" Van Buren, Ogle alleged, had used the money Congress had appropriated to make the president's house "a palace as splendid as

King Andrew the First. (Prints and Photographs Division, Library of Congress)

that of the Caesars, and as richly adorned as the proudest Asiatic mansion." While Van Buren basked in the luxury of French chefs, sterling silver cutlery, "massive" gold plates, expensive champagne, imported silk draperies, and plush carpets, the American people struggled to find work and feed their families.[5]

The charge that Van Buren aped monarchy was a central motif in Whig criticism of Van Buren's tour of New York in 1839. When the Whig press was not pounding Van Buren for undignified electioneering, it was bombarding "His Democratic Majesty" with allegations that he was "imitating Royalty." The *Albany Evening Journal* relentlessly ridiculed Van Buren for "strutting and swelling like some manic Hero or Monarch in all the mockery of pasteboard and spangles." The magnificent procession accompanying Van Buren's entrance into Albany was likened to Queen Victoria's royal coronation the previous summer. Like England's new queen, "His Majesty, Martin the First" was "ushered into the City by his loyal subjects, with all the 'pomp and circumstance' that Cannon, Soldiery, Music and Office-Holders could impart to the Pageant." How different, the *Journal* reminded its readers, had been the behavior of Jefferson and Madison, who "in their simplicity, when traveling as Chief Magistrates of the Republic, repressed Processions and Pageants as Anti-Republican." In contrast to these paragons of republican virtue, who "mingled with their fellow-citizens as one of the People," Van Buren was unable to "move among the people without reminding them by external insignia that he is something a little above the multitude." Had there been even "a spark of Republicanism about him," the president would "have spurned all these trappings of Royalty." But Van Buren's head had been turned by the adulation and pageantry. His republican "disguise" had been "torn off" and he was revealed as he truly was: "the admirer and imitator of monarchy."[6]

Whigs had aimed similar barbs at the allegedly regal character of Jackson's tour in 1833. The *Baltimore Chronicle*, for instance, groused that the "King of England travels with less parade than is made for our republican President, General Jackson." Like the *Albany Evening Journal* during the Van Buren presidency, the *Chronicle* contrasted "the ostentatious display" of Jackson's tour with the practice of "the fathers of the republican party," Jefferson and Madison, who "moved to and fro without the ringing of bells, the firing of cannon, the wreathing of garlands, or the disgraceful genuflections of sycophantic courtiers." As deplorable as the pomp and ceremony accompanying Jackson's movements was the "truckling tribe of scribblers" angling for presidential favor by "their vile flatteries." Reading the "disgusting and nauseating accounts" of the president's tour in the Democratic press—"'The President raised his left foot with grace,' 'the President mounted the step of the barouche with dignity,' 'the President smiled graciously'"—prompted the *Chronicle* to despair for the republic's future. "We are rapidly losing our republican simplicity," the *Chronicle* warned, "and sliding into the fashions, follies, and corruption of monarchies."[7]

However, the charge that Jackson's tour savored of monarchy fell flat. Although

DEMOCRATIC SIMPLICITY.
Or the Arrival of our Favourite Son.

The artist satirizes Van Buren as both too regal and too political. The president's splendid carriage is from England, while Tammany Hall looms in the background. Van Buren says: "These are my loyal subjects! Old Tammany never fails to do her duty." One of the onlookers comments: "This is truly royal—great as the coronation—what a humbug is this Democracy." (Prints and Photographs Division, Library of Congress)

Whigs couched their attack on Jackson's tour in familiar republican language, defending republican simplicity against monarchical trappings and pretensions, their rhetoric often seemed to betray a distrust of an emergent democracy. When Duff Green, editor of the *United States Telegraph*, complained that the tour represented the "degeneracy of the age," he pointed to the way the president was marched "up and down the streets, here and there and everywhere, as if he were a wild beast to be exhibited gratis." The *Baltimore Chronicle*, too, complained of "the vulgar shout" and the "ridiculous exhibition of the President as the 'Punch at a faree show.'" Appalled at the public's fawning over Jackson, Whigs often found it difficult to criticize the pageantry of the tour without also calling into question the people's good judgment. The people, it was suggested, were sick with "Jackson fever" or they were derided as "the thoughtless majority." Whigs might rail against Jackson's "Royal progress" but what seemed to bother many of them most was the sight of a popular, democratic leader mingling with crowds, flattering the women, shaking hands with the men, and kissing the babies.[8]

Jackson's supporters seized upon such rhetoric to expose the president's critics as

THE GRAND NATIONAL CARAVAN MOVING EAST.

A satirical rendering of Jackson's tour of New England. Jackson confesses to having "kissed and . . . prattled to fifty fair maids," while the effeminate Van Buren rides sidesaddle, legs crossed. Bringing up the rear, in a circus-like cage, is the party of Chief Black Hawk, whom Jackson met with in Baltimore at the outset of his tour. The hypocrisy of Jackson's Indian policy is brought home by the large "Rights of Man" flag aloft from the cage. (Prints and Photographs Division, Library of Congress)

elitists who distrusted the people. The opposition's denunciations of King Andrew, Democrats argued, masked the Whig distaste for democracy. The president, in Jackson's view, was the people's direct representative, their national tribune. Unlike a king, the president was a man of the people. The president's will was the popular will; his voice the voice of the people. Congress, Jackson insisted, represented a monied elite, an aristocracy, parochial interests. The real threat to the nation was neither the one nor the many but the few.[9]

Jackson helped to give the presidency a democratic justification that it had previously lacked, but though that justification could quell or at least combat fears of monarchy, presidents in the nineteenth century remained careful to accent the republican character of their travel. Whig as well as Democratic presidents reminded audiences that they traveled in a plain, republican manner, without ostentation. They preferred, they claimed, not to be met with elaborate public receptions and parades. Typical was the paean to Zachary Taylor offered by the administration's mouthpiece, the Washington *Republic*, at the close of the president's 1849 tour.

It was the desire of Gen. Taylor to pass through the country with as little display as possible. It was more his object to see his fellow-citizens at their homes, in their shops, and mines, and manufactories, upon their farmsteads, and in their cities, than to be seen by them. . . . Wherever the people assembled to greet him in thousands and tens of thousands, it was a spontaneous homage to one of themselves who had won their gratitude by services [rendered to the country]. . . . [T]his informal and republican mode of social intercourse was more agreeable to Gen. Taylor than the most pompous and brilliant pageants. He left home to see [the people], to know them, that he might better serve them. They met him as their President, their servant, and their friend.

The president traveled not to lord it over the people but to serve them.[10]

The model republican president traveled essentially alone, surrounded by his fellow citizens, with no entourage or guard. When Democrats defended Van Buren against charges that his 1839 tour had been an ostentatious "royal progress," they emphasized that the president had traveled "on horseback, surrounded by his fellow citizens." In contrast, they pointed out that Whig candidate Henry Clay traveled in a "triumphal chariot" with a "crown of flowers" upon his head. Carriages, in the overactive republican imagination, smacked of royalty, luxury, and privilege. Traveling astride a horse, in contrast was a marker of republican simplicity.[11]

By the time of Taylor's tour, however, carriages and horses were growing obsolete as modes of long-distance transportation. Jackson was the first president to board a train—for a 12-mile ride into Baltimore on the opening day of his 1833 tour—but his short rail journey was a novelty. The rest of Jackson's journey was traversed on horseback or by carriage and steamboat. Fifteen years later, however, train travel had become standard. John Tyler's tour of 1843 and James Polk's 1847 tour were conducted largely by train. Van Buren, too, though he did occasionally ride a horse, traversed most of his six-week tour in 1839 by train and boat.

Concerned about being perceived as traveling in luxury or as erecting barriers between themselves and the people, presidents in the Jacksonian era were often left exhausted and sometimes made seriously ill by their tours. "Continuous mingling with large masses of people" was physically punishing. Taylor's comment that the people were "nigh killing him with kindness" was only half in jest. Indeed the "fatigue of travel" proved too much for the 64-year-old Taylor, who became so weak and sick that he was compelled to call off the tour before it had reached its halfway point.[12]

The same fate befell the 66-year-old Jackson, who had to terminate his 1833 tour prematurely after his aging frame broke down under the rigors of traveling and of greeting massive crowds. In Philadelphia, a morning reception at Independence Hall was crashed by an exuberant "mob [that] forced its way into the building" and "for two hours . . . surrounded [Jackson] and shook his hand." In the afternoon Jackson reviewed a military parade, sitting "bolt upright in his saddle" for five hours in a scorching sun that left his face "compleatly blistered." At the end of the day, only his fifth of the tour, Jackson confessed to his adopted son that he "sincerely wish[ed the] trip was over," and vowed it would be his last. Greeting "upwards of two hundred thousand people" in one day, as Jackson did in New York City, may have been good politics but it was terrible for his health.[13]

Even younger—and less popular—presidents struggled under the strain of the travel and the crowds. When the 48-year-old Franklin Pierce returned from his 1853 tour, "he had to take to his bed, sick with fatigue and cold." Tyler, who was 53 at the time he embarked on his tour, was left "harassed and worn-out . . . almost prostrated by the long journey." Unlike Taylor and Jackson, Pierce and Tyler completed their tours, but only just. Democracy demanded an unmediated relationship between the people and their president, but the president's health and well-being seemed to need a buffer between president and people.[14]

It was not only the people's kindness from which presidents needed protection. Presidents also needed insulation from those few who wished them harm. Yet the potent republican dread of monarchy meant that Americans were extraordinarily slow to press for protective security for the president. Many Americans in the nineteenth century seemed to regard dead presidents as the cost of a democratic presidency.

A protective entourage had long been regarded as one of the telltale signs of Old World monarchies and degenerate empires. Monroe had attempted to defuse this anxiety by traveling with a small escort. Apart from two servants, his retinue consisted only of his personal secretary and one government official, the chief of the Corps of Army Engineers. Jackson's traveling suite was also slight. Only his private secretary, Andrew Donelson, and his frequent traveling companion, Ralph Earl, accompanied Jackson for all of his 1833 tour. But Jackson also traveled for significant segments of the journey with members of his cabinet, something neither Washington nor Monroe had done. Traveling with Jackson as far as New York was Secretary of War Lewis Cass. Secretary of the Navy Levi Woodbury joined the president in New York and traveled with the party to the secretary's home state of New Hampshire. The recently installed Secretary of State Louis McLane traveled with the president as far as New Haven, Connecticut.[15]

A number of antebellum presidents followed Jackson's model of traveling with members of the cabinet. Franklin Pierce, for instance, was accompanied on his 1853 tour by three cabinet members: Secretary of the Treasury James Guthrie, Attorney General Caleb Cushing, and Secretary of War Jefferson Davis. Millard Fillmore conducted his May 1851 tour accompanied by Secretary of State Daniel Webster, Secretary of War Charles Conrad, and Secretary of the Interior Alexander Stuart. When Tyler toured the northeast in 1843 he dragged along half his cabinet: Secretary of Treasury John Spencer, Postmaster General Charles Wickliffe, and Secretary of War

James Porter. Polk took Attorney General Nathan Clifford with him on his 1847 tour of the northeast and was joined by Secretary of State James Buchanan for a significant segment of the journey. Of the antebellum presidents, only Taylor did not tour with members of the cabinet, though Taylor was accompanied by Pennsylvania's Whig governor during the two weeks he journeyed through the Keystone State.[16]

Travel with cabinet members accentuated the president's role as party leader. The cabinet was the president's creation; its selection an affirmation of the regional and ideological diversity of the party as well as a statement of the president's vision of the party. Presidents rarely included anybody in their cabinet who was not a loyal party member. One might wonder why nineteenth-century presidents, who were so often careful to declaim any political or partisan purposes for their tours, would travel with the very individuals most likely to remind people that the president was the head of a political party.

One answer is that traveling with cabinet members may have helped to disarm republican anxieties about monarchy. Although the president was the main attraction, he shared the spotlight and the speech-making with the cabinet members who accompanied him. The president appeared as the first among equals—more like a prime minister than a monarch. Secretary of State William Henry Seward, who traveled with Andrew Johnson on his 1866 tour, drew attention to this in a speech he delivered in St. Louis. Speaking from the balcony of a hotel immediately after the president, Seward noted how unusual it was in the annals of political history to have the secretary of state speak to the public "in the presence of the Chief Magistrate." "Kings and emperors" have "ministers whose duty it is to be silent, and advise, and record, never to open their lips in the common service of all the people." In Seward's view, Johnson's tour thus demonstrated that the American presidency was a very different sort of institution from the monarchies of the Old World.[17]

Traveling with cabinet members was also a useful way for the president to share the burden of speech-making. Nineteenth-century presidents who toured the nation faced a tremendous public appetite for speech-making. Political speeches were almost a way of life for nineteenth-century Americans, and presidents were not exempt from the demands of that rhetorical culture, although the substance of presidential rhetoric was constrained by the president's distinctive role as head of state. But the president was no monarch. Waving benignly was not enough. The American people expected a traveling president to speak to them, whether from a hotel balcony, at a public dinner, or at a formal welcoming ceremony. Sharing the platform with cabinet members enabled presidents to meet the public craving for speech-making without leaving them exhausted.

Savvy presidents could even use their cabinet members to help them reconcile their roles as head of state and head of party. The president could take the high road, delivering a message of unity, while the cabinet member could sound more explicitly partisan on political themes. In 1853, for instance, Franklin Pierce wanted

Seward's comments in St. Louis may have helped to inspire this Thomas Nast cartoon portraying President Johnson as "King Andy" and Seward as a sycophantic prime minister. An even more important impetus was a question Seward had posed to a crowd in Battle Creek, Michigan, on September 5: "Do you want Andrew Johnson President or King?" Seward's point was that for Johnson to be a democratic president rather than a monarchical ruler the southern states needed to be enfranchised. But the opposition quickly seized on this comment to lampoon "King Andy" and his Court. "Like other Kings," wrote the New York Herald, *"he is always talking about himself, what he has done, what he is doing, what he means to do, and what Congress cannot make him do. . . . [N]o President ever before made such a parade of his authority. . . . [H]e meanders up and down the land as if he were a separate estate of the realm, omnipotent, omniscient, and (by virtue of railways) omnipresent" (September 15, 1866). Secretary of the Navy Gideon Welles is at Johnson's right hand, and in the distance Radical Republican leaders are being led off to the guillotine. The cartoon was published in* Harper's Weekly *on November 3, 1866. (Provided courtesy HarpWeek, LLC)*

to use his tour to endorse—or at least float—the idea of building a transcontinental railroad line. Since Democrats generally opposed government subsidies for private corporations, the position represented an ideological deviation from "strict constructionist" Jacksonian principles. Pierce, however, was also aware of the issue's popularity, especially in the West, and was conscious that leading Whigs were eyeing the issue as a means to revive the party's flagging electoral fortunes. Traveling with his fellow partisans enabled Pierce to capitalize on a division of labor in which his cabinet members could "give administrative endorsement to the railroad idea . . . and leave the President the Union and American ideals." At a public dinner in Philadelphia the travelers followed the script exactly. While Pierce sounded general patriotic themes in response to the mayor's toast to the president, Secretaries Davies and Guthrie responded to a toast to "The Cabinet" by pressing the case for extending the railroad to the Pacific and arguing that the policy was consistent with core Democratic principles.[18]

Traveling with the cabinet was politically useful but it also represented a departure from Monroe's plain republican model of travel and signaled the beginnings of a presidential entourage. When Andrew Johnson traveled to New York in 1866 he was accompanied not only by his secretary of state, postmaster general, and secretary of the navy (as well as the secretary's wife and son), but also by two personal assistants as well as General Ulysses Grant and his chief-of-staff, and Admiral David Farragut and his staff secretary. When Hayes traveled to the West Coast in 1880 the official traveling party totaled around twenty people. Those accompanying the president included the secretary of war Alexander Ramsey and the army chief-of-staff William Tecumseh Sherman, their family members and staff assistants, Hayes's wife and two sons, as well as the personal aide and some friends of the president.[19]

The railroad companies made these larger entourages possible by providing presidents with special cars or trains. The relative privacy afforded by a special car enabled the president and his party to rest and to work while traveling. But the car also symbolically separated the president from his fellow citizens, belying the republican myth that the president met his fellow citizens as an equal or as a servant of the people. How many servants—indeed how many Americans—traveled in a "splendid private car" supplied by the railroads?[20]

The perceived luxury of these special cars occasionally offended republic sensibilities and invited partisan complaint. But it was the efforts to protect the president from the people that most directly transgressed republican principles and triggered republican fears. Americans of the nineteenth century continued to tell themselves that the president, unlike the monarchs of old, needed no protection from the people. As James Polk expressed it on his 1847 tour of the northeast, "in other countries, where the representative of the government is the ruler and not the servant of the people, if he ventures abroad amongst them, he must be protected by an escort of soldiers; but here . . . the head of the government finds his only protection in the approbation and the hearts of the people." This belief was central to nineteenth-century Americans' understanding of the president's place in the political system and America's place in the world.[21]

The emergence and institutionalization of a protective guard around the president called into question the cultural significance of presidential travel. In the nineteenth century, presidents traveled in order to dramatize their connection to the American people. Mixing with the people enabled the president to show he was not a prisoner of the White House, and that he was in touch with the needs and interests of real people. But how can a president mingle freely with the people once his entire traveling apparatus is set up to create a barrier between the people and the president?

If historically one of the basic functions of presidential travel has been to underscore the bond between the president and the people, the contemporary president faces a difficult task. A president today rolls into public events hidden in a bulletproof black limousine with darkly tinted windows. Any curious onlookers would not only be unable to catch a glimpse of the president but they would be unable to determine which of the cars in the vast motorcade contains the president. Presidents are thus compelled to travel in ways that make them vulnerable to the charge that they are out of touch with or hiding from the people, as George H. W. Bush discovered in 1992 when Ross Perot jabbed that Bush was so afraid of the American people that he "only moved among the people in a 'motorcade two blocks long.'" Instead of demonstrating the president's connection to the people beyond Washington, D.C., presidential travel may reinforce the image of a president enclosed in a bubble.[22]

In a nation still animated by republican anxieties about a regal presidency, presidents fear being accused of having become out of touch with the people. That was why Lyndon Johnson was loathe to do away with the open-top limousine despite Kennedy's assassination. And why Gerald Ford was so resistant to suggestions that he should avoid crowds and give up shaking hands. After Ronald Reagan was shot, the White House's first instinct was to wrap the president in a protective cocoon. But as the economy slid into recession in the spring of 1982, administration officials worried that the president was being perceived as "remote from the problems of average Americans" and recommended the president travel more to counteract growing impressions that his was a "regal presidency." In March, for instance, Reagan tried to show he understood the troubles of ordinary Americans by visiting the "flooded and unemployment-battered town" of Fort Wayne, Indiana. But traveling often required even more visible security arrangements and so undercut the effort to make the president appear accessible. In May, for instance, when Reagan visited the World's Fair in Knoxville, Tennessee, he appeared at a podium that was separated from the audience not only by a glass screen but by a "wide moat." Hardly the sort of thing to banish fears of a regal presidency.[23]

Designed to display presidential accessibility, travel today unavoidably spotlights the regal nature of the presidency. When George W. Bush traveled to Chile after the November 2004 elections, for instance, he was accompanied by over 250 "staff and security aides" and around 100 members of the press, not to mention "enough planes, cars and communications gear for a third-world army." When the presidency travels, as James Mann points out, it is virtually a "universe onto itself." Contemporary presidential travel dramatizes the regal presidency rather than dispels it.[24]

Aboard Air Force One the president is as isolated from ordinary people as he is in the Oval Office. Nineteenth-century train travel, no matter how lavish the special cars used by the president, did not separate the president from the people in the way that Air Force One does. Train travel was punishing work for a president because it required him to appear at countless stops to speak to or at least greet the people. When President Polk traveled by train to North Carolina in May 1847, for instance, he encountered crowds of people assembled "at intervals of every few miles, and especially at the railroad depots." "At most of these places," Polk wrote in his diary, "I descended from the cars and shook hands with as many of them as my time would permit." Even when a presidential train did not stop at a town it often slowed sufficiently for the president to appear at the rear platform and acknowledge the crowd. And when the president wasn't waving, shaking hands, or speaking from the back of the train, he was meeting committees of local dignitaries and citizens who boarded the train to greet the president. Whereas rail travel relentlessly exposed the president to the people, Air Force One is more like a "flying cocoon" in the way that it insulates the president from the people.[25]

Nineteenth-century rail travel posed a problem for democracy, however, because presidents were traveling at the expense of the privately owned railroads. Public financing of presidential travel represented a democratic advance, but air travel posed new challenges. The military, which had played a limited—though not insignificant—role in the transportation of presidents during the heyday of the railroads, was given the primary responsibility for transporting the president in the age of the airplane. Air Force One is owned, operated, maintained, and protected by the military. Everyone responsible for the flying of Air Force One, from the pilots to the mechanics, is an employee of the military. The president's plane is housed at Andrews Air Force Base and typically touches down at other military bases. Most of the immense costs associated with transporting the president today are borne by the military, hidden within a secretive and sprawling bureaucracy. Freed from the grip of the railroad barons, the president has landed squarely in the lap of the military.[26]

In the early republic, republicanism had at its core not only an antipathy to monarchy but a deep and abiding distrust of a professional military. Or, to be more precise, republicans feared marrying the military to executive power. Jefferson and Madison would surely be appalled to find that the largest unit within the White

House is the White House Military Office (WHMO), which is funded by the Department of Defense. The great majority of the over two thousand military professionals in WHMO are dedicated to servicing the travels of the president as well as his cabinet and staff. WHMO includes the Presidential Airlift group, which is responsible for Air Force One; the Marine Helicopter Squadron One; the White House Transportation Agency, which is made up of some fifty military chauffeurs; and Camp David, which is a military facility operated by the navy. By far the largest WHMO unit is the White House Communications Agency, which is responsible for setting up communications between the White House and the president wherever he might be in the globe. WHMO—pronounced "Wham-oh"—is a republican nightmare come true.[27]

The bureaucratization of presidential travel is not, of course, limited to WHMO. What Michael Burton has aptly called the "presidential travel establishment" also includes the White House Travel Office, the Secret Service, and the Advance Office. The development of a travel establishment has made presidential travel much more predictable as well as safer and more secure than it was in the nineteenth and early twentieth centuries. The first century of presidential travel was littered with grisly accidents and unpleasant near misses. When President Jackson landed in New York City, for instance, he narrowly escaped injury when the bridge connecting the Battery and Castle Garden collapsed, plunging "dignitaries of every age and shape . . . cabinet members, presidential aides, governors, congressmen, mayors . . . into the shallow depths, all drenched, all frightened, and all struggling to regain solid ground." Fortunately for Jackson, who had been at the head of the procession, he and his horse had just reached the other side when the bridge gave way. President-elect Franklin Pierce narrowly escaped being killed when a broken axle hurled his passenger car off the rails and down a steep, rocky embankment, shattering the car into a "mass of broken glass and splintered wood." Pierce's 12-year-old son was not so lucky—he was killed instantly, his skull "almost mashed to a jelly." President Theodore Roosevelt, as recounted in chapter 4, also had a near miss when a trolley car hurtled into the presidential carriage, demolishing the carriage and killing the Secret Service agent accompanying the president.[28]

But the safety and security of the modern presidency have come at a cost. That cost is the creation of a regal presidency. The travel establishment works loyally and professionally to ensure not only that there are no nasty accidents but that there are no unpleasant surprises or even embarrassing moments for the chief executive. The convenience and image of the president are everything. But inconvenience is part of the human condition. Mere citizens wait in traffic jams and airports and train stations. The presidential travel establishment works to ensure that a president never has to wait and is never inconvenienced. As soon as the president boards Air Force One, the plane takes off. When the president is driven to an event, traf-

An 1875 woodcut portrays Jackson's arrival at Castle Garden and the collapse of a segment of the bridge that Jackson had just crossed over. (New York Public Library)

fic is halted so he can pass. The comparison of president and monarch is more apt than we would like to admit. Certainly nineteenth-century Americans would have seen it that way.

But weren't nineteenth-century Americans hopelessly paranoid? From the perspective of the twenty-first century, nineteenth-century fears of monarchy seem almost absurd. After all, the nineteenth-century national executive was small and weak by almost any historical or comparative standard. Even when occupied by Jackson or Lincoln, the nineteenth-century presidential office bore scant relationship to a monarch. However, the exaggerated fears were less irrational than they might seem at first glance. Fear of monarchy kept the executive on a short leash. Anxieties about a regal executive underlay the norm against presidents traveling abroad, Congress's resistance to a presidential travel allowance, and the nation's reluctance to provide protection for the president. These were among the instruments the nineteenth-century polity used to keep the president tethered to republicanism.

It may seem ironic that fears of the president becoming a de facto monarch were so great in an era when there was relatively little to fear from a regal presidency, and even more ironic that those fears are so muted at a time when the presidency has become so magnificently regal. But it is less ironic than it seems. For the rise of the regal presidency required the dimming though not the demise of the republican persuasion. If republican fears kept the president in check, the diminution of those fears enabled the presidency to break free from its republican tether and develop into its modern form.

Distrust of executive power and jeremiads against the regal presidency have not, of course, disappeared from American political life. Aggressive assertions of executive power periodically spur alarms about "the imperial presidency." As we saw in chapter 7, the unveiling of the splendid new Air Force One in 1990 stoked republican anxieties about a regal presidency. Lavish presidential inauguration ceremonies are commonly likened by critics to coronations. After Nixon's renomination in 1972, *Time*'s cover story was titled "The Coronation of King Richard." Some of George W. Bush's critics, including Senator Russ Feingold, have likened him to King George; on rare occasions Clinton was even tagged "King William the First." History, however, does us no favors if it leaves us only with the reassuring thought that we have seen it all before.[29]

The jeremiad about the regal presidency undeniably has deep roots in American history. But more striking than the similarities in rhetoric across the centuries is the gulf in practice. Twenty-first-century Americans have grown comfortable with a regal presidency that would have been unimaginable to nineteenth-century Americans. After the abuses of Watergate, Gerald Ford vowed to avoid a "kingly Presidency," but the electorate seemed unimpressed by his efforts to downgrade the royal trappings of the office. At the first opportunity the electorate voted him out of office. Jimmy Carter's commitment to "depomping the Presidency" was even more ostentatious than Ford's. Carter walked from his inaugural, donned a cardigan for televised fireside chats, turned the thermostat down in the White House, cut the size of his staff and forbid the staff from availing themselves of door-to-door limousine service, and even requested that "Hail to the Chief" not be played upon his every entrance. The self-consciously antiregal Carter was turned out after a single term in favor of Ronald Reagan, who reveled in the regal presidency. Voters rewarded Reagan with a second term. Presidents could be excused for thinking that the nation was not particularly bothered by a regal presidency.[30]

Indeed most Americans seem to enjoy the royal spectacle. The glamour of John Kennedy's "Camelot" continues to hold a powerful appeal for many people more than four decades after his assassination. "Hail to the Chief"—which the military designated as the president's official entry music in 1954—remains as popular as ever. The president after all is not just the head of the government and his party but the ceremonial head of state and symbol of the nation. Britain gets its dose of regal spectacle through the pageantry of the monarchy; Americans get theirs from watching the presidency.

Although the rise of the regal presidency is a twentieth-century development, it is less a perversion of the original institution than its logical culmination. Edmund

One of many depictions of President Nixon as a monarch. (Prints and Photographs Division, Library of Congress)

Randolph and Patrick Henry were, in an important sense, right. Of course, most of the founders would not recognize the presidency they created; indeed they would probably be horrified by it. But they are responsible for its creation nonetheless. For the constitutional framers, as Clinton Rossiter pointed out a half-century ago, "took a momentous step when they fused the dignity of a king and the power of a Prime Minister in one elective office." Unlike the president, a prime minister is dispensable. If a prime minister's support slips his party can remove him and replace him with another. The president, in contrast, cannot be removed by a vote of the legislature, except in cases of egregious wrongdoing, and even then not without precipitating a major constitutional crisis. Presidential removal is more akin to deposing a king than a vote of no confidence in a prime minister. Nobody plays "Hail to the Chief" when the prime minister enters the room, and no prime minister graces the nation's coins. Only presidents and monarchs, both symbols of the nation, receive that kind of treatment.[31]

The White House is central to the regal presidential spectacle. Its magnificent exterior is far more akin to Buckingham Palace than to the drab exterior of Number 10 Downing Street. And the White House's elegantly decorated interior is even more impressive. The plush red carpets that adorn the Grand Staircase as well as the regal hall connecting the State Dining Room and the East Room are visual evidence of the majesty of the presidency. Glittering state dinners, beautiful cut-glass chandeliers, classical European furniture all contribute to the regal symbolism of the White House.

The White House's regal symbolism makes getting beyond the White House all the more important for presidents. Savvy presidents exploit the pomp and ceremony of the White House but are also aware of the dangers of appearing isolated or out of touch with the people. An important function of presidential travel has long been to enable presidents to show that they are connected to the people and to their problems. As President Truman told a crowd in Crestline, Ohio, at the first stop on his June 1948 cross-country tour, it was invaluable "for the president to get away from the White House and get to see people as they are." Traveling among the people enabled him to "find out what people are thinking about," and thus made him able to "do a better job as President of the United States."[32] Traveling made the president not only look better but perform better.

Contemporary presidents offer much the same rationale for traveling as presidents always have, but the justifications seem increasingly labored and indeed transparently false. Presidential travel today enacts a regal spectacle that belies the democratic rhetoric. Air Force One is every bit as regal as the White House. In his whistle-stop speech at Crestline, Truman likened the White House to a "jail" in which the president was surrounded by guards "all the time," but today the guards surrounding a president are even more in evidence when the president is on the road than when he is home at the White House. No amount of traveling can break down the impassable barriers that have been erected between the president and the people. All that is left is spectacle, and by definition that is a relationship between president and people in which the people spectate instead of participate. We may regard this development with nostalgic regret or with hard-headed realism, but nothing short of a political or constitutional revolution will change it.[33]

Notes

INTRODUCTION

1. Robert V. Remini, *Andrew Jackson: The Course of American Democracy, 1833–1845* (New York: Harper and Row, 1984), 60. James Parton, *The Life of Andrew Jackson* (Boston: Houghton Mifflin, 1883), 486–87. Also see John M. Belohlavek, "Assault on the President: The Jackson-Randolph Affair of 1833," *Presidential Studies Quarterly* 12 (Summer 1982), 361–68. Belohlavek mistakenly suggests that the attack was on the return trip (361).

2. Remini, *Jackson: The Course of American Democracy*, 60–61. *Washington Globe*, May 7, 1833. Randolph claimed he only pulled the president's nose.

3. Remini, *Jackson: The Course of American Democracy*, 61.

4. Robert V. Remini, *Andrew Jackson: The Course of American Freedom, 1822–1832* (New York: Harper and Row, 1981), 177–78.

5. Ibid., 177.

6. Daniel Preston, ed., *The Papers of James Monroe: A Documentary History of the Presidential Tours of James Monroe, 1817, 1818, 1819* (Westport, CT: Greenwood Press, 2003), 352. *Democratic Telegraph and Texas Register* (Houston, Texas), July 26, 1847. The *New York Times* did not include photographs until 1896, and not until 1926 did the *Times* place a photograph on the front page.

7. "Wilson a Stranger in Old Yorktown," *New York Times*, July 4, 1913, p. 1.

8. Bruce Miroff, "Monopolizing the Public Space: The President as a Problem for Democratic Politics," which was originally published in Thomas E. Cronin, ed., *Rethinking the Presidency* (Boston: Little, Brown, 1982), 218–32.

9. The Reagan and Bush numbers are from Mark Knoller, "Bush's Use of Camp David for Foreign Guests," available at http://www.cbsnews.com/blogs/2006/06/09/publiceye/entry1698528.shtml (accessed June 25, 2006). Nixon's numbers are from "Why Presidents Flee the White House," *U.S. News and World Report*, August 28, 1978, p. 15. A recent history of presidents and their retreats is Kenneth T. Walsh, *From Mount Vernon to Crawford: A History of Presidents and Their Retreats* (New York: Hyperion, 2005). The name "Camp David" was given to the retreat in 1954 by President Dwight Eisenhower. Prior to that it had been known by the more evocative name Roosevelt had given to the idyllic retreat: "Shangri-La."

10. "Memorandum of absences of the Presidents of the United States from the national capital during each of the several Administrations, and of public and Executive acts performed during the time of such absences," May 4, 1876, in *Congressional Record-House*, 44th Congress, May 4, 1876, 2999–3000. Matthew Pinsker, *Lincoln's Sanctuary: Abraham Lincoln and the Soldiers' Home* (New York: Oxford University Press, 2003), 1–2. The "Memorandum of absences," which includes a count of the number of days each of the first fifteen presidents was away from the capital, was prepared by the Grant administration in response to a congressional resolution requesting that the president inform the Congress of any presidential actions that had been performed when Grant was away from the capital. Grant refused to

supply such information, but did have his administration dig up historical data showing that many presidents had been away from the capital for extended periods of time and had exercised the responsibilities of the office while away. The report was again inserted into the *Congressional Record* on March 20, 1902 (3054–55), during a debate over presidential protection. The report was produced in 1902 as evidence by Republicans that "the Presidential character is never laid aside" (3054) no matter where the president happened to be.

11. The domestic travel data are from Jeffrey E. Cohen and Richard J. Powell, "Building Public Support from the Grassroots Up: The Impact of Presidential Travel on State-Level Approval," *Presidential Studies Quarterly* 35 (March 2005), 11–12. The foreign travel data are calculated based on the information available at the U.S. Department of State's Web site, at http://www.state.gov/r/pa/ho/trvl/pres/c7383.htm (accessed May 1, 2006). Other sources of data on modern presidential travel include Samuel Kernell, *Going Public: New Strategies of Presidential Leadership* (Washington, DC: Congressional Quarterly, 1986), 97; Gary King and Lyn Ragsdale, *The Elusive Executive: Discovering Statistical Patterns in the Presidency* (Washington, DC: Congressional Quarterly, 1988), 270, 273. Bradley H. Patterson, Jr., estimates that President Clinton "made some 2,500 appearances in over 800 foreign or domestic cities or destinations, plus some 450 appearances at public events in the Washington area." See *The White House Staff: Inside the West Wing and Beyond* (Washington, DC: Brookings Institution Press, 2000), 241.

12. States visited by Johnson on his "swing around the circle" were Pennsylvania, New Jersey, New York, Ohio, Michigan, Indiana, Illinois, Missouri, and Kentucky. The other states visited by President Johnson were Connecticut, Maryland, Massachusetts, North Carolina, and Virginia. For a defense of Grant against the charge of absenteeism, see "The Crime of 'Absenteeism,'" *New York Times*, August 5, 1872, p. 4. The nineteen states visited by Grant were Connecticut, Delaware, Illinois, Indiana, Iowa, Pennsylvania, Maine, Maryland, Massachusetts, Missouri, Nebraska, New Hampshire, New Jersey, New York, Ohio, Rhode Island, Texas, Vermont, and Virginia. He also visited the territories of Colorado, Utah, and Wyoming. Apart from Maine, the only states Hayes failed to visit were Arkansas, Florida, Louisiana, Mississippi, South Carolina, North Carolina, and Texas, and the only territories he failed to visit were Montana, Idaho, and what was then called the Indian Territory but is now Oklahoma. Hayes passed through Delaware several times but does not appear to have stopped there. The information on states visited by Hayes is based on a search of the *New York Times*; Hayes Scrapbook, volume 78: September 2–December 5, 1880 (Great Western Tour and Misc.), p. 113, Rutherford B. Hayes Papers, Library of Congress, microfilm, series 6, roll 225; information provided by Nan Card, Curator of Manuscripts at the Rutherford B. Hayes Presidential Center; and Edward O. Frantz, "Goin' Dixie: Republican Presidential Tours of the South, 1877–1933," chapter 1, Ph.D. dissertation, University of Wisconsin-Madison, 2002. The "Rutherford the Rover" label is quoted in Lewis L. Gould, *The Modern American Presidency* (Lawrence: University Press of Kansas, 2003), 7.

13. Bob Withers reports that "an old ledger in the presidential travel office" indicates that Taft traveled 114,559 miles by rail. See Bob Withers, *The President Travels by Train: Politics and Pullmans* (Lynchburg, VA: TLC Publishing, 1996), 90. That is consistent with the figure (114,500) reported by Herbert G. Monroe in a 1945 article. See Herbert G. Monroe, "President's Special," *Railroad Magazine* (1945), 39. The only state President Taft did not visit was North Dakota (Withers, *The President Travels by Train*, 90). The other numbers on domestic rail travel cited in the text are from Withers, *The President Travels by Train*, 86, 108, 117, 122,

131. Franklin Roosevelt traveled 26,775 miles by plane and 83,562 miles by boat. See Monroe, "President's Special," 14.

14. Michael John Burton, "The Flying White House: A Travel Establishment within the Presidential Branch," *Presidential Studies Quarterly* 36 (June 2006), 298.

15. Robert M. Johnstone, Jr., *Jefferson and the Presidency: Leadership in the Young Republic* (Ithaca, NY: Cornell University Press, 1978), 58. Richard Ellis and Aaron Wildavsky, *Dilemmas of Presidential Leadership: From Washington through Lincoln* (New Brunswick, NJ: Transaction, 1989), 70. As Johnstone points out (58), the poor roads in the nation's fledgling capital may have contributed to Jefferson's decision to employ a horse rather than a carriage; New York and Philadelphia—the capital cities when Washington was president—had roads that were far superior to those in Washington, D.C.

16. The twelve states Monroe visited on his 1817 tour were Maryland, Delaware, Pennsylvania, New Jersey, New York, Connecticut, Massachusetts, Rhode Island, Maine, New Hampshire, Vermont, and Ohio; he also briefly traveled through Virginia but it's unclear whether he stopped there. The eight states on the 1819 tour were Virginia, North Carolina, South Carolina, Georgia, Tennessee, Alabama, Kentucky, and Indiana. See Preston, *Papers of James Monroe*, 6, 552.

17. Richard J. Ellis and Mark Dedrick, "The Rise of the Rhetorical Candidate," in Phillip G. Henderson, ed., *The Presidency, Then and Now* (Lanham, MD: Rowman and Littlefield, 2000), 185.

18. James Buchanan's travel was admittedly slight. His only significant travel came in June 1859 when he accepted an invitation to attend the commencement ceremonies at the University of North Carolina at Chapel Hill. Although the occasion for the invitation was "literary, and not political" (*New York Times*, May 20, 1859, p. 1), Buchanan spoke at several stops along the way on the most pressing political issue of the day: secession. At Raleigh, North Carolina, Buchanan responded to a welcoming address by vigorously affirming the value of the Union and warning the South against secession. "It has become fashionable," Buchanan said, "when any little discontent arises in the country to threaten to break up this glorious Union.... It is not every transitory or real evil in the administration of the government which ought to induce us to think of disunion.... If, in the frenzy of political excitement, this great Union should be dissolved, ages yet unborn will curse the day.... Let this Union cease to exist... and liberty upon Earth is gone forever." See "The President's Tour," *Pittsfield Sun* (Massachusetts), June 9, 1859. Jeffrey K. Tulis's claim that Buchanan offered "only 'greetings' on tour" is wrong. See *The Rhetorical Presidency* (Princeton, NJ: Princeton University Press, 1987), 78.

19. Two useful histories of manners in America are John F. Kasson, *Rudeness and Civility: Manners in Nineteenth-Century Urban America* (New York: Hill and Wang, 1990); and C. Dallett Hemphill, *Bowing to Necessities: A History of Manners in America, 1620–1860* (Chapel Hill: University of North Carolina Press, 1999). A history focused on the evolution of *political* manners in the nineteenth-century United States would be a valuable addition.

20. Kenneth M. Stampp, *The Era of Reconstruction, 1865–1877* (New York: Vintage, 1965), chapter 3. *New York Herald*, September 26, 1866. *Milwaukee Daily Sentinel*, September 1, 1866.

21. In *Democracy in America* (New York: Library of America, 2004; trans. Arthur Goldhammer), which was originally published in 1835, Tocqueville observed that "the president of the United States possesses prerogatives that are almost royal in magnitude." However, the president "has no occasion to use" these powers because the United States has been "sepa-

rated from the rest of world by the Atlantic Ocean, . . . has no enemies, and only rarely do its interests intersect with those of other nations of the globe." As those circumstances changed, presidential power could be expected to increase since "it is chiefly in the realm of foreign relations that the executive power of a nation finds occasion to demonstrate its skill and strength" (141–42).

22. Kenneth T. Walsh, *Air Force One: A History of Presidents and Their Planes* (New York: Hyperion, 2003), 7. The quotations are from Mark Penn, an adviser in Bill Clinton's White House.

23. Dumas Malone, *Jefferson the President: First Term, 1801–1805* (Boston: Little, Brown, 1970), 92–93. Not until Woodrow Wilson assumed the presidency in 1913 would the president again deliver the State of the Union message in person.

24. The quotation is from Burton, "The Flying White House," 305.

CHAPTER 1. THE ORIGINS OF PRESIDENTIAL TRAVEL:
THE TOURS OF GEORGE WASHINGTON AND JAMES MONROE

1. Nicholas Biddle to James Monroe, April 10, 1817, in Daniel Preston, ed., *The Papers of James Monroe: A Documentary History of the Presidential Tours of James Monroe, 1817, 1818, 1819* (Westport, CT: Greenwood Press, 2003), 10 [hereafter in this chapter cited as *PJM*]. Biddle would later achieve fame as the president of the Bank of the United States, a post to which he was appointed by Monroe in 1823. Biddle was at the helm of the national bank when President Andrew Jackson declared his "bank war."

2. Monroe [to Congress], January 12, 1825, *PJM*, 776. The explanation he offered to Congress was consistent with what he had told William Jones (president of the Bank of the United States and Madison's secretary of the navy) before embarking on the tour. Visiting fortifications along the coast and northern frontier, Monroe explained, would help not only by "enabling him to perform the duties assigned to [him]" but also "by drawing the public attention to such works" (Monroe to William Jones, April 22, 1817, *PJM*, 13).

3. The phrase first appeared in the Boston *Columbian Centinel*, July 12, 1817, *PJM*, 226; also see the *New Hampshire Patriot*, July 22, 1817, *PJM*, 321; and *Salem Gazette*, August 1, 1817, *PJM*, 393. Ironically, Boston was the one city on the president's tour in which partisanship was not put aside in greeting the president. In a letter to Thomas Jefferson, Monroe recorded that "In all the towns thro' which I passed there was an union between the parties, except in the case of Boston. I had suppos'd that that union was particularly to be desir'd by the republican party, since as it would be founded exclusively on their own principles, every thing would be gain'd by them. Some of our old and honest friends at Boston were, however, unwilling to amalgamate with their former opponents, even on our own ground, and in consequence presented an address of their own" (July 27, 1817, *PJM*, 418; also see Monroe to Madison, July 27, 1817, *PJM*, 419).

4. This motive was first urged on Monroe in a letter from David Humphreys, dated April 25, 1817: "While the principal object of your journey is understood to be, the inspection of the ports, arsenals, navy-yards &c. your presence will be very useful in another point of view. It will have a tendency to harmonise the public mind; &, as it were, to impart a national tone to it. Conciliation seems to be the order of the day. . . . [Y]our visit will . . . go far towards accomplishing the good work of uniting Parties" (*PJM*, 16–17). The phrase "the stain of the Hartford Convention" is from Jeremiah Mason to Rufus King, June 26, 1817, *PJM*, 163. In a similar vein, the *Albany Argus* viewed the elaborate parades in Boston as "an atonement for her po-

litical and moral sins during the war" (June 27, 1817, *PJM*, 169), and Abigail Adams wrote to Monroe's confidant (and acting secretary of state, pending the arrival of Abigail's son, John Quincy Adams) Richard Rush that "the splendor of [Boston's] reception of the president [was] by way . . . of expiation." (July 14, 1817, *PJM*, 236). Monroe also recognized this as a prime motive: "In the Eastern section of our union I have seen distinctly that the great cause which brought the people forward was a conviction that they had suffered in their character by their conduct in the late war, and a desire to show that unfavorable opinions, and as they thought, unjust, had been form'd in regard to their views and principles. They seiz'd the opportunity of which the casual incident of my tour presented to them of making a strong exertion to restore themselves to the confidence and ground which they had formerly held in the affections of their brethren in other quarters" (Monroe to Jefferson, July 27, 1817, *PJM*, 418; also see Monroe to Madison, May 12, 1822, *PJM*, 775).

5. Monroe to Madison July 27, 1817, *PJM*, 419. Also see Monroe to Jefferson, July 27, 1817, *PJM* 418, and *National Intelligencer* (Washington, D.C.), April 23, 1817, *PJM*, 15.

6. "Introduction," *PJM*, xviii. Harry Ammon, *James Monroe: The Quest for National Identity* (Charlottesville: University Press of Virginia, 1990), 374–75. *Baltimore Patriot*, June 2, 1817, *PJM*, 37.

7. Monroe to George Hay, August 5, 1817, *PJM*, 425; also see Monroe to Richard Rush, July 20, 1817, *PJM*, 413. Unless Monroe is guilty of great exaggeration, Jeffrey Tulis's count of President Monroe's speeches on tour underestimates the amount of public speaking performed by Monroe (see *The Rhetorical Presidency* [Princeton, NJ: Princeton University Press, 1987], 64). By Tulis's count, Monroe gave forty speeches on his two tours, whereas by Monroe's count the number would be closer to four hundred speeches in his first tour alone. The records in *PJM* suggest that there were at least fifty occasions on which Monroe delivered public speeches on his first tour. There were apparently fewer public speeches on his second tour but even a conservative estimate would add about twenty additional speeches.

8. *Baltimore Patriot*, June 2, 1817, *PJM*, 37. John Adams to Benjamin Waterhouse, June 18, 1817, *PJM*, 101. Rufus King to Christopher Gore, June 12, 1817, *PJM*, 73. John Pintard to Eliza Davidson, June 12/13, 1817, *PJM*, 71. Also see Henry Meigs to Josiah Meigs, June 3, 1817, *PJM*, 60. The "novelty of beholding the Chief Magistrate" (*PJM*, 47) was a frequent theme in press commentary on Monroe's visit. See, for instance, *New York Daily Advertiser*, June 12, 1817, *PJM*, 69, and *National Intelligencer* (Washington, D.C.), June 17, 1817, *PJM*, 112.

9. Monroe to Jefferson, July 27, 1817, *PJM*, 418. Monroe to Richard Rush, July 20, 1817, *PJM*, 413.

10. "Introduction," *PJM*, xix.

11. R. Malcolm Smuts, *Court Culture and the Origins of a Royalist Tradition in Early Stuart England* (Philadelphia: University of Pennsylvania Press, 1987), 17. Mary Hill Cole, *The Portable Queen: Elizabeth I and the Politics of Ceremony* (Amherst: University of Massachusetts Press, 1999), 39, 1, 22. The design of the great country houses is discussed in Mark Girouard, *Life in the English Country House: A Social and Architectural History* (New Haven, CT: Yale University Press, 1978); also relevant is Cole, *Portable Queen*, chapter 4, esp. 66–67.

12. Smuts, *Court Culture*, 17–18. The source for this account is John Nichols, *The Progresses and Public Processions of Queen Elizabeth I*, 3 vols. (1823; New York: AMS Press, 1977).

13. Cole, *Portable Queen*, 73; quotation at 3.

14. Ibid., 2–3, 35, 63, 135.

15. Smuts, *Court Culture*, 66. E-mail communication with Monica Piotter, August 12, 2004.

Cole, *Portable Queen*, 4. On royal progresses during the reign of James I, see Philip Harrison and Mark Brayshay, "Post Horse Routes, Royal Progresses and Government Communications in the Reign of James I," *Journal of Transport History* 18 (1997), 116–33, and John Nichols, *The Progresses, Processions, and Magnificent Festivities of King James the First*, 4 vols. (New York: Burt Franklin, 1828).

16. The definition of "progress" is from the *Oxford English Dictionary*.

17. Richard Norton Smith, *Patriarch: George Washington and the New American Nation* (Boston: Houghton Mifflin, 1993), 25.

18. Diary entry of October 5, 1789, Donald Jackson and Dorothy Twohig, eds., *The Diaries of George Washington* (Charlottesville: University Press of Virginia, 1979), 5:453. Archibald Henderson, *Washington's Southern Tour, 1791* (Boston: Houghton Mifflin, 1923), 1. Hancock to Washington, October 21, 1789, and Washington to Hancock, October 22, 1789, Dorothy Twohig, ed., *The Papers of George Washington: Presidential Series* (Charlottesville: University Press of Virginia, 1993), 4:212, 214. Also see Washington's diary entry for October 23, where he noted that "this ceremony was not to be avoided though I had made every effort to do it" (Jackson and Twohig, *Diaries*, 5:472).

19. Hancock to Washington, October 21, 1789, *Presidential Series*, 4:212. October 24, 1789, Jackson and Twohig, *Diaries*, 5:474–75. Also see Washington's diary entries between October 17, 1789, when he arrived in Stratford, CT, and November 4, when he left Portsmouth, NH.

20. Smith, *Patriarch*, 25. Richard Ellis and Aaron Wildavsky, *Dilemmas of Presidential Leadership: From Washington through Lincoln* (New Brunswick, NJ: Transaction Publishers, 1989), 44. Edgar S. Maclay, ed., *Journal of William Maclay: United States Senator from Pennsylvania, 1789–1791* (New York: Appleton, 1890), entry for May 9, 1789, p. 25. Maclay's journal is available from the Library of Congress at http://memory.loc.gov/ammem/amlaw/lwmj.html (accessed July 1, 2006). Also see Jackson and Twohig, *Diaries* 5:475n2, 5:491.

21. *Journal of William Maclay*, entry for May 9, 1789, p. 10.

22. Smith, *Patriarch*, 25. Maclay's diary entry is quoted in Simon P. Newman, *Parades and the Politics of the Street: Festive Culture in the Early American Republic* (Philadelphia: University of Pennsylvania Press, 1997), 51. The "high tone" quotation is from Alexander Hamilton who told Washington that "Men's minds are prepared for a pretty high tone in the demeanor of the Executive; but I doubt whether for so high a tone as might in the abstract be desirable. The notions of equality are as yet in my opinion too general and too strong" (Newman, *Parades and the Politics of the Street*, 50).

23. James Tagg, *Benjamin Franklin Bache and the Philadelphia Aurora* (Philadelphia: University of Pennsylvania Press, 1991), 166, 163–64. Newman, *Parades and the Politics of the Street*, 62.

24. *General Advertiser* (Philadelphia), April 23, 1791; the same report is reprinted in the *Independent Gazetteer and Agricultural Repository*, April 30, 1791. Also see *Presidential Series*, 8:73–74. In *Washington's Southern Tour*, Bache is quoted ridiculing Washington's "stately journeyings through the American continent in search of personal incense" (xxiii). No source or date is provided for the quotation.

25. *Presidential Series*, 8:73–74. Also see Smith, *Patriarch*, 93, and David Waldstreicher, *In the Midst of Perpetual Fetes: The Making of American Nationalism, 1776–1820* (Chapel Hill: University of North Carolina Press, 1997), 121. Similar in spirit was the welcome from the residents of Salisbury, who told Washington that "Words are wanting to express our gratitude to heaven for continuing your life, on which our national glory, and domestic tranquility, are

even at this day, depending. . . . That your life, justly dear to the people of this Country, a life precious to freedom, an ornament to human nature, and a blessing to the United States of America, may long be preserved, is the fervent and unanimous prayer of the people of this village" (*Presidential Series*, 8:225–26).

26. Kenneth Cook, "Washington Passes through Halifax," prepared for presentation to the Halifax County Chapter, United Daughters of the Confederacy, April 2, 1976, available at http://www.oldhalifax.com/county/GeoWashington.htm (accessed July 1, 2006). *General Advertiser*, January 29, 1793, quoted in Tagg, *Benjamin Franklin Bache*, 164. Also see Newman, *Parades and the Politics of the Street*, 52.

27. Henderson, *Washington's Southern Tour*, 150, 155–56, 171, 178. Jackson and Twohig, *Diaries*, 6:126–30. Terry W. Lipscomb, *South Carolina in 1791: George Washington's Southern Tour* (Columbia, SC: South Carolina Department of Archives and History, 1993), 21.

28. Jackson and Twohig, *Diaries*, 6:131. Henderson, *Washington's Southern Tour*, 182, 184.

29. Henderson, *Washington's Southern Tour*, 184, xxiii–xxiv.

30. Richard Buel, Jr., *Securing the Revolution: Ideology in American Politics, 1789–1815* (Ithaca, NY: Cornell University Press, 1972), 156. Thomas Jefferson to James Madison, December 28, 1794, John Catanzariti, ed., *The Papers of Thomas Jefferson* (Princeton, NJ: Princeton University Press, 2000), 28:228.

31. *Muskingum Messenger* (Ohio), September 3, 1817, *PJM*, 457. *American Telegraph* (Brownsville, Pennsylvania), September 9, 1817, *PJM*, 470. For praise of Monroe's "republican simplicity" and/or his "plain" appearance, see *PJM*, 43, 111, 124–26, 320, 378.

32. *National Intelligencer* (Washington, D.C.), June 17, 1787, *PJM*, 111–12; also see *National Intelligencer*, June 2, 1817, *PJM*, 33–34; *Eastern Argus* (Portland, Maine), July 22, 1817, *PJM*, 306; *Georgetown Messenger*, June 2, 1817, *PJM*, 33; and the *Baltimore Patriot*, June 2, 1817, *PJM*, 37. The *National Intelligencer* is identified as the "semiofficial newspaper" of the Monroe administration in Mel Laracey, *Presidents and the People: The Partisan Story of Going Public* (College Station: Texas A&M University Press, 2002), 65. The *Intelligencer*'s claim that the ceremonies were spontaneous popular celebrations was not entirely true. The administration played a significant role in choreographing at least some of the demonstrations of respect. According to one press report, the secretary of war and the secretary of the navy, both of whom "conceived it incompatible with all usage, and derogatory to the high office [the president] holds, to wave [*sic*] the accustomary military and naval honors on his visit to the different posts and stations," issued directives to ensure that the president was appropriately greeted when Monroe visited the many military outposts and naval stations on his tour (*Baltimore Patriot*, May 28, 1817, *PJM*, 45, quoting from the *Philadelphia Gazette*). The navy secretary instructed commanding officers at naval yards across the East to ensure that "suitable preparations may be made to receive in a becoming and appropriate manner the President of the United States and pay to him those honours worthy to be offered and to which he is entitled as the Chief Magistrate of a free and enlightened people" (Benjamin Crowninshield to Alexander Murray, May 20, 1817, *PJM*, 29). Secretary of Treasury William Crawford also facilitated the president's travel, instructing the Baltimore collector of customs (a federal post) to "furnish every facility which the revenue Cutter under your direction will enable you to give" to help the president should he be "in need of water conveyance" (Crawford to James McCulloch, May 31, 1817, *PJM*, 32–33).

33. *American Telegraph* (Brownsville, Pennsylvania), September 9, 1817; *PJM*, 470. *Georgetown Messenger*, July 2, 1817, *PJM*, 171–72. *Boston Patriot*, July 4, 1817, *PJM*, 201. Also see *Boston*

Patriot, July 18, 1817, *PJM*, 381–82; *Vermont Gazette* (Bennington), June 24, 1817, *PJM*, 168; and Henry Dearborn to Thomas Aspinwall, July 11, 1787, *PJM*, 409.

34. *Baltimore Patriot*, July 2, 1817, *PJM*, 172. *National Intelligencer*, July 3, 1787, *PJM*, 173. Edward D. Bangs to Nathaniel Howe, August 1, 1817, *PJM*, 237. Also see *Columbian Centinel* (Boston), July 12, 1817, *PJM*, 234; *Virginia Patriot* (Richmond), June 17, 1817, *PJM*, 111; *Albany Argus*, June 20, 1817, *PJM*, 116; *Eastern Argus* (Portland, Maine), July 22, 1817, *PJM*, 306; and *Boston Yankee*, July 4, 1817, *PJM*, 365.

35. *New Hampshire Gazette* (Portsmouth), July 15, 1787, *PJM*, 378. Address by the American Society for the Encouragement of American Manufactures, in *New York Evening Post*, June 14, 1817, *PJM*, 78. Also see *Mercury* (Newport, Rhode Island), July 19, 1817, *PJM*, 384, in which Monroe is praised for "bring[ing] the Chief Magistrate and people nearer to each other." Also see Lyceum of Natural History resolution, June 16, 1817, reported in *Columbian* (New York), June 23, 1817, *PJM*, 90.

36. *Columbian* (New York), May 30, 1817, *PJM*, 59–60; also see June 7, 1817, *PJM*, 105–6. Henry Meigs to Josiah Meigs, June 3, 1817, *PJM*, 60–61.

37. *Richmond Enquirer*, July 18, 1817, *PJM*, 381; also see July 29, 1817, *PJM*, 392–93. Ritchie would later reportedly say that "he approved of Mr. Monroe's administration and all of his conduct, excepting the tour which he made through the States, soon after his first election to the Presidency" (John Clarke to Monroe, April 18, 1822, *PJM*, 774).

38. Monroe to George Hay, August 5, 1817, *PJM*, 423. On July 27, Monroe's assistant Joseph Swift informed the president that "the Kentucky Paper contains insinuations that your tour is wrong & that your objects are sinister" and that "Some of the Virginians, by the Enquirer, affect to be disgusted by the kind of attention Paid to, as the Enquirer disrespectfully terms, the Peoples Agent" (Swift to Monroe, July 27, 1817, *PJM*, 421).

39. *Richmond Enquirer*, August 5, 1817, *PJM*, 398–99; also see the letters to the editor published in the *Richmond Enquirer*, August 12, 1817, and September 5, 1817, *PJM*, 405–406, 490–91.

40. Noble E. Cunningham, Jr., *The Presidency of James Monroe* (Lawrence: University Press of Kansas, 1996), 38. Ammon, *James Monroe*, 378. *Kentucky Gazette* (Lexington), June 28, 1817, *PJM*, 171; also see September 6 and 20, 1817, *PJM*, 491, 495–96.

41. *Niles Weekly Register*, June 7, 21, 1817, *PJM*, 43, 166.

42. Ibid., August 2, 1817, *PJM*, 396.

43. *National Advocate* (New York), June 9, 16, 21, 23, 1817, *PJM*, 62, 80, 94–95, 385–86.

44. *Federal Republican* (Baltimore), April 24, 1817, July 25, 1817, September 2, 1817, *PJM*, 16, 389–90, 488.

45. *New York Daily Advertiser*, May 30, 1817, August 7, 1817, *PJM*, 58, 401–2.

46. *Virginia Patriot* (Richmond), July 24, 1787, *PJM*, 389; the "puffed and flattered" quotation is the view that the *Virginia Patriot* attributed to Ritchie's *Richmond Enquirer*. For the suspicion that Monroe had his eyes on getting reelected, see the letters from James Wilkinson to Henry Dearborn (June 23, 1817, *PJM*, 162) and to Joseph Reed, Jr. (September 23, 1817, *PJM*, 507), as well as the defense of Monroe on this charge in the *Boston Patriot*, June 13, 1817, *PJM*, 108.

47. *Southern Patriot* (Charleston), July 10, 1787, *PJM*, 370–71. The *Southern Patriot* argued that while "the constitution does not explicitly enjoin its performance as indispensable, . . . it is plainly indicated in the third section of that instrument. Speaking of the President's duties, it says—'He shall, from time to time, give to the Congress information of the state of the

Union; and recommend to their consideration such measures as he shall judge necessary and expedient.' Now, as accurate knowledge of such weighty concerns can never be as correctly obtained through means of appointed agents, too often negligent or incapacitated, as by the head of the nation himself, on whom rests a great responsibility. In time of war, when his presence is necessary in the centre of the Union, the President must depend on others for this information. But it is during a season of peace that, by his own observation, the representations of public agents should be tested" (370).

48. *New York Daily Advertiser*, August 7, 1817, *PJM*, 401.

49. Monroe also embarked on a smaller, roughly three-week tour of the Chesapeake Bay in late May and June 1818. This little-known presidential tour (Tulis, for instance, ignores this tour in his count of Monroe's tours [*Rhetorical Presidency*, 64]) is chronicled in *PJM*, 517–49.

50. *Kentucky Gazette* (Lexington), April 16, 1819, *PJM*, 732. Clay had declined an offer to enter the Monroe administration as secretary of war, which he regarded as an inferior post to that which had been offered to his rivals William Crawford (secretary of treasury) and John Quincy Adams (secretary of state). Because Clay was outside the administration, while all of his major rivals for the presidency (Crawford, Adams, and also John Calhoun, who was made secretary of war after Clay declined the post) were in the president's cabinet, Clay not surprisingly settled into an oppositional stance. Clay also had important policy differences with the administration on the federal support of internal improvements, a policy popular in the West but opposed by many Republicans in the South who supported Crawford. On Clay's opposition to the Monroe administration, see Ammon, *James Monroe*, esp. 358–59; and Robert V. Remini, *Henry Clay: Statesman for the Union* (New York: Norton, 1991), esp. 149–61.

51. *Western Monitor* (Lexington), April 24, 1819, *PJM*, 732–33; also see June 8, 1819, *PJM*, 740.

52. *Kentucky Reporter* (Lexington), May 26, 1819, *PJM*, 739.

53. *Western Monitor* (Lexington), June 1, 1819, *PJM*, 701–2. Also see Louisville *Public Advertiser*, April 28, 1819, *PJM*, 733.

54. *Kentucky Gazette* (Lexington), June 25, July 2, 1819, *PJM*, 704–5.

55. *Western Monitor* (Lexington), July 6, 1819, *PJM*, 706–7; also see *Kentucky Gazette* (Lexington), July 9, 1819, *PJM*, 706.

56. Quotations are from the "brief outline" of Monroe's July 3, 1819, speech, as printed in the Lexington *Western Monitor*, July 27, 1819, *PJM*, 709, and from the text of Monroe's speech on July 5, 1819, printed in the *Western Monitor*, July 6, 1819, *PJM*, 715. Monroe's speech echoed, in part, what was said in the speech to him on behalf of the citizens of Lexington: "We feel that we honor ourselves in honoring you, and that republicanism, when rightly understood, does not proscribe, but invites and cherishes refinement of sentiment and manners, and the best forms of politeness and hospitality, as well as an attachment to the principles of liberty, to just laws, and to equal civil rights. We are not aware that we descend from the elevation which, as the friends of a free government, we ought to maintain, or that we impair our claim to think for ourselves, and to judge independently concerning the characters and measures of public men, when we mingle our congratulations, as you pass through the land, with those of the millions, whom our affections lead us cordially to embrace as our fellow freemen in a country of freedom. Republican simplicity, and the spirit of a just independence, are neither rude nor jealous, nor are they most safe when accompanied by habitual suspicion and a promptness to censure. The virtues of the enlightened patriot easily blend with confidence, courtesy and haste" (*PJM*, 713).

57. Text of president's July 5, 1819, speech, printed in *Western Monitor* (Lexington), July 6, 1819, *PJM*, 714.

58. Ibid.

59. See Tulis, *Rhetorical Presidency*, especially chapter 3. In a brief discussion of Monroe's tours (71–72), Tulis approvingly quotes Stuart Gerry Brown's erroneous conclusion that during the tours "Monroe never referred, even in passing, to the issues of the day." See Stuart Gerry Brown, *The American Presidency: Leadership, Partisanship, and Popularity* (New York: Macmillan, 1966), 12.

60. Both speeches, delivered on June 30, 1819, are reprinted in *Commentator* (Frankfurt), July 2, 1819, *PJM*, 695–96.

61. *Carolina Centinel* (New Bern, South Carolina), May 8, 1819, *PJM*, 586–87. *Charleston Courier*, April 28, 1819, *PJM*, 601. Draft of Monroe's response in Beaufort, South Carolina, in *PJM*, 627–28. *Huntsville Republican*, June 1, 1819, *PJM*, 664.

62. *Kentucky Gazette* (Lexington), July 2, 1819, *PJM*, 769. Two examples of praise for Monroe's policy position are the Nashville *Clarion*, July 13, 1819, *PJM*, 744, and the Baltimore *Morning Chronicle*, July 24, 1819, *PJM*, 750–51.

63. *Southern Patriot* (Charleston), April 27, 1819, *PJM*, 606.

64. Ibid. See Richard E. Neustadt, *Presidential Power: The Politics of Leadership from Roosevelt to Reagan* (New York: Free Press, 1990).

65. *Southern Patriot* (Charleston), April 27, 1819, *PJM*, 606–7.

66. *Southern Patriot* (Charleston), April 27, 1819, *PJM*, 606–7. President Monroe's speech, printed in *Nashville Whig*, June 12, 1819, *PJM*, 673.

CHAPTER 2. THE LIFE OF THE PARTY: THE TOURS OF
ANDREW JACKSON AND MARTIN VAN BUREN

1. *Hartford Times*, January 14, 1833; also see the advertisement for the day of celebration on December 24, 1832.

2. *Hartford Times*, January 14, 1833. The resolution was widely reported in the Democratic press in New England. See, for instance, *Eastern Argus* (Portland, Maine), January 16, 1833; *Pittsfield Sun* (Massachusetts), January 24, 1833; and *Rhode-Island Republican*, January 28, 1833. Judson was elected to Congress in 1835 and was subsequently appointed to the district court, where he was the presiding judge in the *Amistad* case. Other members of the committee included Orrin Holt, who took Judson's place in Congress after Judson was named to the bench, and Gideon Welles, a state legislator and co-owner and editor of the *Hartford Times*. Welles would succeed Niles as Hartford's postmaster general after Niles was appointed to the U.S. Senate in 1835, and he would later become secretary of the navy in the Lincoln administration.

3. The electoral statistics are from Richard P. McCormick, "Political Development and the Second Party System," in William Nisbet Chambers and Walter Dean Burnham, eds., *The American Party Systems: Stages of Political Development*, 2nd ed. (New York: Oxford University Press, 1975), 98.

4. Richard P. McCormick, *The Second American Party System: Party Formation in the Jacksonian Era* (Chapel Hill: University of North Carolina Press, 1966), 67–68. *Hartford Times*, February 4, 1833. *Connecticut Courant*, December 25, 1832.

5. *Washington Globe*, March 15, 1833.

6. The argument that the second party system had its origins in the competition for the presidency is advanced in McCormick, "Political Development and the Second Party System." On the first party system see Paul Goodman, "The First American Party System," in Chambers and Burnham, *American Party Systems*, 56–89. The border states of Kentucky and Maryland were also closely contested in both 1828 and 1832.

7. *Historical Statistics of the United States*, Millennial Edition Online. The states in which the state legislatures selected presidential electors were Delaware, Georgia, Connecticut, Massachusetts, South Carolina, New York, Vermont, Louisiana, and Indiana. The one-in-one-hundred white males estimate is by historian Lynn W. Turner, as quoted in Evan Cornog and Richard Whelan, *Hats in the Ring: An Illustrated History of American Presidential Campaigns* (New York: Random House, 2000), 46.

8. See Fletcher M. Green, "On Tour with President Andrew Jackson," *New England Quarterly* (June 1963), 212–13.

9. *Washington Globe*, March 15, 1833. Jackson's letter to the committee of Connecticut Democrats is dated March 7, 1833.

10. On March 30, for instance, Democrats in Concord, New Hampshire, met to select a committee to extend an invitation to Jackson, and on April 1 the designated committee wrote to Jackson, inviting him to visit Concord and communicating their approval "of all the leading measures of the administration." The invitation and the president's response—which was not written until June 13—were published in the *New Hampshire Patriot* on June 24, 1833. The *Boston Statesman* reported that "immediately after it was announced that it was possible [Jackson] might visit this section of the country this season, . . . he was so inundated with letters of invitation that it was found impossible to answer them all without neglecting every other duty: the President was therefore reluctantly compelled, after replying to one or two, to omit answering the remainder altogether" (May 18, 1833).

11. The letter from Boston's Democrats was dated March 11, 1833, but Jackson did not respond until May 21. Jackson explained that he "deferred its acknowledgment until I could decide with certainty whether it would be in my power, this summer" to visit New England. Jackson announced that he would indeed be taking a six-to-eight-week trip beginning in early June, and that he would find it "particularly gratifying . . . to embrace an opportunity of tendering to yourselves and those you represent on this occasion, as well as to my fellow-citizens generally, my personal respects." He would not, however, be able to stay for July 4, though he did look forward to examining "those revolutionary scenes which give Boston so exalted a distinction in our national history." He also cried off "any public celebration" on account of his health. See *National Intelligencer* (Washington, D.C.), May 30, 1833. The legislative resolution was published in the *Boston Statesman*, March 30, 1833. Jackson did not respond to the legislature's communication until June 13, when he was in New York City; Jackson's letter, announcing he would arrive in Boston on June 21, can be found in the *New Hampshire Patriot*, June 24, 1833.

12. *Hartford Times*, April 1, 1833. *New Hampshire Patriot*, May 6, 1833. The *New Hampshire Patriot* had reacted with similar trepidation to news of the invitation from the Massachusetts legislature: "Now by all gods of heathen idolatry, we hope the committee will not recommend that the Boston Aristocracy accompany the President to New Hampshire, for we begin to fear we shall never get a chance to see Old Hickory after all" (April 1, 1833). For examples of the *Hartford Times'* opinion being attributed to the *Washington Globe*, see *Boston*

Post, April 18, 1833; *Salem Gazette* (Massachusetts), April 19, 1833; and *New Hampshire Patriot*, April 22, 1833. The *Globe*'s disavowal was also carried widely. See, for example, the *Richmond Enquirer*, April 26, 1833.

13. *New Hampshire Patriot*, May 6, 1833; also reprinted in *Eastern Argus* (Portland, Maine), May 8, 1833; and (without attribution) in the *New Hampshire Gazette*, May 7, 1833. The *Gazette* had earlier expressed the same concern that the "Federal Legislature of Massachusetts . . . intend doubtless, in the reception of the man they so much abused, to eclipse his fast and staunch friends, who have stood by him in the worst of times, and oblige them as in the visit of Mr. Monroe, to fall in their wake, and be suffered only, to be a sort of make-weight in the business" (April 23, 1833).

14. *New Hampshire Patriot*, May 20, 1833.

15. *New Hampshire Gazette*, May 14, 1833; May 28, 1833. Greenleaf was appointed postmaster by Jackson. See Donald B. Cole, *Jacksonian Democracy in New Hampshire, 1800–1851* (Cambridge, MA: Harvard University Press, 1970), 86.

16. *Portsmouth Journal and the Rockingham Gazette*, May 18, 1833; June 1, 1833.

17. *New Hampshire Gazette*, May 21, 1833.

18. Ibid. Democrats remembered Mason's role with particular bitterness because in 1828 President John Quincy Adams had appointed Mason as president of the Portsmouth branch of the national bank—which was the only branch of the national bank in the state. Unhappy about Mason's lending policies, Democrats in the state had tried without success to get Mason removed. The conflict over Mason had played an important role in igniting the bank war. See Cole, *Jacksonian Democracy*, chapter 5.

19. *New Hampshire Gazette*, May 28, 1833; June 18, 1833. The members of the committee of arrangements are listed in the *Portsmouth Journal and the Rockingham Gazette*, June 15, 1833. Only two of the five selectmen (Ichabod Goodwin and John Smith) could be fairly described as opponents of Jackson, a fact that is implicitly conceded in the *New Hampshire Gazette*, May 28, 1833. Also see a letter from "Jacksonites" claiming that a majority of the selectmen were Jackson supporters (*Portsmouth Journal and the Rockingham Gazette*, June 1, 1833). The *Journal* agreed that "a majority of the board of the Selectmen . . . were the President's political friends" (July 13, 1833).

20. *New Hampshire Gazette*, June 4, 18, 25, 1833; July 16, 1833. Among the fault lines in this conflict was the divide between Democrats loyal to Secretary of the Navy Levi Woodbury and those loyal to New Hampshire Senator Isaac Hill. His was the state's most influential Democrat; his office in Concord was known as the "Dictator's Palace." Owner and editor of the *New Hampshire Patriot*, Hill had been the chief architect in the construction of the state's Democratic Party. A close adviser to Jackson—he was one of those considered part of Jackson's informal "Kitchen Cabinet"—Hill skillfully wielded influence over patronage. After the U.S. Senate, in the spring of 1830, rejected Hill's appointment to a lucrative Treasury post, Jackson backed a move to get Hill elected to the Senate. The only trouble with this plan was that it meant that Woodbury, who currently occupied that post, would have to give way. Woodbury sought assurances that Jackson would offer him a cabinet post instead, but nothing was immediately forthcoming. When Woodbury did not resign, the *Patriot* tore into him for disloyalty and selfish ambition. The Portsmouth *Gazette*, which was edited by Abner Greenleaf, a close ally of Woodbury's and an opponent of Hill's, responded by condemning Hill. The rivalry between Hill and Woodbury was eased when Jackson appointed Woodbury sec-

retary of the navy in 1831, but the relationship between the two men as well as their followers was often strained. Fueling the *Gazette's* suspicion of the selectmen was that one of the
five Portsmouth selectmen was Richard H. Ayer, Hill's brother-in-law (Hill married Ayer's
sister in 1814). For the *Gazette's* attack on Ayer, see May 28, 1833. On the conflict and tension
between Hill and Woodbury, the *Patriot* and the *Gazette*, Concord and Portsmouth, see Cole,
Jacksonian Democracy. Also see the *New London Gazette* (Connecticut), July 17, 1833, which
reported that the New Hampshire legislature, on its last day in session, proposed moving the
capital to Portsmouth "as a mark of disapprobation of the conduct of the citizens of Concord on the occasion of the President's reception." Although passed by the house, the resolution was not acted upon by the senate.

21. *Portsmouth Journal and the Rockingham Gazette*, June 22, 1833.

22. *New Hampshire Gazette*, June 25, 1833; July 16, 1833.

23. *New Hampshire Gazette*, June 25, 1833; July 2, 1833. *Portsmouth Journal and the Rockingham Gazette*, June 29, 1833.

24. *New Hampshire Gazette*, June 25, 1833; July 9, 1833.

25. William B. Lewis to Edward Livingston, November 18, 1833, as quoted in Robert V.
Remini, *Andrew Jackson: The Course of American Democracy, 1833–1845* (New York: Harper
and Row, 1984), 83. *Portsmouth Journal and the Rockingham Gazette*, July 13, 1833. Jackson
left Concord on Monday morning, July 1. Jackson's letter to Abner Greenleaf, dated Sunday June 30, explained that he would not be able to continue on to Portsmouth because
"my strength is not equal to the labor which the further prosecution of my journey requires;
and that it will not be safe for me to proceed beyond this point" (*New Hampshire Gazette*,
July 9, 1833). This was somewhat different from what he had told the New Hampshire state
legislature the day before. Speaking in the legislative chamber, Jackson announced with regret "that neither the state of my health *nor the time which I can conveniently spare from my
public duties*, will allow me to continue my journey further than this point" (*New Hampshire Patriot*, July 8, 1833; emphasis added). In other words, it would appear that politics as
much as health shaped Jackson's decision to terminate the tour. A letter from Levi Woodbury, published in Maine's *Portland Evening Advertiser* on July 2, also intimated that the decision was motivated by more than merely Jackson's health. Woodbury wrote: "I regret to inform you that the ill health of the president is such, *connected with other causes*, as to induce
him to return directly to Washington" (*Niles Weekly Register*, July 13, 1833; emphasis added).
Remini mistakenly suggests that Jackson visited Portsmouth and "left the city as quickly as
decency allowed and pushed on to Concord" (Remini, *Jackson: The Course of American Democracy*, 82).

26. *Portsmouth Journal and the Rockingham Gazette*, May 11, 1833. Consider, for instance,
Jackson's visit to the avowedly partisan Tammany Society in New York City. "Received at the
door of the Great Wigwam by a committee consisting of the Sagamore and three Sachems,"
Jackson was escorted inside where he was introduced to the "Grand Sachem, the other officers
and their numerous Brothers that were present." According to a contemporary press account,
Jackson "expressed great satisfaction in having an opportunity to visit that association whose
exertions had so long and so faithfully been devoted to the establishment and maintenance of
Democratic principles." See *Boston Post*, June 22, 1833 (from the *New York Post*).

27. *Hartford Times*, June 15, 1833. Also see John Niven, *Gideon Welles: Lincoln's Secretary of
the Navy* (New York: Oxford University Press, 1973), 157–59. Another prominent Democrat to

accompany Jackson on part of the tour was New Hampshire's Isaac Hill. See *Essex Register* (Salem, Massachusetts), July 4, 1833. Hill had been among those Democrats to extend Jackson an early invitation to visit New England, writing to Jackson on April 3, 1833, two days after Concord's Democrats penned their letter of invitation. See Cole, *Jacksonian Democracy*, 160.

28. *New Hampshire Patriot*, March 25, 1833.

29. The front seat of the carriage was occupied by two other loyal Jackson allies: Joseph Worrell and Peter Wager. Jackson had recently appointed Wager to be a national bank director (*New London Gazette* [Connecticut], January 30, 1833), though the U.S. Senate would reject the appointment before the end of the year. Worrell was a prominent Jackson partisan. Shortly before the November election, for instance, he had presided over a large pro-Jackson meeting in Independence Square (*Richmond Enquirer*, November 2, 1832). The meeting of Philadelphia's Democrats (held on July 23, 1832) chaired by Horn is described in the *Richmond Enquirer*, July 27, 1832. Over the next several decades Horn remained a loyal Jacksonian, though Philadelphia became increasingly inhospitable political territory for Democrats. Horn was the "perennial chairman of the Jackson Hickory Club in Philadelphia" (Charles McCool Snyder, *The Jacksonian Heritage: Pennsylvania Politics, 1833–1848* [Harrisburg: Pennsylvania Historical and Museum Commission, 1958], 187), and Polk twice nominated Horn to be Collector of the Port of Philadelphia but both times the Senate rejected the nomination (193). According to Snyder, twenty-four of the twenty-six-member Pennsylvania delegation (seventeen of whom were Jacksonian Democrats) voted to recharter the bank, one opposed it, and one abstained (25).

30. The resolutions adopted by the mass meeting were published in the *Richmond Enquirer*, May 21, 1833. The *Commercial Herald* complained that the "notice, calling a meeting for the purpose of making arrangements for the reception of the President excluded all who could not harmonize in judgment and feeling with those who originated it. We mean it did this negatively by inviting those who were the friends of the President and numbered themselves among his political admirers" (quoted in *Pennsylvania National Gazette* [Philadelphia], June 17, 1833). The *New Hampshire Gazette* looked to Philadelphia (and New York) as a model, however: "There the President has not only received committees of his political friends, but it seems the city authorities acknowledge such committees with them in their general arrangements" (June 18, 1833).

31. *Pennsylvania National Gazette* (Philadelphia), June 17, 1833. *Eastern Argus* (Portland, Maine), June 14, 1833.

32. *New London Gazette* (Connecticut), June 19, 1833. *Washington Globe*, June 13, 1833. Also see Remini, *Jackson: The Course of American Democracy*, 70.

33. *United States Telegraph*, June 12, 14, 1833. *Niles Weekly Register*, June 29, July 13, 1833. Similar complaints were voiced about the president's reception in New York City. The *New York American*, for instance, complained that "the whole matter and manner of receiving and showing the President, here, and we believe it was so in Philadelphia, were of party origin and management. The mass of citizens, the clergy, the learned professions, and the great middle class, could not approach him at all" (*National Intelligencer* [Washington, D.C.], June 18, 1833). The *National Intelligencer* agreed that the partisan character of the tour was evident from "the list of [Democratic] committees . . . who have taken the President into custody wherever he has passed" (June 18, 1833).

34. Daniel Preston, ed., *The Papers of James Monroe: A Documentary History of the Presidential Tours of James Monroe, 1817, 1818, 1819* (Westport, CT: Greenwood Press, 2003), 46–48.

35. Allan Nevins, ed., *The Diary of Philip Hone, 1828–1851* (New York: Dodd, Mead, 1927), 94, 96–97. Also see Remini, *Jackson: The Course of American Democracy*, 72.

36. *Washington Globe*, June 4, 1833. *Boston Statesman*, June 15, 1833. *Rhode-Island Republican*, June 26, 1833. Also see *Hartford Times*, April 29, 1833; and *Washington Globe*, June 14, 29, and July 2, 1833. The *Rhode Island Republican*'s only regret was that Jackson had not taken the trip in his first term, for then "the opposition to him would have been sooner and more effectually quelled than they have since been." However, the *Republican* also recognized that had Jackson taken the trip before the election it would have been difficult to avoid "imputations of selfish design"—that is, charges that the president was electioneering. Although a preelection trip would "not have been hailed by so complete a union of all parties in giving him a cordial welcome," the *Republican* felt that it would still have been worthwhile because "it would almost to a certainty have secured for him the divided vote of New England" (June 26, 1833).

37. *Hartford Times*, June 24, 1833. *New Hampshire Patriot*, July 8, 1833. *Washington Globe*, June 12, 1833. A decade later, Dallas would become James Polk's vice president.

38. *National Intelligencer* (Washington, D.C.), June 18, 1833. An example of a scene from Jackson's tour that could have been taken straight out of Washington's tour was "the President's levee" at a New York City hotel. There Jackson was approached by a "young lady" who, "on being introduced to the President, placed upon his brows a beautiful wreath of artificial flowers, bearing the following inscription:–'The tribute of Virtue and Gratitude to the Patriot and Hero who has asserted and defended the honor and glory of his country, in every station to which he has been called by the voice of fellow-citizens.'" The incident is recounted in the *Boston Statesman*, June 22, 1833.

39. Remini, *Jackson: The Course of American Democracy*, 12. The Nullification Proclamation is available at http://www.loc.gov/rr/program/bib/ourdocs/Nullification.html (accessed December 6, 2006).

40. *Washington Globe*, June 25, 1833. Also see *Washington Globe*, June 29, July 1, 1833; *Salem Gazette* (Massachusetts), June 28, 1833; *Lowell Journal*, July 3, 1833; and *Essex Gazette* (Haverhill, Massachusetts), June 27, 1833. The circumstances of Jackson's 1830 toast are recounted in Robert V. Remini, *Andrew Jackson: The Course of American Freedom, 1822–1832* (New York: Harper and Row, 1981), 233–37.

41. *Rhode-Island Republican*, June 26, 1833. *Essex Register* (Salem, Massachusetts), July 1, 1833. *Salem Gazette* (Massachusetts), June 25, 1833. The Newport address was delivered to the president in writing, and apparently the committee did not get the opportunity to deliver the welcome verbally. It went further than other welcoming addresses in endorsing Jackson's first-term record. The people, the address noted, "deliberately upon a review, of all you had done and contemplated doing in your first Presidency, sustained you for a second election, by increased suffrages and confirmed opinions." After praising Jackson's stance against nullification, the address concluded: "We advert not to other topics. We will not further intrude upon that time which is now so pressingly devoted to public duty, nor venture to indulge in the expression of feelings of gratitude and regard with which your political course has inspired us." The committee's chair, Chris G. Champlin, was a strong Jacksonian Democrat. The Roxbury welcoming address was delivered by Jonathan Dorr, a National Republican and soon-to-be Whig.

42. *Pennsylvania National Gazette*, June 13, 1833. Also see the opinion offered by *Niles Weekly Register* that there "is reason to believe that the eyes of the 'old chief' have been opened

by his tour" (July 13, 1833; also see June 29, 1833). Although Jackson was impressed by New England's thriving manufacturing, he evidently drew the opposite conclusion from the one his opponents hoped. On the boat ride home the president reportedly said that such prosperous "establishments, conducted with such skill, . . . could need no protection" from the government (*Essex Register* [Salem, Massachusetts], July 8, 1833; also see July 11, 1833).

43. *Washington Globe*, June 8, 1833.

44. Richard P. McCormick, *The Presidential Game: The Origins of American Presidential Politics* (New York: Oxford University Press, 1982), 136. Jackson added that he also intended to "unite the whole and produce the greatest prosperity to our beloved country." Jackson's views about parties, as McCormick points out, evolved considerably during his time in office. In 1824, Jackson told his nephew: "If I am elected to fill the Presidential chair . . . it must be done by the people; and I will be President of the nation, and not of a party" (144). By 1833, as his comment to Van Buren suggests, Jackson had accepted that he was both head of a party and head of the nation.

45. Green, "On Tour with President Andrew Jackson," 228, 213.

46. Remini, *Jackson: The Course of American Freedom*, 266–67. Jackson to Major William B. Lewis, June 21, 1830, in John Spencer Bassett, ed., *Correspondence of Andrew Jackson* (Washington, DC: Carnegie Institution of Washington, 1929), 4:156; also see Jackson to Lewis, June 26, 1830, 4:156–57. Opposition newspapers, in contrast, played down the enthusiasm of the greetings and size of the crowds and interpreted the "rather . . . tame exhibition" of popular feeling as evidence that the people did not support the veto. See, for instance, "Arrival of the President," June 29, 1830, and "The President's Transit," July 3, 1830, both in the *Cincinnati Gazette*.

47. "The President in Cincinnati," *Cincinnati Gazette*, July 1, 1830. Among the other Jacksonian officeholders in the welcoming committee were William Burke, whom Jackson had appointed as Cincinnati's postmaster, and former Ohio Governor Ethan A. Brown, who had just been nominated by Jackson to be chargé d'affaires to Brazil. The *Gazette* deplored the partisan cast of Lytle's remarks ("our ranks," "our real strength"), claiming that although such partisan sentiments were "common among party politicians . . . it is a new thing to avow it openly, in an address to the President of the nation." The *Gazette* did not, however, criticize the propriety of Jackson's speech defending his veto.

48. "The President in Cincinnati," *Cincinnati Gazette*, July 1, 1830.

49. The account of the movements of Jackson and the welcoming committee is based on the *Cincinnati Gazette*, June 29, July 1–3, 1830. The "noble mansion" quotation is from the *Cincinnati Republican*, as quoted in the *Cincinnati Gazette*, July 1, 1830.

50. Jackson was well aware that attending a partisan barbecue or dinner would invite opposition criticism. Upon learning that a "Barbecue was preparing for General Jackson at Lexington," the *National Intelligencer* groused, "This is certainly a new mode of electioneering. We do not recollect before to have heard of a President of the United States descending in person into the political arena" (October 5, 1832). Robert Remini misinterprets this quotation as evidence that Jackson actually attended the Lexington barbecue (*Jackson: The Course of American Freedom*, 384), but the local press accounts make it clear that Jackson did not attend. See "The President in Lexington," *Frankfort Argus*, October 3, 1832. Elsewhere Remini writes that in 1832 Jackson "attended barbecues on his way to and from Washington" (*Jackson: The Course of American Freedom*, 380), but he provides no evidence in support of this proposition. Later he writes that Jackson "attended one or two [partisan barbecues] but only when

they happened to occur along the route of his travels," but the above quotation from the *National Intelligencer* is the only evidence he offers in support of this claim (384). More accurate is Remini's next sentence: "Normally [Jackson] tried to follow the accepted decorum of presidential candidates by keeping aloof from the campaign" (384).

51. Jackson to Andrew J. Donelson, August 19, 1832, *Correspondence of Andrew Jackson*, 4:468. The letter to Donelson is also quoted in Remini, *Jackson: The Course of American Freedom*, 380. Jackson's letter—written from the Hermitage and dated August 16—declining the invitation of the public dinner is printed in the *Richmond Enquirer*, September 7, 1832. Jackson's visit to Nashville on August 21 is also described in the *Richmond Enquirer*, September 7, 1832. The latter two quotations in the text are from the *Frankfort Argus* (Kentucky), October 3, 1832; and the *Washington Globe*, October 12, 1832. The five thousand estimate is from a letter Jackson wrote to Andrew Donelson dated October 5, 1832 (Remini, *Jackson: The Course of American Freedom*, 385). Another witness put the crowd at between four thousand and five thousand people (*Washington Globe*, October 12, 1832).

52. *Washington Globe*, October 12, 1832. Remini, *Jackson: The Course of American Freedom*, 385. Jackson did more than just see the people; he talked with them as well. In the small town of Owingsville, Kentucky, for instance, Jackson reportedly had "a very interesting conversation" with some citizens "respecting the fate of poor unhappy Poland" (*Washington Globe*, October 12, 1832).

53. *Nashville Banner*, August 14, 1834, as quoted in Remini, *Jackson: The Course of American Democracy*, 181. Also see Jackson to Martin Van Buren, August 16, 1834, *Correspondence of Andrew Jackson*, 5:282.

54. Remini, *Jackson: The Course of American Democracy*, 336; also see 331–32.

55. Ibid., 337.

56. James W. Ceaser, *Presidential Selection: Theory and Development* (Princeton, NJ: Princeton University Press, 1979), 124–25. Ralph Ketcham, *Presidents above Party: The First American Presidency, 1789–1829* (Chapel Hill: University of North Carolina Press, 1984), 135. Also see Michael Wallace, "Changing Concepts of Party in the United States: New York, 1815–1828," *American Historical Review* (December 1968), 453–91.

57. *Albany Argus*, July 1, 1833 (from *York Gazette* and *Harrisburg State Capitol Gazette*).

58. *Albany Argus*, July 1, 1833 (from *Boston Morning Post*); July 3, 1833 (from *Harrisburg Reporter*); and July 9, 1833 (from *Reading Democratic Press* and *Berks and Schuylkill Journal*). Also see the description of the president's escort, the following day, into Allenstown, in the *Albany Argus*, July 12, 1839 (from *Allentown Bulletin*).

59. *Albany Argus*, July 12, 1839. Van Buren had received an invitation from Harrisburg's Democrats to spend the Fourth of July with the "Democratic citizens" of the county; Van Buren responded that although he "hope[d] to pass through Harrisburg" and would be "happy to see my friends," his schedule prevented him from being in Harrisburg for July 4. Van Buren's letter, dated June 17 (three days before the president left the capital), is excerpted in the *Hudson River Chronicle*, July 23, 1839. On June 14, to take another instance, Van Buren responded to a letter of invitation from "the Democratic General Committee" of New York City, informing the committee that he intended to reach the city by July 1. See *Newark Advocate* (Ohio), June 29, 1839 (from *New York Evening Post*).

60. *Albany Evening Journal*, July 3, 1839.

61. Ibid. Van Buren's letter is quoted in the *North American* (Philadelphia), June 28, 1839. The response to the letter is from the *Madisonian*, as reprinted in the *Albany Evening Jour-*

nal, July 6, 1833. Also see the *Hudson River Chronicle*, which objected that "in all of Van Buren's letters concerning his visit, he talks of his 'democratic friends,' and not of his *fellow citizens*" (July 9, 1839). The *New Bedford Mercury* jumped on the president's June 14 letter to the Democratic General Committee—which was published in New York papers toward the end of June—as evidence that the president "chose to come among us as a Loco Foco partisan" and as justification for having him be "left to Loco Foco partisans." Although Van Buren's June 14 letter simply acknowledged the committee's desire to provide a "public expression of regard for myself and approbation of my official conduct," the *Mercury* seized on that acknowledgment to show that Van Buren "gave notice beforehand that he would look upon the compliments paid, not as paid to the station, but as evidence of 'personal regard to himself and of approbation of his official conduct'" (July 12, 1839).

62. Sean Wilentz, *The Rise of American Democracy: Jefferson to Lincoln* (New York: Norton, 2005), chapter 15; quotations at 457, 463. Also see Donald B. Cole, *Martin Van Buren and the American Political System* (Princeton, NJ: Princeton University Press, 1984), 285–348.

63. *Albany Argus*, July 6, 1839. Also see John Niven, *Martin Van Buren: The Romantic Age of American Politics* (New York: Oxford University Press, 1983), 453.

64. Edmonds to Van Buren, June 21, 1839, and June 27, 1839, Van Buren Papers, Library of Congress. Handwritten copies of Edmonds's speech as well as Van Buren's are available in the Van Buren papers. Both speeches were printed in full in the *Albany Argus*, July 6, 1839. Cf. Jeffrey K. Tulis, who claims erroneously that "singling out Democratic listeners was the extent of [Van Buren's] partisanship" (*The Rhetorical Presidency* [Princeton, NJ: Princeton University Press, 1987], 75).

65. *Albany Evening Journal*, July 13, 1839. *Hudson River Chronicle*, July 23, 1839. In a lengthy preamble, the Hudson Common Council defended its action by detailing Van Buren's partisan behaviors on tour. First, the council pointed to his June 17 letter to a committee of Harrisburg Democrats, who had invited Van Buren to "unite with the Democratic citizens" of the county. Van Buren's declaration that he would be "happy to see my friends" was offered by the council as evidence that "party demonstrations were pleasing to the President of the United States." The second piece of evidence was the correspondence between Van Buren and a committee representing the Democrats of Northampton County in Pennsylvania. Although Van Buren declined the committee's invitation of a public dinner, the council nevertheless charged Van Buren with unseemly partisanship because he responded by affirming the truth of the committee's claim that "the people of 'Old Northampton' [had] for nearly half a century, stood forth firm and fearless, in their undeviating support of Democratic men and measures." The final arrow in the council's quiver was Edmonds's partisan welcome in New York City and Van Buren's equally partisan reply. Cf. Tulis, *Rhetorical Presidency*, 75.

66. *Albany Argus*, July 12, 1839; July 13, 1839; July 17, 1839. The president's friends made no apologies for the speech. Typical was the New York *New Era*, which wrote that the president's speech would "be found to be of the highest interest throughout the Union, inasmuch as it is a perfectly explicit and decided expression of his views upon several great questions of national policy" (*Washington Globe*, July 5, 1839).

67. Cole, *Van Buren and the American Political System*, 347. Sean Wilentz, *Chants Democratic: New York City and the Rise of the American Working Class, 1788–1850* (New York: Oxford University Press, 1984), 257. Also see Wilentz, *Rise of American Democracy*, 462.

68. After Van Buren left New York City on July 9, he traveled up the Hudson Valley, arriving at Kinderhook on July 20. After spending a few days in the place of his birth, he continued

on to Albany via Schenectady, arriving in Saratoga Springs on August 1. Van Buren spent most of the next three weeks resting in Saratoga Springs, although he ventured south to Troy for a weekend in early August. The president left Saratoga on August 20, heading north to Plattsburgh (with a brief stopover in Burlington, Vermont), and then swinging west to Ogdensburg where he boarded a steamer that took him south to Oswego and then west to Niagara Falls, which he reached on the last day of August. Van Buren then took three weeks to make his way back to Albany, where the three-month tour finally came to a close. On this last stage of the tour, Van Buren visited not only large towns, like Buffalo, Rochester, and Syracuse, but also a host of smaller towns and villages, such as Cooperstown, Herkimer, and Cherry Valley. The coverage of the president's tour in the *Albany Argus* makes it clear that Van Buren gave far more than the twenty-three speeches that Tulis (*Rhetorical Presidency*, 64) estimates the president delivered on his trip. The number is probably closer to fifty.

69. *Albany Argus*, August 5, 1839 (from the *Schenectady Democrat*); also see July 22, 1833.

70. Ibid., August 15, 1839 (from *Troy Budget*); also see July 31, 1833. Also see the welcome and president's speech in Sandy Hill, reported in *Albany Argus*, August 30, 1839; Oswego, reported in *Albany Argus*, September 11, 1839; Keeseville, reported in *Albany Argus*, September 16, 1839 (from *Keeseville Herald*); and Cooperstown, reported in *Albany Argus*, October 4, 1839.

71. Ibid., September 23, 1839 (from *Onondaga Standard*).

72. Ibid.

73. Ibid.

74. Ibid., July 29, 1839 (from *Kinderhook Sentinel*). According to Tulis, Van Buren had intended to deliver a partisan address at Kinderhook, but opted instead for an "extemporaneous autobiographical" speech (*Rhetorical Presidency*, 76; also see Denis Tilden Lynch, *An Epoch and a Man: Martin Van Buren and His Times* [New York: Horace Liveright, 1929], 433–34). Donald Cole mistakenly attributes the welcoming address at Kinderhook to former governor William Marcy (*Van Buren and the American Political System*, 347); Marcy delivered the welcoming address at Albany.

75. *Albany Argus*, October 5, 1839 (from the *Cherry-Valley Gazette*). During much of the 1830s, Beardsley had served in the New York state senate, where he supported the conservative Democrat Nathaniel Tallmadge for the U.S. Senate. Beardsley was on the board of directors of the Otsego County bank and was sympathetic to the conservative Democratic position that opposed both a national bank and an Independent Treasury, preferring instead to hold federal deposits in state banks. Despite Beardsley's misgivings about Van Buren's Independent Treasury, he voted for him in 1840. Whether Van Buren's visit played a role in keeping Beardsley on board or not, the president's comments were clearly aimed at not antagonizing Beardsley. So even where Van Buren avoided partisan politics in his speech, there was a political subtext for the nonpartisan comments, a subtext that is often lost on the contemporary reader. This biographical information about Beardsley is derived from Levi Beardsley, *Reminiscences; Personal and Other Incidents* (New York: Charles Vinten, 1852).

76. *Albany Argus*, July 18, 1839 (from *Poughkeepsie Telegraph*); September 10, 1839 (from *Keeseville Herald*), emphasis added.

77. Ibid., July 26, 1839; September 23, 1839 (from *Onondaga Standard*).

78. *Albany Evening Journal*, July 19, 1839.

79. Richard Hofstadter, *The Idea of a Party System: The Rise of Legitimate Opposition in the United States, 1780–1840* (Berkeley: University of California Press, 1969), 2.

80. *York Gazette,* August 14, 1848. *Pennsylvanian* (Philadelphia), August 14, 1849.

81. Clinton Rossiter, *The American Presidency* (New York: Harcourt, 1960), 32, 34.

CHAPTER 3. DEMOCRATIC MANNERS AND PRESIDENTIAL DIGNITY: THE TOURS OF ZACHARY TAYLOR AND ANDREW JOHNSON

1. *Troy Daily Whig* (New York), August 16, 1849 (from the *Philadelphia News*). In the nearly eight hundred pages of the documentary history of President Monroe's tours there is only one reference to Monroe shaking hands with citizens. At Concord, reports the *New Hampshire Patriot,* Monroe shook revolutionary war veterans "cordially by the hand" (Daniel Preston, ed., *The Papers of James Monroe: A Documentary History of the Presidential Tours of James Monroe, 1817, 1818, 1819* [Westport, CT: Greenwood Press, 2003], 320).

2. See John William Ward, *Andrew Jackson: Symbol for an Age* (New York: Oxford University Press, 1955), 55–56.

3. Charles S. Sydnor, *American Revolutionaries in the Making: Political Practices in Washington's Virginia* (New York: Free Press, 1965), 49. *Hampden Federalist* (Springfield, Massachusetts), October 3, 1816. Also see the *Hartford Times* (Connecticut), September 2, 1817, which derides the "handshaking gentry." Catherine Allgor writes that in the late eighteenth century "shaking hands among the gentry was becoming a common custom in the United States" (*Parlour Politics: In Which the Ladies of Washington Help Build a City and a Government* [Charlottesville: University of Virginia Press, 2000], 19).

4. Sean Wilentz, *The Rise of American Democracy: Jefferson to Lincoln* (New York: Norton, 2005), 260. Charles Francis Adams, ed., *Memoirs of John Quincy Adams* (Freeport, NY: Books for Libraries Press, 1969; first published 1874–1877), 7:335–36; 8:50. The persistence and evolution of the norm against electioneering are documented in Gil Troy, *See How They Ran: The Changing Role of the Presidential Candidate* (New York: Free Press, 1991); and Richard J. Ellis and Mark Dedrick, "The Rise of the Rhetorical Candidate" in Philip G. Henderson, ed., *The Presidency Then and Now* (Rowman and Littlefield, 2000), 185–200. Also see John F. Reynolds, *The Demise of the American Convention System, 1880–1911* (Cambridge University Press, 2006), especially chapter 3 ("The Emergence of the Hustling Candidate"), which demonstrates that the nineteenth-century norm against electioneering also constrained candidates for Congress and statewide office, particularly the governorship.

5. While on tour, President Monroe was often hailed as "his Excellency," though objections were also registered against this usage for being overly regal (see, e.g., Preston, *Papers of James Monroe,* 35, 94, 116, 170, 365). Despite the regal connotations, nineteenth-century presidents on tour were commonly greeted in this manner. For instance, a newspaper in Staunton, Virginia, heralded the arrival of Franklin Pierce, "His Excellency, the President of the United States" ("The President in Staunton, Va.," *New York Times,* August 22, 1855, p. 1) and a report in the *New York Times* noted the arrival in Buffalo of "His Excellency President Grant" ("The President's Tour," August 17, 1875, p. 1; also see June 11, 1873; April 18, 1875; October 5, 1876). The title was also often affixed to President Rutherford Hayes on his cross-country tour in 1880; see Hayes Scrapbook, volume 78: September 2–December 5, 1880 (Great Western Tour and Misc.), pp. 30, 58, 85, 94, 95, in Rutherford B. Hayes Papers, Library of Congress, microfilm, series 6, roll 225. When Yale University presented an honorary degree to President McKinley (in absentia) in 1898, he was introduced as "his Excellency William McKinley, President of the United States" (*New York Times,* June 30, 1898, p. 6). Also see the Delmonico's Hotel din-

ner menu for "His Excellency" President Andrew Johnson, which is printed in Paul Bergeron et al., eds., *The Papers of Andrew Johnson* (Knoxville: University of Tennessee Press), 11:165. In addition, see Wayne Cutler, ed., *North for Union: John Appleton's Journal of a Tour to New England Made by President Polk in June and July 1847* (Nashville, TN: Vanderbilt University Press, 1986), 8.

6. *Philadelphia Public Ledger*, August 11, 1849 (from the *Baltimore Sun*). *New York Herald*, August 11, 1849. Taylor's entourage was limited to his "faithful attendant" Lawrence Smith and his son-in-law and army doctor Robert C. Wood. Smith is described by the *Pennsylvania Telegraph* as a "very intelligent and respectable Irishman" who was "constantly with [Taylor] to attend to his wants" (August 22, 1849). Also see *New York Herald*, August 12, 1849.

7. *New York Herald*, August 11, 1849.

8. Preston, *Papers of James Monroe*, 36–37.

9. *Troy Daily Whig* (New York), August 16, 1849 (from the *Philadelphia News*).

10. Ibid. *Lancaster Examiner and Herald*, August 15, 1849. *Pennsylvania Telegraph* (Harrisburg), August 15, 1849. *Philadelphia Public Ledger*, August 13, 1849.

11. *Pittsburgh Gazette*, August 17, 1849. *Pennsylvania Telegraph* (Harrisburg), August 22, 1949.

12. *Pennsylvania Telegraph* (Harrisburg), August 22, 1849. *Philadelphia Public Ledger*, August 17, 1849. *Albany Evening Journal*, August 16, 1849.

13. *New York Herald*, August 19, 1849. *Pennsylvania Telegraph* [Harrisburg], September 12, 1849 (from *Greensburg Intelligencer*). *Albany Evening Journal*, August 29, 1849. *Lawrence Journal* (New Castle), August 25, 1849. *Albany Evening Journal*, August 16, 1849 (from *New York Tribune*). For examples of the use of the word "mingled" to describe Taylor's interactions with the people, see the *New York Herald* of August 23, 1849, where the president is described as having "mingled freely with the crowd" at a tavern en route to Somerset, and the *Pennsylvania Telegraph*, which reports that Taylor "mingled with the people" in a Harrisburg "bar-room" (August 22, 1849). Also see *Troy Daily Whig* (New York), September 8, 1849, and the *Beaver Argus* (Pennsylvania), August 22, 1849.

14. *Pennsylvania Telegraph* (Harrisburg), August 22, 1849. *New York Herald*, August 29, 1849. Also see the *Lawrence Journal* (New Castle), August 25, 1849, which reports that at New Castle, "thousands passed in to shake the hands of 'Old Zack,' as they called him."

15. *Pittsburgh Daily Post*, August 14, 1849 (quoting from the *Baltimore Republican*). *Harrisburg Democratic Union*, August 22, 1849.

16. *The Republic* (Washington, D.C.), August 23, 1849. *Philadelphia Public Ledger*, August 13, 1849.

17. *Pittsburgh Gazette*, August 20, 1849; August 22, 1849. *New York Herald*, August 29, 1849. Also see the *Albany Evening Journal's* judgment that where the president "has had the opportunity of coming into direct communication with the people" his popularity "among all classes of the community . . . seems unlimited" (*Albany Evening Journal*, August 29, 1849).

18. *Pennsylvania Telegraph* (Harrisburg), August 22, 1849. *Daily Union* (Washington, D.C.), September 1, 1849. *Pittsburgh Daily Post*, August 17, 1849. Also see "Gen. Taylor as an Orator!!" *Erie Weekly Observer*, August 25, 1849. Among the president's speeches that the Democratic press suggested could not be heard was the speech in Harrisburg (according to the *Harrisburg Democratic Union*, August 15, 1849, it "might just as well not have been delivered, so far as the people were concerned, for no one off the platform heard a word") and the speech in Lan-

caster, which, the Philadelphia *Pennsylvanian* reported, "was impossible to hear, as he spoke very low" (August 14, 1849). For a Whig defense of Taylor that concedes the president's "want of eloquence," see *Beaver Argus* (Pennsylvania), September 5, 1849.

19. Much of what follows in this section is adapted from Richard J. Ellis and Alexis Walker, "Policy Speech in the Nineteenth-Century Rhetorical Presidency: The Case of Zachary Taylor's 1849 Tour," *Presidential Studies Quarterly* 37 (June 2007), 248–69. Taylor had planned a six-week tour of the northeast, the bulk of which was to be spent in Pennsylvania and New York. His plan was to travel westward through Pennsylvania, then up to Buffalo, before heading east toward Albany. The president intended to then continue on to Boston, returning to the capital via New York City and Philadelphia (K. Jack Bauer, *Zachary Taylor: Soldier, Planter, Statesman of the Old Southwest* [Baton Rouge: Louisiana State University Press, 1985], 268). After his collapse on August 24, he still journeyed to Albany, New York City, and Philadelphia, but he was under doctors' orders to head home as rapidly as possible. By that point he was too weak to do much more than acknowledge the occasional crowd and thank them for their welcome.

20. Michael F. Holt, *The Rise and Fall of the American Whig Party: Jacksonian Politics and the Onset of the Civil War* (New York: Oxford University Press, 1999), 445.

21. *Lancaster Examiner and Herald*, August 15, 1849. *Baltimore Sun*, August 10, 1849. Also see *Pittsburgh Gazette*, August 17, 1849.

22. *Lancaster Examiner and Herald*, August 15, 1849; emphasis added.

23. Ibid. Taylor made the same promise in Harrisburg; see the *Pennsylvania Telegraph* (Harrisburg), August 15, 1849, and August 29, 1849.

24. Clayton to Taylor, August 13, 1849, Zachary Taylor Papers, Library of Congress. *Pittsburgh Gazette*, August 21, 1849. Also see Holt, *Rise and Fall of the American Whig Party*, 445. K. Jack Bauer (*Zachary Taylor*, 269–70) quotes Clayton's reaction but mistakenly suggests it was in response to the Pittsburgh speech of the 18th, which was five days *after* Clayton wrote the letter. Clayton was in fact reacting to the president's Lancaster speech. The meeting and tour with the Pittsburgh industrialists took place on Monday, August 20.

25. *Beaver Argus* (Pennsylvania), August 22, 1849. In the Beaver speech, Taylor also repeated his pledge to pursue federal policies—that is, tariff adjustments—that would promote the state's "Agricultural, Commercial and Manufacturing resources." He vowed again that "so far as is proper in the executive to interfere, I shall co-operate with the National Legislature in all measures best calculated to develop and sustain [Pennsylvania's] prosperity." The welcoming address in Pittsburgh was delivered by Walter Forward, one of Pennsylvania's most prominent Whigs. Forward, who had been secretary of the treasury when the Whigs pushed through tariff increases in 1842, welcomed the president by hailing Pennsylvania's industries and declaring: "We think that these things have a National value, and that they merit the favorable notice of the National Government." See *Pittsburgh Gazette*, August 20, 1849.

26. *Trumbull County Whig* (Warren, Ohio), August 30, 1849. Taylor's remarks were widely reprinted in the Whig and antislavery press. See, for instance, *Pittsburgh Gazette*, September 3, 1849; *Western Reserve Chronicle* (Warren, Ohio), September 5, 1849; *Troy Daily Whig* (New York), September 8, 1849; and *Pennsylvania Telegraph* (Harrisburg), September 12, 1849. Cf. Holt, *Rise and Fall of the American Whig Party*, 1057n89. The description of the conversation as "free and general" is from the article in the *Pennsylvania Telegraph*.

27. *Pennsylvania Telegraph* (Harrisburg), September 12, 1849 (from *Beaver Argus*). Bea-

ver *Argus* (Pennsylvania), August 22, 1849. *New York Herald*, August 27, 1849; August 28, 1849 (from *Philadelphia News*).

28. *Philadelphia Pennsylvanian*, August 11, 1849. *Harrisburg Democratic Union*, August 22, 1849. "There cannot be a doubt," concluded the *Democratic Union*, "that this visit was forced upon Gen. Taylor by Gov. Johnston and the Whig managers at Washington . . . for political purposes."

29. For a description of Taylor as "the man of the people," see the *Carlisle Herald and Expositor*, August 15, 1849: "There they stood—farmers, mechanics, laborers—the bone and sinew, in truth, eager to bid the man of the people welcome to Cumberland Valley." The other quotations are from the *Republic* (Washington, D.C.), August 23, 1849 ("He has gone amongst them like one of themselves, that he may speak with [the people] face to face and learn for himself their condition and their desires"), and the *Troy Daily Whig* (New York), September 8, 1849 ("As the servant of the people, he set out to go among them . . . and by mingling freely with the people themselves . . . ascertain their wishes, that he might do his part in endeavoring to execute them").

30. The articles of impeachment drawn up against Andrew Johnson are available at http://www.law.umkc.edu/faculty/projects/ftrials/impeach/articles.html (accessed October 9, 2007).

31. Jeffrey K. Tulis, *The Rhetorical Presidency* (Princeton, NJ: Princeton University Press, 1987), 87.

32. *New York Tribune*, August 28, September 4, 1866; also see September 5, 1866 ("the train was filled with committees from every little town along the road").

33. *New York Tribune*, August 27, 1866. *Boston Daily Advertiser*, August 27, 1866.

34. *New York Times*, August 30, 1866. *New York Tribune*, August 30, 1866. Also see Gregg Phifer, "Andrew Johnson Takes a Trip," *Tennessee Historical Quarterly* 11 (March 1952), esp. 10.

35. *Natchez Daily Courier* (Mississippi), September 13, 1866. *New York Times*, September 10, 1866. Also see Phifer, "Johnson Takes a Trip," 11–12.

36. *New York Tribune*, August 29, 1866. *North American and U.S. Gazette* (Philadelphia), August 29, 1866.

37. *New York Tribune*, September 3, 1866.

38. *New York Times*, August 28, 1866; August 30, 1866.

39. *New York Times*, August 30, 1866; September 10, 1866; September 3, 1866. The call for the president to extend his tour through the South was also sounded by the *New York Herald* on September 1, 1866. Secretary of the Navy Gideon Welles praised Johnson for having spoken "freely, frankly, and plainly" to the American people (*The Diary of Gideon Welles* [Boston: Houghton Mifflin, 1911], 2:589). Praise for Johnson's plain speaking can also be found in the *New York Herald*, August 31, 1866, as quoted in Gregg Phifer, "Andrew Johnson Delivers His Argument," *Tennessee Historical Quarterly* 11 (September 1952), 224.

40. President Johnson, insisted the *New York Times*, was "discussing national affairs, and not politics" (September 3, 1866).

41. Phifer, "Johnson Takes a Trip," 9. In Philadelphia, the Republican municipal authorities made themselves conspicuously absent during the president's visit. According to the *New York Tribune* (August 30, 1866), "of the forty-five members of the Common Council and the twenty-five members of the Select Council . . . less than twenty are at present in the city; and of these a considerable majority are Democrats." The Republican mayor also left the city.

42. *National Intelligencer* (Washington, D.C.), September 19, 1866, quoted in Greg Phifer, "Andrew Johnson Loses His Battle," *Tennessee Historical Quarterly* 11 (December 1952), 298.

43. *New York Times*, August 28, 1866. Many welcoming speeches included an endorsement of the president's policies. In Schenectady, for instance, the welcoming address emphatically affirmed that the president's actions met with the approval of "a very large majority of our citizens." Johnson was informed that the citizens of Schenectady "subscribe to and support your policy of the restoration to their relations to the government and the Union of the late insurrectionary States." It was "a wise, constitutional and beneficent policy" (*Albany Evening Journal*, September 1, 1866).

44. Albert Castel, *The Presidency of Andrew Johnson* (Lawrence: University Press of Kansas, 1979), 90. Phifer, "Johnson Takes a Trip,"12–13; Phillips's letter was written on September 3. 1866. The *New York Herald* stories are from September 1 and September 4.

45. *New York Times*, August 29, 1866. *New York Tribune*, August 29, 1866.

46. *Milwaukee Daily Sentinel*, September 1, 1866. Similar in tone was the *Chicago Journal* of the same date, which condemned the president for continuing "to make himself ridiculous and to disgust sensible people by his egotistic and self-glorifying harangues" (Phifer, "Johnson Takes a Trip," 12). The late night speech from the balcony of Delmonico's Hotel was covered in the *New York Times*, August 30, 1866.

47. *New York Times*, August 31, 1866. *New York Tribune*, August 31, 1866.

48. *New York Tribune*, August 30, September 1, 1866. *Auburn Advertiser* (New York), September 4, 1866.

49. *New York Evening Post*, September 1, 1866, reprinted in *Auburn Advertiser* (New York), September 4, 1866.

50. On September 3, according to the *New York Tribune*, "the President made a speech at every station where the train stopped long enough, except at Ashtabula, where the people would not give him the opportunity, laughing and cheering the four minutes of his stay" (September 4, 1866). The *Chicago Republican* reported that although the crowd was not angry "they simply did not wish to hear him. They laughed and talked, and cheered for Grant and Farragut, and plainly showed that they wanted nothing. [The president] waited patiently for some time and then abandoned the attempt" (September 5, 1866, quoted in Phifer, "Johnson Takes a Trip," 13). Cf. *New York Times*, which suggests only that the "The President and other prominent members of the party appeared on the car platform and received the plaudits of the multitude" (September 5, 1866). The *New York Herald* reported that at the tour's last stop in New York, at Westfield, the president was briefly interrupted by a "solitary man in the crowd," but Johnson "put an extinguisher on him by saying—'Keep quiet till I have concluded. Just such fellows as you have kicked up all the rows of the last five years." According to the *Herald*'s correspondent, "the fellow subsided suddenly, stepped out of the crowd, and was heard from no more" (September 4, 1866).

51. *New York Times*, September 5, 1866.

52. Ibid.

53. Ibid.

54. Ibid. *New York Tribune*, September 5, 1866. Also see the text of the speech printed in Bergeron et al., *Papers of Andrew Johnson*, 11:177.

55. *New York Times*, September 7, 1866, p. 4. The *Times* editorial was widely reprinted and excerpted in the northern press. See, for example, *Albany Evening Journal*, September 8, 1866.

56. *New York Times*, September 5, 1866. *New York Tribune*, September 5, 1866. *Elyria Democrat* (Ohio), as quoted in Phifer, "Johnson Takes a Trip," 13. Among those who advised Johnson to say less rather than more were the savvy New York politico Thurlow Weed, Wisconsin senator James Doolittle, and at least two members of the president's cabinet, navy secretary Gideon Welles and interior secretary Orville Browning. See Eric L. McKitrick, *Andrew Johnson and Reconstruction* (University of Chicago Press, 1960), 428; Hans L. Trefousse, *Andrew Johnson: A Biography* (New York: Norton, 1989), 263; Castel, *Presidency of Andrew Johnson*, 90; and *Diary of Gideon Welles*, 2:647–48. Welles's view was that "no President [or] Cabinet Minister should address promiscuous crowds on excited controverted questions. If they ever speak, their thoughts should be carefully prepared and put on paper; but it is better not to speak publicly at all." President Johnson, wrote Welles, "always heard my brief suggestions quietly, but manifestly thought I did not know his power as a speaker" (2:648). The president, however, received contrary advice from his secretary of state, William Henry Seward, who insisted that Johnson "was doing good and was the best stump speaker in the country." The tour, Seward insisted, was neither "impolitic" nor "injudicious" (2:594).

57. Phifer, "Johnson Takes a Trip," 14. *New York Times*, September 8, 1866, September 14, 1866. *New York Tribune*, September 13, 1866. The "low electioneering" quotation is from the *Albany Evening Journal*, September 4, 1866.

58. *New York Tribune*, September 11–12, 1866. Phifer, "Johnson Takes a Trip," 16–17.

59. *New York Tribune*, September 14, 1866. Phifer, "Johnson Loses His Battle," 302. Phifer, "Johnson Takes a Trip," 18.

60. *Auburn Advertiser* (New York), September 14, 1886. *Albany Evening Journal*, September 4, 1866; also see "The Presidential Disgrace," *Albany Evening Journal*, September 8, 1866. Similarly, the *Daily Cleveland Herald* opined that "the scene at Indianapolis is the direct fruits of the President's style. True, no man is justified in interrupting the President much less in insulting him, but when a man, peasant or prince, plebian or patrician, puts himself on a level with a promiscuous crowd, it is not for him to complain if he gets rough-and-tumble treatment" (September 11, 1866).

61. *New York Herald*, September 26, 1866; also see McKitrick, *Johnson and Reconstruction*, 438.

62. *North American and U.S. Gazette* (Philadelphia), September 8, 1866. *New York Independent*, September 13, 1866, quoted in Trefousse, *Andrew Johnson*, 266.

63. *Albany Evening Journal*, August 30, 1866; August 31, 1866; also see *New York Tribune*, August 30, 1866.

64. *New York Tribune*, September 12, 1866; September 15, 1866. Also see *New York Times*, September 13, 1866; Phifer, "Johnson Takes a Trip," 14–15, 18. The Pittsburgh mayor wrote a public letter explaining his refusal to participate in the welcome of Johnson. He could not participate, he wrote, because he could not trust the president to "refrain . . . from stigmatizing those" with whom he disagrees as "traitors" (*New York Herald*, September 14, 1866, quoted in McKitrick, *Johnson and Reconstruction*, 437). Republican governors too "fled" at Johnson's approach. The governors of Illinois, Indiana, Ohio, Pennsylvania, Michigan, and Missouri were among the many Republican politicians who refused to share a stage with Johnson. See *Diary of Gideon Welles*, 2:589, 594.

65. *New York Times*, September 14, 1866. The final quotation is from Johnson's reply to the welcome in Baltimore; see *New York Tribune*, September 17, 1866.

66. *New York Tribune*, September 15, 1866. *Albany Evening Journal*, August 30, 1866. Greg

Phifer, "Andrew Johnson Argues His Case," *Tennessee Historical Quarterly* (June 1952), 162. In Johnstown, Pennsylvania, Johnson was introduced by Pennsylvania senator Edgar Cowan as "the great tribune of the American people" (*New York Tribune*, September 15, 1866).

67. *Milwaukee Daily Sentinel*, September 7, 1866.

68. *Diary of Gideon Welles*, 2:584–85. William B. Hesseltine, *Ulysses S. Grant: Politician* (New York: Dodd, Mead, 1935), 72. Phifer, "Andrew Johnson Loses His Battle," 305. Geoffrey Perret, *Ulysses S. Grant: Soldier and President* (New York: Random House, 1997), 368.

69. James Harrison Wilson, *The Life of John A. Rawlins* (New York: Neale Publishing Company, 1916), 334; also see 330. Two days later, with the party now in Niagara Falls, Rawlins again wrote his wife about the "unbounded . . . enthusiasm" they had encountered "everywhere along the route," though Rawlins also noted that "there is more cheering for Grant and Farragut than for the President. The President's friends alon[e] cheer him, but all parties cheer Grant and Farragut." The warm receptions persuaded Rawlins that "the chances are favorable to the conservatives and Democrats in this State this fall." Rawlins observed, too, that Johnson "makes innumerable speeches every day" that are cheered "lustily" by the people. Grant, Rawlins added, "was at first quite fidgety over the matter, but has finally grown tranquil and seems to enjoy himself very much." Rawlins, though close to the president, evidently did not at this point know Grant's true feelings, which he had communicated to his wife in a letter he wrote the night before (335–36).

70. John Y. Simon, ed., *The Papers of Ulysses S. Grant* (Carbondale: Southern Illinois University Press, 1988), 16:306, 308. Also see *Diary of Gideon Welles*, 2:591. Johnson's intemperate and partisan rhetoric was not the only aspect of the tour that Grant found offensive. At St. Louis the presidential party was joined by Irish-born Democratic congressman John Hogan, who accompanied the party back to Washington and used his "strong lungs" to introduce the president and his traveling party to crowds at train stations all along the route. Grant despised Hogan, who he believed was a "Copperhead"—an opponent of Lincoln's war on the South—and a "Rebel sympathizer." "A Rebel he could forgive," Grant told Gideon Welles, "but not a Copperhead." To be introduced by such a man was, the general explained, "extremely distasteful" (*Diary of Gideon Welles*, 2:591–92).

71. *New York Herald*, September 7, 1866. Albert D. Richardson, *Personal History of Ulysses S. Grant* (Hartford, CT: American Publishing Company, 1868), 528; the revised edition of Richardson's *Personal History*, published in 1886, omits the account of Johnson's tour, including Grant's critical comments about Johnson. According to Sylvanus Cadwallader, a reporter with the *Herald*, Grant made his "disgusted" remark to his brother Orville on the day the party arrived in Chicago, which was September 5 ("Four Years with Grant," p. 788, in the Abraham Lincoln Presidential Library in Springfield, Illinois); the comments were "overheard by one of his brother's clerks, and duly reported." In *Let Us Have Peace: Ulysses S. Grant and the Politics of War and Reconstruction* (Chapel Hill: University of North Carolina Press, 1991), Brooks Simpson writes that the "no business" comment was confided to Grant's close friend and old schoolmate Daniel Ammen (150), but this is an error. Simpson's source for the quotation—Richardson's *Personal History*—does not reveal to whom Grant made the comment but it does clearly indicate that Grant made it "soon after" leaving Buffalo on September 3. Grant did not meet up with his old friend Ammen until he reached York, Pennsylvania, on September 15, the final day of the tour. Ammen reports that an agitated Grant expressed strong displeasure with Johnson's "swinging around the circle." "Perhaps on no other

occasion," Ammen recorded, had he "seen General Grant discomposed." See Daniel Ammen, *The Old Navy and the New* (Philadelphia: J. B. Lippincott, 1891), 427. Also see Phifer, "Johnson Loses His Battle," 305–6; and Simpson, *Let Us Have Peace*, 149–51.

72. *Diary of Gideon Welles*, 2:592. Johnson to Benjamin C. Truman, August 3, 1868, quoted in Phifer, "Johnson Loses His Battle," 307. Writing in 1935, historian William Hesseltine offered a similarly uncharitable—and incorrect—interpretation of Grant's behavior: "With no knowledge or understanding of the fundamental nature of the American Constitution, Grant shared the erroneous belief that the supreme law of the land was the will of the people, not the Constitution. Accordingly, when he perceived that the elections were certain to go against Johnson, he acquiesced in the decision of the majority and became a supporter of Congress" (*Grant*, 75).

73. Simon, *Papers of Grant*, 22:141–42, 26:345. *New York Times*, October 10, 1875. A notable exception to Grant's usual brevity was a "quite long" speech that he read ("very much, we presume, to everyone's surprise," commented the *New York Times*) at a reunion of the Army of the Tennessee held in Des Moines, Iowa, at the end of September 1875. In the speech, Grant called for the importance of a "good common school education, unmixed with sectarian, pagan, or atheistical dogmas." No longer would the "threat to free institutions" come from the divide between North and South, but instead it would stem from the divide "between patriotism and intelligence on the one side, and superstition, ambition and ignorance on the other." Grant underscored the need to "keep the Church and the State forever separate." Although Grant denied he was introducing politics, "certainly not partisan politics," in fact his message had clear partisan overtones, since it was a direct assault on the use of public monies to support Catholic parochial schools. And, of course, Catholics were much more likely to be Democrats than Republicans. See *New York Times*, October 1, 1875. The text of the speech can also be found in Simon, *Papers of Grant*, 26:342–44. Grant's speech drew considerable praise; see Simon, *Papers of Grant*, 26:347–51.

74. Simon, *Papers of Grant*, 22:157. Adding to the poignancy of the moment was that Grant was introduced by Judge Wilson McCandless, the same "staunch Democrat" who five years earlier had introduced Johnson to the Pittsburgh crowd that had prevented Johnson from speaking.

75. *New York Times*, August 16, 1869. Occasionally the press did censure the crowds that surrounded Grant. The *New York Times*, for instance, clucked its disapproval of the crowds of "curious and ill-mannered people" (October 17, 1871), who "not at all in accordance with the rules of ordinary courtesy . . . pressed him on all sides" (September 11, 1869) or "followed like a rabble after his carriage" (August 13, 1873). For examples of Grant shaking large numbers of hands, see *New York Times*, July 30, 1873, August 22, 1873, and September 28, 1876.

76. John F. Kasson, *Rudeness and Civility: Manners in Nineteenth-Century Urban America* (New York: Hill and Wang, 1990), 142. *New York Times*, October 18, 1871. *Galveston Daily News* (Texas) April 3, 1893 (from the *Brooklyn Standard-Union*). Also see the *Times'* lament about dancing, which it reported was "a new device, worse . . . than hand-shaking, [that] has been invented to vex the soul of General Grant" (June 17, 1869).

77. Interview [August 29, 1877], Simon, *Papers of Grant*, 28:256.

78. *Rocky Mountain News* (Denver), March 10, 1889. Karen Orren, "Benjamin Harrison," in Alan Brinkley and Davis Dyer, eds., *The Reader's Companion to the American Presidency* (Boston: Houghton Mifflin, 2000), 269.

1. *Commentator* (Frankfort), July 2, 1819, and *Columbian Centinel* (Boston), July 12, 1817, in Daniel Preston, ed., *The Papers of James Monroe: A Documentary History of the Presidential Tours of James Monroe, 1817, 1818, 1819* (Westport, CT: Greenwood Press, 2003), 697, 205.

2. *Vermont Gazette* (Bennington), June 24, 1817, and *Boston Patriot*, July 18, 1817, in Preston, *Papers of James Monroe*, 168, 381–82.

3. *New-London Gazette and General Advertiser* (Connecticut), June 19, 1833. "Progress of the President," *Philadelphia Public Ledger*, June 14, 1843. Rutherford B. Hayes Papers, Library of Congress, volume 78: September 2–December 5, 1880 (Great Western Tour and Misc.), p. 100. Also see "The Affections of the People," *Washington Globe*, June 4, 1833: "One of the great advantages of our Republican Government is that there is no necessity for body guards for our Chief Magistrates." When Jackson passed through Lexington, Kentucky, in the fall of 1832, a citizen of the town rhapsodized to the *Washington Globe* that Jackson's "life-guard is the affections of the American people" (October 12, 1832).

4. Donald Jackson and Dorothy Twohig, eds., *The Diaries of George Washington* (Charlottesville: University Press of Virginia, 1979), 6:128, quoting from *Gazette of the U.S.* (Philadelphia), May 21, 1791.

5. Robert V. Remini, *Andrew Jackson: The Course of American Democracy, 1833–1845* (New York: Harper and Row, 1984), 61.

6. The incident is recounted in Remini, *Andrew Jackson*, 227–30.

7. Pretty much the same, but not unchanged. The first president to have a full-time bodyguard was Franklin Pierce, who assumed the office in 1853. See "Protection of the White House Complex and the President in the Nineteenth Century," in section four of the *Background Information on the White House Security Review*, pp. 66–67. This Treasury Department report was prepared in the wake of two alarming incidents on the White House grounds—a plane crash on the White House lawn in September 1994 and, the following month, a man spraying several rounds from a semiautomatic rifle through the White House fence. The sections of the report that are not classified are available at http://www.prop1.org/park/pave/rev7.htm (accessed January 6, 2006).

8. "Remarks at Poughkeepsie, New York," February 19, 1861, Roy Basler, ed., *The Collected Works of Abraham Lincoln* (New Brunswick, NJ: Rutgers University Press, 1953), 4:228; also see 4:204–6. David Herbert Donald, *Lincoln* (New York: Simon and Schuster, 1995), 274–75.

9. Donald, *Lincoln*, 273.

10. "Speech in Independence Hall, Philadelphia, Pennsylvania," February 22, 1861, in Basler, *Collected Works*, 4:240. Donald, *Lincoln*, 277. A month earlier, Lincoln vowed to a close associate: "I will suffer death before I will consent to . . . any concessions or compromise which looks like the privilege of taking possession of this government to which we have a constitutional right" ("Remarks Concerning Concessions to Secession," *Collected Works*, 4:175).

11. Donald, *Lincoln*, 277–79.

12. F. B. Carpenter, *The Inner Life of Abraham Lincoln: Six Months at the White House* (Lincoln: University of Nebraska Press, 1995), 63–64. Ward Hill Lamon, *Recollections of Abraham Lincoln*, ed. Dorothy Lamon Teillard (Lincoln: University of Nebraska Press, 1994; reprinted from 1911 edition), 275. Also see George Bryan, *The Great American Myth* (New York: Carrick and Evans, 1940), 48.

13. Carpenter, *Inner Life*, 65, 66–67.

14. Donald, *Lincoln*, 282. Bryan, *Great American Myth*, 54. "Appendix 7: A Brief History of Presidential Protection," in *Report of the President's Commission on the Assassination of President Kennedy*, 506, available at http://www.archives.gov (accessed January 6, 2006).

15. Carpenter, *Inner Life*, 67. Matthew Pinsker, *Lincoln's Sanctuary: Abraham Lincoln and the Soldiers' Home* (New York: Oxford University Press, 2003), vii. Donald, *Lincoln*, 548. Lincoln objected to the cavalry protection, telling General Halleck that "he and Mrs. Lincoln "couldn't hear themselves talk," for the clatter of their sabres and spurs, and that, as many of them appeared new hands and very awkward, he was more afraid of being shot by the accidental discharge of one of their carbines or revolvers, than of any attempt upon his life or for his capture by the roving squads of Jeb Stuart's cavalry" (Carpenter, *Inner Life*, 67).

16. Donald, *Lincoln*, 593–94, 597. Edward Steers, Jr., *Blood on the Moon: The Assassination of Abraham Lincoln* (Lexington: University Press of Kentucky, 2001), 116.

17. In the immediate aftermath of the assassination, there were alarmed calls for enhanced presidential protection. For instance, ten days after Lincoln's murder, the *New York Times* worried that Andrew Johnson, "being unwilling to evince any distrust of the people," was failing to take sufficient "precautions for his personal safety." The *Times* warned Johnson not to succumb to "any false notions of democracy." The president's life, the *Times* pointed out, "is of infinite value to the nation, and it is due to the nation that every wise and useful precaution should be taken for its preservation. It is not needful that he should be surrounded by any ostentatious array, or by a military cordon of troops and guards. But there should always be near him and about him trained men, vigilant and competent for his protection. The more quiet and unobserved their service, the better; but that service should be constant and effectual" (see "Personal Safety of the President—The Duty of Precaution," *New York Times*, April 24, 1865). Such calls largely went unheeded both by Johnson and by Congress. Congress did conduct an investigation into the assassination but, as the Warren Commission reported, "called for no action to provide better protection for the President in the future" (Appendix 7, 507).

18. Kenneth D. Ackerman, *Dark Horse: The Surprise Election and Political Murder of President James A. Garfield* (New York: Carroll and Graf, 2003), 355, 372. Allan Peskin, "Charles Guiteau of Illinois: President Garfield's Assassin," *Journal of the Illinois State Historical Society* 70 (1977), 136.

19. Garfield had planned a busy summer and fall travel schedule. He intended to spend August at the family farm in Ohio and had agreed to speak in the early fall at a celebration marking the one-hundredth anniversary of the Battle of Yorktown. Following that event he would undertake a tour of the southern states that would include a stop in Atlanta "to deliver a major speech unveiling his Southern and racial policies." Allan Peskin, *Garfield: A Biography* (Kent State University Press, 1978), 595; also see Ackerman, *Dark Horse*, 366–67.

20. Ackerman, *Dark Horse*, 357.

21. Ibid., 407–8.

22. Peskin, "Charles Guiteau," 137, 139. Justus D. Doenecke, *The Presidencies of James A. Garfield and Chester Arthur* (Lawrence: University Press of Kansas, 1981), 95. Also see "The Nation in Its Grief," *New York Times*, September 20, 1881, p. 5.

23. Margaret Leech, *In the Days of McKinley* (New York: Harper and Brothers, 1959), 591. Philip H. Melanson with Peter F. Stevens, *The Secret Service: The Hidden History of an Enigmatic Agency* (New York: Carroll and Graf, 2002), 29.

24. Melanson, *Secret Service*, 24. Frederick M. Kaiser, "Origins of Secret Service Protection of the President: Personal, Interagency, and Institutional Conflict," *Presidential Studies Quarterly* 18 (Winter 1988), 105–8.

25. Kaiser, "Origins of Secret Service Protection," 112. Melanson, *Secret Service*, 27–29.

26. Melanson, *Secret Service*, 30. Kaiser shows that the demotion of Hazen, a Cleveland appointee, was far more than just a reaction to the uproar surrounding his unauthorized decision to divert agency resources to protect Cleveland's family at their summer residence. See Kaiser, "Origins of Secret Service Protection," esp. 108–9, for the complex political circumstances and calculations that underlay Hazen's removal.

27. *Congressional Record—Senate*, March 1, 1902, 2275–76, and March 20, 1902, 3050. The bill called for this protection to be provided "without any unnecessary display." This provision was Section 7 of Senate Bill 3653, the main purpose of which was to make killing, or attempting to kill, the president a federal crime.

28. *Congressional Record—Senate*, March 20, 1902, 3049–50.

29. Ibid., 3050. Hoar credited Pettus with being the person who had suggested adding the military guard provision to the bill (March 1, 1902, 2275). Pettus, however, opposed other aspects of the bill—particularly provisions making it a federal crime to advocate the assassination of the president—and so ended up voting against the bill (March 21, 1902, 3129; also March 1, 1902, 2276; March 18, 1902, 2953)

30. *Congressional Record—Senate*, March 20, 1902, 3050. Kaiser, "Origins of Secret Service Protection," 105.

31. *Congressional Record—Senate*, March 20, 1902, 3053–54.

32. Ibid., 3056.

33. Ibid., 3057, 3060, 3062.

34. Ibid., 3062–63. This brought a concession from the Democrat Thomas Patterson, who said he was "willing to allow the fiction to stand that [the president] is always performing his duty" (3063).

35. Kaiser, "Origins of Secret Service Protection," 115. "Protection of the President and the Suppression of Crime against Government," Report to Accompany S. 3653, House Report No. 1422, 57th Cong., 1st Session (Washington, DC: Government Printing Office, 1902), 12–13.

36. Melanson, *Secret Service*, 32.

37. Colt's speech, entitled "The Protection of the President of the United States," was delivered on March 2, 1902, in Concord, New Hampshire. The speech was inserted into the *Congressional Record* on March 6, 1902. See *Congressional Record—Senate*, March 20, 1902, 2428–29. The address was also later included in a 1906 book, *Addresses of Le Baron Bradford Colt* (Boston: Little, Brown, 1906). Colt served as presiding judge on the First Circuit Court of Appeals until 1913, when he was elected to the U.S. Senate, where he served until his death in 1924.

38. *Congressional Record—Senate*, March 20, 1902, 2428–29.

39. Ibid.

40. For instance, Roosevelt's Secret Service protection is mentioned in stories in the *New York Times* on December 1, 1901, p. 2; February 26, 1902, p. 1; September 11, 1902, p. 3; September 14, 1902, p. 13; September 22, 1902, p. 1; September 24, 1902, p. 1; December 21, 1902, p. 13; May 1, 1903, p. 1; May 9, 1903, p. 9; May 22, 1903, p. 7; June 28, 1903, p. 1; June 29, 1909, p. 1; July 24, 1903, p. 3; July 27, 1903, p. 3; August 3, 1903, p.1; September 8, 1903, p. 1; September 9,

1903, p. 2; November 28, 1904, p. 1; April 4, 1905, p. 1; October 23, 1905, p. 9; July 5, 1906, p. 1; June 2, 1907, p. 1; and July 1, 1906, p. 1. Often the agents were identified by name. See, for example, November 13, 1902, p. 1; July 29, 1904, p. 7; September 23, 1904, p. 1; May 12, 1905, p. 1; May 31, 1905, p. 4; June 30, 1905, p. 4; and September 3, 1905, p. 7.

41. *New York Times*, August 20, 1905, SM11.

42. *New York Times*, July 3, 1902, p. 1. Also see "To Guard the President," *New York Times*, March 28, 1903, p. 1, in which the *Times* again reported the president's security arrangements on the front page, this time for a visit to Chicago. The precautions being taken for Roosevelt's safety for this trip included careful control over who would receive tickets to hear the president speak, for it was feared that "a free-for-all distribution" might result in tickets ending up in the hands of anarchists or others "radically opposed to the present form of government." The police, the *Times* assured its readers, had located "every known Anarchist in Chicago and . . . set a watch upon him or her to see that no secret meetings are held and no plans laid for concerted action."

43. *New York Times*, June 16, 1903, p. 6.

44. *New York Times*, September 7, 1903, p. 1; also see "The Trip across the City," *New York Times*, June 28, 1903, p. 1.

45. *New York Times*, September 11, 1903, p. 6.

46. Ibid.

47. Ibid., September 12, 1903, p. 8; also see September 13, 1903, p. 6.

48. Ibid., September 16, 1903, p. 8.

49. Ibid., November 28, 1903, p. 2.

50. "The President's Peril," *New York Times*, September 4, 1902, p. 8. The accident is reported in *New York Times*, September 4, 1902, p. 1. Also see Edmund Morris, *Theodore Rex* (New York: Random House, 2001), 142–43.

51. Roosevelt to Henry Cabot Lodge, August 6, 1906, Henry Cabot Lodge and Charles F. Redmond, eds., *Selections from the Correspondence of Theodore Roosevelt and Henry Cabot Lodge, 1884–1918*, (New York: Da Capo Press, 1971; originally published 1925), 2:224. "Sought President with Loaded Revolver: Dangerous Lunatic Taken into Custody at Sagamore Hill," *New York Times*, September 3, 1903, p. 2. "Woman Visitor Stirs President's Guards: Secret Service Men Halt Her on Her Third Appearance," *New York Times*, September 3, 1905, p. 7. "Cranks Call on Roosevelt," *New York Times*, July 17, 1907, p. 1. Also see "Woman Tried to Halt President in Church," *New York Times*, August 13, 1906, p. 1.

52. *New York Times*, June 29, 1903, p. 1. Also see Morris, *Theodore Rex*, 123; and *New York Times*, June 13, 1907, p. 1.

53. "Tafts out in the Rain," *New York Times*, December 25, 1911, p. 3.

54. "Dry Humor Marked Coolidge Comment," *New York Times*, January 6, 1933, p. 7.

55. Warren Commission Report, Appendix VII ("A Brief History of Presidential Protection"), p. 510; available at http://www.archives.gov/research/jfk/warren-commission-report/appendix7.html (accessed January 5, 2006). Public Report of the White House Security Review, May 1998, chapter 4 (section entitled "The Tradition of Public Access to the Executive Mansion"), available at http://www.fas.org/irp/agency/ustreas/usss/t1pubrpt.html (accessed January 5, 2006). "Truman Signs Bill Making Secret Service Permanent," *New York Times*, July 17, 1951, p. 15. "Congress Votes Candidate Guard," *New York Times*, June 7, 1968, p. 24. The killing of a federal officer "in the performance of his duties" had long been a federal offense, but the existing statute "was not deemed to cover such public appearances as President Ken-

nedy was making in Dallas when he was shot" ("Senate Committee to Investigate Assassination of Kennedy and Killing of Oswald," *New York Times*, November 27, 1963, p. 19). President Johnson proposed the legislation protecting presidential candidates on June 5, and the bill was signed into law the following day. Robert Kennedy was shot and killed on June 4. The assassination attempt against Truman is detailed in Stephen Hunter and John Bainbridge, Jr., *American Gunfight: The Plot to Kill Harry Truman—and the Shoot-out That Stopped It* (New York: Simon and Schuster, 2005).

56. "Secret Service Decision," *New York Times*, February 20, 1909, p. 2. "United States Secret Service, Budget for Fiscal Years 1975 thru 2003," available at http://www.usdoj.gov/jmd/budgetsummary/btd/1975_2002/2002/html/page133-135.htm (accessed January 6, 2006). The three million dollars figure is given in *New York Times*, July 22, 1951, p. 106; the same story puts the number of Secret Service agents at four hundred.

57. Alvin Shuster, "The Forty Watchdogs of the President," *New York Times Magazine*, October 21, 1962, pp. 67, 77. "Guards for Kennedy; GOP Criticizes Bid for More Secret Service Agents," *New York Times*, March 27, 1962, p. 27. Shuster, "Forty Watchdogs," p. 67.

58. Felix Belair, Jr., "Panel Opposes New F.B.I. Role in Johnson Guard," *New York Times*, November 22, 1964, p. 1. Felix Belair, Jr., "Secret Service Acts to Bolster Johnson's Guard," *New York Times*, November 28, 1964, p. 1. "Extra Funds Voted to Guard President," *New York Times*, April 2, 1965, p. 22. The only small hiccup along the way came when President Johnson objected to $522,000 being spent on two new armored limousines and insisted that they be withdrawn from the budget request, even though the House had already approved the money. See "President Declines 2 New Cars Sought for His Protection," *New York Times*, April 14, 1965, p. 29. The 1973 number comes from Philip Shabecoff, "Flap over Guarding Nixon," *New York Times*, February 18, 1973, 4:3.

59. Warren Commission Report, chapter 8 ("The Protection of the President"), available at http://www.archives.gov/research/jfk/warren-commission-report/chapter-8.html (accessed January 6, 2006); also see Anthony Lewis, "Presidential Security—Warren Report Raises Large Questions," *New York Times*, October 4, 1964, E3. Roy Reed, "Guarding President: Flaws Still Exist," *New York Times*, June 25, 1967, p. 24. Fred Graham, "Arrests for Threats to the President Up Sharply since the Assassination," *New York Times*, January 7, 1968, p. 59. "Security Remains a Major Problem," *New York Times*, October 12, 1964, p. 17. Philip Shabecoff, "The President's Safety vs. Citizens' Rights," *New York Times*, September 10, 1975, p. 29.

60. Report of the U.S. Secret Service on the Assassination of President Kennedy, pp. 12–14. The report was written in December 1963 and was transmitted to the Warren Commission on December 18, 1963. It is available at http://www.aarclibrary.org/publib/jfk/wc/wcdocs/pdf/wcd3v1.pdf (accessed January 10, 2006). Testimony of James J. Rowley, June 18, 1964, available at http://www.jfk-assassination.com/warren/wch/vol5/page467.php (accessed January 10, 2006). Advance work had been part of the Secret Service's job since the early twentieth century. When Presidents Taft or Harding or Hoover embarked on a trip they were preceded by an advance agent whose job was to "visit in advance every city at which the President is scheduled to stop" ("Elaborate Planning Eases Way for President's Alaskan Tour," *New York Times*, June 17, 1923, 8:9). The advance agent inspected the places that the president planned to speak or to stay, made sure that the welcoming committee was not overly large and that the local police would be able to cope with the crowds. When Franklin Roosevelt traveled the advance work was usually done by Colonel Edmund Starling whose work was described glowingly in the *Times*: "[W]ith a watch in hand, [Starling] has measured every inch of ground a Presi-

dent planned to cover, whether by foot, train, automobile, elevator, airplane or ship. He has selected vacation spots, hotel rooms, banquet chambers. He has taught railroad employees, local policemen, automobile drivers, hotel attendants and ministers how to act and what to do in the Presidential presence. He has forced the repair of streets and the alteration of railroad stations and buildings in his advance scouting. He has given apoplexy to emotional chefs whose original menus might have disagreed with the distinguished guest's digestion" (Ray Tucker, "The One Man the President Must Obey," *New York Times*, March 17, 1935, SM4). Forrest Sorrels, a Secret Service agent in the Dallas field office, told the Warren Commission that the advance preparations for Kennedy's 1963 visit were "pretty much the same" as those employed during President Roosevelt's trip to Dallas nearly thirty years before, in 1936. It is hard to imagine a Secret Service agent in the 1990s saying the same thing in comparing advance work in the 1990s with advance work in the early 1960s. Sorrels's testimony is quoted in chapter 8 of the Warren Commission Report, available at http://www.archives.gov/research/jfk/warren-commission-report/chapter-8.html (accessed January 12, 2006).

61. "Secret Service Bill Signed," *New York Times*, October 17, 1962, p. 60. See, too, the timeline at http://www.treas.gov/usss/history.shtml (accessed January 6, 2006). Prior to 1962 the vice president had to ask for protection in order to receive it. Vice President Nixon requested and received Secret Service protection, but Vice President Johnson refused the agency's protection. See "Plan on Security Sent to Congress," *New York Times*, April 25, 1961, p. 20. In 1995 Congress amended the 1965 law, limiting Secret Service protection for former presidents and their spouses to ten years. Those presidents elected before 1995 were exempted from the provision, as were their spouses. A former president's children who are under the age of sixteen are also provided Secret Service protection. A 1984 law allowed former presidents and their spouses to decline protection.

62. "Funds to Protect President Asked," *New York Times*, March 29, 1965, p. 18.

63. Felix Belair, Jr., "Mansfield Urges Care by Nominees," *New York Times*, October 2, 1964, p. 1. Anthony Lewis, "Johnson Doubts Crowd Dangers" *New York Times*, October 1, 1964, p. 1. James Reston, "President's Responsibility to the Presidency," *New York Times*, September 30, 1964, p. 42.

64. Anthony Lewis, "Johnson Doubts Crowd Dangers" *New York Times*, October 1, 1964, p. 1. "Transcript of President Johnson's News Conference on Foreign and Domestic Affairs," *New York Times*, October 4, 1964, p. 69. The last two sentences of Rowley's memo to the president were read to the press but kept "off the record." Those sentences were: "The greatest danger is when buildings are involved as this height greatly broadens the view of the President by people. Far more dangerous than anyone lurking in the crowds is the 'sneaky type' of individual who secretes himself away from the crowd in a hiding place.'" While still off the record, the president spoke at length in order "to educate . . . and inform" the reporters. He insisted repeatedly that the Secret Service "are never concerned when I am shaking hands with people in the crowd. . . . You are much more in danger . . . speaking to a group than you are riding in a car or waving to high school kids on each side. These people that get awfully concerned because the President shakes hands—it shows first a lack of knowledge on their part, and maybe that they have some problems themselves." Johnson did not explain what those problems might be. See Off the Record Press Conference No. 32-A of the President of the United States, October 3, 1964, White House Press Office Files: Backup Material for Pres., Box 70, Lyndon Baines Johnson Library; and Memo, James Rowley to the President, October 3, 1964, WH8 9/1/64–12/31/64, White House Central Files, Box 18, LBJ Library.

65. The memo is available at http://www.aarclibrary.org/publib/jfk/wc/wcvols/wh17/pdf/
WH17_CE_866.pdf (accessed January 8, 2006). The memo was handed over to the Warren
Commission (it was Exhibit No. 866) and Hoover's caution about the impossibility and un-
desirability of absolute security was quoted at length in chapter 8 of the commission's final
report. However, Hoover's specific recommendations about how a president might limit his
exposure were not included in the report.

66. Melanson, *Secret Service*, 290–91.

67. Richard J. H. Johnston, "Johnson Guards Inspect Grounds," *New York Times*, April 22,
1964, p. 22. Richard J. H. Johnston, "Shouts Mar Johnson's Talk at Pavilion," *New York Times*,
April 23, 1964, p. 26.

68. Felix Belair, Jr., "Security Is Evident as Nixon Goes By," *New York Times*, January 21,
1969, p. 24. Felix Belair, Jr., "Tight Security Shield Devised for Inauguration," *New York Times*,
January 19, 1969, p. 56. Also see Robert B. Semple, Jr., "Nixon, Sworn, Dedicates Office to
Peace," *New York Times*, January 21, 1969, pp. 1, 22.

69. Anthony Lewis, "A Palace Guard?" *New York Times*, February 18, 1974, p. 25. James M.
Naughton, "Tap on a Brother of Nixon at Issue," *New York Times*, September 7, 1973, p. 73.
"Presidential Bar on Dissent Eased: Judge Enjoins Secret Service from Curbing Protesters,"
New York Times, August 1, 1973, p. 23. Also see John Herbers, "Secret Service Protection Now
Includes Its Flanks," *New York Times*, March 10, 1974, 4:4. Philip Shabecoff wrote a number
of articles for the *New York Times* covering the story of Nixon's home improvements. See, for
instance, "Secret Service Director Says That Most of $1.9 Million Spent on Nixon's Home Was
for Security," *New York Times*, June 28, 1973, p. 41; "Secret Service Chief Estimates Security at
Two Nixon Estates Adds $500,000 to $10-Million U.S. Cost," *New York Times*, October 11, 1973,
p. 31; and "G.A.O. Critical of Outlays on Nixon's Private Homes," *New York Times*, December
19, 1993, p. 1. In the wake of these revelations, Congress passed legislation in 1974 that required
the Secret Service to fund all security improvements out of its own budget. See John M.
Crewdson, "Fund Role Shifts to Secret Service," *New York Times*, November 3, 1974, p. 23.

70. Warren Commission Report, chapter 8 ("The Protection of the President"), available
at http://www.archives.gov/research/jfk/warren-commission-report/chapter-8.html (accessed
January 6, 2006).

71. The first assassination attempt was on September 5, 1975, and the second on September 22, 1975.

72. Letter from Helena Burch (September 8) and response, folder "JL 3-1/Ford 9/24/75
(2)," Box 23; Letter from Donald Blackwell (September 20) and response, folder "JL 3-1/Ford
9/25/75 (2)," Box 24; Letter from Sam Rishe (September 6), folder "JL 3-1/Ford 9/23/75 (3),"
Box 23; Letter from Louis Heisler (September 5), folder "JL 3-1/Ford 9/19/75 (1)," Box 22. Each
of these letters and the letters cited in the subsequent endnote are in the White House Central Files/JL, Gerald R. Ford Library.

73. James Reston, "Political Adventures," *New York Times*, September 7, 1975, 4:17. Also see
James M. Naughton, "Suddenly the Questions Are as Far-Reaching as Ford's Travels," *New
York Times*, September 19, 1975, p. 18. Carl T. Rowan struck a similar note in his syndicated
column in the *Washington Post*, which ran in newspapers across the country under titles such
as "Please, Mr. President, Stay Home," and "Message to the President: Please Stay in Washington." Some citizens clipped the Rowan column and sent it to the president, urging him
to heed its advice. See, for instance, letters from Elizabeth Van der Veer (September 20, 1975,

folder "JL 3-1/Ford 9/24/75 [2]," Box 23) of Birmingham, Alabama, and Mr. and Mrs. Truman Shipp of Raytown, Missouri (September 13, 1975, folder "JL 3-1/Ford 9/23/75 [3]," Box 23).

74. James Reston, "Political Adventures," *New York Times*, September 7, 1975, 4:17. James M. Naughton, "Ford Vows Not to Be Hostage to Threats" *New York Times*, September 13, 1975, p. 28.

75. "Interview with Reporters in St. Louis," September 12, 1975, *Public Papers of the Presidents, Gerald R. Ford, 1975* (Washington, DC: Government Printing Office, 1977), 1374-76.

76. Gerald R. Ford, *A Time to Heal* (New York: Harper and Row, 1979), 312. "Ford Won't Stop Seeing the Public," *New York Times*, September 23, 1975, p. 1.

77. News Conference, September 24, 1975 (no. 328), pp. 2-4, 6, Box 13, Ron Nessen Files, Gerald R. Ford Library.

78. James M. Naughton, "Secret Service 'Intuition' Kept Ford out of Crowd," *New York Times*, September 25, 1975, p. 1. James M. Naughton, "President Asks $13-Million More for Protection," *New York Times*, October 1, 1975, p. 1. Also see "Ford Is Reconsidering His Plans for Extensive Travel," *New York Times*, September 26, 1975, p. 16, which quotes the president's wife, Betty Ford, as saying that her husband should "keep going, but stay away from people."

79. "A More Secure President," *New York Times*, October 5, 1975, 4:2.

80. "3 Committees Investigating Conduct of Security Services," *New York Times*, April 1, 1981, A21. Melanson, *Secret Service*, 113-17.

81. "The Presidency under Glass," *New York Times*, April 1, 1981, A30.

82. Steven R. Weisman, "Stiff Security Steps Keep President at a Distance," *New York Times*, May 1, 1981, A22.

83. Turner Catledge, "Guarding the President's Train: A Big Job," *New York Times*, October 2, 1932, 8:2. Also see "Roosevelt Guard Made Up of 7 Men," *New York Times*, February 16, 1933, p. 3. Both of these articles suggested, charitably, that presidents were generally the "unwilling subjects" of this sort of pomp and ceremony. For an example of a presidential complaint about protection, see Nixon's comments during an August 1973 press conference: "I don't like it. And my family doesn't like it. Both of my daughters would prefer to have no Secret Service. . . . My wife doesn't want to have Secret Service. . . . I think that one man is probably as good against a threat as a hundred." See "Transcript of President's News Conference on Foreign and Domestic Matters," *New York Times*, August 23, 1973, p. 28. Also see "Nixon Would Pare Protective Detail," *New York Times*, August 23, 1973, p. 30. A conflict between presidential staff and security detail in the Nixon administration bubbled up into public view when the head of the president's protective detail, Robert Taylor, was transferred out of the White House in 1973. Although the director of the Secret Service insisted there was no political motivation behind the job change, the evidence suggests he lied and was covering up for the administration. The real story, according to inside sources, was that the agent had been transferred because he had clashed with Nixon's chief of staff, H. R. Haldeman. In one instance, during a campaign stop in Providence, Rhode Island, Haldeman apparently wanted to remove ropes that separated the president from a crowd of well-wishers in order to give the impression of a "spontaneous" demonstration of support for the president. Taylor refused to permit Haldeman to bring down the ropes because it would endanger the president. See Philip Shabecoff, "Chief of Nixon's Guard Is Removed," *New York Times*, February 14, 1973, p. 85. Also see "Flap over Guarding Nixon," *New York Times*, February 18, 1973, 4:3; and Melanson, *Secret Service*, 221.

1. Noble Cunningham, Jr., *The Presidency of James Monroe* (Lawrence: University Press of Kansas, 1996), 35–36. Daniel Preston, ed., *The Papers of James Monroe: A Documentary History of the Presidential Tours of James Monroe, 1817, 1818, 1819* (Westport, CT: Greenwood Press, 2003), 776. *National Intelligencer* (Washington, D.C.), November 16, 1825, Preston, *Papers of James Monroe*, 778. After Monroe left the presidency, he asked Congress to reimburse him for some of the expenses he had incurred while in public office, particularly expenses incurred while representing the U.S. government in Europe during the last decade of the eighteenth century and the opening decade of the nineteenth century (Harry Ammon, *James Monroe: The Quest for National Identity* [University Press of Virginia, 1990], 554). But he refrained from asking Congress to reimburse him for expenses incurred during his presidency, including his travels. In February 1823, Monroe apparently told his friend Charles Jared Ingersoll that he "ought to be reimbursed" for the $1,912 since he had "made that tour with a view to the promotion of the public defenses" (Diary entry, February 9, 1823, in William M. Meigs, *The Life of Charles Jared Ingersoll* [New York: Da Capo Press, 1970; orig. pub. 1897], 117). Monroe must have subsequently decided that it would be unwise to press his claim for reimbursement of presidential travel.

2. Ammon, *James Monroe*, 546, 534. Also see Meigs, *Life of Charles Jared Ingersoll*, 117.

3. Minutes of the Common Council of the City of New York, Preston, *Papers of James Monroe*, 65; Thomas R. Smith to John Jacob Astor, June 17, 1817, Preston, *Papers of James Monroe*, 93; Monroe [to Congress], January 12, 1825, Preston, *Papers of James Monroe*, 777.

4. On September 22, 1789, a week before the close of the inaugural legislative session, the first Congress set the mileage allowance at $6 for every 20 miles of travel. In 1818 the mileage allowance was increased to $8 for every twenty miles. However, congressional salaries were set well below that of the president. The president received $25,000 a year whereas salaries of members of Congress were $6 a day in 1789 and $8 a day by 1818.

5. Kenneth Cook, "Washington Passes through Halifax," talk delivered to the Halifax County Chapter, United Daughters of the Confederacy, April 2, 1976, available at http://www.oldhalifax.com/county/GeoWashington.htm (accessed April 20, 2007).

6. George W. Berge, *The Free Pass Bribery System* (Lincoln, NE: Independent Publishing Company, 1905).

7. For the full list of exemptions, and the debate it engendered in the Senate, see the *Congressional Record—Senate*, May 16, 1906, 6942–49, esp. 6948.

8. "Luxury for Mr. Harrison: A Train Such as No President Ever Rode in Before," *New York Times*, April 14, 1891, p. 1. Homer E. Socolofsky and Allan B. Specter, *The Presidency of Benjamin Harrison* (Lawrence: University Press of Kansas, 1987), 171.

9. "Luxury for Mr. Harrison," p. 1.

10. Edmund Morris, *Theodore Rex* (New York: Random House, 2001), 215. "President's Train Ready," *New York Times*, April 1, 1903, p. 8. Also see the description of Roosevelt's train in "The President's Southern Trip," *New York Times*, September 5, 1902, p. 3.

11. *Congressional Record—House*, June 20, 1906, 8809.

12. Ibid., 8809–10.

13. Ibid., 8811–12.

14. Ibid., 8809.

15. Ibid., 8809–10.

16. Ibid., 8810.

17. Ibid.

18. Ibid., 8810–11.

19. Ibid., 8811.

20. Ibid., 8810–11.

21. Ibid., 8811.

22. Ibid., 8812.

23. Ibid., 8812–13.

24. Ibid., 8813. Democrats provided only twenty of the 176 "yes" votes.

25. *Congressional Record—Senate*, June 21, 1906, 8847.

26. Ibid., 8847–48.

27. Morris, *Theodore Rex*, 430. *Congressional Record—Senate*, June 21, 1906, 8848. For further evidence that Democrats believed Roosevelt was the "most popular president . . . since the [Civil War]," see William B. Gatewood, "Theodore Roosevelt and Arkansas, 1901–1912," *Arkansas Historical Quarterly* 32 (1973), 21.

28. *Congressional Record—Senate*, June 21, 1906, 8860.

29. Ibid., 8861.

30. Ibid., 8849.

31. Ibid.

32. Ibid., 8849, 8861.

33. Ibid., 8862.

34. Ibid., 8865.

35. Ibid., June 22, 1906, 8921.

36. Ibid., June 21 and 22, 1906, 8865–66, 8936.

37. Ibid., June 22, 1906, 8938.

38. Ibid., 8924–25, 8927.

39. Ibid., 8933.

40. Ibid., 8931.

41. Ibid., 8929, 8931.

42. Morris, *Theodore Rex*, 424.

43. *Congressional Record—Senate*, June 22 and 22, 1906, 8864, 8929.

44. Ibid., June 22, 1906, 8941.

45. *Congressional Record—House*, February 24, 1909, 3028.

46. Ibid., 3029, 3032. The congressman, Nebraska's Gilbert Hitchcock, derived this estimate by including the cost of maintaining the White House and the president's greenhouses and stables, as well as the salaries of White House "clerks and employees" and guards. The total, Hitchcock pointed out, did not include many other costs "hidden away in the appropriations bill and charged to various departments," such as the funding for a barber as well as two "Presidential yachts," the *Mayflower* and the *Sylph* (3029).

47. *Congressional Record—House*, March 3, 1909, 3776–79. "Taft Plans a Trip to Alaska in Fall: Will Make Long Swing through the Country If Congress Provides Funds," *New York Times*, April 19, 1909, p. 1. Also see "Taft's Summer Plans: Hopes to Make Western Trip, but May Be Prevented," *New York Times*, March 29, 1909, p. 1. Through the end of the fiscal year (June 30) Taft was able to cover his travel expenses by spending the unused portion of the $25,000 Congress had appropriated for Roosevelt's travel.

48. "Taft Cancels Trip to Press His Bills," *New York Times*, May 7, 1910, p. 7.

49. *Congressional Record—House*, May 26, 1910, 6939, 6948.

50. Ibid., 6939–40.

51. Ibid., 6940.

52. Ibid., 1910, 6944; also see 6942.

53. Ibid., 6940–41. The editorial was dated May 17, 1910. The other editorials read by Tawney were from the *Atlanta Constitution* and the *Pueblo Star-Journal* (Colorado).

54. *Congressional Record—House*, May 26, 1910, 6941–42.

55. Ibid., 6945.

56. Ibid., 1910, 6946.

57. Ibid.

58. Ibid., 6947.

59. Ibid., 6947–48.

60. Ibid., 6948.

61. "Taft Vindicates South's Hospitality," *New York Times*, May 29, 1910, p. 6.

62. "Offer Taft $5,000 to Pay for Travel," *New York Times*, May 29, 1910, p. 4.

63. Ibid. "Taft to Get Travel Fund," *New York Times*, June 11, 1910, p. 1.

64. "President for All, Taft Says," *New York Times*, July 27, 1910, p. 2. The effect was short-lived, however. In 1912, Democrat John Joseph Fitzgerald, chair of the House Appropriations Committee, assailed Taft for using taxpayer money to fund "partisan junkets." The nation, Fitzgerald said, "has been shocked at the manner in which the Executive has absented himself from this capital, traveling here and there, seeking delegates and votes, denouncing his fellow-citizens, members of a different political party or of factions of his own political party not in accord with himself, at the expense of the people of the United States" ("Taft Trips Assailed as Partisan Junkets," *New York Times*, June 14, 1912, p. 5).

65. See title 3, chapter 2, section 103 of the U.S. Code. The 1978 law (Public Law 95-570) also removed entertainment expenses from this section so that the $100,000 was earmarked for presidential travel only. Entertainment expenses were covered in an amendment to section 105; the amendment set no limit on the amount that Congress could appropriate for the president's "official entertainment expenses."

66. U.S. General Accounting Office, "Presidential Travel: Costs and Accounting for the President's Trips to Africa, Chile, and China," September 1999; and U.S. General Accounting Office, "Presidential Travel: DOD Airlift Cost for White House Foreign Travel," August 2000. The GAO's 1999 report pegged the per-hour flight cost at $34,400 based on figures provided by the White House Military Office. But in the 2000 report, the GAO dramatically revised the per-hour cost estimates based on new information provided by the air force. The actual rate for presidential travel fiscal year 1998, the GAO now concluded, was $56,800 per hour. The 2000 GAO study estimated that the 1999 flight costs for Air Force One were $49,900 per hour and the 2000 flight costs were $54,100 per hour.

67. On his 1817 tour, Monroe traveled aboard a naval vessel between Staten Island and Manhattan, and while on Lake Champlain, Lake Ontario, and Lake Erie. During his 1818 tour of the Chesapeake, Monroe was also a passenger aboard a naval ship. In none of these cases did the navy charge Monroe for its services, nor did Monroe offer to reimburse the navy. Information supplied in e-mail communication to author by Dan Preston, August 20, 2005.

68. U.S. General Accounting Office, "Presidential Travel: Costs and Accounting for the President's Trips to Africa, Chile, and China," September 1999.

69. These numbers are from a 2003 GAO study, the results of which were published in Thomas B. Edsall, "GAO: Bush Tops Clinton in HHS Funding of Trips," *Washington Post*,

July 12, 2003, A4. Also see Thomas B. Edsall, "Bush Tapped HHS Funds to Pay for Trips," *Washington Post*, October 20, 2002, A5. In 2004 the General Accounting Office was renamed the Government Accountability Office.

70. "Taft Trips Assailed as Partisan Junkets," *New York Times*, June 14, 1912, p. 5. When President Truman made a ten-day tour aboard a special train in May 1950 the railroads were paid about $40,000 in fares, but the actual cost of transporting the president was more like $240,000, largely because of the security precautions that were necessary. That extra $200,000 was reportedly absorbed by the railroads. So even though the free pass had been abolished the railroads still subsidized presidential travel. See "Truman's Trip Will Cost 7 Railroads $200,000," *New York Times*, May 3, 1950, p. 26.

71. U.S. General Accounting Office, "Presidential Travel: Costs and Accounting for the President's Trips to Africa, Chile, and China," September 1999, pp. 3, 21.

72. Many of these military personnel are employees of the White House Military Office, the largest administrative unit in the White House, which includes the White House Communications Agency, the White House Mess, the White House Transportation Agency, and the White House Medical Unit. According to the 1999 GAO report, the travel expenses of the White House Military Office were paid for by the Department of Defense. See GAO, "Presidential Travel," September 1999, p. 4. On the administrative structure and function of the White House Military Office, see Peri E. Arnold, Bradley H. Patterson, Jr., and Charles Walcott, "The Office of Management and Administration," in Martha Joynt Kumar and Terry Sullivan, eds., *The White House World: Transitions, Organization, and Office Operations* (College Station: Texas A&M University Press, 2003), 289–93.

73. United States General Accounting Office, "Presidential Travel: Costs and Accounting for the President's Trips to Africa, Chile, and China," September 1999, pp. 4, 7. United States General Accounting Office, "Presidential Travel: DOD Airlift Cost for White House Foreign Travel," August 2000, p. 5. On the work of the Advance Office, see Bradley H. Patterson, Jr., "Manager of Apparently Effortless Success: The Advance Office," in *The White House Staff: Inside the West Wing and Beyond* (Washington, DC: Brookings Institution Press, 2000), 240–62.

74. U.S. General Accounting Office, "Presidential Travel: DOD Airlift Cost for White House Foreign Travel," August 2000, p. 5.

75. U.S. General Accounting Office, "Presidential Travel: Costs and Accounting for the President's Trips to Africa, Chile, and China," September 1999, p. 9.

76. Ibid., pp. 13, 16–17.

77. The days of foreign travel are calculated based on the information available at the Department of State's Web site, at http://www.state.gov/r/pa/ho/trvl/pres/c7383.htm (accessed May 1, 2006). In estimating days of domestic travel for George H. W. Bush and Clinton I have relied on data supplied to me by Brendan Doherty as well as Doherty's "Traveling Strategically? George H. W. Bush, Bill Clinton, and the Electoral College," Paper prepared for presentation at the Western Political Science Association, Oakland, California, March 17–19, 2005, p. 9. Doherty counts 618 days of domestic travel for Clinton, not including travel to Virginia and Maryland (e-mail communication with author, June 26, 2006). If those two states are added into the count, it would add at least another 100 days of domestic travel.

78. *Code of Federal Regulations* (Revised as of January 1, 2006), Title 11, §9004.7 ("Allocation of Travel Expenditures"). Available at http://www.fec.gov/law/cfr/11_cfr.pdf (accessed May 19, 2006). "The Cost of Presidential and Vice Presidential Travel," U.S. House

of Representatives Committee on Government Reform—Minority Staff, Special Investigations Division, March 2006. Available at: http://www.democrats.reform.house.gov/Documents/20060316113550-47530.pdf (accessed May 24, 2006). The 2 percent figure almost certainly overestimates the actual rate of reimbursement. Among the travel costs the study did not include were those associated with Secret Service protection, the president's backup plane, motorcade costs, and helicopter transport, all of which are paid for by the government even if the travel is campaign-related (p. 8). Also the report assumed that "reimbursement is paid for five staff members for each political trip," but as the report also acknowledged, that figure likely overestimates the number of staff members for whom reimbursement was paid (p. 4).

79. Mike Allen, "Bush Capitalizes on Travel Bargain," *Washington Post*, March 5, 2004, A21. Charles Pope, "Campaign 2004: Bush Visit Is a Bargain for Nethercutt Camp," *Seattle Post-Intelligencer*, June 16, 2004, available at http://seattlepi.nwsource.com/national/178018_bush16.html (accessed May 29, 2006). If there is no first-class commercial service between two cities then the reimbursement rate is the coach fare, and if there is no commercial service the reimbursement must be at the charter rate. See Title 11 of the *Code of Federal Regulations*, §100.93 ("Travel by airplane or other means of transportation"), available at http://www.fec.gov/law/cfr/11_cfr.pdf (accessed May 19, 2006).

80. Title 11 of the Code of Federal Regulations, §9004.7 ("Allocation of travel expenditures"), at http://www.fec.gov/law/cfr/11_cfr.pdf (accessed May 19, 2006). Federal election regulations do not allow the president to split flight costs when combining a campaign-related stop with a non-campaign-related stop in the same city. Instead the campaign-related costs are "determined by calculating what the trip would have cost from the point of origin of the trip to the first campaign-related stop and from the stop through each subsequent campaign-related stop to the point of origin." Other on-the-ground expenses incurred on a presidential trip involving both campaign and official events are typically prorated using a formula codified in §734.503 ("Allocation and reimbursement of costs associated with political travel") of Title 5 of the Code of Federal Regulations (available at http://www.gpoaccess.gov/cfr/retrieve.html [accessed May 19, 2006]), which governs administrative personnel. The percentage of a trip that is deemed "political"—and therefore requiring reimbursement to the government—is the "time spent in political meetings, receptions, rallies" divided by the sum of the time spent on political activities and the "time spent on official meetings, receptions, etc." In other words, if the official event lasts three hours and the campaign event lasts one hour, then only one quarter of the travel costs must be reimbursed by the party or campaign. These federal regulations evidently have their origins in White House guidelines for presidential travel drawn up in 1982. See L. Elaine Halchin, "Presidential Travel: Policy and Costs," CRS Report for Congress, May 6, 2004 (RS21835), p. 3.

81. "Press Gaggle with Claire Buchan, Aboard Air Force One En Route Louisville, Kentucky," available at http://www.whitehouse.gov/news/releases/2004/02/20040226-2.html (accessed May 19, 2006). According to a study done by the Democratic staff of the House Appropriations Committee, 84 percent of Bush's domestic travel in 1992 (through early October) was "mixed" and so allowed for shared costs. According to the staff estimates, only about 43 percent of Clinton's travel in 1994 and 1998 mixed political and official events (Thomas B. Edsall, "Bush Tapped HHS Funds to Pay for Trips," *Washington Post*, October 20, 2002, A5). The Democrats' calculations overstate the difference since much of Bush's travel in the remainder of October and the beginning of November 2002 was almost entirely political. See "Depart-

ments of Transportation and Treasury, and Independent Agencies Appropriations for 2004," Hearings before a Subcommittee of the Committee on Appropriations, House of Representatives, 108th Congress, First Session (Washington, DC: Government Printing Office, 2003), 720–21. Still, the evidence suggests that George W. Bush pursued this strategy of pairing political and official events more aggressively than his predecessor.

82. Mike Allen, "On the Way to the Fundraiser: Stopovers Let Bush Charge Taxpayers for Political Trips," *Washington Post*, May 20, 2002, A1. A 1998 article, which pointed out that Clinton "often adds public events onto cash-raising trips," cited White House aides who "freely concede[d] the 'policy' events are tacked on after the fund-raisers, because raising cash takes more advance planning." See Deborah Orin, "Bill's Jaunt Costs You," *New York Post*, July 26, 1998, p. 12.

83. Peter C. Stuart, "Who Pays Presidential Plane Fare?" *Christian Science Monitor*, July 21, 1980, p. 7.

84. "Truman Trip Held Politics by Reece: GOP Chairman Ridicules 'Nonpolitical' Label," *New York Times*, June 1, 1948, p. 48. "President Departs to Speak in West," *New York Times*, June 4, 1948, pp. 1, 12. "President Quips Nonpolitical Trip," *New York Times*, June 5, 1948, p. 2. Oral history interview with Charles S. Murphy, May 2, 1963, available at http://www.trumanlibrary.org/oralhist/murphy1.htm#transcript (accessed April 17, 2006).

85. "Pentagon Lists Election Flights," *New York Times*, April 16, 1965, p. 11.

86. "President's Trip Annoys His Aides," *New York Times*, June 27, 1964, p. 22. "Johnson Took Trip without His Doctor or Code on Plane," *New York Times*, September 9, 1964, p. 31.

87. David Rosenbaum, "Incumbency Helping Ford on Campaign Travel Cost," *New York Times*, May 5, 1976, p. 27. Charles R. Babcock, "Campaigning via Air Force One: Public Foots Much of Bill," *Washington Post*, December 31, 1991, A15.

88. J. F. terHorst and Ralph Albertazzie, *The Flying White House: The Story of Air Force One* (New York: Coward, McCann and Geoghegan, 1979), 83. "Air Fare for Carter Is Figured at $182,000," *New York Times*, January 11, 1978, B8. "Flights Costs in '91: $41,875 per Hour," *Washington Post*, December 31, 1991, A15. "43 on the White House Payroll Top $100,000," *New York Times*, September 20, 1992, p. 23. The per-hour flight cost for Eisenhower's presidential aircraft in 1957 was only $348 an hour. See "Columbine Cost Cited," *New York Times*, July 24, 1957, p. 28.

89. Title X of H.R. 2183, which passed the House of Representatives on August 6, 1998, required "any political committee of a national political party for whom the President, Vice President, or any executive department head uses Air Force One for transportation for any travel which includes a fund-raising event for committee benefit to reimburse the Federal Government for the actual transportation costs for the use of Air Force One by the individual involved." Presidential challengers, too, benefit from travel subsidies but they are private sector subsidies rather than government subsidies. In both the 1988 and the 1996 presidential campaigns, for instance, Bob Dole relied extensively on corporate-owned jets. Corporations supplied the jets to Dole, according to one press report, "at a fraction of the actual cost" of flying the plane. As Bill Hogan of the Center for Public Integrity explained: "These are basically invisible or unreported campaign contributions. In the Presidential race, we outlaw direct corporate contributions, yet we put corporate jets at the disposal of candidates." See Leslie Wayne, "Report Faults Dole and Clinton on Flight Costs," *New York Times*, December 13, 1996, B15, and "Dole Using Corporate Jets in Campaign Trips," *New York Times*, September 19, 1987, p. 9.

90. White House Personnel Authorization Act of 1978: To Review Transportation Expenditures under the Act, Hearings before the Subcommittee on Human Resources of the Committee on Post Office and Civil Service, House of Representatives, 102nd Congress, March 31, April 8, 9, 30; July 21, 1992 (Washington, DC: Government Printing Office, 1993), 27. Mike Allen, "On the Way to the Fundraiser: Stopovers Let Bush Charge Taxpayers for Political Trips," *Washington Post*, May 20, 2002, A1. The final quotation is from Greg Ganske, a Republican member of the House who challenged Iowa Senator Tom Harkin in 2002.

91. The $100,000 limit on the president's traveling expenses can be found in the U.S. Code, Title 3, chapter 2, section 103. The provision relating to the travel of presidential aides is U.S. Code, Title 3, chapter 2, section 105 ("Assistance and services for the President"). GAO reports from the late 1980s and early 1990s found that presidents spent between $275,000 and $400,000 on travel expenses under section 105. See, for example, U.S. General Accounting Office, "Unvouchered Expenditures: Executive Office of the President, Fiscal Year 1991 Expenditures Subject to Audit Were Proper," May 1993; U.S. General Accounting Office, "Unvouchered Expenditures: Presidential and Vice Presidential Expenditures for the Periods Reviewed Were Proper," September 1990; and U.S. General Accounting Office, "Unvouchered Expenditures: Presidential and Vice Presidential Fiscal Year 1986 Expenditures Were Proper," April 1988.

92. U.S. General Accounting Office, "Presidential Travel," August 2000, p. 7; U.S. General Accounting Office, "Presidential Travel," September 1999, p. 29. U.S. General Accounting Office, "Month in Review: September 1999," p. 17. For examples of the White House refusing to respond to press inquiries about the costs of presidential travel, see "Presidential Gas Bill Gets Steeper," CNN.com, August 24, 2005; Scott Lindlaw, "Bush Enjoys Travel Advantage on Taxpayer-Financed Air Force One," Associated Press State and Local Wire, May 31, 2004; "The Perks of Presidential Travel," CNN.com, March 22, 2004. Also see Dana Milbank, "The Cost of Presidential Travel Is Anyone's Guess," *Washington Post*, October 29, 2002, A19.

93. White House Personnel Authorization Act of 1978: To Review Transportation Expenditures under the Act, Hearings before the Subcommittee on Human Resources of the Committee on Post Office and Civil Service, House of Representatives, 102nd Congress, March 31, April 8, 9, 30; July 21, 1992 (Washington, DC: Government Printing Office, 1993), 8, 13. Also see *New York Times*, September 20, 1992, p. 23.

CHAPTER 6. GOING ABROAD:
BREAKING THE "IRONCLAD CUSTOM"

1. Roosevelt to Andrew Carnegie, August 6, 1906, H. W. Brands, ed., *The Selected Letters of Theodore Roosevelt* (New York: Cooper Square Press, 2001), 423.

2. "The President's Tour," *New York Times*, September 3, 1866, p. 5. Grant to Lemuel A. Wilmot, September 1, 1871, and Grant to James G. Blaine, August 31, 1871, John Y. Simon, ed., *The Papers of Ulysses S. Grant* (Carbondale: Southern Illinois University Press, 1998), 22:125–26; also see 25:349. In 1869 Grant turned down an invitation from the Pacific Mail Steamship Company to visit China and Japan (Grant to Allan McLane, March 29, 1971, Simon, *Papers of Grant*, 21:276–77).

3. Walter A. McDougall, *Promised Land, Crusader State: The American Encounter with the World Since 1776* (Boston: Houghton Mifflin, 1997).

4. Ibid., 113–14, 119.

5. Jules Cambon to Theophile Delcasse, July 13, 1901, volume 8, Archives of the Ministry of Foreign Affairs, Paris. My thanks to Lewis Gould, who supplied me with his translation

of this memorandum. Also see Lewis L. Gould, *The Modern American Presidency* (Lawrence: University Press of Kansas, 2003), 8. Gould also brought to my attention a letter McKinley wrote to Mrs. Sanford B. Dole on July 20, 1900, assuring her that "it would be a pleasure" for him to travel to Hawaii. In April 1900, Hawaii had become an incorporated territory, that is, an area under the control of the United States in which the Constitution applies in exactly the same way as if that territory were a state. The countries acquired in the Spanish-American War were treated as unincorporated territories, and so individuals in these areas did not have the same constitutional rights as those in the United States.

6. *New York Times*, May 7, 1901, p. 1.

7. Ibid.

8. A description of Harrison's reception in El Paso can be found in the *New York Times*, April 22, 1891, p. 1.

9. "Text of the Canal Treaty," *New York Times*, November 21, 1903, p. 2. Also see Nathan Miller, *Theodore Roosevelt: A Life* (New York: William Morrow, 1992), 407.

10. Theodore Roosevelt to Kermit Roosevelt, November 20, 1906, in Brands, *Selected Letters*, 441. This letter was written aboard the U.S.S. *Louisiana*, after the president had completed his inspection of the Panama Canal. Also see Miller, *Theodore Roosevelt*, 399.

11. *New York Times*, November 9, 1906, p. 1.

12. Ibid. *New York Times*, November 11, 1906, SM1.

13. "I'm Off for the Ditch: President's Farewell," *New York Times*, November 9, 1906, p. 1. Roosevelt left the White House on November 8 and returned on November 26. He was in Panama from November 14–17 and in Puerto Rico from November 21–22.

14. "Appendices: The President's Speech," *New York Times*, December 18, 1906, TM7. Also see *New York Times*, November 19, 1906, p. 3.

15. *New York Times*, November 16, 1906, p. 1. *New York Times*, November 17, 1906, p. 1. Also see Edmund Morris, *Theodore Rex* (New York: Random House, 2001), 468–70.

16. Lewis L. Gould, *The Presidency of Theodore Roosevelt* (Lawrence: University Press of Kansas, 1991), 98. The *Boston Globe* opined that Roosevelt's transgressions against tradition were "not only forgiven, but . . . heartily applauded" by the people because he was himself a man of the people, "a man in the street, a hail-fellow-well-met." He could "ignore precedent" because he did "it openly and frankly, and therefore, in the opinion of the great mass of mankind, honestly" ("The Roosevelt Charm," *Boston Globe*, November 19, 1906, p. 6).

17. The term "invisible lines" is used to describe the border between the Canal Zone and the Panamanian Republic in "What the President Will See When He Gets to Panama," *New York Times*, November 11, 1906, SM1. *New York Times* coverage of President Taft's 1910 visit to Panama includes "Taft Sails for Panama," November 11, 1910, p. 7; "Panama Canal to Be Ready Dec. 1, 1913," November 16, 1901, p. 1. "Taft Reassures People of Panama," November 17, 1901, p. 4; "Taft Lands in Cuba; Off Again for Home," November 17, 1910, p. 4; and "Taft's Cruise Ends at Capital To-day," November 23, 1910, p. 6. The December 1912 visit, which occurred after Taft had been defeated by Woodrow Wilson, received less prominent coverage in the *Times*. See "President Sails for Colon," December 22, 1912, p. 4; "Taft Arrives at Panama," December 25, 1912, p. 1, "Taft Homeward Bound," December 27, 1912, p. 4; and "Taft to Visit Cuba on Way Home To-day," December 29, 1912, p. 9. Neither trip attracted the same publicity as Roosevelt's Panama trip. That may explain why the two trips President Taft made to Panama are mistakenly omitted from the State Department's website (http://www.state.gov/r/pa/ho/

trvl/pres/12787.htm), which purports to be a complete listing of presidential travel abroad. The State Department's listing "does not include Presidential trips to U.S. territories overseas, days spent at sea in international waters, or stops at uninhabited islands," but both of President Taft's visits to the Canal Zone, like Roosevelt's visit, took him outside the 10-mile-wide Canal Zone and into the Panamanian Republic. In greeting the Panamanian president in November 1910, Taft said: "As once in the case of Mexico, so now in the case of Panama, I ventured to violate the customary limitation upon the movements of the President of the United States by leaving the soil of my own country to come beneath the flag and protection of a friendly neighbor." Taft also assured the Panamanian president and people that, contrary to rumors, the United States had no plans to annex Panama. "Nothing would justify" such an action, Taft said, "so long as Panama performed her part under the treaty" granting United States absolute control over the canal (*New York Times*, November 17, 1910, p. 4).

18. Donald F. Anderson, *William Howard Taft: A Conservative's Conception of the Presidency* (Ithaca, NY: Cornell University Press, 1973), 265. In a letter to his wife dated October 15, 1909, Taft confides his fear that "two billions [in] American capital in Mexico" would be "greatly endangered if Díaz were to die and his government go to pieces" (Taft Papers, Series 2, 1909 Feb 18–Jan 31 1918, Reel 26, Library of Congress). In a subsequent letter to his wife, dated October 17, Taft describes at length the meetings with Díaz.

19. *New York Times*, October 17, 1909, p. 1.

20. Ibid., October 17, 1909, p. 1.

21. Ibid.

22. "Mr. Taft's Trip," *New York Times*, September 14, 1909, p. 8.

23. Ray Stannard Baker, *Woodrow Wilson, Life and Letters* (Garden City, NY: Doubleday, 1935), 5:30–32.

24. McDougall, *Promised Land, Crusader State*, 122. Wilson's May 27, 1916, speech is in Arthur S. Link, ed., *The Papers of Woodrow Wilson*, 69 vols. (Princeton, NJ: Princeton University Press, 1966–1994), 37:113–16. In a speech on May 30, 1906, Wilson explained: "I shall never myself consent to an entangling alliance. But I would gladly assent to a disentangling alliance—an alliance which would disentangle the peoples of the world from those combinations in which they seek their own separate and private interests and unite the people of the world upon a basis of common right and justice" (*Papers of Woodrow Wilson*, 37:126).

25. *New York Times*, November 1, 1918, p. 8, as quoted in James D. Startt, "Wilson's Mission to Paris: The Making of a Decision," *Historian* (August 1968), 599.

26. *New York Times*, November 19, 1918, p. 1.

27. A Memorandum by Robert Lansing, "Will the President Go to the Peace Conference?" November 12, 1918, *Papers of Woodrow Wilson*, 53:65–66.

28. A Memorandum by Robert Lansing, "The President's Going to the Peace Conference," November 18, 1918, *Papers of Woodrow Wilson*, 53:127–28.

29. Key Pittman to Woodrow Wilson, November 15, 1918, *Papers of Woodrow Wilson*, 53:94.

30. Peter Gerry to Woodrow Wilson, November 16, 1918, *Papers of Woodrow Wilson*, 53: 103–4.

31. "On Wilson at Peace Table the 'Noes' Have It," *New York Times*, November 15, 1918, p. 1.

32. Ibid. Most significant was the opposition expressed by the *World* (New York), which was sometimes referred to as "the mouthpiece of the Administration." The *World*'s editor,

Frank Cobb, initially believed Wilson should go to Paris, but after traveling to London with Wilson's adviser Colonel Edward House in October, he changed his mind. On November 4, Cobb wrote a memo to House detailing various reasons the president should stay in Washington. The president, Cobb concluded, "could only lose by 'playing the game of European diplomacy.'" See Startt, "Wilson's Mission to Paris," 602–3. The *World* agreed with Lansing that "the place of the President of the United States . . . is in this country and at the seat of Government of whose vast affairs he is charged with direct administration." Although nothing in the Constitution prevented the president from going to Paris, the *World* stressed that "there is a tradition of this kind which goes back to the beginnings of the Republic" and "its validity has been repeatedly recognized." The president should thus respect that tradition and stay at his "official post" in Washington ("On Wilson at Peace Table the 'Noes' Have It," *New York Times*, November 15, 1918, p. 1).

33. John Hessin Clarke to Woodrow Wilson, November 18, 1918, *Papers of Woodrow Wilson*, 53:120. Also Woodrow Wilson to John Hessin Clarke, November 18, 1918, *Papers of Woodrow Wilson*, 53:120.

34. Woodrow Wilson to Gavin McNab, *Papers of Woodrow Wilson*, November 18, 1918, 53:116. The idea of traveling to Europe at the end of the war to attend the peace conference was one that Wilson had been considering since at least the beginning of 1918. See Startt, "Wilson's Mission to Paris," 601.

35. "Mr. Wilson Falls into Grave Error," *Detroit Free Press*, November 20, 1918, p. 4. James Startt surveyed 168 newspapers, and found that of the 85 percent that editorialized after the White House's announcement of the trip on November 18, 48 percent backed the decision, 25 percent opposed it, and 27 percent were noncommittal. See James D. Startt, "Wilson's Trip to Paris: Profile of Press Response," *Journalism Quarterly* 46 (1969), 737–42.

36. "The President's Journey," *St. Louis Daily Globe-Democrat*, November 20, 1918, 2:12.

37. Startt, "Wilson's Trip to Paris," 738.

38. "The President's European Visit," *Outlook* (New York), November 27, 1918, p. 488.

39. Startt, "Wilson's Trip to Paris," 739. In a memo to Colonel House, Wilson explained why he should have a seat at the Peace Conference: "I play the same part in our government that the prime ministers play in theirs. The fact that I am head of the state is of no practical consequence" (Wilson to Edward Mandell House, November 16, 1918, *Papers of Woodrow Wilson*, 53:97). The French premier Clemenceau disagreed. In a telegram to Lloyd George, the British prime minister, he argued that "Since [Wilson] is a chief of state he is consequently not on the same line as ourselves. To admit one chief of state without admitting all seems to be an impossibility" (Charles Seymour, ed., *The Intimate Papers of Colonel House* 4:209–10; quoted in John Michael Pyne, "Woodrow Wilson's Abdication of Domestic and Party Leadership: Autumn 1918 to Autumn 1919," Ph.D. dissertation, Notre Dame University, 1979, 113).

40. *New York Times*, November 23, 1918, p. 3. *New York Times*, November 25, 1918, p. 2. Murat was a descendant of Napoleon Bonaparte's sister.

41. *New York Times*, November 26, 1918, p. 2. Lawrence's column originally appeared in the *New York Evening Post* on November 25.

42. "President Wilson's Projected Trip to Europe Argued before the Supreme Court of Public Opinion," *New York Times*, November 26, 1918, p. 14. The previous week, on November 20, the *Times* had editorialized against the trip, calling it an unwarranted and "astonishing departure from custom." The nation should send delegates or commissioners to Paris,

not the head of the executive branch. "Has the President," queried the *Times*, "so little confidence in his judgment in the choice of men for these high errands that he must needs go himself?" (p. 14).

43. "Questions Never Raised Before in Washington," *New York Times*, November 28, 1918, p. 2.

44. *New York Times*, November 21, 1918, p. 1.

45. State of the Union Message, December 2, 1918, *Papers of Woodrow Wilson*, 284–86. "Address Fails to Stir," *New York Times*, December 3, 1918, p. 1.

46. *Congressional Record—Senate*, December 3, 1918, 23. The resolution introduced in the House was identical except that the vice president would only exercise the presidential powers and duties while the president was absent from the country. When the president returned he would again be president. On November 30, the *New York Times* opined that "the weight of authority seems to be on that side," citing in support the view of the venerable former senator George F. Edmunds (whom the *Times* judged "the greatest constitutional lawyer now living who has served in any American Senate") that by "going abroad [the president] will, for the time being, cease to possess his executive powers" and that it was "the duty of the Vice President to carry on the Government" in the president's absence (*New York Times*, November 30, 1918, p. 10). Several days before the *Times* editorial, George Wickersham, who had been attorney general in the Taft administration, argued this same position in a speech to the Council of Foreign Relations in New York. Wickersham added that the fact "that these questions in the past have never arisen for actual decision is a tribute to the wisdom of our Presidents in conforming with the traditions of their great office, with that unbroken custom which ripens into law, and in not suffering the whisperings of personal ambition to lead them to depart from the paths of accustomed action, thereby avoiding the creation of new, uncertain and perhaps dangerous questions of constitutional right and power" (*World* [New York], November 27, 1918, p. 3; also see *New York Times*, November 27, 1981, p. 1).

47. *Congressional Record—Senate*, December 3, 1918, 26.

48. Ibid.

49. Ibid., 25. The case is *Ex parte Hawkins* (1900) 1913 OK CR 313.

50. Ibid. In claiming Taft visited Canada, Williams was perhaps thinking of Taft's 1910 trip to Eastport, Maine, which borders Canada. To reach Eastport, the president's yacht, the *Mayflower*, did cross into Canadian waters but the vessel, on which the president slept, remained carefully "anchored on the Maine side of the line." When the president came ashore at Eastport to give a brief speech, he spoke of his desire to establish closer commercial ties with Canada, drawing cheers from an audience that included "many Canadians." But despite the proximity of Canada, and the importance of Canadian-American relations at this time, Taft did not enter Canada. His wife and her friends, however, did set foot in Canada, as they visited the island of Campobello, which is now famous as the site of Franklin Roosevelt's summer home. See "Taft Spends Night on Canadian Border," *New York Times*, July 20, 1910, p. 3.

51. Diary of Henry Ashurst, December 3, 1918, *Papers of Woodrow Wilson*, 53:313.

52. These quotations are taken from various newspapers as cited in "Making War on Our Chief Peacemaker," *Literary Digest*, December 14, 1918, p. 9. The day after the president left Washington, D.C., Secretary of War Newton Diehl Baker wrote to Wilson informing him that "now that you have actually gone the press of the country has taken a generally settled and sensible view of your going" (December 5, 1918, *Papers of Woodrow Wilson*, 53:323).

53. "Taft Defends Wilson's Trip; Says Advantages Are Clear; Constitution Confers the Right," *Public Ledger* (Philadelphia), December 5, 1918, quoted in *Papers of Woodrow Wilson*, 53:323–24.

54. Mann's statement is quoted in *Papers of Woodrow Wilson*, 53:308. Wilson immediately sent Mann a note thanking him and praising him for his "patriotic and thoroughly fair and sportsmanlike position" (Wilson to James Robert Mann, December 3, 1918, *Papers of Woodrow Wilson*, 53:308).

55. Lodge to Roosevelt, December 2 and 9, 1918, quoted in Pyne, "Woodrow Wilson's Abdication," 132–33.

56. *Congressional Record—Senate*, January 3, 1919, 967–68. A revealing portrait of Sherman can be found in Ralph A. Stone, "Two Illinois Senators among the Irreconcilables," *Mississippi Valley Historical Review* 50 (December 1963), 443–65.

57. *Congressional Record—Senate*, January 3, 1919, 970.

58. Ibid., 971–72.

59. Ibid.

60. Pyne, "Woodrow Wilson's Abdication," 135–37. Also see Kurt Wimer, "Woodrow Wilson's Plans to Enter the League of Nations through an Executive Agreement," *Western Political Quarterly* 11 (December 1958), 800–812.

61. Pyne, "Woodrow Wilson's Abdication,"176, 180.

62. Ibid., 166, 189. On occasion, Wilson admitted that he lacked the information necessary for constructive engagement on domestic issues. On January 23, 1919, for instance, he cabled his aide Joseph Tumulty that he would have to leave it to Congress to decide a particular question because "I might make a sad mess of it by interfering with so little knowledge" (*Papers of Woodrow Wilson*, 54:227). Historian James Morton Blum agrees that Wilson's "full energy [was] claimed by events in Paris, [and he] was not thinking about American opinion" (*Joe Tumulty and the Wilson Era* [Boston: Houghton Mifflin, 1951], 173). McCormick, a member of the American delegation, had been Wilson's campaign manager in 1916.

63. Pyne, "Woodrow Wilson's Abdication," 212–13. Telegrams from Joseph Patrick Tumulty, January 6, 1919, and February 15, 1919, *Papers of Woodrow Wilson*, 53:625, 55:198. Also see Tumulty to Wilson, November 21, 1918, December 12, 31, 1918, January 30, 1919, February 1, 1919, and March 13, 16, 25, 30, 1919, *Papers of Woodrow Wilson*, 53:156, 371, 571; 54:390–93, 428; 55:493, 540; 56:373, 436.

64. From Joseph Patrick Tumulty, March 14, 1919, *Papers of Woodrow Wilson*, 55:500. Wilson to Herbert Bayard Swope, February 7, 1919, *Papers of Woodrow Wilson*, 54:550. As early as January, Tumulty communicated to Grayson his concern that "American newspapers [were] filled with stories . . . of [a] critical character about [the] rule of secrecy adopted for peace conferences, claiming that the first of the fourteen points has been violated. In my opinion, if President has consented to this, it will be fatal" (January 16, 1919, quoted in Pyne, "Woodrow Wilson's Abdication," 217).

65. "'Nobody Home' in Washington, Yet the Government Goes On," *World* (New York), March 23, 1919, p. 1.

66. Ibid.

67. Wilson to Josephus Daniels, January 31, 1919, *Papers of Woodrow Wilson*, 54:408. Pyne, "Woodrow Wilson's Abdication," 212; also see 218.

68. Pyne, "Woodrow Wilson's Abdication," 185, 179.

69. "Back to Normal," Address before Home Market Club, Boston, May 14, 1920, in Frederick Schortemeier, *Rededicating America: Life and Recent Speeches of Warren G. Harding* (Indianapolis: Bobbs-Merrill, 1920), 227.

70. "Mr. Wilson at Court," Republican National Committee (Washington, DC, 1920). Thanks to Lewis Gould, who provided me with the campaign pamphlet. A copy of the pamphlet is available in the Gould Papers, Research and Collections Division of the Center for American History, University of Texas at Austin.

71. *Ohio State Journal,* January 29, 1919, as quoted in Randolph C. Downes, *The Rise of Warren Gamaliel Harding, 1865–1920* (Ohio State University Press, 1970), 323.

72. Address by President Warren G. Harding on Canadian-American relations delivered at Vancouver, B.C., July 26, 1923, in Warren G. Harding, *Western Addresses, 1923* (Washington, DC: Government Printing Office, 1923), no page numbers.

73. A complete listing of FDR's foreign travel is available on the State Department's Web site, at http://www.state.gov/r/pa/ho/trvl/pres/c7383.htm (accessed June 3, 2007).

74. The first usage of the phrase "leader of the free world" in the *New York Times* was in 1948 in a commentary that described the United States as "potentially the political leader of the free world." See Barbara Ward, "The Marshall Plan Is Not Enough," *New York Times,* November 14, 1948, p. 71.

75. The number of days spent on foreign travel is calculated using the State Department's list of "Presidential Visits Abroad," available at http://www.state.gov/r/pa/ho/trvl/pres/c7383.htm (accessed June 3, 2007). The least traveled president since World War II was Harry Truman, who averaged fewer than five days of foreign travel per year; all of that travel came in his first term. In *The Elusive Executive: Discovering Statistical Patterns in the Presidency* (Washington, DC: Congressional Quarterly Press, 1988), Gary King and Lyn Ragsdale offer misleadingly low estimates of days of presidential foreign travel between 1949 and 1984. For instance, they calculate that Eisenhower spent only three days in foreign travel in his first term (p. 270), when in fact the correct number is twenty days.

76. Skip Thurman, "Clinton Tops Frequent Flier Club," *Christian Science Monitor,* November 21, 1997, p. 1. Andrew Rosenthal, "From His Position of Power, Bush Swings into a Defense," *New York Times,* October 5, 1991, p. 1. Paul Brace and Barbara Hinckley have shown that foreign travel had a strongly negative effect on Bush's popularity. See "George Bush and the Costs of High Popularity: A General Model with a Current Application," *P.S.: Political Science and Politics* (September 1993), 501–6, esp. 504.

77. George C. Edwards III, *The Public Presidency: The Pursuit of Popular Support* (New York: St. Martin's, 1983), 75. Gallup approval ratings from Truman to Reagan are conveniently reproduced in King and Ragsdale, *Elusive Executive,* 295–307.

78. The forty-one hours figure is from Newton N. Minow, John Bartlow Martin, and Lee M. Mitchell, *Presidential Television* (New York: Basic Books, 1973), 67; it is also cited in Samuel Kernell, *Going Public: New Strategies of Presidential Leadership* (Washington, DC: Congressional Quarterly Press, 1986), 95. Bush visited China on October 18–21, 2001, February 21–22, 2002, and November 20–21, 2005.

79. James Bennet, "Clinton Packs Up His Care and Woe to Trot the Globe," *New York Times,* March 23, 1998, A1. Paul Brace and Bruce Hinckley, "Presidential Activities from Truman through Reagan: Timing and Impact," *Journal of Politics* (May 1993), 382–98, esp. 391. A study by Robert E. Darcy and Alvin Richman ("Presidential Travel and Public Opinion," *Presidential Studies Quarterly* 18 [1988], 85–90) found that in the period between 1953 and 1980 foreign

travel by presidents had a "very small and very insignificant" effect on popularity. However, they did find a significant effect for longer trips to Western nations and to "major Communist powers." A study published in 1989 by Dennis M. Simon and Charles W. Ostrom, Jr. ("The Impact of Televised Speeches and Foreign Travel on Presidential Approval," *Public Opinion Quarterly* 53: 58–82) found that foreign travel had no significant effect on presidential popularity. Also see Robert F. Marra, Charles W. Ostrom, Jr., and Dennis M. Simon, "Foreign Policy and Presidential Popularity: Creating Windows of Opportunity in the Perpetual Election," *Journal of Conflict Resolution* 34 (December 1990), 588–623, esp. 611.

80. Thurman, "Clinton Tops Frequent Flier Club," p. 1. George W. Ball, "Is This Trip Necessary," *New York Times*, February 13, 1972, SM11.

CHAPTER 7. TRAINS, PLANES, AND THE PARADOX
OF THE TRANSPORTATION REVOLUTION

1. Robert F. Dorr, *Air Force One* (St. Paul, MN: MBI Publishing, 2002), 29. In July 1932, Roosevelt had flown from New York to Chicago to accept the Democratic nomination for president, but he had not been in a plane since that dramatic flight.

2. The journey is recounted in Harry Hopkins's diary, entries from which are to be found in Robert E. Sherwood, *Roosevelt and Hopkins: An Intimate History* (New York: Harper and Brothers, 1948), 668–73. Also see J. F. terHorst and Ralph Albertazzie, *The Flying White House: The Story of Air Force One* (New York: Coward, McCann and Geoghegan, 1979), 125–33.

3. "Capital Sees Plan," *New York Times*, January 27, 1943, p. 1; "Numerous Hints of Meeting," *New York Times*, January 27, 1943, p. 3. "Axis Kept Guessing; Wrong as Usual," *New York Times*, January 27, 1943, p. 3. Doris Kearns Goodwin, *No Ordinary Time: Franklin and Eleanor Roosevelt: The Home Front in World War II* (New York: Simon and Schuster, 1994), 401.

4. Harold E. Tabor to Roosevelt, February 11, 1943. Doris Kinney to author, November 3, 2005. The letter from Tabor and the other letters to FDR cited in the subsequent paragraphs are located in "World War II: Casablanca Conference: Miscellaneous Comments," which can be found in container 3 of an Official File on World War II (OF 4675) at the Roosevelt Library in Hyde Park, New York.

5. Cooper Davis to Roosevelt, January 27, 1943. Grace Jenson to Roosevelt, January 31, 1943. Mrs. C. Winn to Roosevelt, February 1, 1943. Samuel Paper to Roosevelt, January 31, 1943. Examples of such letters could easily be multiplied. See, for instance, the letter from Abe April, a purveyor of "fine furs" in New York City, who wrote to FDR: "As a citizen and friend, I beg of you not to take such a chance again. God, forbid that anything should happen to you in this crucial period when we need you so much" (to Roosevelt, February 9, 1943). Similarly, Frank Kopp of New York City wrote to tell FDR that he was "convinced that the risky trip you made was in the interest of the American people," but also to remind the president that the nation's "131 million people together with several hundred more million people throughout the world have too much at stake now, and we cannot have anything happen to you.... I cannot put a price on your life, because in my opinion there is no replacement ..., therefore, my dear Mr. President, please do not take any more such risks in the future, because too many of us depend upon you, and you owe us this consideration" (to Roosevelt, February 2, 1943).

6. Sumner S. Ferris to Stephen Early, February 3, 1943.

7. Joseph Kramer to Roosevelt, January 27, 1943. George W. Allen to Roosevelt, undated, emphasis in original.

8. The quotations are from Goodwin, *No Ordinary Time*, 409; and the Spokane (Washington) *Chronicle*, as quoted in *New York Times*, January 28, 1943, p. 4. The Secret Service ruled out making the trip to Casablanca by boat because of the dangers posed by German submarines. Roosevelt's attitude toward flying is discussed in Goodwin, *No Ordinary Time*, 409; terHorst and Albertazzie, *Flying White House*, 127; and Kenneth T. Walsh, *Air Force One: A History of Presidents and Their Planes* (New York: Hyperion, 2003), 43.

9. "U.S. Press Studies Casablanca Talks," *New York Times*, January 28, 1943, p. 4. "Press Hails Roosevelt-Churchill Meeting as 'Epoch-Making,'" *Evening Star* (Washington, D.C.), January 27, 1943, A3. *New York Times*, February 6, 1943, p. 4. A few newspapers, particularly those that leaned Republican, took a more skeptical view. The *Los Angeles Times* described the trip and meeting as "grandstanding" and the *Chicago Tribune* dismissed them as "theatrical" (*Evening Star* [Washington, D.C.], January 27, 1943, A3). The *Springfield Union* (Massachusetts) noted disapprovingly, "Both Mr. Roosevelt and Mr. Churchill love the spectacular, the unusual. Unquestionably the melodrama of this excursion appealed to both of them. We do not believe the trip was justified and hope sincerely that no similar adventure will be undertaken by Mr. Roosevelt while we remain at war" ("U.S. Press Studies Casablanca Talks," p. 4). But even Roosevelt's enemies had difficulty concealing their admiration for the president's boldness. Seventy-five-year-old William Allen White, an ardent Republican and long-time owner and editor of the *Emporia Gazette* (Kansas), for instance, hailed Roosevelt's "impudent courage": "We, who hate your gaudy guts, salute you" (quoted in James MacGregor Burns, *Roosevelt: The Soldier of Freedom* [New York: Harcourt, 1970], 331).

10. "Rendezvous at Casablanca," *New York Times*, January 27, 1943, p. 20. "The President's Safety," *Evening Star* (Washington, D.C.), January 27, 1943, A11. The first quotation in the paragraph is from an editorial in the *Seattle Post-Intelligencer*, which was excerpted in the *New York Times*, January 28, 1943, p. 4.

11. "Meeting in Africa Hailed by Butler," *New York Times*, January 28, 1943, p. 6.

12. McKinley's itinerary, which included a visit to Salem on May 22, was published on page one of the *New York Times*, April 14, 1901. The president and his wife got as far as San Francisco before calling off the northwest portion of the trip. See "Mrs. McKinley in a Critical Condition," *New York Times*, May 16, 1901, p. 1.

13. Hayes Scrapbook, volume 78: September 2–December 5, 1880 (Great Western Tour and Misc.), p. 113, Rutherford B. Hayes Papers, Library of Congress, microfilm, series 6, roll 225. Capi Lynn and John Marikos, "Notable Salem Stopovers," *Statesman Journal* (Salem, Oregon), February 21, 2005, A2. *Daily Capital Journal* (Salem, Oregon), October 12, 1911, p. 1. According to the census, Salem's population had grown to 4,258 in 1900 and had reached 14,094 by 1910. The two speeches Hayes delivered in Salem were reprinted in the *Oregonian*, October 1, 1880, p. 1. The speeches are also available in Speeches and Messages, October 1879–March 1881, Hayes Papers, series 9, roll 293. The *Oregon Statesman* described the memorable scene at the capitol when Harrison visited: "The big state house belonged to the people yesterday, and they made use of it. They packed it from pit to dome. They couldn't begin to get into the hall of the house, which was tastefully decorated for the occasion, and where the addresses were made; so they took possession of the whole big building. . . . A loving couple from Rickreal occupied the governor's sofa in his private office, and a family from Eola ate their lunch on the table where the gubernatorial messages and vetoes were written—and spattered butter over the ink stand" (May 6, 1891, p. 1). The *New York Times* commented only that the people of Salem were "out in force and gave the distinguished visitors a royal reception" (May 6, 1891, p. 1).

14. Admittedly Hayes carried Oregon by a slender 3.5 percent margin in 1876, but he had vowed from the outset to be a one-term president and when he toured Oregon at the end of his term the Republican standard bearer was James Garfield. Taft lost Oregon in 1912 but that defeat was due to Roosevelt entering the race as the nominee of the Progressive Party. In 1908 Taft and the Republicans had carried Oregon by a comfortable 23-point margin. Between 1900 and 1924 the Democrats only once garnered more than 40 percent of the vote: in 1916, when the incumbent Woodrow Wilson narrowly lost the state to Republican Charles Evans Hughes.

15. Chester Arthur, for instance, received criticism in 1883 when he failed to appear when passing through towns on his trip to Wyoming. The *Chicago Journal* wrote: "We think President Arthur made a mistake when passing through the country on his recent trip in persistently refusing to appear at the railroad stations where the people had assembled to pay their respects to the chief magistrate. Many of these persons had traveled a considerable distance in order to get a sight of a live President, and were no doubt sorely disappointed when the train stopped and there was no response to their urgent appeals. . . . Mr. Lincoln, Gen. Grant, and Mr. Garfield were popular with the masses of the people because they loved to mingle with them, and never refused to shake hands with or speak a pleasant word to their fellow-citizens" ("President Arthur's Mistake," *Chicago Journal*, August 6, 1883, reprinted in *New York Times*, August 9, 1883, p. 3).

16. "The President at Portland; A Series of Ovations along the Route to That City," Hayes Scrapbook, p. 112. "President Hayes: From Roseburg to Portland," *Oregonian*, October 1, 1880, p. 1.

17. Homer Socolofsky and Allan B. Spetter, *The Presidency of Benjamin Harrison* (Lawrence: University Press of Kansas, 1987), 171, 176, 177. "Harrison's Trip Finished," *New York Times*, May 16, 1891, p. 5. When Hayes traveled to Oregon he had to travel by overland coach between Redding in northern California and Roseburg in southern Oregon because the railway track between these two towns had not yet been completed. By the time Harrison arrived a decade later, that segment of track had been completed. Whereas it took Hayes five days to get from Redding to Portland, Oregon, Harrison made the same trip in under twenty-four hours.

18. "Washington Welcomes Returning President," *New York Times*, June 6, 1903, p. 1.

19. *Western Times* (Sharon Springs, Kansas), May 8, 1903, pp. 1, 4. Roosevelt to John Hay, August 9, 1903, in H. W. Brands, ed., *The Selected Letters of Theodore Roosevelt* (New York: Cooper Square Press, 2001), 312. Also see "The President's Sunday at Sharon Springs, Kan.," *New York Times*, May 4, 1903, p. 2. The estimate of the crowd's size can be found in the *Topeka Daily Journal*, May 4, 1903, p. 1.

20. "President Roosevelt in Sunflower State," *New York Times*, May 3, 1903, p. 2. The estimates for WaKeeney are from *Western Kansas World* (WaKeeney, Kansas), May 9, 1903, p. 4; and the *Independent* (WaKeeney, Kansas), May 8, 1903, p. 3. The estimate for Junction City is in the *Salina Evening Journal*, May 2, 1903, p. 1.

21. "President Roosevelt in Sunflower State," *New York Times*, May 3, 1903, p. 2. *Ellis County Free Press*, May 9, 1903, p. 1. *Western Kansas World* (WaKeeney, Kansas), May 9, 1903, p. 4.

22. *Wilson Echo* (Wilson, Kansas), May 7, 1903, p. 3. *Ellis County Free Press*, May 9, 1903, p. 1.

23. Roosevelt to Henry Cabot Lodge, May 29, 1903, and Roosevelt to John Hay, August 9, 1903, *Selected Letters*, 295, 311. Writing to William Howard Taft, Roosevelt anticipated that his

tour, apart from the time in Yosemite and Yellowstone, would be "as exacting a work as a human being can imagine" (April 22, 1903, Elting E. Morison, ed., *The Letters of Theodore Roosevelt* [Cambridge, MA: Harvard University Press, 1951], 3:465).

24. Roosevelt to Hay, August 9, 1903, *Selected Letters*, 313, 307–8.

25. "What the President Must Endure on His Trip to the West," *New York Times*, April 7, 1901, p. 21.

26. Edward O. Frantz, "Goin' Dixie: Republican Presidential Tours of the South, 1877–1933," Ph.D. dissertation, University of Wisconsin, Madison, 2002, p. 320. "President Taft Ends His 15,000 Mile Tour," *New York Times*, November 12, 1911, p. 1. Bob Withers, *The President Travels by Train: Politics and Pullmans* (Lynchburg, VA: TLC Publishing, 1996, 90). According to Withers, Taft traveled 114,559 miles as president. On Taft's limitations as a public speaker, see Paolo E. Coletta, *The Presidency of William Howard Taft* (Lawrence: University Press of Kansas, 1973), 72–73; and Peri Arnold, "Effecting a Progressive Presidency: Roosevelt, Taft, and the Pursuit of Strategic Resources," *Studies in American Political Development* 17 (Spring 2003), 80. "If it were not for the speeches," Taft told White House military aide Archie Butt, "I should look forward with the greatest pleasure to this trip [to the West Coast in the fall of 1909]. But without the speeches there would be no trip, and so there you are" (*Taft and Roosevelt: The Intimate Letters of Archie Butt, Military Aide*, 2 vols. [Garden City, NY: Doubleday, 1930], 1:185).

27. The information about Bush's travels has been gathered from the news releases and press briefings available on the White House Web site: http://www.whitehouse.gov. In addition, information has been checked against information available in press accounts of the trips.

28. "Presidential Visits by State," http://www.whitehouse.gov/infocus/social-security/map.html (accessed March 1, 2006).

29. Harry S Truman, *Memoirs: Year of Decision*, 295. "President to Apply 'Whistle Stop' Technique to Air Travel in Fast 4-Speech Schedule," *New York Times*, August 17, 1949, p. 2. "Events of Interest in Aviation World," *New York Times*, February 7, 1953, p. 31. "Truman Air Travel Sets New Record—Over 135,000 Miles," *Planes* (January/February 1953), 1–2. Although Truman's flight to Olympia was the first time a president had used a plane to make a domestic trip, it attracted virtually no comment in the contemporary press. Air travel had by then become widely accepted. Tellingly, two accounts of presidential air travel misidentify the date of the historic flight. In *The Flying White House*, J. F. terHorst and Ralph Albertazzie write that "Truman made his first flight . . . on May 5, 1945, barely three weeks after taking office. . . . It was a one day round trip between Washington and Kansas City, Missouri, to visit his home in nearby Independence. It was also the first domestic presidential flight in history" (149). But in fact Truman was ensconced in the White House on May 5, as his appointment calendar confirms. This error is repeated in Walsh, *Air Force One*, which follows the account of terHorst and Albertazzie closely, indeed almost verbatim in places. Walsh writes: "Truman made his first flight . . . on May 5, 1945, less than a month after taking office. . . . That day trip from Washington to Kansas City—to visit his home in nearby Independence—was the first domestic flight for any president" (45). Compounding the sin, Walsh does not cite terHorst and Albertazzie.

30. *New York Times*, June 14, 1948, p. 1. *New York Times*, June 19, 1948, p. 6. More precisely, 8,534 miles of the trip were by rail, and only 225 miles were by air. Most of the remaining miles were traversed by car.

31. "Text of Taft's Retort to Attacks on Congress," *New York Times*, June 12, 1948, p. 7. Taft's speech was delivered on June 11 in Philadelphia, the same city that was set to host the Republican national convention beginning on June 21. Dewey triumphed on the third ballot, but Taft was Dewey's main competition, finishing second on both the first and second ballots.

32. "Democrats Ask Cities If They're 'Whistle Stops,'" *New York Times*, June 18, 1948, p. 5. "Taft Draws Down Cross-Country Civic Ire for His 'Whistle Stop' Gibe at Truman Trip," *New York Times*, June 20, 1948, p. 7. Robert J. Donovan, *Conflict and Crisis: The Presidency of Harry S Truman, 1945–1948* (New York: Norton, 1977), 399. Also see "The America of the Whistle Stops," *New York Times*, June 8, 1952, p. 3. President Truman first used the expression "whistle-stop" on June 14, 1948, in a speech in Los Angeles, which he described as "the biggest whistle-stop" on his tour. Address before the Greater Los Angeles Press Club, June 14, 1948, Public Papers of the Presidents, which is available at http://www.trumanlibrary.org/publicpapers/ (accessed April 17, 2006).

33. Rear Platform and Other Informal Remarks in Michigan and Ohio, September 6, 1948; Rear Platform and Other Informal Remarks in Ohio, October 11, 1948; also see Address at the Armory, Akron, Ohio, October 11, 1948. In *Public Papers of the Presidents*, available at http://www.trumanlibrary.org/publicpapers/ (accessed April 17, 2006). Truman's unqualified promise, which received prominent press coverage (see "Truman to Speak at 'Whistle Stops,'" *New York Times*, September 7, 1948, p. 18), was made from the back of a train in Toledo, Ohio, at around midnight, after Truman had spent the day speaking in a half dozen locations across Michigan. Perhaps the late hour explains why the promise was made in a more unqualified form than his more cautious comment at a press conference a few days before in which he explained that "everybody wants you to stop at every whistlestop [and] that's what we want to do, if we can." The President's News Conference, September 2, 1948, *Public Papers of the Presidents*.

34. Gil Troy, *See How They Ran: The Changing Role of the Presidential Candidate* (New York: Free Press, 1991), 194.

35. *New York Times*, November 3, 1952, p. 15.

36. E. W. Kenworthy, "Campaign Special: TV or Train?" *New York Times*, April 29, 1956, pp. 12, 30.

37. Ibid., pp. 34, 36.

38. Ibid., p. 34.

39. Cabell Phillips, "Torchlight, Train, Television," *New York Times*, September 18, 1960, pp. 111, 116.

40. Walsh, *Air Force One*, 43–44.

41. terHorst and Albertazzie, *Flying White House*, 158. In his press conferences and public speeches, Truman only made reference to the Sacred Cow once, in a June 27, 1945, press conference at which he drew a laugh from the press corps when he announced that he would be back in Washington on Sunday morning "provided the Sacred Cow stays in the air."

42. "Name of 'Sacred Cow' for Truman's Plane Causes Embarrassment at White House," *New York Times*, October 27, 1946, p. 14. terHorst and Albertazzie, *Flying White House*, 161. Walsh reports the nickname came from "an irreverent press corps" (Walsh, *Air Force One*, 43; also see 49), a claim that is taken verbatim from terHorst and Albertazzie, *Flying White House*, 161. This claim, however, seems at odds with a *New York Times* report from 1946 that the name was bestowed by "the personnel of the Army Transport Corps" (October 27, 1946,

p. 14) and an earlier 1944 *New York Times* story, which reported that although the plane is "unnamed" the pilot "Colonel [Henry] Myers and his men unofficially refer to it as the 'Sacred Cow'" ("Marshall and Byrnes Fly to Paris to See Eisenhower," *New York Times*, October 7, 1944, p. 2).

43. terHorst and Albertazzie, *Flying White House*, 163–64. Walsh emphasizes Truman's desire to use the *Independence* as a way to attract attention and look presidential (*Air Force One*, 44, 48–50). On FDR's shadow and the invidious comparisons made between Truman and FDR, especially among the liberal wing of the Democratic Party, see William E. Leuchtenburg's *In the Shadow of FDR: From Harry Truman to George W. Bush*, 3rd ed. (Ithaca, NY: Cornell University Press, 2001), and Alonzo Hamby, *Beyond the New Deal: Harry S Truman and American Liberalism* (New York: Columbia University Press, 1976).

44. terHorst and Albertazzie, *Flying White House*, 176.

45. Walsh, *Air Force One*, 54. terHorst and Albertazzie, *Flying White House*, 191.

46. Dorr, *Air Force One*, 51. terHorst and Albertazzie, *Flying White House*, 66. The first mention of Air Force One in the *New York Times* was in a May 29, 1961, story, which noted that the president's plane is known as Air Force One "for communication purposes" (3). A couple months later, on July 5, the *Times* reported that the president would be traveling on Air Force One, "his 707 jet plane" (p. 4). And on July 29, the Times wrote of "Air Force One, [the president's] military jet." By November of 1961, Air Force One made its way into the title of a profile of President Kennedy's air travel, though the words "Air Force One" were placed in quotation marks. Alvin Shuster, "A Trip aboard 'Air Force One,'" *New York Times*, November 19, 1961, SM59. Not until well into Johnson's presidency would it become commonplace for the press to reference Air Force One without any kind of explanatory clause (e.g., "Mr. Kennedy's plane," "the official designation of the President's blue-and-white jetliner," "[the president's] jet transport," "the president's plane") preceding or following use of the term "Air Force One." See *New York Times*, May 19, 1963, p. 48; May 29, 1964, p. 12; March 18, 1964, p. 1; September 12, 1964, p. 1; contrast these with, e.g., February 18, 1966, p. 13, and August 22, 1966, p. 1, where the term "Air Force One" appears without any attempt to identify or explain the term.

47. Walsh, *Air Force One*, 55, 62.

48. terHorst and Albertazzie, *Flying White House*, 176, 200.

49. Walsh, *Air Force One*, 2, 17. John Corry, "The Presidents' Planes" *New York Times*, March 7, 1985, C26. The survey was conducted in 2002 and asked respondents "to name the plane that the president flies on" (Walsh, *Air Force One*, 17).

50. Walsh, *Air Force One*, 13, 15–16. Von Hardesty, *Air Force One: The Aircraft That Shaped the Modern Presidency* (Chanhassen, MN: Northword Press, 2003), 68.

51. Hardesty, *Air Force One*, 18. Walsh, *Air Force One*, 15. The "hordes of people" quotation is from an interview with Douglas Brinkley conducted by Walsh. Carter recounts that when he was governor of Georgia his "most exhilarating moment" was when "Richard Nixon flew into Atlanta Airport in Air Force One" to commemorate the passing of Senator Richard Russell. At the sight of the plane touching down, Carter was "overwhelmed with excitement and pride in my country" (Walsh, *Air Force One*, 14).

52. William Safire, "Deroyalization," *New York Times*, November 12, 1973, p. 33.

53. "Mr. Nixon Goes Public to Enhance His Image," *New York Times*, December 30, 1973, 4:3. "Nixon Feels Flight to Coast on Commercial Plane 'Scored Points' with the Public," *New*

York Times, December 28, 1973, p. 12. Also see Lou Cannon, "Nixon Flies West on Commercial Jet," Washington Post, December 27, 1972, A1.

54. terHorst and Albertazzie, Flying White House, 88. William V. Shannon, "How Long for Nixon?" New York Times, December 27, 1973, p. 27.

55. Marjorie Hunter, "Top of the Line in Magic Carpets," New York Times, December 25, 1977, p. 1. Hunter quotes Rosalyn Carter confessing that "inside, my first reaction was how luxurious it was" (p. 5).

56. Tom Wicker, "Little 'd' = A Little Humility," New York Times, November 9, 1976, p. 35. On Johnson's "throne" see Walsh, Air Force One, 83. Wicker's final piece of advice was aimed at the Times's managing editor, Abe Rosenthal: "take the capital 'P' out of 'President' in the Times stylebook." Over twenty years later, in November 1999, the Times would finally take Wicker's advice and change "the President" to "the president."

57. See Hugh Sidey, "A $650 Million Flying Palace," Time, January 15, 1990, 31; and "Could They Hit Air Force One? Time, February 5, 1990, 59. Also see Dorr, Air Force One, 109. The $650 million figure came from Air Force estimates that the two planes were nearly $385 million over the original $262 million contract with Boeing; the cost overrun was absorbed by Boeing, which "refused to comment . . . on the cost overruns." See Bill Richards, "Air Force One's Maiden Flight Goes Very Well," Seattle Post-Intelligencer, January 27, 1990, B3. When the plane was officially unveiled late in the summer of 1990, White House Press Secretary Marlin Fitzwater indicated that the total cost of the two planes, including a new presidential hangar, was $410 million, and that was the figure that appeared in most press accounts in late August and early September. See, for instance, "Nearly 2 Years Late, Air Force Receives New Presidential Jet," New York Times, August 24, 1990, A15; "'Air Force One' to be Two 747s," St. Louis Post-Dispatch, August 24, 1990, B1; and Andrew Rosenthal, "200,000 Miles Later, the President Gets His Wings," New York Times, September 9, 1990, p. 26.

58. Hugh Sidey, "The Loftiest Chariot," Time, July 21, 1986, p. 25.

59. "No Guilt Trips on AF One," St. Petersburg Times (Florida), September 13, 1990, A16. Also see James Gerstenzang, "Political Flak May Fly with President's Jet," Seattle Times, August 24, 1990, A1, A5.

60. Jean Heller, "Jumbo Price for Jumbo Jets," St. Petersburg Times (Florida), January 22, 1990, A1. Sidey, "$650 Million Flying Palace," 31. Also see Gerstenzang, "Political Flak May Fly with President's Jet," A5. Rosenthal, "200,000 Miles Later," p. 26. "Cook's Tour," Seattle Post-Intelligencer, September 7, 1990, B5. After he was out of office, Bush described Air Force One as "grand" but not "fancy." There were no "gold bathroom fittings and plush carpets. . . . No mirrors on the ceiling, no circular beds, no Jacuzzis, no bidets even. But man oh man, is it comfortable" (George Bush, "Man Oh Man, Was It Comfortable," Forbes [Winter 1996], 120–22).

61. "Stow the Flak—New Air Force One Meets a Vital Need," Seattle Times, August 25, 1990, A19. Letter to the Editor, Seattle Times, August 31, 1990, A9. Sidey, "Loftiest Chariot," 25.

62. Walsh, Air Force One, 2. "Majestic" is a word often used to describe Air Force One. Bush's father used the word in a short piece he wrote for Forbes four years after leaving the White House in which he described Air Force One as "that majestic aircraft ("Man, Oh, Man," 120), and Carter's chief of staff, Hamilton Jordan, reached for the same word in describing the presidential aircraft as "that majestic plane" (Hardesty, Air Force One, 10).

63. Rosenthal, "200,000 Miles Later," 26. terHorst and Albertazzie, Flying White House, 67.

1. James Mann, "The Imperial Presidency," *New York Times*, February 27, 2005, 7:21. Mann's essay is a book review of Stephen Graubard's *Command of Office: How War, Secrecy, and Deception Transformed the Presidency from Theodore Roosevelt to George W. Bush*. The phrase "monarchy in republican clothing" was used in an editorial in the *New York Times*, May 26, 1973, p. 30. The Randolph and Henry quotations can be found in Richard J. Ellis, ed., *Founding the American Presidency* (Lanham, MD: Rowman and Littlefield, 1999), 35, 260.

2. *Federalist 69*, in Ellis, *Founding*, 274.

3. Jefferson to Madison, June 9, 1793, *The Papers of Thomas Jefferson* (Princeton, NJ: Princeton University Press, 1995), 26:241. Simon P. Newman, *Parades and the Politics of the Street: Festive Culture in the Early American Republic* (Philadelphia: University of Pennsylvania Press, 1997), 51. Richard Ellis and Aaron Wildavsky, *Dilemmas of Presidential Leadership: From Washington through Lincoln* (New Brunswick, NJ: Transaction, 1989), 61n47. "The Anas," in Adrienne Koch and William Peden, eds., *The Life and Selected Writings of Thomas Jefferson* (New York: Modern Library, 1944), 126. Ellis, *Founding*, 266–67. Robert Johnstone writes that in Jefferson's "own mind 'monarchism' and 'Federalism' became almost interchangeable terms." See Robert M. Johnstone, Jr., *Jefferson and the Presidency: Leadership in the Young Republic* (Ithaca, NY: Cornell University Press, 1978), 51.

4. The famous picture of Jackson is reproduced in Noble E. Cunningham, Jr., *Popular Images of the Presidency: From Washington to Lincoln* (Columbia: University of Missouri Press, 1991), 192.

5. Robert Gray Gunderson, *The Log-Cabin Campaign* (Lexington: University of Kentucky Press, 1957), 101–4. Michael F. Holt, *Rise and Fall of the American Whig Party: Jacksonian Politics and the Onset of the Civil War* (New York: Oxford University Press, 1999), 107. In concluding his marathon oration, Ogle urged his House colleagues to reject the pending appropriation for "alterations and repairs of the President's house" lest Van Buren spend the money to erect a throne or buy "a crown, diadem, sceptre, and royal jewels." Although "deprived of the title of royalty," Van Buren was aiming to add the "trappings" of royalty to the royal "prerogatives" he already claimed for himself (Gunderson, *Log-Cabin Campaign*, 105).

6. *Albany Evening Journal*, July 9, 19, 20, 24, 25, 1849.

7. *Baltimore Chronicle*, as reprinted in *United States Telegraph* (Washington, D.C.), June 18, 1833. The same jeremiad was sounded in the *Philadelphia Commercial Herald*: "We used to be thought republican, and to be at least three thousand miles from the fetes and trappings of royalty; and the shouts of a degraded and enslaved people. But our democracy has become strangely diluted, and we are at this moment not over eighty-seven miles and a half from the scene of as much adulation and sycophancy as ever the slaves of the old world paid to the tyrants that lorded it over there. What are we coming to? Is it thus the 'people's President,' he, who was to have gone through the country an emblem of republican simplicity, is to be glorified, and bowed down to the freemen, whose servant he is. We protest, in the name of Liberty, and of that democratic simplicity which is now converted into royalty and its trappings, against all this flummery, all this war upon simplicity and the dignity of freemen" (as reprinted in *United States Telegraph*, June 18, 1833). Also see the editorial from the *Philadelphia Gazette*, reprinted in *United States Telegraph*, June 20, 1833. At least one prominent Democrat was also made uneasy by Jackson's tour. For the *Richmond Enquirer*'s editor, Thomas Ritchie, Jackson's tour brought back unpleasant memories of President James Monroe's tour. The adulation showered upon Monroe, Ritchie reminded his readers, "partook more of the pomp of

monarchy—than of the simplicity of the Republic. [It was] more like the homage of subjects to their ruler, than of a free people towards their first magistrate." Ritchie was convinced that adulation would not turn Jackson's head, but he was nonetheless distressed at the "excessive attentions" and "sycophantic panegyrics" directed toward the president. Still, Ritchie perceived in Jackson's reception, despite its "vulgar" and "superfluous" excesses, confirmation of "the great popularity of the man and his administration." See "The Tour," *Richmond Enquirer*, June 18, 1833.

8. *United States Telegraph* (Washington, D.C.), June 14, 1833; June 12, 1833; June 18, 1833. Robert V. Remini, *Andrew Jackson: The Course of American Democracy, 1833–1845* (New York: Harper and Row, 1984), 70. Fletcher M. Green, "On Tour with President Andrew Jackson," *New England Quarterly* (June 1963), 216–17. Attacks on Van Buren's tour also, at times, veered into an attack on the people themselves for being taken in by the spectacle. Van Buren's entrance into Albany, for instance, not only revealed Van Buren's predilection for monarchy but showed him to be "a would-be Monarch, *with an abject and craven populace at his heels*" (*Albany Evening Journal*, July 25, 1839). Generally, though, the *Albany Evening Journal* placed the blame squarely on the shoulders of Van Buren, who was "a Fop in manners and an Aristocrat in feeling." When Whigs criticized the president's "servile" following or "his loyal subjects," they generally had in mind not "the people" but rather Democratic officeholders and other partisans hopeful of offices.

9. On Jackson's role in developing the concept of the presidential mandate, see Richard J. Ellis and Stephen Kirk, "Presidential Mandates in the Nineteenth Century: Conceptual Change and Institutional Development," *Studies in American Political Development* 9 (Spring 1995), 117–86.

10. *Republic* (Washington, D.C.), reprinted in *Daily Missouri Republican*, September 20, 1849.

11. *New York Evening Post*, reprinted in *Pittsfield Sun* (Massachusetts), August 22, 1839.

12. "The President's Return," *Semi-Weekly Eagle* (Brattleboro, Vermont), September 20, 1849. *Daily Missouri Republican* (St. Louis), September 20, 1849. *Barre Patriot* (Massachusetts), August 17, 1849.

13. Remini, *Jackson: The Course of American Democracy*, 70. Jackson to Andrew Jackson, Jr., in John Spencer Bassett, ed., *Correspondence of Andrew Jackson* (Washington, D.C.: Carnegie Institution, 1931), June 14, 1833, 5:109.

14. Remini, *Jackson: The Course of American Democracy*, 83. Roy Franklin Nichols, *Franklin Pierce: Young Hickory of the Granite Hills* (Philadelphia: University of Pennsylvania Press, 1958), 283. Oliver Perry Chitwood, *John Tyler: Champion of the Old South* (New York: Russell and Russell, 1964), 323. Before joining President Fillmore on his May 1851 tour, Daniel Webster confided to an associate that he "dreaded" the forthcoming trip. "I see four elements of distress in it: 1. Heat. 2. Crowds. 3. Limestone water. 4. The necessity of speech-making" (Merrill D. Peterson, *The Great Triumvirate: Webster, Clay, and Calhoun* [New York: Oxford University Press, 1987], 482).

15. Jackson to Vice President Van Buren, in Bassett, *Correspondence of Andrew Jackson*, June 6, 1833, 5:106. Also see Remini, *Jackson: The Course of American Democracy*, 64.

16. James Buchanan was accompanied on his trip to the University of North Carolina by Secretary of the Interior Jacob Thompson—a native North Carolinian. Polk also traveled to the University of North Carolina for commencement exercises in 1847 and took with him Secretary of the Navy John Mason. Both Mason and Polk were graduates of the University of

North Carolina. Van Buren began his tour without any cabinet member in tow, but at Saratoga, New York, he was joined by Secretary of War Joel Poinsett, who accompanied the president for the final month of his 1839 tour.

17. *New York Times*, September 10, 1866, p. 1.

18. Nichols, *Franklin Pierce*, 281. "The President's Tour," *New York Times*, July 14, 1853, p. 1.

19. Kenneth E. Davison, *The Presidency of Rutherford B. Hayes* (Westport, CT: Greenwood Press, 1972), 213–14.

20. Johnson's special car is described approvingly as a "splendid private car" in *New York Times*, September 27, 1866, p. 5.

21. Wayne Cutler, ed., *North for Union: John Appleton's Journal of a Tour to New England Made by President Polk in June and July 1847* (Nashville, TN: Vanderbilt University Press, 1986), 74; also see 8–9.

22. Michael Kelly, "Perot Carries His Message to Arkansas," *New York Times*, May 31, 1992, p. 20.

23. Steven R. Weissman, "Aides Urging More Contact with 'Real People,' " *New York Times*, May 19, 1982, B6. Howell Raines, "A Rare Presidential Journey into Public View," *New York Times*, March 18, 1982, B14.

24. Mann, "The Imperial Presidency," 7:21.

25. Allan Nevins, ed., *Polk: The Diary of a President, 1845–1849* (London: Longmans, 1929), 236. The phrase "flying cocoon" is from Elisabeth Bumiller, "Peace and Political Status at 39,000 Feet," *New York Times*, October 29, 2002, A24.

26. When nineteenth-century presidents traveled by water they generally traveled on vessels owned, operated, and paid for by the navy.

27. Peri Arnold, Bradley H. Patterson, Jr., and Charles Walcott, "The Office of Management and Administration," in Martha Joynt Kumar and Terry Sullivan, *The White House World: Transitions, Organization, and Office Operations* (College Station: Texas A&M University Press, 2003), 289–93. Other units in WHMO include the White House Medical Unit and the White House Mess. The pronunciation of WHMO is from Michael John Burton, "The Flying White House: A Travel Establishment within the Presidential Branch," *Presidential Studies Quarterly* 36 (June 2006), 307.

28. Burton, "The Flying White House," 298. Remini, *Jackson: The Course of American Democracy*, 71. *New York Times*, January 7, 1853 p. 1; January 10, 1853, p. 2; September 4, 1902, p. 1.

29. See Arthur M. Schlesinger, Jr., *The Imperial Presidency* (Boston: Houghton, Mifflin, 1973), and Andrew Rudalevige, *The New Imperial Presidency: Renewing Presidential Power after Watergate* (Ann Arbor: University of Michigan Press, 2005). The *Time* magazine story was from August 28, 1972. The Feingold charge is from "Senator Says Bush Is Acting Like 'King George,' " available at http://abcnews.go.com/GMA/Politics/story?id=1418046 (accessed July 10, 2006). The "King William the First" tag is from http://eatthestate.org/02-02/ KingWilliamFirst.htm (accessed July 10, 2006).

30. Ford, quoted in Marjorie Hunter, "President, Now Confident, Shuns Isolation," *New York Times*, July 25, 1975, p. 11. The "depomping the Presidency" quote is from Carter's press secretary, Jody Powell, as quoted in Hedrick Smith, "Carter So Far: Mix of Style and Substance," *New York Times*, March 6, 1977, p. 144.

31. Clinton Rossiter, "The Presidency—The Focus of Leadership," in Aaron Wildavsky, ed., *The Presidency* (Boston: Little, Brown, 1969), 47; the essay originally appeared in the *New*

York Times Magazine, November 11, 1956. Also see Clinton Rossiter, *The American Presidency* (New York: Harcourt, 1960).

32. Robert J. Donovan, *Conflict and Crisis: The Presidency of Harry S Truman, 1945–1948* (New York: Norton, 1977), 395–96.

33. See the penetrating analysis by Bruce Miroff in "The Presidential Spectacle," in Michael Nelson, ed., *The Presidency and the Political System,* 7th ed. (Washington, DC: Congressional Quarterly Press, 2003), 278–304.

Index